THE VANISHING INDIAN UPPER CLASS

THE VANISHING INDIAN UPPER CLASS

LIFE HISTORY OF RAZA MOHAMMED KHAN

TERRY WILLIAMS AND RAZA MOHAMMED KHAN

[The Vanishing Indian Upper Class: Autobiographical, part memoir, part biographical, and while not purely biographical, covers a macro view, by looking at sociopolitical and economic forces that affect a person's life and his connection to the family and the larger society to which Raza Mohammed Khan is central. In the final analysis, it is both an ethnography of the country and a personal narrative.]

ANTHEM PRESS

Anthem Press
An imprint of Wimbledon Publishing Company
www.anthempress.com

This edition first published in UK and USA 2022
by ANTHEM PRESS
75–76 Blackfriars Road, London SE1 8HA, UK
or PO Box 9779, London SW19 7ZG, UK
and
244 Madison Ave #116, New York, NY 10016, USA

First published in the UK and USA by Anthem Press in 2020

Copyright © Terry Williams and Raza Mohammed Khan 2022

The author asserts the moral right to be identified as the author of this work

All rights reserved. Without limiting the rights under copyright reserved above,
no part of this publication may be reproduced, stored or introduced into
a retrieval system, or transmitted, in any form or by any means
(electronic, mechanical, photocopying, recording or otherwise),
without the prior written permission of both the copyright
owner and the above publisher of this book.

British Library Cataloguing-in-Publication Data
A catalogue record for this book is available from the British Library.

Library of Congress Control Number: 2020946136

ISBN-13: 978-1-83998-132-6 (Pbk)
ISBN-10: 1-83998-132-6 (Pbk)

Disclaimer

The authors take responsibility for the entire content of this book. The contents are
not intended to harm, willingly or unwittingly, any person living or dead, named or
unnamed. Comments and questions about the content may be directed to the authors.

This title is also available as an e-book.

Dedicated to
Kazim Mohammad Amir Khan
and the memory of his parents who passed away in relative penury
Anita Saddler
Yumna Zahra Khan
John Fraser

CONTENTS

PART ONE		1
Chapter 1	Introduction	3
Chapter 2	The Family Tapestry	13
Chapter 3	Amadabad's Zenith: The Life and Times of Nawab Ali Mohammad	19
Chapter 4	Nawab Dawood Ahmad	27
Chapter 5	Raza's Early Childhood	31
Chapter 6	Raza's Later Childhood and Adolescence	53
Chapter 7	Beginning of an Exile: Boarding School	65
Chapter 8	The Wedding of Zainab and Hurr	81
Chapter 9	Abid Arrives to Join Raza	93
Chapter 10	The School Rebel	107
Chapter 11	Crammers	113
Chapter 12	Secret Love	127
Chapter 13	Journey Home	141
Chapter 14	Return to London and Shireen	147
Chapter 15	Farewell to Shireen	161
Chapter 16	Down but Not Out	169
Chapter 17	The Garret	177
PART TWO	Ithaka	187
Chapter 18	An Indian Odyssey	189
Chapter 19	Nawab Dawood Ahmad in Pakistan	205
Chapter 20	Bombay Itinerary	221
Chapter 21	The Return	229
Chapter 22	Raza's Second Aldermaston March	237
Chapter 23	Tess and Raza	243

PART THREE — 255

Chapter 24	The Decline	257
Chapter 25	Ibn Dawood's Claim	273
Chapter 26	Ibn Dawood's Victory	283
Chapter 27	Raza and Maysam	289
Chapter 28	The Ugly Portraits of Ibn Dawood and Begum	299
Chapter 29	The Sad and Tragic Deaths of Hurr Bhai and Zainab Baji	305
Chapter 30	Raza Visits His Ailing Sister	311
Chapter 31	Tragic Ends	325

Epilogue — 331
Acknowledgments — 333
Bibliography — 335
Index — 337

PART ONE

CHAPTER 1

INTRODUCTION

The story begins in June 2010, when I was a guest in Raza Mohammed Khan's apartment in London. I was in London to give a lecture at the London School of Hygiene & Tropical Medicine. Raza suggested I stay over at his duplex flat near Islington in north London. We met several years earlier in Paris at a drug conference he organized. Raza, as his friends called him, was making breakfast of fresh peas, fried fish, potatoes, toast, and assorted fruits, when the phone rang. As he animatedly spoke to the party on the line in what I soon learned was Urdu, his voice and mannerisms changed from those of the calm, fluent, English-speaker I knew into how I visualized from my travels animated Indian, and also other non-English-speaking people talking to each other. I was discovering an entirely new aspect of Raza, even though I had known him as a friend and professional colleague for many years.

Ending the call, he sat pensively, cupping his face, his arm supporting his head. It was clear that all of his thoughts concerning breakfast were now forgotten. His wife Tess asked about the caller: "One of your relatives?" Raza nodded. He said that the telephone call was from his nephew, Maysam. Tess became excited. She knew her husband and nephew had recently been in contact about a family dispute regarding an inheritance. His cousin Ibn Dawood, who Raza referred to by the nickname "Shaikhoo," had taken control of the estate and family fortune.

The dispute is among various family members—cousins, sisters, uncles, including Raza—all of whom have claims to the family wealth. This breach of sharing, which was being lost, had apparently been a historical family tradition, as something no one had visited in their lifetimes. Tess did not go further into explanations about Raza's family because she still found it difficult to work out the various relationships with different family members. Finding the story of human interest, I asked Raza to tell me about it.

He felt uncomfortable at first about admitting to his aristocratic background. "You could say," he responded sheepishly, "that I was brought up as a prince.

I don't really talk about it, not that there's anything to hide, one is not responsible for one's birth, but it's a thing of the past, even if the past, it seems, is always with us. What we have made of ourselves, what I have become is through my own efforts. Some of my friends think that I am someone who is ferociously independent. That may be because of the life I've led, where I have had to work to make a living, work that has taught me much and much of which I've enjoyed."

Now that his past was out in the open, Raza relaxed. He began to talk more openly about the family dispute. "Maysam is my nephew, that is to say he is the son of two first cousins of mine, Hurr and Zainab, who were betrothed to each other and later married. His mother is also one of the three older sisters of Zainab, Shaikhoo, or Ibn Dawood, two of whom live in London. We keep in touch by phone because I live quite far from them and my work makes it difficult for me to find time, but sometimes I go over to see them, particularly Maysam's parents. We have also visited Delhi together when Tess and I first met. That's how Tess has come to meet these relatives who she's so confused about."

"I had come to know some years back from Maysam about his mother [my Zainab Baji], continuing to live in straitened circumstances, unable to meet her mortgage payments, nor afford to support her children. Hurr Bhai's patrimony was already all used up. When I contacted her about her situation, she admitted as much to me. I knew that she had some money and property left to her in Pakistan by her father, Nawab Dawood Ahmad, in her own right. He had made the same arrangements for his other daughters. This was natural. He loved them both. The main inheritance was expected to go, by common understanding, to the only son, Ibn Dawood [Shaikhoo] in line with the rule of primogeniture, along with all the inherited culture and tradition of sharing with other members of the family."

It turned out Shaikhoo had swallowed up the proceeds under the pretext of managing the assets on his sisters' behalf, admittedly with their own trusting and naïve consent.

Raza said it was a long, complicated story and Maysam comes into it because he had been on to "his uncle's game for some time." In fact, ever since he was persuaded to give up his job in another bank by his uncle and became employed as an official at the notorious Cosmopolitan Bank of Commerce and Debit (CBCD) branch in London at the time to look after his uncle's affairs—affairs which involved secret numbered accounts in Swiss banks, shady Pakistani financiers, offshore accounts in the Caymans and hedge funds, high living, and secret affairs.

"The long and short of it is that Maysam eventually convinced his mother of what her brother had been up to because it filled her with such a sense of remorse and shame that it took time for her to admit or face up to her own brother's misdeeds—her dear brother she had tended to as a baby when he was seriously ill."

Maysam's mother agreed to let her son go with her cousin Raza to consult some lawyers on what could be done to challenge her brother in an Indian court. She was happy that Raza was accompanying Maysam to the lawyer's office, because she trusted him. That is what the telephone conversation was about. I admitted to Raza how much the story intrigued me and how outraged my egalitarian spirit was on his behalf at what I had just heard. I asked would he mind if I were to write and tell the family story as a kind of life history account.

Tess, as the loyal and dutiful wife, was all for encouraging the idea and yet honest in her sayings. She felt Raza was too close to the situation, on one hand, and too academic on the other to write this family account himself. Someone removed from the family could make the story more accessible to readers. She had met Shaikhoo before and knew how greedy and niggardly he was. With her frequent interruptions and comments, she gave me the impression that Raza needed encouragement to pursue the idea of a book, but eventually Raza agreed that a book would be a good idea since it could illuminate the various scenarios and intrigues in a way that exposed what Shaikhoo had done and continues to do with the inheritance.

"Besides," Raza continued, "pursuing the affair through solicitors is going to be a costly business, with some fees required in advance by the solicitor's Indian office, and Baji, my cousin, doesn't have that kind of money. Besides, even if some money was to be rustled together, Indian courts take a lifetime, which I haven't got. So I'd be very happy to have your help, as I'm sure would Maysam."

Unbeknown to his cousin, Shaikhoo was busy preparing his claim to the central government for the release of the family estate from the Custodian of Enemy Property, a claim being couched in all the legal artifice that would airbrush any other potential claimants' names from history and leave him, Ibn Dawood, as the "sole legitimate heir," a phrase he would often use about himself, and would have his cronies in Lucknow do the same.

A true-life history involves more than conversations and I was assured other forms of documentation were available: digitized family documents, letters, emails, boxes of photographs, notes, poems, even stories and accounts written by different family members. Raza added: "I even have an estimate from the solicitors' Indian office of the value of the liquid and solid assets of the family estate, which comes to hundreds of millions of pounds, not rupees, even if some is still being held by the Custodian of Enemy Property. That sad story I can also tell you about." We agreed to do the book and I would draw up release forms. Later that day and for the remaining days of my stay in London, there were long conversations with Raza, sometimes well into night: explanations about his family and its ancient provenance, about his childhood in India, how he came to be in England, his career and work, about anything that I thought could be relevant to the story.

I notice he is casually dressed as everyman, no suit or tie, travel by bus or the underground, lived in a working-class neighborhood. Raza seemed to me like a lost prince disguised as an everyday worker, and I, an ethnographer, was about to engage in an exciting, life-altering ethnographic excavation.

As our conversations continued while sitting in his London flat, the more stories he told the more real they became, replete with details that were too real to be contrived. Yet, as I was beginning to pay serious attention to them and though I thought they might simply pass, I realized these were not just stories about Raza's family, but because of his writerly inclinations, which we will hear more about later in the narrative, will reveal a master storyteller, a raconteur. His recounting gave the distinct impression of joy on his face. His face does not give the look of anger or disgust, so much as askance, you could say.

His nose is evenly placed, his eyes look straight at you. When something strikes him as humorous, though not perhaps to anyone else, he wears a mischievous look, and one I imagined he must have gotten from childhood. I could not, nor could anyone who took the time to listen as he gave value to the pageantry and pictorial description of events, ignore the sheer delight in the telling of the incredible and the commonplace, so evenly blended as if he were living every moment all over again.

"My family dates back at least to the time of the Mughal Empire," he quietly explained. "But most present-day Americans seem to be only interested in their world and not much else [...] when they hear 'Amadabad,' I'm sure that they think Osama Ben Laden at Amadabad, not Abbottabad."

We both laughed, yet knew it to be founded on some element of truth. The fallout from 9/11 has been indiscriminate. Raza confirms that just having a Muslim name made him identifiable, even though we can joke about it now. British Muslims are the last legitimate targets of racism in Britain today, thanks to Blair. But the joke about Abbottabad made me realize how funny and witty he could be at times. These sorts of anecdotes occurred in the kitchen when I was busy cooking for my hosts as an act of repayment for their hospitality, or on buses into town, or just a walk down the street to find some okra for a Mississippi gumbo I was preparing.

By the time my stay had ended, I had amassed loads of notes and materials to sift and analyze when I got back. Raza agreed to keep supplying me with his life story and to fill in any gaps or explanations that I prompted him about. I also ask him to send copies of photographs he had shown me earlier. I had looked at some old sepia photographs of his great-grandfather as an adult and then again in old age, surrounded by a battalion of courtiers, retainers, servants, sentries and so on. There were also photographs of his grandfather, his uncle Nawab Dawood Ahmad, his father, his brothers and cousins. These were family photographs that made the story come alive.

I also noticed there were no women in the photographs, except his sister as a young girl. He said that the females were in *purdah*, curtain or screens that separate women from the sight of men, nor was there one of his cousins Shaikhoo, whose real name is Ibn Dawood. Raza told me that photographs of him were not allowed to be taken from his birth due to superstition, and that even when he traveled to Pakistan in 1951, his name was added to his mother's passport rather than his photograph. However, I did manage to scan some photos of him from websites. The photographs were usually taken in the palace of Amadabad, or in the town palace of Hyderbagh. Ibn Dawood appears as an effete, diminutive figure in glasses trying to appear taller and more imposing as becomes a man of his position.

From these images, I also received an idea of the size, layout, and architecture of these fabulous places. I stopped and looked at some of the photographs again. They stretched my imagination, and by looking at Raza's ancestors from a bygone age, I noticed the uncanny likeness he bore to his great-grandfather. The eyes, facial features, and stature are all there. These images reveal something unique about the social world of which Raza is an essential character and will form a keen insight in the analysis.

In London the following summer, I had a chance to interview Maysam but decided against it since I felt the main interest was with Raza and opted to concentrate only on his version of events, at least for the time being. Since he was getting on in age, I didn't want to spend the limited time at my disposal traveling all over the place gathering other family tales when the gist of it is documented in letters from Maysam and other members of the family. Yet, I was aware of the need to triangulate and get as many voices from as many different perspectives as possible. Raza has since obliged by sending me not only Maysam's letters and documents but also letters and documents from his uncle, his father, his brothers and sister, his cousins, and testimonies of eyewitnesses, so much so that my files are now bulging.

Two further meetings over the next year with Raza followed since I began getting the book together. He continued to supply me with pages of writing in his own inimitable style. Both of these meetings took place in New York. The first time we shared something about his life and family, a detail here, an anecdote there, but soon I had amassed even more "data" about his family, his life, and those close to him. I might add, unless I was doing a study, I had never been given so many quotes, adages, aphorisms, poetical references, and turns of phrases from any one person.

The second time, I insisted he stay at my apartment in New York on his way back from Boston where he had been visiting his daughter. At this time, we both sat and talked more earnestly about writing his story and I began by continuing an interviewing technique I had employed in London, treating Raza as a "project subject."

On one evening, I probed deeper into the outcome of publishing Raza's narrative. As we were finishing dinner, I asked him: "Out of curiosity, what would you do if your cousin were to hear of the book being written, as can happen some times. Supposing he offered to settle with you, what would you do?" After some thought, Raza replied: "Seriously speaking, you know me. You know how I live. Besides, I am now in my 70s. What realistically do I need in the way of a settlement for my remaining days? I could be a bit more comfortable, sure. Couldn't we all? Money's not the issue. Things between Shaikhoo and me have gone so far down the road that settlement is now out of the question from his side and from mine. For him, it is because he is so greedy and so utterly controlled by his wife, who is even greedier, more lusting for power, if you can imagine that."

"For me, a settlement is impossible because, if he has already broken his word to my father, which he has, all I'm going to be greeted with are either phony 'manana, manana' (tomorrow, tomorrow) excuses, or the same stone-hearted silence that he normally treats his sister with. No, the only thing I'm after is the redemption and the closure that my story can bring for my parents. There's no more powerful weapon for the average person than shaming those protected by wealth and privilege. Let him find out that there's a book in which he figures, but let him also find out that when all is told, the game is up.

Our ancestors behaved differently, not by the rules of primogeniture, which is alien to Islamic tenets, but by sharing things. All male children received equal shares, and in Shi'a Islam daughters received half of what sons received. Let everyone know that he's not the central character, but a sorry apology."

"The story that I am going to tell you is bigger than him, it's bigger than all of us. It's a story about a family and its legacy of honor, compassion, love, sacrifice and betrayal; of sharing and dividing up land. The story that I tell you will expose the contrast that exists between our family's life as it was and Shaikhoo's life in the new India of the super-rich and the consumerist middle classes. Remember he is actually among the top 15 percent of the wealthiest income earners, protected by the absence of any enforcement of the law, and preening themselves in the midst of an ocean of teeming poverty, the other 85 percent."

"I can see by your expression that I seem to be talking in riddles. But all will become clear. When you finish the story, and if it's published, the reader will see at its very core the barbaric nature of the functioning of the law of primogeniture, the rights of the first-born male, often to the exclusion of the second or third born, let alone the females who are often just dowry fodder. Is such a law fit for a modern democratic society? Ours is not the only family where primogeniture has raised discord, misery and bitterness. That's the issue my story raises."

Listening to him relate his sentiments so forcefully, I was somewhat surprised; yet, I had some crucial questions. The quote is significant because it provides the basic narrative tension for the story (or ethnographic excavation). This tension is between the values he espouses and those he practices as a member of the upper class; but here, Raza says nothing, comparatively speaking, about the law of Shi'a Islam as it relates to inheritance. Under either system, the male is privileged. What does Raza think about this? He does not say. He admits that women are "dowry fodder," but as a progressive, left-leaning, educated, cosmopolitan man, what is his "modern" view of this?

I believe it is because that modern view might see women have much more agency than the term "dowry fodder" imagine them to have. This quote is the basis—a kind of narrative analytical roadmap—for Raza's analytical voice in the text. In a social context, it is missing. This is another way of evoking the tension mentioned before since I am not just noting that Raza seems unable to situate his narrative in the appropriate social context of wealth in India at the time; in part, for example, the idea of the superrich in India is relative. For Raza, this narrative gives voice to a family history that is slowly being unworked by other family members, and Raza's account serves as something like testimony of chicanery; and these wrongdoings he is attempting to correct in order to reclaim a heritage. In this passion project in a somewhat idiomatic way, I feel like a Mississippi blues man since I am trying to understand Raza's tragic story as a blues manifesto, part of a much larger historic process, the disintegration of a dynastic link and the self-cannibalization of aristocracy.

As our conversation evolves, Raza talks endlessly about the palatial homes he grew up in and his first-rate education.

He is sheltered. But he never mentions any encounters with the Indian "underclass"; more specifically, I refer to the caste system. How is this possible? How does any discussion about modern India and its independence not take into account, even at a cursory level, the prominent caste system in India? And, on top of this, you have the religious clash between Hindu and Muslim, the lynching of Muslims in Kashmir, and the attacks of Muslims students and teachers at Jawaharlal Nehru University, not to mention the permanent subordination of women in Indian society.

Moreover, Raza's (family) idea about social justice seems to be characterized and encapsulated in Urdu poetry—the writing and recitation thereof. This is alluded to in subsequent conversations and I will come back to that later, but, as interlocutor, I ask where are the on-the-ground applications of the social justice ideas represented in various forms of Urdu poetry? The linkage? I thought this issue important for the text. Does Raza acknowledge and see the social justice shortcomings of Shi'a Islam (or Islam period) in India (old or new)? He sees the law of "primogeniture" as barbaric; but there is no acknowledgement of the inherent sexism in Islamic practice and thought.

This would be, I surmise, very difficult even for a nominal Muslim like Raza who, nonetheless, came from a devout and traditional Muslim family to do. But I do think this is one of the narrative's (reflective) shortcomings of what is revealed to me and Raza's retrospective recall of his life couched in Indian social and political history. The family law aspect is truly significant (marriage, inheritance, and divorce) and here I wonder what feminist scholars (as such) would make of his account. I should also mention that the idea of social justice is a kind of couture justice because it is applicable only to a small subset of people.

In many ways, the rest of this narrative is a combination of oral stories and written literature. Raza's remarkable vocabulary of Arabic, Persian and Urdu terms (he still speaks the latter fluently) and the words he inserted in the text might be unfamiliar to the reader, but I have inserted their meanings into the text as much as possible for clarification. As far as the names of individuals and their need for privacy and a measure of protection, I have changed the names of only those who are alive where it might prove embarrassing or hurtful, but the names of the places remain as recalled. By devising the few aliases I did record, the attempt was to be faithful to the sources and meanings attributed to the original names and locations.

CHAPTER 2

THE FAMILY TAPESTRY

Early in the semester, I invited Raza to come to my experimental seminar "The Organic Novel," which I teach at the New School for Social Research. Raza brought with him the genealogy of his family, a tradition followed by Muslims who settled in India, as noted by the imminent professor of Mughal India, Irfan Habib. It was done in order to keep alive their ancestry and where they came from. This was more like a tapestry connecting distant relatives than what we call family trees. In the case of the Amadabad family, the genealogy has been reproduced and written in Urdu by his brother Abid on a large scroll of paper, and which itself was based on one started by their father.

It was a huge scroll of white paper that stretched across the long seminar table, with all the names in the family tree written in a neat small Urdu script. To my students, it seemed dauntingly complex and extremely impressive. Explaining it, Raza became emotional because it was more than just a scroll of a family tree; for him it was his family tree. I remarked how different it was from family trees as we know them in the West. It was a record of all the extended family connections and intermarriages through and across generations, and fraternities or brotherhoods as well as sorority alliances, impossible to contain within conventional family tree formats.

One of the first pieces related to the tapestry Raza sent about the family was written in Boston, while visiting his daughter.

"Because the tapestry evokes for me some quite striking figures, symbols, motifs and decorative features, a little like Persian or Mughal miniatures from a dim and distant past, all linked by a common thread of continuity. By unraveling this thread and trying to decipher it I hope to understand what, if any, future awaits our family, or whether it will simply fade away into history, as so many families do."

The idea of a "family bloodline within the context of a nation" is a formulation that comes to mind here, and I see it as inextricably linked to the question of "continuity." Yet, it also seems evident that the idea of inheritance is essentially based on this idea of continuity—the material reality of ancestors and immediate family members who came before Raza. I decided to follow Raza's route through all the material he sent, but rather than beginning with a genealogy shrouded in the mists of history and still waiting to be researched, I decided to begin with reference to the piece Raza sent me starting with his great-great-grandfather, Nawab Ali Khan, as a distant but real enough ancestor of the main protagonists of the story.

NAWAB ALI KHAN

Nawab Ali Khan was the adopted son of the widow of the deceased nawab of Amadabad. Children confirmed not only that women could succeed their deceased husbands, but that they could also adopt a successor. Since her husband had left her without children, she had adopted Nawab Ali from a neighboring noble family. This practice was common among the local rulers and nawabs of Awadh who formed a kind of brotherhood in the region. He followed the Shi'a Muslim faith, a topic that is of some cultural and historical importance for this and subsequent periods of this story.

"I'll come to the subject matter, but let's begin by discussing it through a film. Have you seen *The Chess Players*? A film by Satyajit Ray?" I nodded that I had. "Good," he continued, "as you know it is set in the Lucknow of 1857, on the eve of the Indian uprising in which my ancestor Nawab Ali was involved. It depicts a debauched king of Awadh, busy playing a form of chess called 'chawsar,' just prior to the Indian uprising, and who has lost control of events to preserve his kingdom from falling into the hands of the British, depicted with the arrival of General Outram, played by Richard Attenborough, at the court of Awadh in Lucknow, a cameo scene." I was struck by an allusion to the "barons waiting in the wings and rallying people to rise up against the British. It made me immediately think of one such baron—my great-great-grandfather."

Having looked deeper into the background, I learned that the kings of Awadh had all been Shi'as, tracing their roots to Khorasan in Iran. Yet, by mid-century, they were leading such dissolute lives. How did this go down with the ordinary Shi'a population? The answer to that is to be found in the ascendancy of *Marsiya* writing and recital in Lucknow during the early nineteenth century.

Marsiyas are an epic form of poetry, often elegiac, heroic, and tragic at the same time with the theme of sacrifice in the name of truth at its core. They are intrinsic to the shared values upheld by their authors and the Lucknow audiences of rich and poor alike.

"Now as chance would happen, I have recently learnt that Nawab Ali also left behind a *Marsiya*, and undoubtedly recited it during Moharram. *Marsiyas* were a rallying cry, a warning against decadence and corruption, public recitals in verse form evoking images of love and truth and honor, sacrifice and compassion, images that bound audiences as one. As such, *Marsiya* is elitist and aristocratic on the one hand, and peasant based and potentially revolutionary on the other. It goes on to illustrate this duality by the way religious chants of 'Ya Husain' turned into demands for bread and land in places like Lebanon and Iraq."

Raza suggests that Amadabad was also an agrarian society. There, on the night of the 10th of Moharram, after the ceremonial burial of the replica coffins of Imam Husain, his family and followers, all pierced with arrows, something strange happens: hundreds of peasant women and children, mostly Hindu, gather in the arches of the palace and wail into the night. It is something remarkable, atavistic, and primordial, about the shedding of blood and rites of fertility so that crops can grow again. "It leads me also to think of the glue that must have bound ruler and ruled like the one that empowered my great-great-grandfather to raise a militia of a few thousand from the local peasants and farmers to take on the British."

The subject matter of *Marsiyas* and Moharram is a bit like the Passion Plays during Easter commemorating the sacrifice Jesus made to save humanity. Think of another film: *Christ Re-crucified*. It shows how during the occupation of Crete by the Turks, villagers took on different roles from the New Testament. It was the same with *Marsiyas*. The subject matter is the account of some very tragic events in the early history of Islam, particularly Karbala, but as this story is also a human story, the recital of the *Marsiya* still had and, dare I say, has a wider appeal, because it transcends time and place of occurrence, and reminds you of the truths contained in all the great civilizations: the necessary struggle against injustice, of compassion and sacrifice, of fathers and mothers parted from their sons, and of brothers and loyal friends departing this life in order to pay the ultimate price for the stand they all had taken.

"To return to the topic of *Marsiya* writing and recital, this reached its peak between the early nineteenth century with people like Mir Anis and Mirza Dabir, and lasted until the mid-twentieth century. Since the practice entails some complexity, I will not describe it all but I will say the recital still continues but of old classical *Marsiyas*. Little new composition now takes place. During my great-grandfather's time, attending a *majlis* or gathering and listening to *Marsiyas* being recited played a vital role in reminding people that truth and social justice were a vital part of the message of Imam Hussain.

During my childhood and early life, I was expected to attend and listen to and at a later time recite *Marsiyas*, written not just by famous Lucknow poets, but also those by my great-grandfather, my grandfather, my uncle and my father in Amadabad. They were like the sword of truth and social justice cutting through the daily dross of existence and giving it meaning by exposing corruption and nepotism. You may be surprised to note but Sunnis also attended the *majlis* during Moharram."[1]

When I asked Raza during our conversations in both London and New York about the relevance of *Marsiyas* for the modern reader, suggesting perhaps it was too abstruse and intellectual, he agreed, saying: "There is a dilemma. We live in dark times when religious extremism is the order of the day. With regard to Muslim extremism, they are engaged in acts of fratricide, and not simply in acts of 'terrorism,' but it was not always thus. If not mutual respect, there was at least tolerance and understanding between the different schools of Islamic belief. This was the case, for example, in the civic life of Lucknow, which was considerable and Lucknow was known for its customs, manners, tolerance, and accommodation of other religions. Muslim Shi'as ruled Awadh, but Sunnis also enjoyed a major role. Lucknow survived until partition and independence and it is vividly depicted in the novels and writings of Attiya Hosein. There was occasional friction between them but this was calmed down and dealt with through discussion and mediation."

By 1858, as foretold in Indian folklore, a powerful means of remembrance for the people, the Indian War of Independence had arrived in 1857. In the end, the British prevailed by supporting those local rulers who were waging their own skirmishes against a weakened and effete Mughal ruler, but were now beset by the problem of raising more revenues required not just for sending the wealth back to Britain but also for administering a whole subcontinent, not just Bengal.

I was curious about the actual sources of the family's wealth, and felt that Raza was reluctant to discuss this, perhaps because he was ambivalent about the wealth. I believed more information would be forthcoming in this regard. I heard in one conversation with Raza, though I was unsure of the source, that the great-great-grandfather was a trader and perhaps a major landowner. I assumed his forefathers were landowners, though this issue is not clear from

---

[1] Imam Hussain was the second son of Fatima, the daughter of Prophet Mohammad, after the martyrdom of Prophet Mohammad in the year 632.

previous discussions with Raza. I also wanted to know if the great-grandfather was a descendant of the "nawab" rulers, and if "nawab" was an official title or just a name. I knew it meant governor or ruler in India under the Mughal Empire, but the fact that he was a governor and not simply referred to as such would of course add to the mystery.

"Nawab Ali died of his wounds in 1858. His brick mansion in Amadabad was partially destroyed by enemy bombardment. So in the end, the British had won what was soon to become part of their empire, the 'jewel in the crown,' the subcontinent of India."

However, henceforward, they would be overstretched in governing the vast territory. Stories about the Black Hole of Calcutta (1756) a century earlier were fresh in the mind. Ruling Bengal had been hard enough, so they had resorted to what is known as the Ryotwari system, a method of raising revenue, largely through indirect means, by holding a zamindar or landowner responsible for collecting monies and handing them over to fill the coffers of Britain. This oiled the machinery of their rule.

"Different methods were employed in different regions. In the United Provinces of Agra and Awadh, as Uttar Pradesh was then called, they restored land to the zamindars and taluqdars. Worried too by the elite's relations with their tenants, that had so nearly succeeded in ousting them by raising local militia, the British tried to limit this risk by introducing a new system of land law in Awadh, embodied in the custom or English law of primogeniture, that is to say that the eldest male child was to be the sole heir. This policy would ensure that an identified landowner could be held to account in case of any dissent or rebellion by younger siblings."

Primogeniture, though alien to the Muslim custom of dividing land or property equally, did not come into play in the case of Raza's great-grandfather, Nawab Hasan, because he was the only son of Nawab Ali Khan. Since he had been a minor at the time of his father's death, his life was spared. Befriended by the local governor, he was sent to college in Calcutta, where he learned English and became quite proficient at it, according to Raza. The states were restored to the family when he came of age in 1885.

Accounts of his achievements were passed down through generations, and as Raza recounts, the family residence, bombed and partially destroyed by the British, was not only restored but considerably extended. Above all, rewards were meted out to the townspeople, to children and the local peasantry in the form of almshouses, madrasas, hospitals, and schools. All were part of his great-grandfather's formidable militia as his renown spread beyond Lucknow as far as Iraq and beyond.

NAWAB HASAN KHAN

It is reported when news of flooding in Iraq in 1893 reached Nawab Hasan Khan, he set sail with a cargo of rice and wheat. Raza says, "My father told me that my great-grandfather's cargo of rice and wheat was mingled with grains made out of gold, and that when he presented his cargo to the governor of Basra, he was given in return a ruby-encrusted solid gold quill pen. He also brought back some date palms to plant at home."

Raza recalls seeing the pen in the palace as a young man and swears it was there even as an adult until Anno, who was the last known member of the family ever to see it. Raza also mentions how one of the date palm trees survived on the main lawn of the palace, but never bore fruit.

Raza was effusive when speaking about Nawab Hasan Khan and his contributions to the social and cultural life of Lucknow. He spoke of his stature, how he cut an imposing figure of almost six feet, as portrayed in photographs. The clothes he left behind were preserved in wooden chests, wrapped in muslin cloth, with mothballs scattered around. Raza remembers his father wearing the striped silk wide-bottomed trousers and an embroidered sherwani coat. He would have also cut an impressive figure in his sober finery in the renaissance of the Indian National movement that had recently started in 1942. It is known that he was a prominent member of both the Congress and the Muslim League.

Nawab Hasan Khan married once and had four children, two sons and two daughters. Both daughters were referred to as Ammijans by Raza's parents, leaving his elder son, Raza's paternal grandfather, to succeed him. Again, the issue of primogeniture is not tested because his younger brother passed away at the young age of 32. Raza stresses this point to me in relation to Anwar Bukhari's claims of being "the sole legitimate heir" on the basis of family tradition, when in reality it is a legacy of British imperial rule that the constitution of the Republic of India somehow overlooked in removing from the statute books when zamindari was abolished in 1953. Raza's great-grandfather passed away in 1909 and was succeeded by his son, Raza's grandfather, known as Nawab Haider Ali Mohammad.

CHAPTER 3

AMADABAD'S ZENITH: THE LIFE AND TIMES OF NAWAB ALI MOHAMMAD

"By all accounts he was quite a man," Raza says, referring to the life and times of Nawab Haider Ali Mohammad. "He was a close friend of Motilal Nehru, and knew the young Jawaharlal, as well as Jinnah. Many of these connections were passed on to the next generation." Raza sent me an account of his father telling him when the family was sitting down to lunch—a time usually reserved for the telling of family stories: When Motilal was imprisoned in a Lucknow jail by the British, Nawab Haider Ali would send him various items.

"You know your Dada Abba, the British provincial governor, and Motilal Nehru were such boon companions that they became known as nawab, kabab, and sharab. Motilal Nehru was known to have a penchant for alcohol. And, you know what else? When the British imprisoned Motilal in Lucknow jail during the 20s, your Dada Abba, with the connivance of the governor, used to send him a bottle of champagne buried beneath a platter of biryani."

With all of these civic and other duties, Dada Abba still managed to marry twice. The first wife was of Irani descent, Raza's paternal grandmother, the lady he was taught to call "Bibi Amma." With her, Nawab Haider Ali had four children: two daughters, both referred to as *Ammijan* or paternal aunt, followed by Raza's uncle or Baba, and lastly the youngest who was Raza's father, born in 1917.

Raza's father at Tajposhi (circa 1939).

Raza reminisces to me about reciting his grandfather's poetry in public in the palace as a young boy. Like his father, who, by the way, was also an accomplished poet, Raza's grandfather continued the tradition of writing Urdu poetry—largely Shi'a religious poetry like threnodies on an epic scale ("*Marsiyas*"), verse poems ("salaams"), and quatrains ("rubaiyat") and handed the tradition down to his sons. The palace will be described in some detail later.

Other stories Raza heard from his father and the old retainers who were there to serve, included those who obliged the further extension of the palace that had been started by the great-grandfather. Photographs of the time show the palace to be that same mixture of Mughal and Rajasthani architecture (a blend of Hindu and Moslem) that characterized palaces, large and small, across the Gangetic plain and into Rajasthan.

Shortly Raza's grandfather took another wife, with whom he had two sons. The second wife and her family were housed in a grand mansion, the White Palace, built by Raza's grandfather in the old part of Lucknow. The thick walls enclose a large more or less rectangular space containing new extensions to the main buildings, an extension to the *zanana* (women's quarters) at the rear, and buildings extending out from the zanana into a renovated, enclosed garden forming the rear of the palace. The large lawn or *chaman* where the great-grandfather had planted some rare trees, other than the date palms, was further enhanced.

The religious charities or "waqfs" built by Raza's grandfather for the poor and the orphans were continued and new ones endowed. These charities are consistent with the Zakat, one of the five pillars of Islam: I wanted to know how much interaction the grandfather or the great-great-grandfather had with the Indian poor. These were questions I continued to inquire about. Like his father before him, Raza's grandfather also engaged with Indian national politics by joining the Indian National Congress as well as the Indian Muslim League, all the while managing to maintain amicable relations with the British governors of the time.

The children of the second wife were provided for and given a settlement by the grandfather during his lifetime in accordance with the *Sanad*, a government charter or patent or deed, which can also be a letter having the force of an edict or ordinance. There were some tensions between the members of the two families from the two marriages over who might succeed, as one would expect, but these were resolved in time. Indeed, many years later, "Uncle" Rasheed, who Raza met by chance in London during the 1960s, told of how he and Mr. "Hubble Bubble" (a nickname given to the temporary head manager of the estate) managed to dissuade the grandfather from signing everything over to his second wife. It was even rumored that during the late 1920s, the then-governor of Uttar Pradesh had threatened to place the Amadabad Estate into the ward of courts, should the law of primogeniture be flouted.

In order to preempt such discontent over inheritance, the British had added a safeguard within the taluqdari law of primogeniture, known as "Taluqdari Sanads." These allowed the ruler to ensure the welfare and well-being of all members of the collective family. In his particular case, the Sanads included the offspring from his two wives. From here on, if tensions were to arise within a family, these could be resolved, if not by informal means, then in the last resort by recourse to Taluqdari Sanads.

In addition to these marriages, the grandfather had another earlier premarital liaison, known as the *Mut'a*, a temporary marriage agreed by a contract that is recognized under Shi'a law. From this liaison, there were three children: two daughters and a son. Raza remembers looking at and wondering about these people living in the palace. The son bears a striking resemblance to

Raza's grandfather in early photographs, and though the relationship was never fully explained, Raza was taught to call him uncle.

Raza's grandfather, Dada Abba later matured.

His two sisters lived in the *Qila* (palace) and he was given a house in the town. Some things were like that, and Raza never asked.

Raza's grandfather Nawab Haider Ali's death at a relatively early age of 53 was tragic, though not unexpected. He had suffered a stroke a few years earlier, leaving him frail and weak, unable to walk, as later photographs reveal. Raza had learned from the older people still around that he had to be carried in a specially designed chair.

"But [looking at him] those eyes still hold their serene pride. The gigantic efforts of this one man in the private and public spheres had begun to take their toll. The enormous efforts in promoting education for Muslims are all well chronicled. Only as recently as 1928 he had hosted the Nehru Commission conference in the large white Baradari of Kaiserbagh, which still stands today and is still hired out by the Yaluqdar Association for large functions."

Raza continues: "The Nehru Commission was intended as a rebuff to the British Simon Commission then visiting India, offering a talking shop instead of real change, which the Indian National Congress had rightfully decided to boycott. The conference was followed by a fabled feast consisting of eight courses each of European, Hindu, and Muslim cuisine. My grandfather had sat next to his old friend Motilal Nehru who had convened the Nehru Commission and they both enjoyed their high calorie meals, despite my grandfather having been diagnosed as a diabetic."

Raza mentioned how a new project his grandfather was involved in at that time was in dire needs of funds. "This new White Palace project in the northeastern part of the city had come to a halt for lack of funds and because of flooding during 1927. He had a reputation for building palaces: an extension of the palace at Amadabad and the building of the White Palace in the old part of the city had already been accomplished. Also, two or three close friends and advisers, amongst them Farugi, a family friend, had persuaded him to desist signing over the estate to the progeny from his second wife. This was done in order to risk the British governor invoking the law of primogeniture and take the estate back once more into ward of court."

Eyewitness accounts relate the impact of Raza's grandfather's early death in particular on the rest of the family, the deep sense of loss his wife and children felt. No sooner had the news been conveyed to his first wife than the rest of the family learned of it through maidservants, who were often the first to know. They all donned black *dupattas* (a long headscarf) to go and bow before the grieving grandmother, who had donned a white *dupatta* as befits a widow. Widows could always be distinguished by this simple difference in the color of the dupattas, and interestingly enough, prayers for the deceased were led by female clerics at a later time.

The widowed grandmother, who Raza referred to as Bibi Amma, you might specifically say had to be strong for her children's sake and hold things together, no matter the personal loss that would remain with her for the rest of her days.

"By all accounts," Raza informed me, "she was someone with a strong personality and a set of values that had made her tolerate and accept many things over the years. She had a largeness of heart and a kind of wisdom of her own. She knew that the news would soon reach everywhere, which indeed it did. She decided to entrust the arrangements of the grandfather's will to the old trusted advisers like Uncle Rashid and Mr. Hubble Bubble. Together with her London-educated younger brother, they were made joint executors of the will that had been left by my grandfather."

The burial took place in the scaled replica of the shrine of Imam Husain in Karbala, Iraq. The traditional period of mourning lasts for 40 days, an occasion when traditional prayers are recited daily and meals were distributed to the poor, as was the custom. Here there was no exception, but the funeral and the mourning were on a grand scale as befits an elder statesman. On the 40th day, a large banquet was held; more than a thousand people attended from far and wide. Everyone who was anyone was invited. The old nawab was laid to rest and buried in the replica of the mausoleum of Imam Husain at Karbala that had been built by ancestors in the outskirts of Amadabad. Black-and-white photographs reveal a huge crowd of males escorting the coffin. The young boys accompanied by old advisers and retainers had led the procession. Women observing purdah went to mourn at the grave in the evening.

"In the male quarter too everyone who was anyone had gathered. The body had already been bathed, covered with a white sheet, and lain to rest on the washed wooden board of the bed and made ready for burial. Clerics had gathered to consult about the funeral arrangements. These had also been hastily made in accordance with religious requirements, as well as the will of the deceased."

In his will, Nawab Dawood Ahmad, his eldest son, his first with Bibi Amma, was declared to be the heir and successor in accordance with the Oudh Settlement Act. A separate settlement had already been made during his lifetime with his second wife and her two young children by leaving the palace in old Lucknow to her and her children.

They had been given a beautiful palace in the old part of Lucknow known as the White Palace, similar to the White Palace that he had started to build in the northern part of the city, as well as a regular monthly stipend from the estate. As for Raza's father, the law of primogeniture prevented the bequeathing of any sizable property to second sons, so he was awarded the same stipend as the other children, the village where he was born, together with parcels of land along the Sitapur Road.

The grandparents were both sensitive to this and quite fond of him and his new bride, so much so they had hoped the young couple would occupy their quarters in the palaces after him.

Raza made it clear this arrangement was the understanding of Uncle Rashid and Mr. Hubble Bubble as well. However, these plans were temporarily changed. What appears from accounts to have happened was this: although daughters are supposed to take up abode with their husbands, which both of Raza's Ammijans did, the recent tragedy and period of mourning meant that the two daughters started staying with their mother on a more permanent basis.

Raza's parents provisionally moved to quarters at the other end of the main courtyard, adjacent to her older sister's, and accessed by a side entrance to the *zanana*, which was the main entrance side.

An era was indeed over for the old stalwarts. This was 1931 when two such friends and boon companions of the Congress Party, Motilal Nehru and the nawab of Amadabad, had passed away within months of each other. Young lions like Motilal's son Jawaharlal and Subhash Chandra Bose had come to the fore, flanking the inveterate and wily old political strategist Mahatma Gandhi, who was in and out of Congress, building a mass peasant-based movement. Raza remembers hearing much about Gandhi in his childhood from his "khaddar," his uncle who wore a handloom-woven, cotton kurta—a sure sign of Gandhi's pervasive populist influence.

During the life and times of Nawab Haider Ali Mohammad, Amadabad reached what seemed to be its zenith according to whatever measure one cares to make: its income and wealth; the further extension of the Lucknow palace, his maintenance of good relations with the British governors and officials, as well as with the Congress and the Muslim League; his connections with other rulers and nobles that has been chronicled by Raza's father; the fame that attracted so many talents and people from the growing Indian middle classes to Amadabad, including physicians, lawyers, architects, those wanting to obtain stipends for helping to collect rent and other managerial duties, architects, craftsmen and artisans, and so on. The town flourished under the fame and fortune of its ruler.

Of course, with it all, the palace and the place also attracted carpetbaggers, sycophants, and flatterers, but the integrity of the estate and its ethos remained intact under the nawab's eyes. It is said that he would always counterbalance the advice of one with the contrary or different advice of another and then make up his own mind about any action that needed to be taken, and ensured that it was carried out.

It is clear that Nawab Haider Ali Mohammad was rich and politically connected, and knew many of the players involved in fashioning a New India—which, is to say, the key players plotting independence from Great Britain. Yet, I was curious to know if Raza's grandfather was regarded as a religious leader of sorts, perhaps what Muslims would refer to as an "Imam." At any rate, his early death left a vacuum in India, one that needed to be filled.

CHAPTER 4

NAWAB DAWOOD AHMAD

The era of Nawab Dawood Ahmad, Raza's uncle, began with his accession in 1931, although it was a period Raza and others would refer to as an "interregnum." "Accounts of the interregnum reveal a profound period of mourning, a somber atmosphere when no one seemed to laugh or smile, particularly not my uncle. This long period came to an end naturally sometime after the 40 days had passed."

The official accession ceremony had been postponed to allow for a suitable period of mourning. The young nawab was in his 17th year, while Raza's father had just turned 14, when their father passed away. Contemporary accounts and medical records reveal that the two young men were of a highly nervous disposition, which in the circumstances is hardly surprising.

That they succeeded in steadying themselves was in no small measure due to the love and protection of their mother. She in turn counted on the loyalty of Uncle Rashid and Mr. Hubble Bubble's governance and management, for handling the selection of tutors for Urdu, Arabic, Farsi, and English, and the religious and secular mentors to instruct them in religious customs and traditions.

Raza recalls hearing from his father about a simple incident that can sometimes bring release. "My uncle, who hadn't been known to smile for a long time after his father's passing away, let alone laugh, was abstractedly looking for an ashtray one day while reading and smoking. As he reached his arm out to flick the ash, Mian Jani, one of the courtiers and retainers, and a known comedian who was seated nearby, leaned forward with his mouth open as a substitute for an ashtray. Anyway, there seemed to be a more relaxed air about the place emerging."

Duplicates of the photographs from the box Raza had sent me and the albums reveal formal photographs of the two young brothers. They appear very close to each other in one. Others show them wearing ceremonial garb at the accession of Nawab Dawood Ahmad. The difference between the two princes is that the older one, the new nawab, wears a crown, while his younger brother wears an ornate *pagri* (turban) with a jewel. The younger, who is Raza's father,

Haidar Ali, is slightly taller than his older brother, and more his father's stature. The nawab is shown wearing glasses.

With the accession over, the expectations were that new nawab would carry on the family tradition in all its pomp and glory. However, this was not to be. Yet vultures had been circling around the young head and had gathered from far and wide, as the most rapacious wore the black garb of clerics. Others of a predatory nature sported beards and were members of politicized religious sects like Firangi Mahal. Some were just greedy for any drops from the gravy boat as it passed them by. Religion is going to be used as a tool to siphon off the wealth of Amadabad, which had become one of the wealthiest noble families during his father's time. In the young nawab, the circling vultures identified easy prey: someone who turned to religion in his grief, and is likely to be easily persuaded to follow their advice. They bide their time. His mother still alive and aware of the potential danger kept a wary eye on her son.

After his father's death, Nawab Dawood Ahmad decided to destroy expensive cases of wine and spirits that the old nawab had invested in for entertaining English and Hindu guests. They were thrown in the small lake or *talaab* as a gesture towards the religiose who had whispered that God had punished his father for providing alcohol, even though he did not drink alcohol himself. The fine cut-glass decanters, glasses, and carafes were somehow saved.

While Nawab Dawood Ahmad attended to these acts, he was also eager to bring offspring as a means of guaranteeing his legacy. "In 1933, and then again in 1934 and 1935, his wife gave birth to daughters one after another, but no son. Then in 1936, he was persuaded by one of his brothers-in-law and his friend, the Raja of Nanpara, to take a trip to Europe, but not before the birth of twin nephews, sons of his younger brother Haidar Ali. He showed his happiness by taking off his glasses and smiling down at the newborn twins."

Soon after the birth of his nephews, Nawab Dawood Ahmad set off on a journey that took him by train to Bombay, where he and his companions booked their onward journey via Thomas Cook, who were the officially recognized organizers of trips to England and the Middle East, including Mecca as a place where many Muslims traveled for Hajj. They had been appointed as such by the imperial government of India.

"This happened to be the first stage of the nawab's journey. Rumor has it that he not only went for pilgrimage to Mecca but also sought and obtained an audience with King Ibn Saud, a supporter and one of the chief financiers of the Muslim League. Of course, as a Wahhabi, he favored the Sunni Muslims of India, but as the honorary treasure, Nawab Dawood Ahmad must have needed a long diplomatic spoon to sup with Ibn Saud, but sup he did."

The second stage of their journey took them along the Red Sea and through Suez to London, where he stayed with his companions at Claridge's, a luxury hotel in the heart of Mayfair. Raza tells me there are no remembered accounts of his stay in London or his tour of Europe, but there are photographs of the three companions.

We can see this trip as a light interlude before his return to the combination of religion and politics that he had been pursuing earlier. It remains to be seen where this would lead him.

Raza's father, Nawab Haidar Ali Mohammad, showed early signs of being different from his brother Nawab Dawood in temperament, interests, stature, and looks. Where the latter took a deep interest in religion and politics, he was apolitical, looking at it as a game for liars. He gave short shrift to sycophants and flatterers and was known for his forthrightness. The circling vultures kept away from him.

Raza's father had other, wider interests, too: in sport, he played polo and tennis; in clothes, he had a fine eye for both Indian and European styles, *sherwanis* (knee-length coat buttoned at the neck), *achkans* (knee length jacket), suits, shirts, ties, hats, *chooridar* pajamas (tight-fitting trouser worn by men and women), *angarkhas* (a long full-sleeved outer wear for men); he smoked pipes and fine cigarettes; he read widely, leading a nephew of his to remark one day to Raza that he was amazed at Raza's father's wide reading and erudition, because whenever he visited the huge library at Amadabad, he would invariably find notes at the beginning of books he picked up, and found notes and comments written in Raza's father's neat handwriting. I was told the library held more than 5,000 hardcover books.

Raza's father had shot up a few inches in his late teens and stood at 5'10", with an athletic figure. His studies at La Martinière had finished in 1934, and with them his dream of going to an English university abandoned in order to help manage his brother's estate. Apart from being a cultured gentleman farmer as we might imagine, he was also very much a family man. He had married the woman of his choosing and he shared with her the tragedy of a baby son who died at birth in 1935. There would be other children since they were still young and they consoled each other.

Raza's mother, Bajia Amma, was the youngest of the female relatives in the household. She was feisty from a young age, indeed she had to teach herself to hold her own in the pecking order.

"My mother was slender, with fair skin, some freckles and red hair, she wore a diamond-studded pin on the left nostril of her fine nose, and, when she looked you in the eye and smiled, your day was made. She also liked clothes and listening to all the gossip that handmaids brought daily about who was saying what, or what anyone was wearing. She knew my father loved her, but didn't need to probe his loyalties because she knew how much he loved his older brother too."

The tone and tenor of the story thus far understates how Raza is connected to dynastic rulership and is not simply part of the rich Indian elite; unless I more consistently inquired, he did not say he was. But I feel he identifies with the dynastic elements and does not disavow his membership in the old ruling class of India. And although this is an account of what he describes as an interregnum, again he does not at first define or articulate what exactly an interregnum is in the Indian custom context. Nor is it clearly stated that Nawab Dawood was an important official and ruler in his own right. Much of these facts are implied in his recall, and otherwise simply left unexplained.

Up to this point in the narrative, the reader has been hinted at that Raza is the descendant of a nawab and only later are you expected to understand fully this is the case. In other words, this business of the nawab is a critical aspect of Indian history and has migration implications, because under what circumstances do we trace the germinal roots of Islam in India? I believe this issue of the nawab is tied into all of this. Another way of articulating this is to see Raza's narrative as at least engaging a duality; on the one side, it is about dynastic continuity and the redefining of the Indian (Muslim) family; on the other, it is a clash between a series of laws enacted by colonial powers, namely the British and the dynamism of Shi'a family law.

It was into these family dynamics and turbulent political times that Raza and his twin brother Abid were born in February 1936.

CHAPTER 5

RAZA'S EARLY CHILDHOOD

RAZA AND ABID

According to various oral accounts, Raza's birth followed the tragic loss of their first baby boy the year before, and his unhappy parents consoled each other and out of that mutual love and consolation his mother conceived again. She was worried about the situation reoccurring, but as soon as the nervousness passed, she began all the precautions and preparations for the birth of the new baby. She informed her husband. The family doctor confirmed the pregnancy.

The rest of the family came to know and there was genuine happiness for the young couple. Raza's uncle, Nawab Dawood, was particularly pleased. There was going to be a new baby in the house. Handmaids and servants were kept busy making clothes, and though most of the excitement was in the female quarters, some repercussions were also felt in the male quarters through the doctor's comings and goings.

A wooden cot covered in silver was ordered. The baby was expected in February. At the moment it was only July. The monsoon was still to come, then some clement weather until the winter starts. By October she would be showing. Time enough.

The regular checkups with the doctor continued. An English nurse was employed to help with exercises and to give advice on health. On the question of hygiene, there was no need. Raza's mother, the youngest daughter of the raja of Bilahra, who was told to call her Bajia Amma, and who performed the ablutions for prayers five times a day, and bathed regularly. She supervised the cleaning of dishes, and nets were placed on top of food dishes to keep flies away during meals.

Monsoons followed the hot summer and turned into winter. At a check-up in early December, Raza's mother complained of a funny feeling because she could feel two pairs of legs kicking about. A consultant accompanying the doctor visited and decided after examination that Raza's mother was expecting not just one baby but twins, and that some of the distress was as a result of the two fetuses moving about. Suddenly something akin to panic engulfed the household. Another cot would need to be ordered.

The next two months were difficult for Raza's mother to walk or sit. Then finally February arrived just as the weather was beginning to warm up, and on February 13, toward midnight, the first baby was born. It was a boy and he was named Raza. Then in the early hours of the morning of the 14th, and after some travail, a second baby, also a boy but much thinner and frailer than Raza was born. He was named Abid.

They were born in the central room of that part of the palace that was to become his mother's quarters. From all accounts, Raza, the earlier born, was quite a big and jolly baby who loved to burst balloons that hung over his cradle, and to gurgle with laughter at the noise they made when popped. Many years later, when it was considered all right for a child to be told about death, he learned he was not the oldest of his parents' children, but that they had had an older son who died soon after birth. The woodworked silver metal cradle he slept in next to his mother's bed had been made for Raza and was very heavy to carry.

As suggested above, Raza's brother Abid had a difficult birth, and when he finally emerged, he turned out to be quite thin and frail and needed more nursing. They were both given a nanny to look after them and Abid slept in a similar cot next to Raza.

Raza always used a term of endearment for his nanny, calling her "Amma," as she was his mother's most trusted handmaid and companion, who had accompanied Raza's mother from the neighboring princely estate when she, the mother, who had been orphaned at an early age and come to live in Amadabad. Raza's Amma was a round-faced, dark-skinned, kindly lady whom Raza loved.

The first sensorium Raza remembers of the kitchen and the palace are the dusty smells after the rain falls and the spicy aroma of fresh mangoes mixed with the cool breeze of winter nights. As he described this scene, he said he could almost taste the smell of cardamom, Indian peppers, and curries as the fragrance drifted through the kitchen window in the morning.

It was from the central room of his mother's quarters that Raza's explorations of the world began. After he had been fed and washed, Amma would carry him out on his mother's instructions to see his aunts in their quarters, or just to run around with him in the central courtyard, of which the other quarters were based, in a race with Abid's nanny.

One of the first people he would be taken to see was his paternal grandmother, his Bibi Amma, who would normally be sitting in her room in the morning sun. She would call to him as he approached in his Amma's arms, and he would be put down on the carpeted floor that was covered with a white sheet. By the time he was a little over 1-year-old, and had grown his first few teeth, she would put a pinch of fennel seeds in his mouth. His two aunts, his father's older sisters, would be there, and they would play with him too, and teach him how to say *adaabs* (hand gestures meaning respect and politeness) with his right hand.

The next most important people to visit and learn to pay respects to were his uncle, Nawab Dawood Ahmad, whom Raza called "Baba," apparently because those were the first sounds that came out of his mouth when his uncle rubbed his face on his belly. Then there was Khalajan, his uncle's wife, who was also the older sister of Raza's mother. She was a quiet lady, five or six years older than his mother. The age difference between her and her husband was also five or six years. Raza and Abid were taught to call her Khalajan. She would rarely emerge from her large, barely lit room, but she could be heard giving orders to her servants. Her three daughters had by now a room of their own with handmaidens and nannies. They were toddlers before Raza and Abid, and by the time Raza was a toddler, they were already being taught to memorize and recite the Kalima, the fundamental tenets of Islam.

By the time Raza became a toddler, his explorations of the house he was born in became unstoppable. When no one was watching, he would scamper out on his fours and be found inside the doors of the women-only *Imambara* (shrine built by Shia Muslims), known as "Fatimain."[1]

But, to continue with our story, the reason for Raza homing on to this room turned out to be his penchant for eating the sweet-tasting ashes left by fat incense sticks that were burnt there. It was decided that the way of stopping him would be by giving him charcoal biscuits as a placebo. They worked.

These strange tastes Raza had were no surprise because Raza turned out to be finicky and picky about his food. Try as they might, he would spit out any solid that tasted of even the slightest amount of spice, and particularly any sort of meat. He would eat plain rice and daal, but no chapatis. Vegetables like potatoes had to be wiped on a chapati before his mouth would accept even a mouthful. He loved Indian sweets like barfi and gulab jamun. By contrast, his

---

[1] It should be explained that Imambaras, ceremonial rooms used by Twelver Shi'as, had been built by Raza's ancestors in the female quarters, and that "Fatimain," a religious ceremonial room for honoring female descendants of the Prophet was used by women only, and that all males, even infant males, were not supposed to even look inside.

brother Abid was more experimental with food, and the parents found it simpler to have meals prepared for him.

Raza was not allowed to crawl around in his mother's kitchen area unattended, nor in his mother's courtyard because of the dirt and dust on the ground. If he needed to be by his mother, he would be sat down in a highchair next to her that folded out to make a little table. From there she would feed him. If he needed to go to the toilet, he would be carried to a pot that had been placed over a water drain at the far end of his mother's courtyard, from where he would look around abstractly as he did his business and see the rest of his mother's quarters. Sometimes his Amma might carry him into his mother's handmaids' quarters, a long darkly lit room leading off the kitchen area. Otherwise he would crawl around in his mother's rooms where she would be sitting and talking with visitors and handmaids.

More importantly, when his father came indoors to the female quarters for breakfast, lunch, or dinner, it was what we might call quality time and learning table manners. Both parents played with the twins. Raza was still bigger than Abid, and when Abid was beginning to crawl, Raza who could already stand, had the habit of sitting down on him. No one found it funny except Raza. His mother would turn her face away and his father would wave an admonishing finger at him. But such habits were finally put to a stop when his father decided to teach him a lesson by sitting on him. But mostly they were happy times.

The father would lie next to the two toddlers on the carpeted floor that was covered by white sheets. The mother would sit on the bed. The father would tell stories, many of them funny ones, and would tease them. Raza did not take teasing easily. Once he started crying when his father called him "straight" while calling himself and Abid as being "contrary." He didn't want to feel left out, so he started crying and went off to search for his uncle. The uncle understood but pretended to be cross for Raza's sake.

"I would say 'come on, let's go find my young brother,' and it turned into a mock mini drama because my father would hide from my uncle and my mother pretended not to know, and smiled at my uncle when I wasn't looking. At other times there would be lessons in good behavior, morality, and manners."

When the two toddlers had dozed off, they would be picked up by their nannies and placed in their respective cots, and the intervening doors between the living room shut, so that the only noise heard came from the fan above the cots. The parents would continue talking quietly for a while next door, then his father would return to do some office work in his rooms in the male quarter, and his mother would return to the chores of ordering food and groceries once she had asked her husband what he wanted to eat.

During 1939, when Raza was a little over 3 years old, his Bibi Amma, who was the head of the family, passed away. One day she was there and the next Raza no longer saw her. Death as a reality was still hidden from toddlers and infants, so Raza was simply whispered to by his Amma that his Bibi Amma had gone to *Jannat*, meaning heaven. And there the matter stayed in a 3-year-old's mind trying to imagine God. The person he would now see sitting in her place was his older paternal aunt, who was now regarded as the head of the family and even his uncle would bow to her and consult her in reference to all important decisions dealing with the family.

"She always looked a little stern. She was married to one of the sons of the Imam family. I remember him only by his photograph which hung in his paternal aunt's quarters. He also passed away at an early age, leaving behind a son called Hurr, who was the oldest member of the family from my generation, a full eight years older than Abid and I." Besides his Ammijan, Raza would see seated his younger paternal aunt, who he remembers as being very round-faced and jolly.

It was during this time, while learning to walk, that Raza began his exploration of the male part of the palace. Three servants were allocated the task of looking after the twins. One of them was his Amma's husband and after the boys had had their breakfast of toast, boiled eggs, a cup of hot Ovaltine, and some freshly squeezed orange juice, Raza's Amma would go to the side entrance that led to his mother's quarters and summon her husband to come and take the boys for a walk.

As interlocutors, let us step back and reenter Raza's mother's quarters through the side entrance to the zanana and take stock of the explorations already made by the toddlers before stepping outside, for it has always conjured up, evoked the heart of what Raza calls home. Let's start with the side entrance that was the route for all the comings and goings.

"It was a simple large wood-framed doorway, covered by a heavy canvas blind to provide purdah. As you enter, it leads to a small courtyard. Across the courtyard, you could see a three-story building that was seldom used except for storage purposes. There are two or three steps leading up from the sunken courtyard on the right hand side that occupy the kitchen and dining area adjacent to the mother's room that, despite its high ceilings, was usually full of smoke from the brick stoves over which food was cooked using both coal and wood for fuel, while the spices, herbs, garlic, and onions were ground by other women using a rectangular piece of chiseled granite and a small loaf-shaped granite stone. Water was drawn with a nearby hand pump, while drinking water was brought in by water bearers from the main well in the male quarters. Sweepers swept the floor and cleaned the toilet regularly."

Raza's mother's living quarters, sheltered from the outside world by the high wall of the adjacent Baradari in the male section of the palace, consisted of three long high-ceilinged interconnecting chambers. The central chamber where his mother slept and where he and Abid were born, and the near chamber, which she used for sitting and receiving other women in, generally the wives of the *daroghas* (police officials) and head chefs, of family retainers and courtiers, and so on. Beyond the central room and leading to the main courtyard, there was a third chamber used for religious purposes. Known mainly, as Abid reports, as the small *Imambara* or *paidayish wala kamra* (literally "the birthing room"), this is where Raza's uncle, as well as his two aunts were born. However, this was not the birthplace of his father, who was born in a house in a neighboring village, that of the grandmother.

One can imagine the noise, the smells, and aromas that engulfed Raza everywhere: the voices of his mother giving orders to the servants, the servants shouting to each other while grinding amazing-smelling spices, which carried another aroma as the onions and spices were fried, the shouts heard from outside the side entrance for provisions being delivered, the racket of the crows, kites, and pigeons as they circled like opportunist scavengers.

Emerging from there Raza and Abid were handed over for supervision by servants, and here they came into a different world, full of hustle and bustle, and chatter and calling, though in a much more open space than the more enclosed white room space of the zanana.

"Kites, eagles, crows, wild pigeons circle and hover, the kites with their long-forked tails, swooping down for morsels of food being carried from the main kitchens. Other birds, like small cockatoos can be seen clinging to the sunlit walls in the early morning, warming their feathers before taking flight. Servants and attendants would shout to one another across the open space, gardeners clipping the henna bushes that grow along the edge of the great lawn." When the twins emerge out of the side entrance in the morning, they see a small lawn in front and alongside its wrought iron, painted railings a broad path that leads to the main water well sheltered by tall trees, and beyond that a large sunken lawn bordered by a broad path. Tall henna bushes edged all the way around the lawn are seen on the other side of the path. To the right lies the immense structure of the main part of the palace.

The palace was a vast, rectangular space, geometrically built into quarters and each quarter had a kitchen and a host of women who cooked food for the retinue of workers: body guards, servants, gardeners, nurses, babysitters, chauffeurs, stable boys; and the vegetables would come year round, even in the wintertime, from one locale or another. The yellow walls of the palace painted white around the arches complement the green doors; the paintings of family members hung in various parts of the place, high above chandeliers and below resting on fine Persian carpets with large dining tables, fine China, porcelain vases, couches, sofas, and furniture purchased by his grandfather from London shops; mirrors reflecting marble-top tables sit amidst European reproductions, which were all signs of wealth.

The palace itself was situated in the center of the small town, which consists of two main districts; on one side, from the portion called Muqeem Manzil you have a view across a large pond, where water chestnuts grew, and which would be harvested in season. Beyond this stretch a medley of houses with narrow lanes and brick dwellings covered with clay where the ordinary folk live.

This was one quarter of the town and beyond these there is another large pond or lake, across which there is a dirt road leading past an orphanage built by his great-grandfather, leading to mausoleums replicating the Shi'a shrines in Najaf and Karbala, as well as a railway station. On the other side of the palace is another quarter of the town where the main bazaar is located, as well as more dwellings. Further beyond there is a large mango orchard called the *hazaara*, meaning "a thousand mango trees," but whether there were that number or not he does not know; then there is what is known as *lakhphera*, or a park with "thousands of trees," and a small lake for water birds.

Along the side from the entrance past the wide staircase leading to a large raised courtyard facing the Baradari, Raza and his brother have been allocated two interconnected rooms that are simply furnished. When the twins walk down the graveled main path, they encounter the people who were living there, and they are taught to pay respects to all elders, even servants they see. These rooms became their rooms for play and socializing with selected peers until 1941 when their school education began, and they would move with their parents to Lucknow.

Raza and his brother were both too young to understand or appreciate and explore, their days still had a structure, and they were chaperoned or followed everywhere. They had been given a tutor to teach them the Quran at a given time, and to recite prayers after following the correct rituals for the ablutions. Next came an obligatory visit to an uncle who lived on the first floor of the palace in rooms overlooking the main gate, whereas his father's rooms were well known to Raza. He was often sent there to wake up his father at his mother's behest, because his father had a habit of lashing out with his leg at any servant who was sent. The mother, trusting that her husband would not kick his toddler son, would ask a servant to carry him and put him down by the bedside. The strategy worked.

"I was told, because I don't rightly remember this, but I was told, I would shake my father and say, 'Abbajan wake up, Ammajan is calling you. Wake up. Please wake up.' I'm sure on hearing my insistent pleas, he would try turning over, but when that didn't work, he would be forced to gather me into his arms, sit up, and promise to get himself ready."

The time that was left for play or leisure was spent in their rooms with a couple of youngsters, who were children of people working in some respectable capacity for the family if the weather was too hot. If it was pleasant enough, they would play a cricket of sorts, with a tennis ball, stumps contrived out of stacked brick, and a child's wooden bat. There were rules of sorts, as taught by one of the retainers, but Raza really liked to bat and was allowed to even if the ball had hit the bricks. However, some sibling rivalry between the twins, and when Abid was given out, he would also refuse to budge, or throw his bat down in a temper and walk off.

The twins were not the first young males of the Amadabad family to have been seen out and about in the male part of the palace.

Raza and his brother Abid in the center with their bearded father wearig glasses. Lucknow (circa early 1940s)

Two old first cousins had been seen around from a few years before. The first, named Hurr, was a full eight years older, and the second, named Husain was some four years older. They had both moved to Lucknow for schooling by this time and came to the palace only during school holidays or for religious occasions.

"For such occasions, they had both been allocated rooms of their own on the third floor, right high up at the top of the palace from which you could not only look down on to the first floor courtyard below, and across to the library, but beyond where the town lay. I remember the excitement I experienced in finding my way around via a wooden staircase that led up to their rooms from the large red veranda on the first floor. Both the cousins showed us a lot of affection. Hurr or his big brother (literally) Baray Bhaisahab was very studious, while Husain was more convivial and full of bravado. They had both been appointed with their own tutors and mentors. At this time, I could only admire and respect Hurr."

Raza was not old enough to relate to similar interests, his mind was on other things—cricket, mainly. He played it whenever he could, and when the lawn in front of the side entrance became too small, he would play in the walled garden beyond, using the trunk of a large fruit tree that grew sweet purple fruit akin to damsons or plums. It was called a jamun tree. Here he could play cricket all day, a trait that often got him into trouble, and servants would be sent to fetch him for lunch, or because his parents had sent for him. He would then have to scurry back and behave like a penitent. He would find Abid already there. His mother would say, "Son, what have you been doing?"

"Nothing, just playing cricket."

"Why didn't you ask your brother to join you?"

"Because he doesn't know how to play, and he loses his temper too easily."

"But he's smaller than you. You should give him a chance. He's your brother after all."

Raza recalls these moments like they were yesterday, and would use the voice of his mother in the telling. He would often mimic the people he spoke about with expressions that were full of so much of life, habit, and custom. He would even recite from memory such events with a charming grace. As his mother would softly admonish him, he'd put his head down and nod in agreement, and he would give Abid a chance, but again the sibling rivalry would erupt.

"I think—no, I know—mother knew Abid was no angel. He would forever be nagging her for this and that, and his temper tantrums were well recognized all round in contrast to me, because I felt I was a bit more good-natured and, you could say, I had a more outgoing personality."

What Raza did not tell me—I heard this from Tess—was that he and his brother became known as "Tweedle Dee" and "Tweedle Dum," names given to them by both their father and their uncle, and repeated by their older cousins as a way of not taking sides, and instead laughing at their antics.

PRIMARY SCHOOL

Although Raza and Abid had by now moved with their parents to the unfinished White Palace in the northeastern part of Lucknow, they would still return to Amadabad for the holidays and, of course, the major religious occasions. If Raza's accounts from his memory are to be believed, then these days in Amadabad and living in the White Palace were idyllic. It was at this time he and his brother were enrolled at the Loretto Convent School for Girls, which admitted boys up to the age of 8. They were taken there in a chauffeur-driven car, and accompanied by their Master Dada.

The little green Austin Minor would return at lunch time with a prepared meal that they would sit and eat on the grass next to the parked car, with a spread cloth for plates and cutlery. Their older girl cousins also attended Loretto, but came in separate cars, acknowledging Raza and Abid, but they were in higher classes. They stayed in the main family palace and Raza did not see much of them at this time. Nor did they see much of their older male cousins, Hurr and Husain, who by then were studying at Colvin Taluqdar's College and the Martiniere School, respectively.

La Martinière College, Lucknow, 1947.

Even today this would be considered well-off and signs of wealth, especially with the tax on cars at that time.

At Loretto, Mother Mary Austin (who had also taught their father) and Sister Frances Therese instructed the boys in basic reading, writing, and arithmetic.

"Mother Mary Austin was very strict but with a soft heart and chastised us if we didn't pay attention, by smacking our palm with a ruler, but I noticed how her face would turn immediately remorseful when once the ruler broke on a palm."

Loretto was also the first place Raza came across a manifestation of racism: the school playground was cordoned off in the middle with British and Anglo-Indian children on the one side and the Indian children on the other side. He recalls lessons concerning the basic history and geography and general knowledge where he learned that history was essentially from a totally Eurocentric point of view, as exemplified in readers like "Britain and Her Neighbors," all about the Cloth of Gold and with no mention of Indian history as such.

"Although this much was to be expected in India under British rule, it also helped me form an imagined unity to the subcontinent as a unified country that historically it had never possessed, except under the British—neither under the ancient empires of the Mauryas and Guptas, nor later under the Mughals."

Raza was only later to come to understand this when he came to study Indian history in England that the ancient inhabitants of India were Dravidians, a much darker-skinned people, who were pushed down to South India by the fairer-skinned Aryan invaders. Much later, when the subcontinent became known as British India, the unity it had was given to it by the English language, the language of the rule of law and of administration.

I was intrigued by Raza's reflections about the Dravidians because the myth states that the "conquerors from the north said that the children of darkness were the Dravidians and the children of light were the Caucasians or Aryans." Though he did not go into detail about this, he did say there was more to this since some theories on caste system support the notion; and a scripture of the Dravidians linked them to the sun and therefore knowledge or seeing the light. Through historical plunder, it was changed to make them appear to be children of the night and therefore ignorant people who should be guided into the light by Aryans or their masters. Raza said his father had evidence and manuscripts that proved this to be the case in the library at the palace.

But still these were happy days, as Raza recalls laughing, and telling his friends ever since. This is when he first came across American GIs, stationed in Lucknow since the surprise attack on Pearl Harbor in 1941. They would saunter past outside the school and be friendly toward the twins eating their lunch on the grass.

"On one occasion, the soldiers were offered a spicy kebab by the driver and found it too hot, they therefore declined a gulab jamun because it looked suspiciously like the kebab. Loretto is also where we learnt to recite nursery rhymes like 'Humpty Dumpty' and 'Little Jack Horner' in Anglo-Indian rhymes."

It's been his stock-in-trade at parties and gathering with his friends ever since. He recites still now as we talked about those days:

Humpty-Dumpty:
Humpty-Dumpty batha ka chat
Humpty Dumpty gir gaya path
Raja ka ghora, rani ki ghori,
Humpty Dumpty kabhi nai jori

Little Jack Horner
Little Jack Horner
Baitha in a kona
Eating his kishmish pie
Usmen angootha dala aur kishmish nikala,
And said: "Bohoth achchha larka hum hai."

The reciting of these poems gave him quite a laugh and his face lit up with smiles and grins. To my mind, when I hear Raza reciting gems like these, they speak of that fleeting phenomenon known as Anglo-Indian culture, and I encourage Raza about the need for them to be collected and preserved in an anthology.

"Anyway, after school, our Master Dada would be waiting for us after school, and we would be driven to Hazrat Ganj, where we would invariably stop at the Kashmir Fruit Mart, and Master Dada would buy fruit, cornflakes and, best of all, salted cashew nuts to take home. All 'rich' food. For schoolbooks we would stop a little further down at the Universal Book Depot before turning back home. On occasions we might go by the Zoo, from where the lions could be heard roaring in the mornings from within the grounds of the White Palace."

There was a major blip in this idyll when Raza returned to Amadabad during the first summer holidays. Raza became ill during this time, when a series of medical issues emerged in his young life.

"Though I was only all of 5 years [old], I remember I was playing cricket on the small lawn outside the side entrance of the zanana leading to mother's quarters. I liked playing cricket all times of the year, and at all times of the day when I could get away from lessons and other duties. On this particular occasion, it was noontime, or about noon, because I remember how the sun was blazing down and I was enjoying hitting the ball, when all of a sudden I stood up and did what was unthinkable for me, at least: I walked away from a game of cricket, albeit complaining of a blinding headache. Servants rushed over to me and brought me indoors to mother.

I had a very high temperature and Dr. Ghyasuddin, our family physician, who wore these heavy glasses and had this odd little goatee beard and mustache. The doctor didn't know what was wrong with me and on examination the doctor asked for a second opinion because he feared I might have typhoid fever. Now this other doctor, I was later told, was a surgeon in the British army who came from Lucknow to examine me. Typhoid was confirmed, and a course of treatment and medication was prescribed. Both my parents were naturally very worried and the return to the New White Palace and to Loretto Convent had to be postponed. I was told to lie down on this small bed which was at the end of mother's living room, where it was quite dark I remember. Also I remember eating or having a diet of baked custard to give me nourishment and some energy. This was just as well because I can tell you now I have all my life loved the taste of baked custard."

"I also remember not-so-pleasant moments when they gave me those enemas, but all in all the whole treatment and recuperation lasted for what seemed like forever because I couldn't play cricket or be with my brother or any friends. My father told me much later that it lasted about six weeks."

There would be days and times when he suffered from delirium and when he would feel a pounding and throbbing in his head. His mother was carrying his yet-to-be-born sister, Zahra, but she could not help worrying about her eldest born. She would let Raza lay his head down on her lap in the quarantined corner of her room. Abid and other children were kept away. Though his father told him of the time it took to recuperate, he was at the time unsure of the time frame and because those records that had been kept by his mother can no longer be found.

The following summer, he was well again and at that time the family returned to Amadabad.

Later that year, during November 1942, Zahra, Raza's little sister, was born in Amadabad, and his parents were overjoyed at the birth of a girl—now they had three children. Raza was kind by nature and took to her immediately as his little sister, but Abid *"felt like piggy in the middle,"* a phrase Raza used, even though he was only a few hours younger than Raza. The parents took care not to appear to take sides, but the nature of sibling rivalry is such that those who come in the middle often feel left out.

Raza mentions it was also around this same time he and his brother noticed their uncle busy about the palace. Mostly he was to be found under a large red-and-white striped marquee that had mysteriously appeared in the middle of the great lawn one day. On an occasion when Raza had ventured forth to play cricket in the garden, his uncle had beckoned to him. Politely saying his *adaabs* to his uncle, Raza had spotted several thick square glass tanks with some kind of acid in them, and his uncle with some of his cronies huddled around and what looked like experimenting.

Later he learned from Abid, who was a curious little boy, that he had heard it whispered that the acid was being used to melt down family gold, which was being used to finance the nawab's political activities, and that silver items were being plated with gold in order to replace them and disguise the fact that anything was missing. This story seemed somewhat far-fetched, but I took it as it was. Another summer, Raza said his uncle asked them to do something quite odd.

"My uncle asked that we both, Abid and I, have our heads shaved, just as he had done. He told us that hair made the head too hot and he said this all the while laughing or smiling at us, as if to say I dare you to do it. Well, Abid and I agreed to do it."

With shaven heads they would wait for the 4:00 o'clock gong to sound four times, which meant it was time to go to the swimming pool in the garden.

"But by the time we got there our uncle was already in the pool in his swimming costume, a modest black affair covering the top of the body as well."

"When we saw our uncle in the shimmering inviting water, we would dash up the steps from the swimming pool to get changed into our, you might say, equally modest swimwear to join him in the water. Sometimes our father would join us too."

But times like these were rare. Those halcyon days that were etched in memory as endless and idyllic lasted only for a summer or two, or maybe three, and included trips to the holiday resort of Nainital in the Himalayas, with the train picking up all the family members at Amadabad Station, and on which a whole compartment with bathroom and toilet en suite would be reserved for Raza's parents and two children; in fact, the whole train would be booked, with other first-class carriages and coupes occupied by his uncle and aunts and cousins, and second-class compartments for all the servants and cooks who would accompany them, the train puffing up the winding track as it ascended the lush foothills of the Himalayas.

Raza remembers his father saying, "I think I can, I think I can, I think I can," slowly in imitation of the engine, before changing it to, "I thought I would, I thought I would, I thought I would." As he mimicked his dad as the engine sped up again down another incline before reaching its destination, where the party would be met by cars to chauffeur them to family-sized bungalows, where they would stay for two or three weeks, and the father would spend his days learning to yacht on the lake, leaving the twins in the care of an acquaintance who would teach them how to roller skate in the adjacent skating rink. As Nainital is close to the border, with Tibet to the north and Nepal to the east, the mother would spend her days buying Chinese silk, and games of mahjong with pieces made of ivory, and other things that Chinese-looking people brought around on their laden bicycles to sell. Those seemingly endless idylls, he would tell me in no uncertain terms, were the calm before the storm.

THE MAN IN THE PALACE

I point out here a new branch in the life of Raza which is evident since it departs from an account of his childhood and instead focus on Nawab Dawood.

Nawab Dawood Ahmad was now more frequently to be seen and for longer stays in Amadabad from around the time that Raza was 5. However, he was not so much back in his palace because he was still constantly on the move between Lucknow, Delhi, Bombay, and Calcutta, giving political speeches and mixing with politicians like Jawaharlal Nehru, Sarojini Naidoo, Jinnah, and so on.

As to the nawab's frame of mind, it was a mystery even to himself at times. At such moments, he would shut himself off in his room and gave orders not to be disturbed. At other times he might share things with cronies and advisers, but there was little conversation with his younger brother, Raza's father, except for polite words.

There was much talk of the Muslim League, but what its demands and program were and what it stood for were not clear. The influence of religion was patently obvious by their presence as friends and confidants of the nawab, but Nawab Dawood kept everyone guessing about his intentions.

He became known as "the man with many masks" because he was trying to play so many different roles that had people guessing: the devoted younger brother to his two older sisters; the devoted husband with three daughters and no son; the devoted older brother to Raza's dad; adopting the twins as if they were his own since he was without son; sincere in his piety and committed to Shi'a Muslim traditionalism, expressed through marsiyas, Salaams, and the observation of religious occasions; and his embrace of the exigencies of a political cause that demanded the sale of much family wealth. For he had by now become the treasurer of the Muslim League. But he rarely allowed any slippage between the different masks. So adept he had become in burying his feelings deep down.

Events at the national level, as well as at the international level, were fast moving between 1941 and 1945, as we know, and they were to impact directly on the Amadabad family due to Nawab Dawood's politics in a dramatic and decisive fashion. I have carried out my own research into this period in order to understand the various accounts of Raza and other informants. The Second World War, which had been waging since 1939 in Europe, had drawn the United States and Japan into conflict in 1941, with the surprise Japanese attack on Pearl Harbor. British India became necessarily more drawn in to the global conflict.

Gandhi's "Quit India" campaign entailed the boycotting of British goods, particularly the import of cotton-made goods grown in India but manufactured in Britain and sold back to India, which had been flourishing until then. Gandhi's *khaddar*, or homespun cotton movement, acted as an irritant to the British. Yet it came to a temporary halt, when suddenly wrong-footed by Jinnah's offer of loyalty and support for the Allies in 1942, the Congress under the leadership of Gandhi and the younger Nehru reluctantly decided on a similar offer of support—but not until a date of departure had been extracted from the British. Lord Wavell, commander of the Allied Forces in India and Burma, conveyed the news to the British prime minister, and a date was set for Britain's departure by 1947.

As to the issue of Muslims in India, Jinnah remained deliberately vague and did not commit himself. Jinnah still hoped for an accommodation with the Congress for Muslims and Hindus to coexist within one united India, albeit one that recognized Muslim majority areas, an idea that was to be ridiculed by Jawaharlal Nehru as politically and economically unviable. Later, Jinnah and Nehru almost switched sides as then were the shifting ideological sands that could not be deciphered ahead of the moment of 1947.

In these circumstances, Raza confirmed in conversation what I had discovered in my research into these historic events. Nawab Dawood had to decide whether to keep both the Congress and the Muslim League on his side, even going as far as giving shelter to the charismatic Subhash Chandra Bose, who had briefly been president of the Congress before being ousted by Gandhi. When Chandra Bose was on the way out in 1940, according to one of the old retainers in Kaiserbagh, there used to be frequent blackouts over Lucknow for fear of Japanese planes attacking the city. During one of these blackouts, Nawab

Dawood Ahmad was seen parading up and down the long verandah with a revolver attached to his belt while his guest, Chandra Bose, slept in the palace.

It was soon after this occasion that Nawab Dawood Ahmad, impatient with the dithering of the Muslim League over the issue of partition or no partition, had been swung over by the group of the youth faction of the Muslim League and delivered his speech in a moment of political folly in favor of a separate, autonomous, and independent Pakistan.

Raza further informs me that, if it were a prediction, he would have been correct. "For reasons given, as stated, Jinnah had rebuked him. Having committed this seeming act of calculated folly, which risked the entire future of the family, the nawab set about repairing fences all around. After offering his profuse apologies to Jinnah, he tried to mend fences with the Congress, communicating frequently with Nehru and remaining on good terms with him and other Congress leaders like Mrs. Sarojini Naidoo, whose photograph, incidentally is still on display in the main entrance of the palace in Lucknow. There's a copy in our family albums, showing me and my brother, Abid, alongside our cousin Husain, walking to the White Haiderbagh Baradari, in the trail behind Nawab Dawood and Mrs. Naidoo."

A Muslim homeland had become Nawab Dawood Ahmad's life's raison d'être and would invariably attract his attention first. At the time, despite his loyalty to Jinnah, who being childless regarded him as a son, his own plans and intentions, if any such had formulated in his mind, remained concealed from the world, including his immediate family. No one knew which way he would move or jump. The nawab's unresolved dilemma created uncertainty and tensions among the older generation of family members, tensions that were not eased by the presence of people from Ferangi Mahal and the same politicos disguised as clerics who had circled around the nawab 10 years earlier in Amadabad.

One of them who the young Raza remembers distinctly was called Kamal Sahab. He and others had now become frequent visitors to the palace in Lucknow. Raza remembers them sitting with his uncle in the lawn, smoking cigarettes and smiling as they talked among each other, that is when they were not closeted with him in his office. Nawab Ali Haidar was certainly affected, and must have felt that the future of the family and its legacy was at stake, but found his older brother evasive and always too busy for a one-to-one chat with him.

This evasiveness on the part of Nawab Dawood Ahmad only served to heighten Raza's brother's (Abid) nervousness and inner tension. He also became moody and given to fits of depression like his brother (Raza) had been for some time.

The nawab also needed to explain his political actions and speeches. What impact might they have on the ordinary public? What might the consequences of partition be for Amadabad? What might follow? His wife was a *rani* (queen) in her own right. What if it came down to a partition of India? The Shi'a Muslims of the United Provinces stood little realistic chance of obtaining a Muslim majority vote in the UP. What would happen to the estates and the land?

Moreover, there were his two older sisters to consider, the older already a widow because Hurr's father had passed away just shortly after Raza's grandmother, and the younger sister's husband was of a more secular nature and scarcely likely to give up his own estate in favor of a move to Pakistan. Finally, there was Haidar Ali, his younger brother. Some clarity was needed, but none came because the nawab was still in the process of undoing his rash speech. Whenever Raza's father tried to find his brother on his own to discuss what was in his brother's mind, the nawab was too busy. These questions are meant to lend urgency to the nawab's decisions, to provide a rationale. To do so, I think they needed some reformulations, however, none were forthcoming.

During that time in the early 1940s, Raza's parents had to leave the White Palace because it had been requisitioned for the officers of the RAF, and move to the main family house. It was not a happy or welcome move for Raza's mother. In the White Palace, she had been able to get away from all the gossip and backbiting of Amadabad because her two boys were seen as too close and dear to their uncle and people whispered that they had been put up to admiring themselves.

Bajia Amma had led a paradisal life in the White Palace: she could see her women friends, she could indulge in new clothes, keep her own milk-producing cow in the palace grounds, have her husband's undivided loyalty for once, and observe him become a family man who would read stories to his children by the fireside. Now this life would end, and she would be back in an atmosphere of petty gossip, since her sister-in-law was now expecting another baby boy, or at least that is what was expected. She made the best of things but longed to be back at the White Palace again, away from the gossip and intrigue that was bound to increase, focusing on her sons. She pleaded with her husband to buy a home somewhere apart.

She warned him that no good would come of being so loyal to his elder brother and help in the management of the family estate, but Nawab Haidar Ali would have none of it, he was not one for giving up on loyalties, split though they were, though his wife and servants and secretaries could trace the signs of this worry in his mood shifts, wrestling with himself, since he could get no clear answer from his brother, who never seemed to be available for a real heart-to-heart.

Naturally, both parents tried to avoid making the children aware of any tensions or worries. Their upbringing and education came first, and after the summer of 1944, Raza and Abid were due to be enrolled at the Martiniere Boys' College, which the father had himself attended. Their 9-month-old daughter also required nursing and attention.

In the family palace in Lucknow, Nawab Haidar Ali was allocated an en suite pair of rooms on the first floor at the front of the palace, overlooking the porch, and the twins were given a room around one of the central courtyards, while Zahra had an adjoining room. Nawab Dawood Ahmad did not take up his father's room on the first floor but had his apartment on the ground floor renovated.

Raza describes the accommodations of Nawab Dawood Ahmad:

> It consisted of a spacious front room with a large desk and some modern 1930s furniture—two chairs, a settee, and a table on a carpeted floor, where visitors and guests were received. Beyond the living room through three wide arches there lay a larger carpeted room containing his bed, with a number of narrower arches that separated it from a long narrow space, wide enough to accommodate a long dining table with chairs.
>
> This is where Nawab Dawood Ahmad entertained guests. Behind the living area there was a large dressing room, and adjacent bathroom and toilet. He alone amongst all the family members lived on the ground floor. Sentries and servants guarded the entrance to the nawab's suite. Important visitors were announced and ushered in. Personally signed photographs of many of these, such as the nizam of Hyderabad, the nawabs of Rampur and Bawahalput, the rajas of Pirpur, Lorepur, Nanpara, politicians such as Jawaharlal Nehru, and many others were on display in his suite. His secretariat lay adjacent to his suite, and there was a telephone situated in the lobby in front, which was also furnished with chairs and a comfortable couch where visitors would wait.

Raza tells me that he has memories of going into the secretariat room to ask for rubber erasers and rulers and pencils for school.

> Adjacent to his apartment and right at one end of the long palace building there was an apartment for the chief manager of the Estate, who kept the

nawab up-to-date with the affairs of Amadabad Estate. Everyone else stayed on the first floor of the palace, which also contained the female quarters where my aunts and their daughters lived. On the male side of the palace there were rooms for my male cousins, Hurr and Husain along one side of a large inner courtyard. Hurr was 15 by then and attending Colvin Taluqdar College, and Husain, who was 11, attended the Martiniere, where Abid and I were also shortly to be registered.

THE BIRTH AND INFANCY OF IBN DAWOOD

Whenever Nawab Dawood Ahmad was around, he came to dine with his wife and daughters in their quarters, and sometimes he would stay behind with his wife in privacy after the daughters had gone for their English lessons, or were away at school in Loretto. The nawab was still a man in his 30s, and even if his wife was several years older, he was still trying to give her a son, but without success. At about this time, rumors were rife in the zanana in Amadabad because he had been seen gazing at a rather pretty handmaid of his wife on more than one or two occasions.

The handmaid was soon not to be seen in the palace. She was held to blame for enticement, not the nawab himself. She was not of noble birth and these were different times to those of his father. It was impossible for him to contract a "Muta" marriage as his father had done. For one thing, he needed to appease his wife, for they were still without a male heir, and thus quenched any flame of salacious gossip gathering force. To see all of this is to understand that it reeks of Indian patriarchy.

"Many 'mannats' [religious vows] had been made for years that the rani and nawab be blessed with a son, many candles lit. Then, as chance would have it, a pregnancy was confirmed in March or April 1943, but there was still no certainty that it was going to be a boy or a girl, which led to more prayers."

Of course, a lot of these prayers and rituals for a boy are still practiced today. I asked Raza would this be an excellent time to discuss gender inequality but he avoided the question by stating superstition was used by some of the old female servants and retainers to ward off evil spirits, and more prayers given for the birth of a healthy living boy.

"When finally the baby was born in early December 1944, it turned out to be a boy, as if everyone's prayers had been answered. He was given the full name of Ibn Dawood. He was a small baby, fragile in health and disposition by all descriptions, and kept swaddled. His two sisters cared for him, but the whole aspect around his health was kept hidden. It is only later that Raza began to notice his cousin walked around like a penguin, and used to refer to him jokingly as penguin. This trait was known as out-toeing. He was later nicknamed 'Shaikhoo.'"

The news of the birth reached Raza's parents when they were living in Haiderbagh, in exile from the White Palace that had been commandeered by the RAF. Raza's father immediately sent a message of mubarak to his brother and sister-in-law and said that he would soon be arriving in Amadabad.

Raza and his family came to hear of the event and Raza got to see their baby cousin during the school holidays that winter when they arrived in Amadabad. The whole palace was in a state of excitement. The birth was greeted with much fanfare, fireworks, and a salvo of gunfire. Prayers were recited in the zanana and food distributed to the poor of the town. Nawab Dawood Ahmad had thus finally succeeded in appeasing his wife and given her an heir. The month of Moharram was about to dawn, so further rejoicing was postponed until the following Spring.

Raza cannot remember too much of Ibn Dawood as a baby boy because his 8-year-old head was by then much too occupied with games and friends to give Ibn Dawood much thought, but when I ask him directly about it, he agrees that he too must have been delighted:

> "Who wouldn't be? I loved my uncle, and I was happy for him," was his short answer before continuing: "In my mind, the first image I have is that of my handsome debonair father, wearing his beige-colored sherwani and maroon velvet cap, carrying the little cuddly boy, with big eyes, wearing a white sherwani out of the female quarters under an arch of drawn sabers formed by the equestrian guard outside the main entrance to the zanana. My uncle was either not around or didn't feel it right and proper for him to parade his own son. My father then carried Ibn Dawood up the stairs to the Baradari to tie a 'girah' or knot, usually of cotton, tied around neck, hands and feet of the supplicant which is tied to a holy relic after prayers."

It was from his mother and his Amma that Raza later heard the many stories and accounts of Ibn Dawood's infancy and childhood. Ibn Dawood's mother was in her 36th year at the time and the birth had been problematic. The infant was frail and small; as a result was nursed and frequently examined by the doctor for the first few months.

At about the age of 2, Ibn Dawood developed an inflammation of the spine, a mild form of polio. This was also later confirmed by Raza's Baji Zainab, who remembers herself and the other sisters tending and nursing Ibn Dawood until the affliction had passed. His mother became concerned for her boy's welfare. A suitable nanny was found to follow the toddler around, and when he was old enough to be sent outside, one of the nawab's trusted retainers was appointed to escort him and bring him to his father's room.

He had a special diet and certain foodstuffs like chicken and aubergines he was not allowed to eat. He was referred to as "Maulvi Munaqqa" by his cousins because he was given munaqqas and kishmish to eat. These are grapes that are dried in a particular fashion and are considered as remedies in Middle Eastern and Ayurvedic medicine for debility. They are even used as a substitute for milk compared to which it is easier to digest.

Since Ibn Dawood was much younger than his male cousins to join in with their games or conversations, he had only one male playmate at this time, and that was Dada Mian's second youngest child. They would go around together escorted by an "ataleeq" or mentor, followed at a distance by a servant. The gloom and depression partially lifted from Nawab Dawood Ahmad when he received the news of the birth of a son, but only partially.

CHAPTER 6

RAZA'S LATER CHILDHOOD AND ADOLESCENCE

Raza and Abid were allotted a room for study across the large dining hall from their parents' quarters, overlooking one side of the inner central courtyard of the palace. This was the family's first stay in the main palace and the boys living and sleeping quarters consisted of an en suite apartment with bathroom, toilet, and a changing area. Directly below that was situated Master Dada's room, which they would go down to for homework and tuition. Across the courtyard they would see their two *Bhaisahabs*, or older first cousins—Hurr and Husain, both of whom were respectively eight and four years older. This disparity in age between them and the twins felt considerable at that age, since they were in secondary education while the twins were at the primary level, albeit no longer at Loretto but at La Martinière Boys College.

LA MARTINIÈRE

Since their father and uncle had attended the college before, it was natural that the children too should follow, and because the other family precedent was their great-grandfather had attended the Calcutta branch of La Martinière. The boys' college, and a separate girls' college in Lucknow, had been founded in accordance with a will left behind by a major general named Claude Martin, a Frenchman, in 1836. La Martinière College, Lucknow, had the distinction of having played a part (on the British side) during the siege of Lucknow in 1856 and against the forces led by Raza's great-great-grandfather.

This distinction was becoming a dubious one to hold up at the time India was demanding its independence, but there it was still declaring the message when Raza and Abid started attending. The staff and pupils at the time had reportedly helped in the defense of the Residency during 1857. Three cannons still stand in front of the enormous magnificent baroque building, named Constantia. This is where Claude Martin had lived in the late eighteenth century, and it was also featured in *Kim*, the film made on location in 1949, starring Errol Flynn, after a story by Rudyard Kipling.

Talking to me about his first experience at the college, Raza says: "We wore uniforms of khaki shorts and shirts. Boys were allotted to different houses called Lyons, Martin, Cornwallis, and Hudson. I remember wearing the yellow-and-black striped canvas belt of Lyons House. Most of the boys at that time were Anglo-Indians, as were most of the teachers. In the primary section of the school, we were taught first by Mrs. England, and after that by Miss Burns, who was an auburn-haired lady with freckles and who spoke with a Scottish accent. Most of the Anglo-Indian boys were known as teachers, "foundationeers," and provided with free tuition, board, lodging, and clothing through the trust established by its founder. Others were day scholars. During summer, school would start at 7.00 a.m. and finish at 1:00 p.m. During the winter, there was a later start at 9.00 and school finished at 3.00 p.m."

Raza did not make many friends at the school, except toward the end. The two boys he and Abid got to know were Andrew and Colin Buck who they were allowed to be invited home by their father. Raza and his brother were invited in turn to their home, which was in part of Lucknow known as the Golf Colony, where most of the Anglo-Indians lived. That friendship lasted because even after leaving for London, Raza's sister kept in touch with Andrew's wife. Raza believes both Andrew and Colin came to London, but he lost touch.

As demographics of Lucknow before the war and prior to independence show, there was quite a sizable population of Anglo-Indians in Lucknow, but they kept largely to themselves. And, of course, during the war there were some Britishers as well.

"In particular I remember two tailor shops run by the English, one of them called Andersons and the other called Drapers. My father, who was very fashionable at the time, would have his suits made there. I remember looking through my father's wardrobe and admiring it. He always had shirts to match his many suits, and silk ties, bow ties, shoes and fashionable socks too. But he didn't socialize much with the English as relations with them were kept at a civilized distance.

We were taught to keep our own values, but I felt a sense of ambivalence in this attitude because we were not encouraged or allowed to see Indian movies, which were considered too vulgar, with one or two exceptions like *Pukaar*. When going out to see a movie, we were also encouraged to wear European clothes and to see English or American films only. The second film I ever saw was Charlie Chaplin's *Gold Rush*, which father took us to see."

Raza remembers him explaining the humorous scenes, especially the one where Chaplin starts eating into the leather sole of a shoe, having mistaken it for a piece of steak. Before that they had only seen one other movie *The Song of Bernadette*, when they were students at Loretto Convent, but this didn't count, as it was part of schooling and Catholic propaganda.

"Dada Mian or Master Dada always accompanied us to the movies. During World War II, which was still ongoing, both British and American soldiers frequented the cinemas in Hazratganj. At the end of the program, the cinemas played 'God Save the King' and everyone was expected to stand up. Occasionally, some American GIs wouldn't stand and this would lead to fisticuffs between the Tommies and the GIs. The few Indians watching the movie would have a quiet laugh about this falling out between white people, and sympathies were generally with the Americans because India was also engaged in its own independence struggle against the English."

Raza cannot remember all the films he saw at that time but they included ones with Laurel and Hardy, as well as a black-and-white film version of *Frankenstein*. He remembers being haunted by that film for long afterwards, and whenever he went late at night to his mother's room to say goodnight, he would always look at the corner of the courtyard roof where he imagined Frankenstein's monster appear suddenly looking down at him. Films became a passion, a wholly new experience in a darkened hall where only the screen was lit up, with stories that seemed like dreams.

He admits to being something of a dullard at school and often being chastised and kept in detention. By contrast, "Abid seems to have been a bit of a precocious twin, was a bit of a swot." In retrospect, Raza admits that this was because all he was interested in was games and friends.

During this period that marked a temporary cessation of anti-British activities in the Indian national movement, he remembers accompanying his father to a garden fete held in the governor's residence, which was just down the road from Loretto.

"This was the first time I remember Attiyah Hussain, an attractive looking lady, a little younger than my parents, and a distant relative of my family through the Kidwais, and a friend and visitor. I remember her because she had made my father buy a raffle ticket in support of the war."

To Raza's surprise and joy, when the winning raffle ticket was announced, his father's raffle ticket number had come up and he had won what looked like a three-foot-long replica of a British airplane carrier, painted in a steel navy grey, and complete with all the details of a flight and landing deck, revolving cannon turrets, everything but the replica men. This was the latest toy to add to his and

Abid's existing set of toys and games that included Meccano sets and even a gramophone. So games and escapades there were aplenty.

One of the latter involved climbing to the rooftop with his cousin Husain to shine mirrors at flying overhead planes. One such incident sticks out in his mind, and this was when the airplanes showered down leaflets. Raza imagined that the pilots must have seen the reflection of the mirror being shone from the rooftop of the main palace. When Husain and he ran to pick up one of the leaflets, they saw a picture of Emperor Hirohito, and the phrase "JAPAN SURRENDERS" emblazoned across it. Without grasping the world-shattering importance of it, Raza had witnessed the news of the dropping of the first atomic bombs on Hiroshima and Nagasaki. He was 9 years old at the time.

Soon after that—Raza cannot recall the exact date—he and his parents and brother and sister returned to the White Palace now that the war was over and the palace was no longer needed by the British. However, the stay there did not last long for within a year they were back in the family palace. Apparently, the same head manager of the Amadabad Estate whose quarters were next to his (Raza's) uncle had decided to lease the White Palace out because of a shortage of revenue. Whether this was done with the knowledge of Nawab Dawood Ahmad or not, it did cause Raza's mother and father considerable upset. At some point in 1946, his father seemed to undergo a nervous breakdown and extreme mood swings.

These were interludes in a family environment where his mother showed increasing anxiety and fear when she saw her husband dance around the dining table with a razor blade near his neck and a strange wild-eyed look on his face, encouraging his young sons to join in and chant: "We are now all monkeys." At moments like these, Raza would catch some of his mother's anxiety and not know where to look. Soon the whole family came to hear of his father's condition.

Raza's maternal aunts were the only ones his father seemed to show any respect toward. His uncle, Nawab Dawood Ahmad, stayed well clear, as did his wife. The women believed that a spell had been placed on Raza's father and tried to tell by the shadow cast by lit candles in the paternal aunts' quarters who it was thought had cast the spell. This was all in Lucknow. When they all went to the palace at Amadabad, and one of these moods came over Raza's father, he would throw a fit and walk barefoot out of the palace, out of Amadabad itself, and along a dirt road to the village some five miles away where his mother, the old rani, had given birth to him.

No one tried to stop him, for when a servant had once tried to restrain him on the instructions of Nawab Dawood Ahmad, Raza's father had used his strength to shrug off the attempt. Instead, servants just followed him from a distance to prevent him from any self-harm. All this was all too bewildering for Raza. Older people did not discuss such matters with youngsters like him.

In due course, it turned out that Nawab Haidar Ali was sent to a sanatorium in Rai Bareilly in southeast of Lucknow for treatment. When he returned home, he seemed to be calmer. He seemed to be aware of the fact that he had been ill, though not in the accepted sense because he had been advised to visit Europe and United States to consult further with psychologists and receive treatment.

Nawab Haidar Ali was just 29 years of age at this time and his elder brother, Nawab Dawood Ahmad, was yet to reach the age of 33. Both of them still young you might say to bear the responsibilities of the family legacy. We have already had reasons to note that the medical records of both had shown that they were of a highly nervous disposition at the time they lost their father. Deprived of his paternal guidance, they had had to grit their teeth and get on with it. Our story has also sketched out the tumultuous times they lived in. Now with the end of the war, the long-awaited promise of independence for India from the British was round the corner during the following year, 1947, and the Amadabad family had a stake in the form it would take.[1]

In the regional elections of 1937, the Muslims in Uttar Pradesh numbered about a third of its population, but had won no seats. This was due to the lack of much grassroots support for the Muslim League, and, therefore, under Nehru the Congress felt that the League could be ignored, and that such support that it had there came from its aristocratic rulers and landowners. The Congress decided against forming any alliance with the League, hoping that many of these Muslim aristocrats and landowners, such as the Amadabad family, could be won over in time.

Our story has already related the fact of the Congress boycott of the declaration of World War II by the British. In fact, it had instructed all its provincial governments to resign, and how the Muslim League under Jinnah

---

1 During the 1937 regional elections to the Legislative Council, Gandhi was no longer leading the Congress. Nehru Junior, that is to say Jawaharlal Nehru's era had for all intents and purposes begun, but he remained loyal to Gandhi, as his writings reveal. Although on the surface he was more progressive and seemed to espouse some form of Socialism, because Gandhi was influenced more by Tolstoy than Marx and certainly not by the British Fabians. So much is still part of the extensive and growing historiography of the Indian national movement and open to interpretation in India and outside.

had stepped into the political vacuum thus created by offering its support to Britain. The Congress subsequently trumped this by also calling off its boycott in return for a date of departure by Britain. This moment was now imminent.

For all of his mending of fences and relations with the Congress leadership, Nawab Dawood Ahmad was troubled how things would pan out personally for him. He remained loyal to Jinnah. He staked everything now on the Muslim League winning seats in Uttar Pradesh during the legislative elections of 1946. He even went so far as to persuade his brother Nawab Ali Haidar to stand for a seat. There is a description that Raza gives of his now-recovered and handsome father wearing a green sherwani with a golden stud pinned to its collar with the letter "P."

Raza remembers too that his father lost out to the Congress candidate Rafi Ahmad Kidwai, who was a distant relative. The Congress had once again trumped the league in Uttar Pradesh as it had calculated way back in 1937, but the British rulers were reluctant to agree to any notion of partition. Muslim thugs had already massacred Hindus in Bengal, and Hindus retaliated with a greater massacre of Muslims. Rather than the policy of "divide and rule" often attributed to them, they still wanted India to have some form of dominion status within the Commonwealth, and rather than the legacy of untold bloodshed, they wanted to leave behind the legacy of the rule of law.

It was Nehru's refusal to deal with Jinnah, who he disliked at a personal level, that was driving things inevitably toward partition. Jinnah had still not made up his mind on what role the League would play in a future independent India. Just as he was giving a speech in Bombay putting forward an 11-point program of demands to the British, into this scene stepped Mountbatten, sent as the latest and last Viceroy of British India. Communal riots were raging in Punjab as Mountbatten arrived. Within a month, he had decided that since the deadlock between Congress and the League could not be overcome, partition was inevitable.

Of course, personal relations are never supposed to influence matters of state, but in this case, they did. The sartorially elegant viceroy formed an instinctive and immediate affinity with the handsome and cultured Nehru, who was also known for his discreet affairs with members of the opposite sex.

The word "Pakistan," signifying a separate homeland for India's Muslims, had only recently been coined, but Indian Muslims could not all be accommodated within Pakistan, so thinly were they spread in some parts of the subcontinent, and no matter what formula for the partition was eventually devised. The wonder of it all was that no referendum was offered to the Indian populace on the question, nor any offered by the British. This meant that legislative district boundaries would determine contiguous majority and minority religious areas, leaving anomalies like Kashmir and Hyderabad Deccan to one side.

As a result, Nawab Dawood Ahmad found himself in a no-win situation whether he decided to stay and become a recognized leader of the Muslims left behind in India, as reportedly he was urged to do by none other than Nehru, or leave the ancient family seat, uprooting himself in the process, and go to Pakistan.

Raza eloquently states that "the nawab had this poisoned chalice to drink, but decided to bide his time before he did so. Secretly, he had already purchased two large properties in Karachi for just such an eventuality in the event a contingency arose."

All these thoughts ravaging the nawab's being went on above the heads and beyond the knowledge of Raza and the other youngsters in the Amadabad family by the older members in order to preserve some sense of *ettihaad* (unity). As 1947 dawned and partition approached, the young Raza only remembers being told that the family would be going on *ziyarat*, a form of pilgrimage to the sacred shrines of the Prophet Mohammad's descendants, to the holy Shi'a shrines in Iraq and Iran.

During April 1947, all the family, except for Raza's older cousin, Husain—who by then had become a boarder at an English-type of public school in the Himalayan foothills—left Lucknow. As mentioned, the ostensible reason given was a ziyarat, though it did not include Mecca and Medina. These descendants are largely buried in Iraq and Iran. You could hazard a guess that behind this laudable reason, as the adults in the family were only too aware, lay the fear of Hindu–Muslim conflict, like the ones already witnessed in Bengal and Bihar, and concern for the safety of their children.

The family left Lucknow, not collectively because that would have been impractical, but in units. Raza, Abid, and Zahra left with their parents and traveled by train to Madras, from where they flew by seaplane to Karachi. It was a BOAC commercial flight, and as Raza recalls, they had a cabin to themselves through whose portholes he could see the waves lapping around the ski-like blades of the plane before it took off for Karachi.

Karachi was where his uncle, Nawab Dawood Ahmad, had bought two large houses in the part known as Clifton. This transaction had taken place on the advice of Jinnah, who had seen two pieces of prime property advertised, and immediately alerted the nawab about it.

"According to Maysam's younger brother [Qays], the story goes that Jinnah saw the two properties for sale in the English daily called *Dawn* and strongly advised the nawab that he should invest in these, since if India is partitioned, there would be a place of refuge for him and his family, a haven to shelter in. The money for the transaction came from the sale of gold and other fabulous wealth of Amadabad which the nawab had been selling for the cause."

They turned out to be two-story houses that could accommodate everyone, all the family members. So when the entire party of retainers and servants traveling with the family arrived, they all stayed in one of the two houses, en route to Baghdad.

One day Raza went swimming with his young cousin Qays in a bright blue pool at one of the houses, and on another day, bored with nothing to do, he decided to make his own amusement by walking up and down the verandah chanting the names of two prominent Pakistani politicians that sounded like rap music. It made Hurr laugh out loud.

"There's a small black-and-white photo in his album that he took. It shows Hurr at around the age of 19, sitting in his khaki shirt and pants, holding a solar topee (safari helmet), and looking out to sea. They stayed there for a few days."

After a few days, Raza's family left for Baghdad, while other members like his aunts and cousins went by boat to Basra and linked up with them later. Ibn Dawood, who must have been about 3 years old at the time and a bit thin, had only recently recovered from a form of latent tuberculosis, and was still being nursed by his sisters, traveled on his mother's passport, thus avoiding the taking of any photograph.

In Baghdad, Raza's family stayed in a rented house in a suburb known as Kazimain, about 5 miles from the centre of Baghdad, and where there is a twin shrine for Imam Musa al Kazim and his grandson, Imam Mohammad al Taqi, is located. They stayed there in a street winding through a bazaar, full of the aromas and smells of grilled kebabs, tomatoes sprinkled with sumac, and the cries of vendors beckoning passersby.

Raza, still a vegetarian, loved the sweet taste of grilled tomatoes wrapped in bread and having made the ziyarat to Kazimain, the family traveled to Karbala, about 60 miles southeast of Baghdad for the ziyarat to the shrine of Imam Husain, the Prophet's grandson, also known as the "martyr of martyrs." Here they linked up with Hurr and his mother. They lived in a house from where there was a clear view of the Dargah of Hazrat Abbas, half-brother of Imam Husain, and his standard-bearer in the battle against the forces of Yazid. The house belonged to the Pirpur family. A few streets further along lies the shrine of Imam Husain. Both these shrines had their domes covered in gold leaf and was on a far grander scale than their replicas in Amadabad.

Staying in Karbala and visiting the shrines daily must have been like a balm for the whole family, escaping the turmoil in India, but the period of *ziyarat* was not yet over. Next they traveled to Najaf, about another 40 miles away, where the shrine of Imam Ali, cousin and son-in-law of the Prophet, is located. A further 8 miles from there lies the mosque of Kufa, where Imam Ali was assassinated. In the surrounding desert, Raza and Abid scrambled about, looking for semiprecious translucent stones known as "duur-e-najaf," which they kept in the flat cigarette tins their father had bought, once they were empty.

The ziyarat in Iraq was almost over by now. They had yet to visit the shrines of the 10th and 11th Imams, Ali al-Naqi, and Hasan al-Askari in Samarra, which is situated almost 200 miles north of Baghdad. For this trip they went back from Najaf to Baghdad by bus, before booking a return journey by coach. By now the summer of 1947 was nearly over. If there was any news from home, the children were not informed.

Yet there was one last ziyarat remaining, to the shrine of Imam Azim. For this the family booked a flight to Tehran, on a Soviet airplane, a converted Dakota. The seating was on a wooden bench along the fuselage and not in rows as in other civilian planes.

Raza remembers the plane hitting air pockets when it would suddenly lose height before regaining its path. Eventually landed in Tehran, and traveled once more by road to Mashhad to the shrine of Imam Ali al-Azim, the 8th Shi'a Imam and to Qum and the shrine of Lady Fatima, another Shi'a saint. The family's *ziyarat* to the various shrines was now nearly complete. From here they traveled back to Tehran, and to complete their trip, their father, Nawab Ali Haidar, treated them to stay in a hotel in the resort of Darband, in the foothills of the Alborz Mountains.

They stayed there for about a week. Raza's mother was particularly happy in the hotel, since she could speak Farsi and loved the fresh pomegranates, grapes, and melons. Their stay in Darband was picturesque yet brief, the ziyarats nearly over for the family.

Here their father left them to go for treatment in Europe and America, while the rest of the family traveled via Zahedan before crossing over into the town of Quetta, which was by then part of Pakistan. From Quetta they traveled to Karachi, which was by then the largest town in West Pakistan, and from there they eventually took a long-winded journey to Lucknow, avoiding trouble spots on the way. Independence and its corollary partition had become facts that the family had to get used to.

It is estimated that millions of innocent people in Delhi, Lahore, and many of the major cities in the north and west, as well as Dacca, then the capital of

East Pakistan, as well as Calcutta in West Bengal were raped, killed, or displaced. Yet Lucknow, the city of culture, was left relatively untouched.

Here the changes were imperceptible to the young at first. True, Raza was told that Amma's husband had left for Pakistan, though Amma and her daughter remained in the service of Raza's mother. Other servants and retainers had also left and formed a huge flotsam and jetsam of Muslim migrants flooding Karachi, and referred to as "muhajir," or migrants. Hindu Sindhi migrants forced to leave their homes in Karachi filled their place in Lucknow. It was the older generation that noticed the changes more.

While the family completed the ziyarats, Nawab Haidar Ali traveled to Vienna and consulted with Alfred Adler's system of psychology and then gone to New York to see another psychiatrist, and staying at the Waldorf Astoria, before returning to London where he had consulted with the king's physician, Dr. Mathias Alexander, at the same time as the royal wedding of Princess Elizabeth to Prince Philip Mountbatten, the Duke of Edinburgh, was taking place, before he finally returned home.

Haidar Ali seemed well and in good spirits, regaling his sons Raza and Abid with his adventures: demonstrating how the Alexander technique involved learning about good posture; how the Americans in New York spoke with a nasal twang; showing off his heavy gold-and-silver American cufflinks; and singing "Oh, what a beautiful morning" from the musical *Oklahoma* that he had seen on Broadway. He filled his boys' ears with wonder. What topped it all was that his wife had conceived, and a fourth child was due to be born in the winter of 1948.

Beneath the surface, though, he was much troubled about the future of the children. As he spoke to his elder brother, to his wife, and to some close friends, he generally assessed the new situation of what independence from Britain might mean for him and the family; given that his sons were now about to enter their teens, he was aware of the exodus of large numbers of Anglo-Indian and British teachers from the Martinière, he thought of other possibilities.

One scenario he thought feasible was to send the boys to the English-style boarding school in the hills where his nephew Husain was still attending; since time was of the essence and the boys' education had already been interrupted, he hastily decided to enroll them there.

Although the idea of moving from home did not seem to worry the boys, they soon changed their mind because the school turned out to have 99 percent of pupils from the elite Hindu upper and rising middle classes, with the exception of a few Sikhs also in attendance. Raza and Abid thus far had a largely sheltered life in the palaces in Lucknow and had rarely mixed with Sunni boys of their own age and social class, let alone Hindu and Christian boys. This factor was compounded by a nascent Hindu pride in the new India. The boys in their class took to laughing at Raza and Abid's English pronunciation of Indian names and places, and making the two Muslim boys feel isolated.

This feeling of isolation resulted in bed-wetting and more ridicule being heaped on them. With the exception of one or two English teachers and one solitary female Muslim teacher, all the other teachers and housemasters were Hindu. The boarding school food, largely Hindu vegetarian, was not much to their liking. However, the clinching factor came in a dramatic fashion.

On January 30, 1948, in less than a month of them being there, Mahatma Gandhi was assassinated. Tensions were palpable, as they must have been everywhere else in India. Muslims came immediately under suspicion.

Thankfully, the police acted very swiftly and caught the suspect within a few days, who turned out to be a Hindu fanatic, blaming Gandhi for continuing to preach nonviolence against Muslims, even in the wake of the post-partition massacres.

However, this did not prevent one Hindu boy at the school coming up to Raza and saying, all Muslims should be killed. This only hastened to increase their misery, and their education for which their father had sent him there suffered. When Nawab Ali Haidar came to visit them, Raza mentioned the incident of the verbal threat he had received from another boy, and immediately decided to take them out, and enroll them at the Martinière once again.

By the beginning of 1949, the future shape of education in India was becoming clearer. Hindi was beginning to be taught as a second language, at least in the Uttar Pradesh, the most populous Indian state. The boys started to master Hindi at school but the matter began to exercise the father's mind. English was the most widely spoken language in the world and likely to remain, and anyone with an English education would stand a far better chance of making a successful career, even in India.

He looked closer to home and observed that his eldest sister had already decided to enroll Hurr at Cambridge, and that the second sister was also making preparations for her son Husain to follow him and go to an English university. As chance would have it, an English couple came to visit Nawab Dawood Ahmad.

The husband was a business partner of some Irani friends of the family in Calcutta, who ran a tea-exporting business. Nawab Ali Haidar had a word with his brother, the outcome of which was that Raza's father decided to speak with the English visitors about possibilities of Raza and Abid's education in England.

Further discussions between Raza's parents followed. The mother needed convincing of being separated from her boys and argued that the boarding school experiment in India had failed. The father scratched his head. Finally, he managed to prevail against his wife's wishes by pointing out that Raza was beginning to be attracted to girls and that he could not be kept under lock and key, and that sooner or later he might be led astray.

Although Raza had been kept out of the discussion, that fateful summer he was informed that he would be going to a boarding school in England, and that Abid would join him a year later, this being the concession their mother had exacted in return for agreeing to be parted from one of her sons. "See how it goes with one, and if it turns out alright, and only then, Abid can go and join him," she said. The date of Raza's departure was set for January 1950, once Moharram was over.

Raza did not realize it but he was about to bid farewell to so many people, places, and things. Since that time was still far off, Raza shut his mind to the future and turned to enjoy the present.

He was now in his 14th year and grown quite tall for his age. Abid was visibly shorter than him though his twin, but the two of them still shared the same room in the palace and enjoyed the same set of friends, though by now for want of space they would go to the immense verandah on the first floor and above their father's suite. The verandah was open on three sides and had a floor made of large bright red tiles. Hence its name "laal baramdah," or red verandah. Here they would sit around a table and play Urdu alphabet cards, or rhyming games of Urdu poetry.

He had made friends with an Anglo-Indian boy at the Martinière whose father had been killed in the army. These connections were further strengthened because the boy had a younger sister, named Sheila, who had become friends with Raza's sister Zahra. At other leisure times, when he had finished his homework, Raza would go to the cinema, for which he had developed a real taste by now. He also began to keep a record of his adventures in a notebook.

That year Moharram began at the end of October. Raza left the Martinière for the last time, even though the school term was not yet over, and accompanied his family back to Amadabad, as was the family's wont, irrespective of things like school, and as was to remain its wont, this meant that Raza would be about two or three weeks late for his school in England.

CHAPTER 7

BEGINNING OF AN EXILE: BOARDING SCHOOL

All places that the eye of heaven visits,/Are to a wise man ports and happy havens./Teach thy necessity to reason thus/There is no virtue like necessity.
Richard II, act 1, scene 2

Now, the poetic license Raza took in the quote above from the speech of John of Gaunt, Duke of Lancaster, to his son Henry Bolingbroke, the future King Henry IV of England, from Shakespeare's play "Richard II," may not seem wholly apt.

The advice Nawab Haidar Ali was to give to his son may sound similar, but Raza was about to reach his 14th birthday, whereas Bolingbroke was a mature man banished by Richard II. Moreover, Nawab Haidar Ali was true to his brother beyond the call of fraternal loyalty, as it were. He was sending his teenage son to London, away from the intrigues, gossip, and an uncertain future hanging over the Amadabad family, yet was also sending Raza to England for education, and to become independent-minded and learn to become a man. The father's and, therefore, the family's expectation were that in due time he would return to help manage the estate, or to find some suitable post in India through family connections, and to look after his parents in their old age.

No sooner had the plane carrying Raza and his father landed in Delhi, they were whisked away in a limousine to stay overnight in the house of a relative, situated in one of the wide avenues of New Delhi, designed by Lutyens and built by architects and engineers as the imperial capitol in the early part of the century. It was adjacent to, but distinct from, the old city of the Mughals and earlier rulers of India. The boy, his eyes now dry after the painful departure from his mother and a place he called home, sat up wide-eyed and looked out of the car window. He had heard so much about Delhi, old and new. His father and the chauffeur pointed out the various landmarks along the way. The next day they would catch a BOAC flight to London.

"I will show you more of Delhi when you come back during your holidays," the father promised, "this is what the French call a soupcon, a taster," he added. The next morning, they drove to the airport and caught a flight to London. They had put on winter clothes, suit, and tie. Raza wore a brown check jacket, the same one he was wearing in photos taken in London, which were found among his box of photos. They both carried overcoats for arrival in London. Raza's father explained that the journey time would be overnight.

They boarded a four-engine BOAC plane only half full and Raza's father, who was of a sociable nature, got talking to the stewards and fellow passengers. He explains his thoughts at the time.

"I sat shyly in my seat trying not to stare. The first stop was Basra, where I'd visited before, followed by Alexandria (Egypt), a short hop from there to Rome, before arriving at Northolt Airport. The first leg to Basra was safely negotiated, then having refueled the plane took off for Alexandria."

Raza hadn't been this Far West before. For the moment, his homesickness was forgotten, until the one engine developed a problem, and the captain informed the passengers they would be put up overnight at the grand Heliopolis Palace Hotel. The next morning the delayed plane left for the third leg of the journey for Rome. Approaching the city, the American passengers insisted because of the delay and inconvenience the least the captain could do was to fly over Vesuvius so they could see the crater. These were business passengers, so the captain duly obliged.

"My father looked at me and smiled with a wink, as if to say this is how you do business as the plane circled over Vesuvius and tipped one wing and then the other so passengers on both sides could take a look at the cloud of smoke rising from the crater. After landing at Rome, the first thing Nawab Haidar Ali did was to spread out his prayer carpet on the corrugated iron-landing strip that was still there from the war days. The American passengers with whom he had made friends looked on with respect."

Raza didn't follow suit because his father would make sure he would say his prayers inside the airport building, which he did. Then, off to the last leg of the journey to London.

"I was pulled from my dreams of wild horses on a great desert dune when the tires hit and could hear sounds of movement as passengers rustled bags from overhead lockers, and hand baggage and clothes, walking down the corridors of the plane."

He had not seen London from the window as the plane circled the sprawling city below until it landed on the tarmac. He heard an announcement had been made overhead but he paid no heed because he simply had to follow his father who knew everything. They stepped into a bus then stepped out again into a chamber of smoke and bodies with heads afloat. He caught up with his father and found himself standing in front of a border officer.

His father was carrying both passports for the official to check. The official in turn looked down at Raza, asked him where he was coming from. The voice that came out of his mouth was louder than he intended.

"Sir, I am with my father. I am to go to school here."

"All Right, then. Welcome to England."

The official winked at Raza's father and stamped the passports.

Raza finally shuffled behind his father and out into the arrivals lounge where some people were waiting to greet their families or friends. His father spotted a friend, Mr. McDoug from London, who invited them to stay at the local hotel. Raza says:

> My father had a car ready, a black Daimler, and I quietly listened and answered questions when prompted by my father. We would be driven to the Cumberland Hotel, by Marble Arch, for lunch and stay there for a few nights. My father explained that it was Marble Arch and it was originally designed for Buckingham Palace but later relocated here because it was not wide enough for the ceremonial royal horse-drawn carriage.

Outside it was cold, dull, and raining. Not like home at all. Not even like Nainital. He felt lonesome as the car approached the center of the city, meeting more traffic, until it rounded that giant arch.

Raza looked at it blankly.

> It's white Carrara marble you know, all discolored now because of the weather and pollution caused by smoke.

Raza continued to give a blank look. Thankfully then McDoug found a parking space behind the Cumberland that was shown to them by the hotel's uniformed commissioner, who also directed one of the luggage porters to follow the car and bring the luggage to the reception.

McDoug, who led the way to the rather grand reception hall, had made a lunch reservation, and before that they checked in at the reception desk, the overcoats handed in at the cloakroom, before Raza followed the two adults into a large marbled gent's toilet, where they washed their hands and combed their hair. The baggage had meanwhile been placed in the cloakroom, to be fetched after they had lunched.

From there they were ushered into the dining room, which did not look too crowded. Menus were brought over by the headwaiter who then discreetly walked away, giving them time to peruse and choose. All this was new to Raza, who watched whatever his father did and followed suit. As opposed to home, the overwhelming majority of people were white.

This was what Raza had to get used to from now on, and to the fact of standing out as a foreigner among them. Following lunch, McDoug said that he needed to return to his office in the city, but since they were not expected at the school until early evening, he would be back to pick them up and drive them to the school. They shook hands, and as McDoug went to his car, father and son went up to the room on the fourth floor where Raza's father's room was located.

They were shown the way down the pink-colored corridor by one of the hotel porters who carried their luggage at the same time. A young chambermaid came swiftly down and opened the door to the room. The luggage porter deposited their luggage while the chambermaid showed them the light switches, how the radio worked, where the room telephone was, where the bathroom and toilet were, and so forth—all the usual formalities of hotel rooms, and all very new to Raza.

"But I should mention that since we'd landed in London, my father had hardly said three words to me. At times he was intimidating and distant. Perhaps he felt that I should have been more responsive to McDoug. He had noticed what seemed like my sullen demeanor and decided to lecture me about manners. He began to tell me that he wanted me not to forget who I was. He said I should remember I would be the only Indian in this school, but this should be something to be proud of, not ashamed. And that I am a Khan. But besides that, he told me 'I was a very bright and industrious boy, and there's no reason I should not be at this school. That I was just as good, and just as intelligent, as any of these English boys, if not more.'"

"I remember my father looking me straight in the face and saying, 'I know this, and so do you. The English do not: until then they will judge you solely by your appearance. This is fact, and there is nothing you can do about it. The only thing you can do is wait, and prove them wrong in your actions and your deeds. Your academic performance will only give these boys reason to envy, not ridicule, you—but only if you work hard, as I have taught you.' As he told me these things and though they stayed etched in my head I had doubts, whether I could really meet his expectations."

Raza, lost in thoughts, gazed out the window, enthralled by the scenes passing by in the streets below. He was in England for the first time, had rarely been abroad, and every sight was new. Of course, his father had traveled extensively, visited the United States, Vienna, France, what have you, and seemed impatient with his inattentiveness.

"You will have plenty of time for sightseeing. Now please listen to what I am telling you. And do not forget to write to mother and remember that this new England place is your adopted land and that I love you."

He was right, of course. The future was there for Raza to explore the intricacies of this modern and lively city, the capital of the Western world, and of course at the moment, the very least he could do was listen to his father, and show some deserved respect. Raza remembered the moment well.

From this moment on Raza still finds the memories too blurred by the moment after all these years, which remained like a rock in the throat of his soul, the abandonment by family is what it meant.

His head was full of thoughts and the first thing he noticed after the conversation with his father was how early it got dark in London. It was January and he'd already made a note of the city's coordinates: 51 degrees North and 0 degrees West. It was from where time around the world was measured.

At home the time would be five-and-a-half hours earlier. That means it was 9:30 p.m., and his mother would have said her evening prayers and eaten, as would have Abid and his sister Zahra, while the youngest, Jafar, born only 13 months earlier would be in his cot. A shiver went through his body as he waited for McDoug to arrive and drive them to the boarding school just north of London. The phone rang in his father's room and reception informed Mr. McDoug had arrived, and the moment he heard the name of Mr. McDoug, he became nervous about leaving and every time he hears Mr. McDoug, he got this shot of anxiety.

Raza's father told reception he'd be right down. His luggage, consisting of a large trunk, a smaller suitcase, and satchel were in the cloakroom so no need to carry anything. He put on winter coats and scarves and locking the door behind him took the lift down. He counted slowly the floors as he descended.

Raza thought at that moment that in all of England he would have just two contacts once his father had returned home—his eldest cousin Hurr, who was at

Cambridge, and McDoug. And just as the thought came to him, Mr. McDoug appeared.

"I saw him (Mr. McDoug) standing there, all pink, well-scrubbed face and blue eyes, smiling and leading my father and I to the car. I tried hard to hold back emotions but just got into the car and sped off up the Edgware Road and on toward Radlett or some such place that McDoug shouted out from the front seat."

Up until the moment of arriving at the boarding school, Raza had managed to forget why he was there; captivated by the cosmopolitan landscape of London, thoughts of home and the fact that he had left home still eluded him. His head was still in the clouds as he thought about the trip to the place. He recalled as the car moved ever closer to the school, the irrevocable reality started sinking in: the stately grounds, the venerable buildings, the clean-cut boys in their black blazers—this was to be his home now. Everything he saw, he did not see as it was but only as it wasn't: not Amadabad, not India, not his family, not his happiness. And soon he would be unpacked, situated in new living quarters, and his father would leave him, to catch his flight back to India. But just as the car pulled to a stop in front of a small yet impressive brick building overgrown with ivy, he was overcome by a sense of urgency and despair. Not wanting to cry in front of his father, he clenched his teeth and tried not to think of his mother and home. He felt sick.

"A tall, thin man with a clipped accent, teeth bulging from his mouth, dressed rather finely in a dark, double-breasted suit, had come out to meet us. He introduced himself as Mr. French, the housemaster, and started talking to my father. After inquiring into my health, he subsequently ignored me, which was fine because I wasn't feeling very conversational.

After a brief tour of the grounds, given by an overeager prefect, solely for the benefit of my father, I was led to the house with its dormitories, where all the bags were waiting. The grey trunk and suitcases, mutely standing in the hallway, in front of what was to be a large shared room, that might as well have been the chopping block and executioner as far as I was concerned."

He burst into tears.

The tour guide blushed, even though he must have seen this sort of thing before. Raza's father, noticing the emotional outburst and feeling a bit embarrassed himself, took his son by the shoulder closing the door behind him. Now for a moment there, he calmed down a bit, and stood in the middle of the room, not knowing what to do. His father sat down on what was going to be Raza's bed, patting the empty space next to him.

"I don't want to go to boarding school in England? I don't like it here."

"But Raza, my son! You only just arrived! How can you already know you don't like it?"

"I just know."

"You just know. Well, you know what else I just know? I know that sometimes life is comprised of difficult challenges, challenges that we have to face in order to make ourselves stronger human beings. Now, I could sit here and tell you that everything will be fine, and that you have nothing to worry about. That your mother and I love you and that home will always be there for you. In other words, I could treat you like a child. But, Raza, you are not a child anymore."

"You are becoming an adult, a man, and so I think it only right that I tell you the truth. Your mother and I do love you: that is true. But home will not always be home for you. In fact, home, Amadabad, will never be that for you again. That place was your childhood, a stage in your life you have outgrown now. Yes, you will come back and be there again, but it will not be the same as it was. You will be older, and you will have changed. Amadabad will have changed. Even I will have changed. And believe it or not, someday sooner that you might think, why, this place will be your home, too. Perhaps you'll even stay here in London after you have finished with school. You never know. But that is precisely my point, my son: there is nothing holding you to Amadabad anymore."

"You are free to be and to do whatever it is you want in life. Of course, I will still expect certain things from you—I will always be your father, of course—but eventually, every sparrow leaves the nest, and every parent must let go, and hope that they have raised their children right. Sometimes you will make mistakes. And sometimes life will be hard, as it seems now. But I hope if anything, I have taught you to be strong and independent. That is the most important thing as a father I could ever give to you. More than money, comfort, happiness, or even love: the strength of will to be free. Everything else is just so much consolation. You need nothing, Raza, as long as you have yourself. Do you understand?"

Raza nodded but didn't really understand. It was beyond him. He suddenly realized his father was leaving the next day for home and he broke down crying. The House matron, by the name of Mrs. Nimmo, heard the cries and came into the dormitory. Glances were exchanged between her and the father, as a result of which it was decided for the sake of calming things down Raza's father would stay the night at the school. Things always seem more dramatic at night. The next day they gain a bit of equilibrium; and Mr. French was informed; and the nawab telephoned McDoug and British Airways, and since it was an open ticket there was no problem in booking his return flight for the next day.

And so, it turned out father and son slept in the Sick Room for the night and the next morning, though not totally consoled, Raza accepted his father needed to return home, and his father promised to return for the Easter holidays and take him to Paris.

Mr. French and his wife Simone lived in the adjacent section of the building that formed one of the five Houses into which the school was divided. They assured the nawab that all duties of care and education would be properly discharged. In the distant past, Mr. French had another Indian boarder at the House with the name of Ranbir Singh, from another princely family, he informed both Raza and his father.

"It was a long time back, mind you, before the war it was." His family had given them a tiger skin as a gift in appreciation of educating and caring for their son and there it was decorating part of the floor of his living room.

The evening of Raza's arrival, Mr. French had informed the whole House of fifty boys or so during evening prayers that an Indian boy was arriving and they were not to stare at him. He had also appointed another new boy called Tim to befriend Raza since they were going to be in the same class, and to show him the ropes.

Thus, it was after waking up in the Sick Room, Raza got dressed with his father and went down to see him off. A local taxi had been called because McDoug was busy that day, and as it pulled up on the graveled drive, Mr. French was already standing there with his son, Tim. Dry-eyed this time, Raza embraced his father according to custom and waved him off. As the taxi turned around and drove off, Mr. French took Raza by the arm and introduced him to Tim.

"Now off you two go, you'll be late," said Mr. French looking at his watch, "you're already late for breakfast, go and catch up with the rest of the boys going to chapel." With that Mr. French turned around and walked away to his private quarters at the side of the building, leaving Raza and Tim to themselves.

Tim, a young boy with a reddish face, a pleasant smile, dark brown hair with a quiff of hair at the front of his forehead, had been selected as Raza's inductee. They were going to be in the same class, and were both older than others in their class, Raza because he had missed out on school, and Tim because he was a little slow. Together the two entered the House they were in just as everyone else was spilling out of the dining hall. Most of the others just gave a glance at the new Indian boy, as they had already been told not to stare, and walked briskly to the Junior or Senior Common Rooms according to the years they were in. Tim just ushered Raza toward the Junior Common Room (JCR) and then out again toward the chapel.

Tim had never seen an actual Indian before; and though he'd heard of India, and knew it was populated by people called Indians, and ruled until very recently by the Brits, people like himself and the rest of the school had seen the place on newsreels in the cinema. He even had a book about a high-flying treasure hunter whose wild escapades take him to India (on a death-defying quest to recover a stolen magical stone from a demonic death-cult called "thuggees"). But in person, seeing someone actually from India, this ancient land of snake charmers and fire-worshipers—of course, he couldn't help but stare at his companion as they walked to chapel.

"Again: Are you just going to stare at me, or are you going to say something?"

"You speak English?" asked Tim, wide-eyed as though it was he who was in a trance.

"Of course I speak English," Raza, thinking to himself: My roommate's an utter imbecile! "What do you think I've been speaking? Some mumbo-jumbo gibberish?"

Raza was quite proud of his English. He had learnt it at Loretto and at La Martinière; he had, in fact, been teased about it at the Indian boarding school where he had spent an unpleasant time.

The question and the use of idiomatic slang seemed to startle Tim out of his hypnotic stupor.

"No, no," he said, realizing just how stupid he must have sounded, "It's just that I don't know, I would have thought you'd have spoken, I don't know, some form of pidgin English or Hindi."

"Urdu actually. But I was also taught English, and everyone in my family is fluent. England colonized India, don't you know?"

"Of course I know."

"And if I'm going to go to school in England, I better damn well speak English, yes?"

They walked along, neither really knowing what to say next. Obviously, this wasn't the best start, considering Tim was going to have to ease Raza into the rules and ways of the school. Tim had lived in suburban Havering with his parents all his life, and now they we were going to have to share time for at least the next term. His family was Anglican and from the comfortable middle class. They walked along in silence for a while, passing the school tuck shop along the way.

"Do you like toffee?"

"Yes."

"Would you like some?"

The English boy, a bit on the chubby side, reached into the bulging pockets of his jacket and pulled out a paper bag of toffees he'd saved. He handed Raza the bag as they walked along chewing.

"So, what's it like?" he asked, still chewing.

"What's what like?"

"Why, India, of course? What's it like? Are there huge, hideous snakes everywhere? And lions and tigers prowling for fresh meat? And hollering troop of monkeys swinging through the trees?" He paused. "Do you live in the jungle?"

"Actually, I live in a palace, or rather palaces should I say."

Tim couldn't believe his luck.

"Wow, really, a palace? You must be joking. What are you, a prince? Was that man, your father, a king? Wait a minute, I'm no mug—are you pulling my leg?" Tim asked, suddenly suspicious.

"No, actually, my family is descended from royalty. My uncle is the nawab of Amadabad."

Satisfied, Tim perked up again.

"If you're royalty, really royalty, even Indian royalty, what are you doing going to school in England? Shouldn't you be out riding elephants or something?"

"My father wanted me to come."

"Oh, my father's making me go to school, too. I don't want to, but he doesn't care what I think." Tim popped another toffee into his mouth. "It's not fair. We're supposed to live in a free country, you know, but then when I don't want to go to school, it's like he's the bloody king and it doesn't matter what I want. Rubbish is what it is, I tell you, rubbish."

Shocked at Timothy's lack of respect, Raza said: "Well, he's my father and it may not matter what I want but I know he's doing it for my best."

"That's not right. Of course it matters! It matters what you want because you're you!"

"It's just tradition, I guess," Raza told the inquisitive lad. "Most families send their children to London for schooling, at least the families I know. I'm supposed to attend boarding school, go to Oxford, get an education, and then return to India."

"Return to do what?" asked Timothy, still chewing as he spoke.

He seriously thought about it for a moment. Nothing came to mind.

"I don't know." He finally said. And he really didn't.

They soon arrived at the Chapel, a more modern-looking building than the rest of the school, situated across the lane. As the boys walked slowly and silently in file, Raza followed Tim and sat next to him in one of the front rows where the new boys sat. Church music was being played on an organ, which reminded

Raza of a dirge. Tears that had been stemmed since his father departed started flowing down his cheeks. Tim looked at him and felt some sympathy.

"Don't cry," he whispered, "It'll soon pass."

But it didn't pass. Raza would often and unexpectedly find himself crying and hated school. It was so regimented, so petty in its hierarchies, and though he was alright in some of the classes (Math and English), he also came across racism from one of the teachers.

This came in the person of a wiry little man with a quirky smile called Mr. Robertson, his geography instructor who had served in the army in Egypt during the war and saw the same sullen look that he had seen in the eyes of the fellaheen. Raza also came across another form of racism, a jocular kind, from the physical education teacher. He longed for the term to be over and for his father to arrive for the Easter holidays and take him to Paris.

Thankfully for Raza, the winter term (Lent) came to an end eventually, but not quickly enough, as his father had returned from India as promised, and telephoned and spoke to Mr. French and agreed a time to pick Raza up.

Raza waited on the graveled drive, watching cars driven by parents of the boarders, taxis for others, trunks and suitcases already there by the side of the drive waiting to be loaded, doors of vehicles slamming, shouts of goodbyes to friends, until finally a taxi drove up and his father emerged, smiling and wearing a black homburg and dark overcoat.

He doffed his hat to Mr. and Mrs. French who had just come out from their private section. A few words were exchanged out of courtesy and politeness.

Mr. French put his hand on Raza's shoulder and pushed him forward toward the taxi: "There you go dear boy, have a good time in Paris, and we'll see you back after the holidays, refreshed and raring to go." Raza said goodbye to Mr. and Mrs. French and got into the car with scarcely suppressed relief and joy.

LONDON/PARIS

The taxi turned out of the drive and sped along the country lane, heading toward central London. The father put an arm around the boy and the boy greeted the father the way he had been brought up to greet him with "Adaab Abbajan." They exchanged news about how all the members of the family were, but the boy said little when asked about the school, because it still touched in him a raw nerve. Within 40 minutes they had reached the Cumberland Hotel where the boy had lunched on arrival in London, and now the father had booked two single rooms there for them.

This was the first opportunity for him to have his own bedroom and not a dormitory. He was feeling excited and adult and agreed to change his school uniform for his holiday wear—clothes he had brought with him from India—and knock on his father's door before going down to lunch. The father had already promised to take him on a holiday to Paris and no doubt that would be discussed. His father was ready as Raza knocked at the door. His father looked at Raza and smiling took the elevator down to the ground floor and reception. At the reception desk, he handed in their keys and walked out.

The entrance to Marble Arch Tube Station was adjacent to the hotel entrance. His father stopped and asked for a weekly magazine called *What's On in London*. Paying for a copy, saying "thank you" politely, and picking up the magazine, he turned to Raza and said: "Where should we go now? It's too early for lunch, so I think we should take a walk down Oxford Street and look at some shops, what do you say?" Raza nodded. He had no ideas: he had not been to London as his dad had. He let his father show him London.

They walked down the wide street with crowds of people along the pavements as far as the eye could see, purposefully marching around. London looked like the grand city that his tutor at home had told him about, though he did look up and notice that a building adjacent to the hotel had no ceiling and upper floors, and that it was boarded up.

As he followed his father down Oxford Street, Raza noticed the shops, the double-decker red buses, the black taxis, the businesslike walk of the pedestrians hurrying to their destinations, the newspaper vendors, and the traffic lights. Two blocks further down the street, his father took him into a large department store through large revolving doors. The store was called Selfridges, and it occupied the whole block on one side of the street.

Raza had never encountered anything like this before. As they entered, they stepped on to a white-marbled floor that went on and on, divided into halls containing different kinds of items, men's clothes, jewelry and watches, cameras and gadgets. There was no time to explore the whole of that floor, let alone the floors above served by elevators they had passed. The father seemed to know where he was going and led him to the camera and photographic department where he asked for a photo of Raza to be taken.

The shop assistant obliged and led them to a large kiosk where he showed all different sizes and styles of people's photos. While father and son looked, the shop assistant drew their attention to what was called a "poly-photo"—a sheet of 48 photos of the same person, from different angles and with different poses and expressions, all for the price of little more than it would cost to have one portrait.

Beginning of an Exile

The suggestion was sold and Raza sat down on the stool, while the assistant adjusted the lighting and the camera, who then asked Raza to look at the camera and smile, asking him to turn and look in different directions and with different expressions, as he clicked away.

When finished he told them that the poly-photo would be ready in a few minutes. Then true to his word, he produced this A4 sized sheet of 48 snaps in sepia of Raza in his brown checked jacket, wearing a tie and occasionally a smile here, a half smile there. The sheet was placed in a large stiff-backed brown envelope and Raza has kept them ever since, as I discovered going through his album.

Emerging from Selfridges, they walked back toward the hotel, window-shopping along the way, his father chatting about this and that, telling him things, Raza looking at the faces of passersby, until his father suggested since it was approaching lunchtime they should go into a place called the Lyons Corner House near the hotel. This was another new experience for Raza, though evidently not for his dad. The Lyons Corner House seemed a bit like a department store to Raza in that it had different kinds of restaurants-self-service, restaurant with waiter or waitress service, and a restaurant with live music. Raza's father steered him toward the salad bar.

"Here you can help yourself to as much and as many kinds of salads as you can carry on a plate, and go back for more if you wanted to," his father explained. The price for the total meal, including dessert, bread roll, fruit juice or soft drink was fixed at 2 shillings and 50 pence, or something, as Raza recalls, making a note for future reference.

Raza's London adventure was just beginning, and between mouthfuls, his father outlined the "program" as he calls it, for the duration of the holidays. At 14 years old, he wanted his son to be happy and feel settled which included spending two or three days for the initial introduction to London, then catching a train for Paris, returning to London for a few more days, and meeting up with Hurr Bhai, his eldest cousin, who was coming down from Cambridge to meet them.

The memories from this time are hazy and merge into experiences that may have occurred the next year, or the year following that, who knows, but he remembers that he got to know the West End, including Soho of the early 1950s. His father first took him to a Turkish restaurant called the Istanbul, because his father wanted to eat meat and felt safe eating in restaurants and cafes either serving kosher or Muslim cuisine. For the same dietary reason, they also went to Veeraswamy's in Regent Street and the Vega near Leicester Square that served vegetarian food. "Sir Stafford Cripps and Mahatma Gandhi used to eat here," his father chortled in the Vega.

These places were also selected because they were reasonably priced and to show Raza where to go for future reference. He also mentored his son on how to behave in restaurants and to always give tips to the waiter or waitress. The weekly magazine *What's On* showed him how to find places to eat, cinemas, places to visit, and how to get there by public transport. Then the time came for them to travel to Paris. His father made reservations for them to travel via train and ferry.

APRIL IN PARIS

Raza arrived at Gare St. Lazare with his father just after midday where his father had booked rooms in an inexpensive hotel nearby. Neither of them knew any French, and it was a Saturday when banks would be closed. They hurried down to Tim Cook's, through whom the trip had been booked and travelers' cheques had been obtained. Luckily the Paris branch was nearby. But they were too late. It was closed by 1.00 p.m. The father had only brought a handful of spending money. What to do? From a distance they spied the red awning of a restaurant, which advertised a sign reading "American Bar."

That decided it since at least English would be spoken. They were ushered into what seemed like a side restaurant of a much bigger establishment, and handed a menu in English. Father and son both ordered omelets. "And for drinks, Monsieur?" Raza asked for a coca cola and the father, the connoisseur and pedagogue, settled for a Perrier with grenadine. After their meal they politely refused a dessert because of limited cash, and the father asked for the bill. When it arrived, the bill came to 5,000 old francs or about £5—a big amount in those days.

The father, not affecting to show any surprise took a note from his wallet and paid without so much as raising an eyebrow, but Raza realized instantly that it was far too much. Much later they were to discover they had lunched at none other than Maxim's, frequented by royalty and the glamorous. But only Raza never said much about money even while at school; money, allowances were implied but never brought to the table for discussion. It was some kind of an upper-class kind of thing where money is not spoken about as if it were rude to do so.

But the rest of their days in Paris were going to have to be more economical. It was meant to be an adventure for a young boy, and they visited the usual places for which Paris is famous: the Eiffel Tower, Notre Dame, the Louvre-Les Invalides (Napoleon's tomb where Raza's uncle, so the story goes, had insisted on performing the namaaz in 1936, by tipping the attendant), the Sacré Coeur and of course the Champs Élysée. Raza's father bought a copy of *Une Semaine à Paris*, which, like the *What's On* in London, listed all the restaurants, cinemas, theatres, and events in Paris. Through that he discovered a small inexpensive restaurant tucked away in a side street near the Arc de Triomphe, called Tehran.

"Let's go there," and so they did, tasting Persian cuisine, something they had last eaten in Iran in 1947.

France and England had reacted to the effects of war in different ways. Whereas in England rationing had been introduced on various foodstuffs and commodities, France had not. Instead, it seemed that unless you went to a good hotel and not an economy one, you were likely not to have a bath, only a toilet and a washbasin. So the father also tracked down a hammam or Turkish bath where they could bathe. The hammam was situated inside a mosque in the eastern part of Paris down along the long rue de Rivoli, as anyone who has ventured in Paris will know. Soon their stay in Paris was over, but Raza had fallen in love with the city and knew in his heart that he would be back.

On their return from Paris, and for the rest of the remaining holidays in London, Hurr joined them from Cambridge. By now, the father, ever mindful of expenses, had moved there to the Lancaster Gate Hotel, on Bayswater Road, and only one "tube" or train stop away from Marble Arch. Raza was indeed happy to see his cousin. He had always looked up to him, and enjoyed his iconoclastic sense of humor. The three passed the days meeting, eating, sightseeing, and dining together. It was Raza's first experience of Speakers' Corner in Hyde Park right opposite the Cumberland. Here there were orators pronouncing on every subject under the sun. One particular orator fascinated him.

It was a black man, the first Raza had seen. He had a disfigured hand, his right, which he waved at the audience. His face was also disfigured, one eye balefully looking out at them, as he harangued and insulted his largely white audience for the audacity of ravaging and enslaving his country and his people, and how as a consequence pigeons were coming home to roost from the former colonies, and he was here in the heart of the colonial power to stay. Raza, still a boy, did not have the maturity of an adult, nor the time to understand, but the words were to resonate for some time to come.

And then it was time to return to school again, time to say goodbye to his father again, but not with so many tears this time because his cousin Hurr was there. He promised to visit Raza at school during the summer term. That was it. It was hard returning to school, but there it was. There was no obvious choice, no way out.

The summer was over, a wedding was in the offing and Dawood's self-exile was imminent.

CHAPTER 8

THE WEDDING OF ZAINAB AND HURR

This was Raza's first English summer experience, the long days that stretched on into the night, and cricket and swimming, which he had always loved and yes, the exams to be negotiated. It would be a bit more bearable this time around even though it would be new entrants to the school as well. He'd be one more rung up the ladder of hierarchy, which is the very essence of public schools—to instill in boys the ability to first take and then to give orders, a skill that would hold Britain in good stead in the empire. The rebel in Raza was saying, "No big deal." He would now be able to put his hands in his trouser pockets outside the House, undo one of his jacket buttons, move on to other slightly less onerous House duties, such as washing up.

On return to school, he found letters from his mother and sister waiting for him. Loving letters he'd missed so much and he would find the time to write to them when letter-writing time was scheduled during the boarders' daily routine.

Raza also made a few new friends and exchanged gossip and news. None of them it seemed had done very much. Raza told them about his holidays, which had evidently been fuller. He told them about Paris, and about the movies he had seen, and the restaurants he had been to. They lived in the suburbs or out in the country and went back to their families, he didn't. Something of the exotic was beginning to attach itself to him.

This was countered by something approaching racism and resentment on the part of other more senior boys who, on one occasion, told him to scrub his neck with a brush because it looked too brown. On another occasion a prefect told him to go and buy some "elbow grease" to help him polish tables better. The people who ran the tuck shop would have it. When he went to the tuck shop, which was run by Mr. and Mrs. Schnabel, they just looked at him with pity. The boys were just being horrid and playing a joke. There was no such thing as "elbow grease."

He wrote to his parents and sister, confiding in her his first views and feelings about his experience of racism, of how it didn't fit in with the moral compass of how he had been brought up. He would write to her how he remembered that he had always wondered about and felt uncomfortable with the distinctions people made even back home between darker-skinned and lighter-skinned people, and why it should be so. He had always found darker skin more attractive as a young boy in the qila in Amadabad.

As if this was not bad enough, his father had decided against him going home for the summer holidays. His father thought that would be too unsettling for the boy. The news from his father felt like a slap, a double rejection, especially since Raza was the only member of the family who would be absent from his cousin Hurr's wedding to his Bari Baji. He thought of the wedding celebrations, and the chance to see Nirmala, perhaps. It was the final straw when in the middle of June Hurr came to see him. His term at Trinity College had already come to an end, and he was on his way to India. Hurr smiled kindly at Raza, understanding his younger cousin's feelings and sympathizing. They spent a short time together and then Hurr was gone.

Meanwhile, the father had already corresponded with his own teacher from the Martinière, a certain Mr. Taylor, who had retired and lived with his wife in the village of Haugh of Urr in Kirkudbrightshire, in the west of Scotland. Toward the end of the summer term, Hurr came to see him too before his departure and wedding, which only served to reopen the wounds of exile.

This talk of exile by Raza made me think about growing up in Mississippi and at 16 coming to New York for a eight-day trip not with my father but with ten other high schoolers to perform a play in Harlem. The reason I mention this is because when people heard me speak with a southern drawl, they were just as amused as Raza was with his British accent and wanted to know more about his background, what it was like living in such a place and all since racial killings and lynchings has a long history in Mississippi, but Raza's life in India was just as intriguing.

The India of myths, palaces, gold, colorful costumes, poor masses, ancient vocabularies, gurus, and maharajas; these are the kinds of images present in my mind about the India Raza is thrust into at this moment as he stepped out of the car as they arrived and helped Mr. Taylor with the luggage as his wife went to open the front door. Somehow Raza swallowed the bitter pill and went on. Mr. and Mrs. Taylor were very polite and pleasant. This was the summer when they had been made aware of Raza's homesickness, and sought to divert the boy's attention.

They lived in a medium-sized cottage set in the middle of farmland and had farmers for neighbors. The summer evenings would be even longer here since the sun sets even later in Scotland than in London. In brief, it was a cozy-looking place he stepped into, and made out of grey stone, and inside it had lower ceilings than he was used to. The living room, kitchen, and larder were on the ground floor, with a door leading out from the kitchen into a south-facing garden.

The floor above consisted of three bedrooms and a bathroom. One of these was to be his. The traditional furnishings included photographs and other items brought back from India, though not the proverbial tiger or leopard skin seen in the homes of other ex-colonials. He soon discovered, the next day in fact, they had laid everything out for him. He was introduced to a boy his own age called Billy, with whom he was to grow friendly over the next few weeks. They had also organized riding lessons for him with his neighbor Mr. Muir, the farmer from next door. The weather was fine except for occasional showers, and everything developed from these beginnings, and soon Raza appeared to get over feelings of homesickness.

There were outings to neighboring towns like Castle Douglas and Dalbeattie, even as far as the principal county town of Kirkudbright, and beyond to the Ayrshire coast. When not out cycling with Billy—for he had learnt to cycle in Lucknow on his father's Raleigh bicycle—or spending time with Mr. and Mrs. Taylor and Billy, he would go horse riding with Mr. Muir's daughter Jean, with the younger brother looking on and curious to find out what Indians were really like. This amused Raza and he and Jean became friends too. She was about the same age as him and had blue eyes and dark brown hair. He found her very direct and that helped, though Mr. Muir kept a wary eye on things.

Raza could see his eye on him, and guessed that it must have been something about dusky skin and foreigners. "Mr. Muir himself had never been to India, but there were many Scots who had served in the British Army. Finally, Mr. Muir decided to test me."

One day, as Jean and Raza sat on their horses in his fields, he asked Raza if he had ever ridden over a hurdle. When Raza said no, he suddenly gave Raza's horse a sharp smack on the rear, and the horse galloped over a gate, and the rider came tumbling down, almost in slow motion, over the horse's neck and fell with a bump on the grass. It didn't hurt and Raza picked himself up with a look of surprise. Raza was okay thereafter in Mr. Muir's eyes, and Jean became Raza's first female pen pal. They carried on exchanging letters for some time afterwards.

The only other thing of note during those holidays was the sudden appearance toward the end of his cousin Husain Bhai, who had arrived to start his studies at Oxford. He had been present at Hurr Bhai's wedding and on arrival by train from London had sought out Raza, but in trying to pronounce Haugh of Urr, he was met with blank faces, until it suddenly dawned on someone:

"Aye, Haugh of Urr, would you mean? Aye, that's a wee place not too far from here. You could ask that cabbie. He would take you there?" Husain Bhai repeated the story to the Taylors and Raza, and they all found it amusing what a posh English accent would sound like in Scotland.

ZAINAB AND HURR

By 1950, the nawab had taken to adopting a more religious attitude as both a garb of atonement for the sin of having called for the creation of Pakistan and, paradoxically, as a uniform of his Muslim identity in the new India. Raza offers a rather elaborate explanation attached with the letter from Abid:

The month of (Ramadan) Ramazan that year would fall halfway through June and terminate in July. He consulted the "istikhara" (guidance prayer) counting the beads on the "tasbeeh" (akin to a rosary), and following that up with consulting Lucknow's chief Shi'a cleric about the most propitious day in the month for the wedding of his eldest daughter Zainab (Raza's Baji) to his nephew Hurr.

The wedding had been fixed for a propitious date that would also coincide with the young man's university holidays. Abid wrote a letter to Raza describing the wedding in detail, although the letter didn't reach Raza until September.

"The wedding took place accordingly on 22 Ramadan, 1369, which is equivalent to 7 July 1950. It is worth including here for (historical) reasons: Extensive preparations for it had been going on for many months as there was no shortage of money. Besides, it was the first such ceremony taking place in the Amadabad family (since my parents' wedding almost 20 years earlier). The actual marriage ceremony was to be at Amadabad. The groom and his party were to go there in a convoy of several cars, where they were to be received by the bride's party."

As such, Khalajan, her daughters and son had been in Amadabad for some days beforehand, and so had been Raza's mother and sister. Meanwhile Raza explained the whole affair.

"My father had been there for some time longer, looking after the arrangements and elaborate preparations. My brother Abid opted to stay in Lucknow with Hurr and Husain and to go as part of the groom's party. Hurr's paternal relations had been invited from Patna: Taqi Chacha and his family, Adil Chacha, his wife and daughter, and various others, including of course Lady D.. All the while our uncle, the nawab had stayed behind in Lucknow to see the groom off. He himself tied the 'sehra' (headdress for weddings) on Bhai Saheb's forehead before rushing off to Amadabad to receive the 'baraat' (wedding procession)."

"The groom's party then left in a fleet of cars for Amadabad, Husain Bhai and Abid traveling with the groom in his car. On reaching the outer iron-railing gate of the palace at Amadabad, they saw father waiting there in person leading the groom's reception party. Bhai Saheb said he saw Mamujan standing and asked to stop but even though the car slowed it did not stop because father signaled to him to keep going, and so he did till the car reached the steps of the Baradari, where the nawab came hastily down the steps to receive the groom. We immediately got out and were directed to our allocated rooms."

"In the evening, dinner was served at a large table in the hall (where portraits of Victoria and Edward VII hung)." Raza said, because of Ramadan, they didn't have lunch but only had dinner there. No fancy or flashy clothes were worn by the menfolk, there was no *zarbaft* (cloth of gold) or *jamewar* (coats made out of ornate Kashmiri shawls) worn by anyone. Instead, they wore simple sherwanis or achkans of different hues and shades."

"Among those invited to be present were those attached to us, like Hurr Bhai's and Husain Bhai's tutors. Among those invited were the rajas and nawabs, there were kukra, who assisted the *daroghas* (maîtres de cuisine) with food preparations and Surat Bahadur Shah (son of Lalla Bum Bahadur Shah). No one was invited from grandfather's second wife's family for the 'nikah' ceremony, or to the banquets that followed a few days later. And, uncle did not ask Raja Nanpara, with whom he had been on such friendly terms for so long, and toured Europe with. The reason being that Nanpara might bring his bottles and he could not tolerate drinking even in one's own room in Amadabad palace."

"The 'nikah' was to be held on the next evening. After dinner the raja retired to the room he had chosen for himself, having vacated his usual room for guests and my father retired to the room he had chosen. Abid went to sit for a while in the red-floored verandah where some others were also seated. Since uncle for the past few years had been putting on his Islamic mask, there was to be no music or singing."

"Two of his old friends, Kamal Sahab and Dr. Afridi, were sitting feeling bored. They sent for Moazzam Ali and requested that he sing some 'qawwali and ghazals'. The man was afraid of offending the nawab sahib, but they insisted. The man, knowing how close the two were to the nawab, complied. Next morning poor Moazzam Ali got some taunts and tongue-lashing from uncle, who must have heard the chanting."

All customary Indian ceremonies had been vetoed by what Raza calls his more "Muslim than Thou" uncle. There were thus no *manjha* (song and dance) and the like. The actual nikah was held in the hall of the baradari. The bridegroom sits on a *masnad* (cushioned seat) under the central arch with the two officiating clerics. The hall had been fully lit up including the big red glass chandelier. People gathered in the baradari. First a cleric ascends the large pulpit to narrate the "hadis-e-kisa," when that is over the nikah is performed. Following which there were general greetings and people bowing and embracing each other.

At night, seating on the floor had been arranged with masnad for the groom and another one as well. People who had penned some verses to celebrate the occasion came forward one by one and read out their verses or got someone to read for them. The next event, called "rukhsati," is what is usually the most emotional since it is the bride's departure with her husband. There are general farewells with the bride in tears at leaving her parental home. During such time a traditional song known as "baabul" is sung. One reason for singing the "baabul" is to muffle the sounds of weeping and crying.

Raza was keen to explain what this meant: "Instead of the baabul, uncle ordered Moazzam Ali to 'Read the Baabul,' but the man remained silent, the nawab repeated his order, at which the man folded his hands and protested 'Sarkar, the Baabul is sung and not read!' The Nawab frowned saying, 'Don't jest with me and just do it without the accompaniment of musical instruments.' Meanwhile, Mantoo Chacha was standing on the place above the estate' treasury with some men carrying bags with tens of thousands of 1 silver rupee coins (which are very expensive now) of which he continuously took fistfuls and threw them for the poor to scrummage for."

"All the while tears of emotion flowed from Mantoo Chacha's reddened eyes. The whole scene is well imprinted in my memory from Abid's letter. At last the canvas screen called 'qanat' was drawn away and the car carrying the newly wedded left for Lucknow. The dowry had been loaded on trucks and was to be accompanied by armed guards. Uncle himself had stayed behind as had my father, mother and sister for the time being."

"Here ceremonies in regards to the bride's reception at Lucknow had to be as my eldest aunt, the bridegroom's mother, wanted and desired. The newly married pair were brought to the drawing room upstairs, known as 'jhule wala kamra,' where the masnad had been placed on a wooden platform, to which the two were led to sit, while the rest sat on sofas and chairs. All ceremonies had to be done as our eldest aunt required and even Bhai Saheb had to comply, with or without hesitation or reluctance."

"Firstly, the bride's feet were to be washed by the bridegroom. For this a silver basin was brought and a silver-spouted jug containing water. Bhai Saheb poured the water from the jug into his hands and washed his wife's feet whose soles had been dyed with henna, as had also the palms of her hands. A small portion of Indian-style milk pudding was then brought in a small silver bowl with a spoon."

"The bridegroom was then required to make his bride eat it from his hands. All these weren't without a little hilarity. The next thing was a little awkward for Bhai Saheb. He was required to offer a short *namaz* (a form of worship) by the side of his bride. He tried to say something like 'but,' but his mother firmly told him to go and perform the required ablutions and offer namaz. He had to do as he was told. He was then required to carry the bride in his arms to the bridal room. The room named as 'burji ka kamra' was all set up for their stay. There were chains of a variety of jasmine flowers known as 'motiya,' which is zambac. I remember that whenever Abid went to see them there was always a very nice fragrance of this zambac."

"The next ritual was that the bride was to be shown to her in-laws. Again she was made to sit on the masnad in the jhule ka kamra. Hurr Bhai's relatives were seated on sofas. One by one they came forward, the bride rising and bowing and saying salaams in the traditional manner each time, and Hurr Bhai's uncles presenting her with cheques wrapped in red handkerchiefs. This is what is known as 'ru numai' (showing one's face)."

In my discussion with Raza, I wanted to know more about this joking aspect of the ritual and he tells me a few stories that Abid conveyed to him.

"There are some kinship relations known as joking relationships and one such relationship is that of the bride's younger sisters with the bridegroom. Younger sisters of the bride try to play pranks on the bridegroom. I remember two such incidents happening, and both misfired. One morning Bhai Saheb was strolling on the front lawn with two people when one of the bride's sisters sent down a prepared 'khasdan,' supposedly containing specially made paan for Bhai Saheb. He immediately said that he never eats paan, and motioned for it be offered to one of the companions who did take paan. With some reluctance and hesitation, he took it."

"The sister-in-law was peeping from upstairs. The khasdan had in fact contained no paan and as soon as Salman Abbas opened it a poor little sparrow flew out which had been trapped and placed inside. This caused much laughter as the prank had clearly misfired. Another prank was tried when Bhai Saheb returned to Amadabad to pay his respects to the bride's elders who had remained behind. Amid had gone along with him. Now, mother had firmly told Zahra not to try any pranks, which she could do as the bride's younger sister."

"One prank that is usually played by the younger sister-in-law on the bridegroom is to try and conceal the bridegroom's shoes, for the retrieval of which he usually pays something to her. When Bhai Saheb went to see our mother, some people tried to encourage our sister to hide the shoes."

"But in view of what mother had said she was very reluctant, however, Buddhan Phuphi who was also there, continued to coax her. Zahra became somewhat confused. Bhai Saheb was wearing very ordinary shoes, while Abid's were a little ornate 'nagra' shoes, and mistaking his shoes for the bridegroom's, and she hid Abid's instead of bridegroom, but this prank had also misfired! However, Bhai Saheb still insisted on giving her some token amount."

"When everyone was back in Lucknow, three banquets were held by the groom's party. These, as you know, are referred to as 'dawat-e-walima.' These were held on successive evenings in the Kaiserbagh Baradari, and each night different categories of people were invited. On day the then governor, Sir Homi Modi, and a number of government officials had been invited and on another day it was the turn of close friends, some lawyers, doctors and other professionals, and politicians. On a third occasion it was the turn of taluqdars, zamindars and more distant relations, members of old established Lucknow families, including some so-called nawabs, hakeems, maulvis, and poets. Usually of course only two banquets are permitted in Islam. The excuse for the third banquet given on this occasion was that one banquet has been given by the groom's mother and the other by his father-in-law. Abid thought that it was a mere excuse and it was in fact a matter of showing off."

"For the whole show it may be worth remembering that the raja had long been putting on a display of frugality and leading a simple lifestyle and in actual fact, for several months tremendous expenses had been undertaken. The houses at Amadabad and Haiderbagh both had a complete refurbishment inside and outside, and the raja himself presided over it at Haiderbagh. There had been an estate contractor employed by the name of Habib-ur Rahman, who was receiving constant orders from the nawab, while the nawab himself asked some family members living there as to what colors they wanted their rooms to be painted. Secondly, for many months there had been continuous clanging and clinking of metalware in Amadabad where large numbers of copper cooking pot of different sizes were manufactured so as to be included as part of the dowry."

Raza says all this is well remembered by his friend Azizoo who pointed out that in Lucknow numerous sets of clothing were tailored and embroidered with gold-and-silver thread to be given, some as part of the dowry, and others to be given to other family members but he did not know the exact quantity. He goes on to say this about Abid at the end of the conversational letter concerning the wedding and the events:

> Amadabad had no electricity till the mid-1960s. Private generators had been installed and used to full capacity, night and day, for several days. These generators had been in Amadabad since the close of 19th century and were fired by coke or coal, and those acquired later were oil driven.

"Some simple lifestyle indeed, and at what expense! The nawab may well be wearing his 'garhe ka kurta' and eating his 'jau ki roti,' yet at his daily table there was a variety of fancy food, both Indian style and Western style. Many, many people saw through the mask he put on. Even Azizoo used to call him a big actor. The editor of the leading Urdu newspaper *Qaumi Awaaz*, named Hayatullah Ansari, wrote a pungent article about the nawab's farce. The fact is that no matter what show he may put on, the nawab was always fully aware and confident in his wealth and his authority. He may have known that the political wind was changing and that the present state of affairs was doomed, but he knew that he was still a nawab." Some of these comments came from a letter from Abid.

When Raza read this letter, he did not immediately take in all that Abid was trying to convey. Abid had his own up and down attitudes toward their uncle. He was concentrating instead on what he had missed, rather than the message about his uncle whom he still held in much esteem.

NAWAB DAWOOD AHMAD: SELF-EXILE

There was a reason for the austere and sober mood the nawab had adopted. He felt he was being punished for having adopted the politics he had, and for his indecision. We have earlier described Raza's experiences of being sent into exile, but perhaps this is too strong a word, but this was for different reasons.

His father had clearly perceived the upheavals that had taken place in his native land, the disruption to the educational system, and that for his son to continue with his schooling in India was no option and, therefore, packed him off for education in England.

But as far as the nawab was concerned it was not the same thing. It was momentous for the whole family. When Raza received the news of his uncle's self-exile, he was surprised. Among his memories and in family photographs the figure of his uncle, the nawab of Amadabad, stood out clearly in his mind, for he had known and loved his Baba since childhood, and the image of him standing at Lucknow Airport waving goodbye was still vivid in the boy's mind. He seemed like a permanent fixture of the place called home.

The uncle's sudden decision to leave India and go to Pakistan was always going to be double-edged. The coming about of a theocratic state called Pakistan, in the creation of which the nawab had invested his whole adult life, had resulted in the idea, which is always so pristine and pure in the mind, becoming mired in so much blood and mud as soon as the idea hit the ground. He had not liked what he had heard or seen from afar: the communal pogroms and slaughter and mass migrations of Muslims from the new India to West and East Pakistan that followed caused ethnic frictions, notably in Karachi, where the "muhajirs" (migrants), people from his home province of Uttar Pradesh, faced when they got there; discrimination in housing and employment; and the ethnic and sectarian prejudice from the local inhabitants.

The option of remaining on in his estate in India was also problematic because the ruling Congress Party was aware of the role that he had played before independence. Would his family connections with its prime minister, Jawaharlal Nehru, and his father's with Motilal Nehru count? More to the point, how secular a democracy would India remain?

By 1945, the era of Gandhi had come to an end, and that of Nehru had begun. Ambedkar, one of the few people with the political intelligence to secure secularism from the jaws of an Indian nationalism tinged with a non-variegated Hindu religiosity and caste, had been sidelined by him being put in charge of drawing up a constitution for the new India—a task that would take him two years, in other words, it would shut him out. The odds were that castes, class, and religion would remain, and Hinduism of the monolithic variety created inadvertently by Gandhi would in years to come become the hidden face of secular democratic India.

Writing the constitution is not insignificant, since it would be akin to downplaying Martin Luther King's role in the struggle. Raza's fine view of the constitution telling of his social class, diluting power must be difficult and unsettling. From reading so far, I would suspect these royals to support secularism but not equal rights for all.

"This made the nawab remain in a state of indecision," so thought Raza. "And would his friend Nehru remain amenable to his presence? He visited Nehru but failed to find any clear indication of welcome were his decision to remain in India the outcome. Nehru was preoccupied with the affairs of state. He seemed to be friendly and warm enough, as someone who hailed from the same aristocratic classes of UP should, but that's all."

The second letter from Abid, sent to Raza a few weeks after the wedding, confirmed the path the uncle had decided on without clarifying what exactly that path was to take. The letter simply reads:

My dear Bhaisahab,

Uncle suddenly just left India, after Zainab Baji's wedding. He has gone to Pakistan. He did so in September. He went with everyone—his wife, his daughters, his son Ibn Dawood, a large retinue of attendants, chefs, servants, everyone except the recently married couple.

Clearly, the decision had astonished everyone in the family too. Raza's father seemed shaken to the core that his brother should do this. The wide-reaching ramifications of this singular act by the head of the family may not have entered into Raza's immediate consciousness, since he was still trying to come to terms with his own exile, but they were to prove so far-reaching that their effects are still being felt to this day by the surviving generations.

CHAPTER 9

ABID ARRIVES TO JOIN RAZA

Raza returned to school in September after his summer holidays in Scotland, and as summer turned to autumn and the evenings started to draw in again, it was time again to experience what the next step up the hierarchical chain had in store for him. I should note how in a student's third and final term as a "fag" (hard worker) you had even lighter duties to perform, before "fagging" itself came to an end. He was also shunted into the Remove Form along with his friend Graham because their school exam results had been so mediocre, rather than into the 4th Form as most of the others had been.

That apart, at the beginning of term, he met up with his old friends and made some new ones too, because he was gregarious by nature. When he talked about his summer holidays in Scotland, and mentioned Jean, "Oh, and who is this Jean then? Is she a girlfriend?," the blond-haired Campbell piped up all eager and excited. Other boys gathered around, all ears to listen to a bit of gossip. "Yes, I suppose she is. She is a girl, and she's a friend. So? I guess you could say we have promised to become pen pals. But she is more a friend than a girlfriend." Whistles and winks greeted him.

Soon afterwards and sure enough a letter duly arrived from Jean. It was full of news about her and her school, her riding lessons, Billy and other friends he'd made.

"She signed off: Yours till Rhubarb grows whiskers."

"That was a new one on me. So when it came to letter-writing time in the House I told her about school. That my exams had only been so-so, and so on, I followed Tim's tip and signed off with: 'Yours till hell freezes over.' It gave me a warm kind of feeling."

Throughout the winter term, Raza continued to struggle, academically taking little interest, though he was turning out to be okay in some sports, particularly a new one for him: squash. That being said he did take an interest in reading when it came to quiet time in the House reading room. He had spotted a whole set of bound novels by Sir Walter Scott—*Ivanhoe*, *The Talisman*, *Rob Roy*, *The Fair Bride of Perth*, and so on, which synced with his new link to Scotland, and he devoured that detailed style Scott had, and which others found boring.

Then not soon enough, along came the Christmas holidays, which all the boarders would spend with their families. Raza did not celebrate Christmas, nor did his cousins at Cambridge and Oxford. Through correspondence and agreement between them and his Dad, he went to see Hurr and went to stay in Cambridge. His cousin Husain also joined them there.

"During holiday times Cambridge was free of most students, except those who were foreign. Digs were, therefore, empty and easy to find, and I and Husain stayed across Midsummer Common not far from the city center, while Hurr Bhai stayed in his rooms at Trinity College. We usually met for breakfast in the market place, and spent most of the days together."

At times when Hurr was revising because he was very diligent, and Husain was elsewhere, Raza would go to the movies. His love affair with movies had now seriously begun. Sometimes he would go with his cousins to see black-and-white noir films, and at other times he would go on his own to see romance and adventure movies, particularly those that starred Yvonne De Carlo.

On one occasion, he had become so enraptured by a film called *Bird of Paradise*, starring Debra Paget, that he lost track of time and sat through it twice. His cousins being forced to come to the cinema to see whether he was there, and have the usherette tell him that his cousins were waiting outside for him brought him out of his reverie. He was crestfallen but his cousins just laughed and said they were responsible for him and thought that something had happened.

"In the afternoons, about teatime, we would go to Dorothy's, where there was a large dance floor. Hurr seemed to like going there to watch and to listen to the music. He was newly married, very happy and deeply in love with his wife Zainab. So he would simply dream of her as he watched couples dancing. One particular slender young woman with long dark ponytail caught all their eyes. Hurr's eyes would seem to light up as she waltzed around, and he would look smilingly at Raza and say: 'You know, I am deeply in love with my wife.'"

And, he was. It was written all over his face.

Over Christmas Day itself, most restaurants were closed. The only place open was the local Indian restaurant, which is where they lunched and dined. The food wasn't too bad, though not like home. Then after the Christmas period, the three would travel to London since the train fair was inexpensive and this way the cousins would make sure that Raza got back to school on time. They knew their uncle would be escorting Abid in January, but that the arrival might be late because it would be after Moharram, just as Raza had been late the previous year. Their own terms at university began later than school terms did, and so it was no hassle for them.

"In London we found bed-sits in the Lancaster Gate/Bayswater area: simply furnished rooms, with a gas fire, toilet and bathroom, and that's about all. The rent was cheaper than in hotels, and this mattered because we were on tight budgets because our families had sacrificed so much to enable us to have a good education."

ABID AND RAZA

The one saving grace for Abid was that Raza was already there at the boarding school, and that he would not have to experience anything like Raza's trauma. He was slightly late of course as predicted, just as Raza had been the previous year, due to the importance the family attached to the observance of 10 weeks of mourning of Moharram at Amadabad. Their Dad, wearing his black homburg and black overcoat, brought him to the school. Raza was at lessons at the time, and had only a cursory opportunity to meet his father, who he learned would be back at Easter. After lessons he made sure to telephone him at his hotel and to pay respects.

Raza was already in the second week of term in his second year, and he had to keep in mind the boarding school regime was such that "fraternization" between boys in different years was frowned upon. A slight exception was made in the case of siblings, but only a slight one. Raza was mindful of this.

Being in his second year meant no more duties. He had made a few more friends, in particular with a boy called John, who had one glass eye and who seemed rather effeminate. This friendship came about when Raza was doing a 5-mile walk around the neighboring reservoir because the games pitches were frozen, and because exercise every day was compulsory.

Raza had put on his heavy boots, thick socks, under which he had tucked in his trouser bottoms, and a thick woolly jumper. It was early February, and it was a biting cold day. Raza was one of the stragglers and found himself in John's company. "My shins are bending," Raza exclaimed. John looked at him and smiled. "Poor lad, how could his shins be bending? What a peculiar expression," thought John to himself, as they walked on in silence.

In all Raza felt befriended by just four people by this time: Mr. and Mrs. Schnabel, both Jewish, who ran the school tuck shop, and who had a complete understanding of some of the cruel jokes the white Christian were apt to play; and the two boys, John and Tom.

PARIS AGAIN IN SPRINGTIME

Easter came and with it another trip to Paris, but only this time he and brother Abid went by train and ferry and then train again. Raza has a black-and-white photograph, showing his father standing on the deck, wearing a black overcoat and his homburg, smoking a pipe. They stayed in the same area in Paris, but in a different hotel—one with a toilet and bathroom. Raza had by now learned about the Paris metro, how to find directions, and buy tickets. He had begun to understand some written and spoken French. Mr. French, who also taught French, was a precise teacher with an insistence on grammar and pronunciation. He remembered being taught a funny pedagogic poem that young French children must have been taught. It went:

> Dans la gendarmerie,
> Tous les gendarmes rient.
> Quand un gendarme rit
> Dans la gendarmerie

It may sound quaint and silly, thought Raza to himself, but as he had begun to learn French in his second year, he had discovered that the language was *plus logique* than English. Trying to speak it and to make yourself understood to a Parisian was a different matter, but he was up for it. His father was quietly impressed by Raza's attempts to ask for things in French: the directions, reading notices, ordering from the menu. He was beginning to master the minimum French words, terms, and phrases required by a foreign tourist.

Raza was 15 by now, grown a bit taller and interested in the opposite sex. Both he and his friend noticed all the mature women and liked movie stars and paid attention to teenage girls, looking but not letting his father see he was looking.

Raza's dad though was a clever man, aware of his son's sexual awakening. On one occasion, after visiting Le Sacré Coeur, they walked down Montmartre past the Moulin Rouge, and other nightclubs. On the hoardings and publicity, they noted the name of a show called the "Folies Bergères."

Sex was everywhere. The three of them had been brought up to be very moral and said nothing. Then a funny thing happened: on their last night, the father said to the two boys, "I am going my own way tonight. I'll have a quiet dinner, probably at the Tehran, and take a walk, but if you two boys want to go out together somewhere then you have pocket money and my permission."

Raza and Abid looked at each other, although they had been getting allowances or pocket money since they were 8 or 9 years old, hesitated because of the carefree way he offered it. And also because they didn't want to leave their father on their own. "No, I'll be happy to eat Iranian food, and I know that Raza, for one, likes his steak and chips. My teeth can't take that kind of food. So goodnight, and be good."

The boys got changed into different clothes, looked at the mirror, combed their hair, went down to the reception and along the way decided to take a walk through Paris. It was about 7:30 in the evening, the sky was partially clouded, but you could still see some stars. The air felt cool on their cheeks. They didn't feel hungry right then and, proverbially speaking, wanted to work up an appetite. From the hotel they walked to the Place de l'Opéra.

They turned back and looked again at the building. Abid confided to Raza: "Two evenings before I came here and tried to buy a ticket for an English performance of 'Antony and Cleopatra', which is my set text in English literature. What's more I had found out that it was starring Anthony Quayle and Peggy Ashcroft. Anyway, as I went up to the booking office, I saw a very pretty French girl behind the ticket desk. She didn't speak any English, and I was trying to say 'one' in French, but she kept on not understanding. So exasperated, I finally said to her—'all right, give me two, if you'll come too.'"

They both laughed. Raza was surprised his brother also had a bit of a wandering eye for girls. "So, what happened?" he asked as they continued walking. "Oh, nothing, because the tickets were too expensive. But the young woman did smile back at me." They had finally reached the île de la Cité and stood looking up at the Notre Dame for a few minutes, "Poor old Quasimodo, I feel sorry for him," Raza, marveling, as countless millions must have, at the architecture, the flying buttresses, the towers at the front, the gargoyles and chimeras, and at the spirit of Hugo's Hunchback hovering everywhere.

After a few minutes they crossed over one of the bridges towards the Left Bank and came up to Boulevard St. Michel. There was life here: lights, restaurants, tourists, and young people. They had worked up a hunger by now, so they didn't venture down any side street but carried up the boulevard, looking at menus and prices, until they found a restaurant in the place de la Sorbonne, which had just the kind of choice they wanted, and at the right price. A set two-course meal for two would set them back a mere £2.00. "Oh, the folly of Maxim's last year" thought Raza, as they entered and indicated a table for two.

A waiter came up and showed them to a table on the terrace. Neither of them drank alcohol because of religious custom, so they both ordered Perrier and some bread and butter. After reading Abid ordered his favorite dish—calf's liver, in a rich gravy and with caramelized onions and some "frites," while Raza had asked for a steak, medium cooked, and "frites" too, accompanied by a tomato and onion side salad. It all looked very appetizing. They dug in and tried not to think of the awful boarding school meals, all fat and gristle. "How come the French lived so well, even when they had been occupied, and the English had rationing and bad cuisine?"

Raza repeated what he had thought the previous year. They shrugged. Abid then ordered a crème caramel but Raza opted for a selection of cheeses, with coffee to follow. The meal over, they paid the bill and walked out following more or less the same route. It was 10 p.m. as they looked at the clock at one of the crossings. By the time they reached the Metro at Chatelet, they thought the night still young and, on a whim, decided to go and catch the show at the Folies Bergère.

For two teenagers from a traditional family in India, attending an English public school, this was quite a daring thing to do, but at least they had manners and tried to act natural. No one questioned or stopped them from buying a ticket because of their age and came into the large theatre, and shown seats. As many tourists has Parisians in the crowd. When the show came on there stood Josephine Baker on the stage, in a near-nude costume.

Both boys enjoyed the show, though it was more the thrill of doing something daring as teenagers that was the real experience of the night, and experience only capped by the surprise on the faces of the two boys when they looked up and saw their father in one of the seats above. As their eyes met those of their father, he smiled slightly and nodded. This was seen as a normal thing to do. After all this was Paris. Thus ended their joint trip to Paris. It was Raza's second visit of course, and he was sure there would be many more.

That summer term, something happened within Raza. He had developed physically and emotionally. His experiences in London, Paris, Cambridge, and Scotland had made him more independent. His school companions recognized it. He found it easy to make friends, just as he had done in India. He was popular among the boys, though not with the teachers, some of whom projected on to him an exotic representation of a dusky-skinned ex-colonial man-boy, whose manners, though polite, did not stretch to trying to endear himself to teachers or to suck up to them, as some others did.

Going back to school after the holidays was not without incident. Here's how Raza explained the situation:

> My father had asked for permission to go to the cinema on the last days of the holidays. I and Abid were due back by 6.00 p.m. because I wanted to

see *Shane*, starring Alan Ladd, which had just come out in the West End and was showing at the Paramount in Lower Regent Street. There was an early showing at 10.30. a.m. My father reluctantly agreed but asked us to meet outside the cinema at 1.30 when the film would be over. But my visit to the cinema proved disastrous. You see I was engaged, or maybe the word was entranced by the film that I decided to risk watching at least the beginning again. With continuous performances that was possible in those days.

But you see I lost track of time so keen was I to see it from the beginning again: the stranger arriving at the homesteaders farm, the wide-eyed look of the little boy at the farm gate tracking him all the way down the valley, the haunting tune of "Shadows fall on the prairie," and I was away in another land. Right then just as Jack Palance entered the bar, dressed all in black, there was a tap on Raza's shoulder. The usherette had shown his father down to where I was seated.

His father looked furious and Raza got up immediately from his seat and looking crestfallen followed his father's steps out of the cinema. He apologized and swallowed the medicine of his father's anger as best he could. Abid was waiting outside and they decided to go and have their lunch quickly, before going back to pack their bags at the hotel, and return to school. They said goodbye to their father at the school gate.

That summer, something else happened. His first friend Graham was removed from the school for not being up to the academic mark. Graham seemed to take it with a shrug and a smile, but also with a bit of uncertainty as to what his future would hold.

Raza struggled academically, at least in some subjects. His father had wanted to push both the sons towards the sciences. It was not to be. Raza showed better marks in history, French, geography, and English language, but was only average in math and English literature. He was quite poor in Greek and Latin.

"I must say straightaway that I did enjoy Mr. Stott, the white-haired classics teacher reading from Homer's *Odyssey* to the class in English. In chemistry and physics, I was failing, and only doing marginally better in biology, where I did some fine anatomical sketches."

In the case of art lessons, Raza's art teacher noticed something interesting in his use of color, but chastised him when he caught him tracing from a photograph of Yvonne de Carlo. The gossip spread among the teachers. This gossip increased when he wrote a story for his English assignment about an Arabian knight who rescues a princess. His way of negotiating through schooling was a combination of rebellion and subterfuge.

"At the end of that summer term, Mr. French retired and was replaced as housemaster by Mr. Rodney Kirkhall, a tall, stiff-backed, stern-looking man given to few words. There were rumors that he had been in charge of a prisoner of war camp in Scotland, keeping an eye on German prisoners. At any rate he did not strike me as the playful type. I felt I had to look out for him."

"He was certainly a man of few words. When asked any question his response usually started with: 'Well, [...] ahhmm.' The betting among the boys was that he wouldn't last long as a housemaster as he was going to find it hard to fill the shoes of old Frenchie. And, so it proved to be. Major Kirkhall decided to make his own mark by introducing some changes, and unsurprisingly, his inclination was to run a house full of civilian schoolboys like an army camp. His approach to running the House was ignored by the House tutor, and the matron kept her mouth shut and her head down. As for the majority of boys, particularly the more senior ones who were not prefects, but senior in terms of age, there was resentment combined with wariness. 'Caveat!' went the whisper whenever he was seen doing the House rounds."

Raza was the first of the senior boys to attract his attention. It happened on the last day of the winter term when he got changed into his holiday suit before departure. Kirkhall, noticing it, called him over.

"He said in a loud voice, 'What's the meaning of this? That is not your school uniform. Kindly go and change back into your school uniform before leaving for the holidays.' I was astounded. I hadn't been stopped from doing it before, but I went back and did as told to do, the incident was humiliating and made me angry."

Things didn't bode well for Raza during the next term, but those forebodings could wait because at least he knew he was due to go home.

FIRST RETURN VISIT HOME

Raza's first journey home came as he flew back with Abid in late July via Delhi. At Delhi his father asked a relative to meet them at the airport because arrivals in India could be a long bureaucratic process, with passengers not being required to form queues for passport or baggage checks. After just 18 months in England, Raza, who had got accustomed to queues in London felt a little flustered with passengers jostling in the arrivals hall and porters milling around to get tips for carrying baggage.

He noticed officials usher in some people through with a nod and a smile and wondered what that was about. Then his eye caught the relative who was waiting by the barriers and waving at him and Abid, and then talking to an official and pointing in their direction. The official waved them to come forward. So this was how it worked: you needed to know someone.

This came as a first culture shock in reverse. He was becoming anglicized. After spending the night in the relative's home, they were given onward tickets for Lucknow for the next morning and the internal flight with Indian Airlines came with the second culture shock. The plane was full of Indian businessmen and their families: a new emerging breed, in an independent India, some of them inclined to wearing gold and silver "bling" and being quite pushy and self-important. So this was the new middle-class businessman.

What was discernible here was that the process of assimilation was beginning to generate feelings of multiple belongings in Raza not just Indian and Islamic ones, but now an English one too. How he would learn to deal with the ethical tensions these would create was a question for the future, but for the moment these were forgotten as Raza and Abid entered the small arrivals hall at Lucknow airport and they spied their father in person who had come to receive them. After the usual greetings and embraces they got into the family car and sped towards home.

Then they were home, Raza for the first time after 18 months. Home to faces and sights familiar since childhood. Here little had changed except when he looked at his uncle's suite of rooms on the ground floor and noticed it was all shuttered up for a year now because his uncle had left for Pakistan.

"As I walked up the white marble stairs, taking two steps in each stride, I arrived at the familiar courtyard, one side of which was boarded up, the green paint of the boards flaked by the sun and rain. I entered the door to mother's quarters through a curtained doorway, I glanced towards mother's room and saw her seated on a bed outside her room, wearing that indefinable look of maternal love. I bowed, as she called in a quiet voice: 'Come son, sit by me.'"

He did as he was told and as she patted the space on the bed, she could see he was taller, and didn't have that "baby fat" look, and, in the customary fashion, embraced her as she tousled his hair. Raza was growing into a fine young man, as his mother stroked his face, a face with a handsome line and bone structure; he seemed to have avoided the aggressive brows many Indian men have and his mother smiled at him with approval.

Some food and tea was set out by the servants and then his brother Abid and sister Zahra came in and soon all the maidservants and his Amma, all with smiling faces; and since it was the end of the mango season (Raza's favorite variety of mangos) some "chuswa" variety was plated with additional fruits.

As he sat down at the table Raza noticed his youngest brother Ravinder, who was not yet 3 years old, come out of the room he shared with Zahra, adjacent to his mother's room. He was still a toddler then, wearing a white vest, but he looked at his eldest brother without really recognizing him. There were only photographs of Raza and Abid dressed in Arab clothes in his mother's room, and this tall boy had a resemblance to one of those photos, but he hadn't seen or heard him to speak to or pay him any attention as far as he could remember. Raza paid scant attention to his little brother then smiled and got on with his breakfast.

When he and Abid had finished their breakfast, their mother asked them to go and get washed and put on some clean Indian clothes and to let her know what they wanted to eat for lunch. When they returned their father was in his room but came out on to the verandah. Their mother who had been performing her "wuzoo" (Muslim ablutions) for prayers emerged from her bathroom and told them that they ought to go and pay their respects to their two Ammijans.

His maternal aunt and Ibn Dawood and two of his older sisters were still with his uncle in Pakistan, but his cousins Zainab and Hurr were for the present living in the suite at the front of the palace, with its doors opening out to the main portico, the same suite that his parents had once occupied when they moved from the new White Palace. So they had better pay their respects there too.

The two boys did as was expected and then returned when they were called for lunch. Nothing can replace home cooking. As the two boys returned, they could see the dining table being laid. As Raza passed his sister's room he didn't know how he had failed to notice the large cage placed to one side outside her room, and at the very end of his mother's verandah, for the cage was full of chirping budgerigars that Zahra had started keeping.

Their mother had finished her early afternoon prayers by then, and was sitting on the bed in the verandah when Raza and Abid returned from their rounds. She didn't eat with them. She hadn't eaten with them for some years because she had kept her own special diet of porridge, occasionally tasting a morsel of food prepared for the rest of the family if she fancied it. This had been the case for as many years as Raza could remember.

She looked up: "How did it go? What did your Ammijan say? Who else was there?" she asked. This was part of his mother's internal communications system. Raza and Abid took it in turns to fill her in. "And, did they give you anything?" "Yes, Rupees. Fifty each." A tally was kept because their mother didn't like to be beholden and would at some time repay by giving money to the Ammijan's children at some point, and Raza understood all this and was filled with an ineffable tenderness for his mother. He knew she too had been lonely without all her children being around.

The boys washed their hands in their mother's bathroom before returning to the dining table, and waited for the father to emerge from his room. One of the maidservants went to his door and called him in a quiet voice to lunch. Nawab Haidar Ali emerged and the boys and Zahra got up from their chairs and waited for him to sit down before they did. This was the usual custom.

"The children chose their different likes. I ordered some arhar dal and shami kababs, Abid has asked for some pasanda saalan, and Zahra some moong khichri. And, there are some chapatis of course. And since Kalloo khansama had been asked also, then some grilled chops, salad and potato chips were ordered as well, since they would be on their way."

"Very good. Bismillah, let's sit down."

Such was the usual established rhythm of things, and Raza realized what he's been missing and following lunch he was free to see his childhood companions who had already been informed of his return. He and Abid still shared the middle of the two rooms directly across the courtyard. However, his father reminded him not to forget to go and see his old Master Dada who lived below their room and on the ground floor.

Afternoon was also the time when his mother would say her midafternoon prayers, order food for the evening about which everyone had already been asked during lunch what they would like to eat, and time permitting she would take a nap or read her Urdu language newspaper, or see visitors and catch up with what was happening around town. Raza also understood that he needed to go and sit by his mother in her room to be with her.

"So sure enough when I went to his room, my friend Azizoo was sitting on the verandah outside his room, a tall slim man, a little older than himself, the nephew of the librarian, and from the family of one of Lucknow's most celebrated poets, Azizoo was learning Urdu calligraphy in order to find work at one of the Urdu newspapers. He got up and smiled as old friends acknowledged each other."

Abid joined them. After a while the conversation turned to Shireen, or rather Raza broached the subject with his friend and confidant.

"I thought you would have forgotten her by now. I thought you would have become too English by now. I'm glad to see that's not the case, but as for Shireen she has gone with her family to England too. Didn't you know?"

Raza didn't know this, but a slow and lasting flame for her still burnt in his heart. They talked about other things too as tea was ordered. Raza followed this sort of daily routine more or less every day. There were a few minor alterations, because some days he would visit sons of a distant relative, Afsar and Sarwar, who was a successful Lucknow barrister and close confidant of Raza's father. He also spent time going to Hazratganj to bookshops or to see a movie.

On one occasion when he was doing his daily rounds of paying respects, he went to see his cousins Hurr and Zainab. Hurr was now in his final year at Cambridge, and were glad to see him. As he sat on one of these occasions, Hurr said to him smiling: "Married life is good. Your Baji and I are so very happy. So tell me Raza, when you have finished your studies, Insha' Allah, who do you have in mind?"

"Shireen," Raza quickly let slip. They both looked at him astonished at his secret, and both simultaneously with one voice said: "Uncle won't like that." This made Raza shut up and wish he hadn't said what was really in his heart. He realized the elephant in the room is that Shireen is Hindu.

The holidays were underscored only because time was passing quickly and soon he would be returning to London. He had wanted to drown that realization by trying to behave as before, as though he had never gone away. But his friends did notice a change in him: in accent, gestures, demeanor he was becoming quite anglicized. They must have wondered how much more Raza would change by the time of his next visit.

Thus, the summer holidays did pass and it was a "wrench," as Raza would say, leaving home again. His mother prepared "peendees" (balls made out of nuts, sugar, and green lentils), some aloo ki bhujia and roghni tikia for the journey to Delhi for the both of them and with a bow and embrace they were off again.

In his bags Raza had packed an album, borrowed from his father, on physical exercises based on calisthenics because he was beginning to become more physically aware of himself, more man-boyish and keen on sports.

"Back at boarding school I finally found myself in the 4th Form. Feeling more independent and able to make choices, I also stood out as one of the taller boys in school. Now in the Senior Common Room there were more of a choice of newspapers, boys could have a brew up of baked beans and toast, and were allowed to play records and listen to the radio in their spare time. I liked the taste of baked beans—anything was better than the awful school grub. I also listened to the voice of John Arlott commentating on the test matches, and half-listened to 'The Archers,' but movies were the real deal, and if I couldn't see any during term time, my father allowed me and Abid to subscribe to magazines, so I took out a subscription to *Picturegoer*, and an American movie magazine, copies of which other boys would peer over their shoulders at."

"During the Christmas and Easter holidays I shared a bed-sit with Abid in the same area as before. Hurr by now had graduated and returned to join his wife Zainab not in India any longer but in Iraq, with his father-in-law, Bawab Dawood Ahmad, where he apparently felt frustrated, and longed to be in England, pursued a career in education. Husain was due to graduate from Oxford the next year, and for now concentrated on his studies."

Raza and Abid had different tastes: Abid was the more studious, preferring to spend his time reading. Raza was more often to be found in the movie shows and even kept a note of all the films he watched, and wrote down the movie titles he had seen in an exercise book, together with who starred in them.

By 1952, in his reckoning he had seen more than 700 movies, and counting. That takes some doing because it means that he must have been in cinema houses from morning until the last show in the evening. Occasionally, he would go with Abid to restaurants in between.

During Ramazan he still fasted, though he didn't pray five times a day. That year Ramadan had fallen during the winter, which made it easier to fast, and he would go with Abid to the Vega to break fast by eating scrambled eggs on toast accompanied with a nice pot of tea. He still stuck to a Muslim diet and drank no wine.

Raza's clothes, the suits, shirts, ties, Indian achkans he once wore when he was younger, those wore clothes made for him by British tailors purchased by Andersons and other drapers were all slowly changing.

"I remember wearing red houndstooth check shorts and jackets, Indian clothes were made at home and the materials chosen by my mother. I only started wearing white when I was about 7or 8 years old, because before they were red or green. I should say my attitude towards fashion changed and I began wearing US fashion every chance I got because I thought it looked more stylish."

SUMMER 1952: SECOND VISIT HOME

During the summer holidays in 1952, Raza and Abid returned for their second journey taking a holiday home. In many respects, things were much the same as the previous time, the only difference Ibn Dawood had returned from Pakistan with his mother, after his father Nawab Dawood Ahmad decided to move to Iraq. Ibn Dawood was now almost 8 years old, attending the Martinière, and still being brought up in an overprotected way, and when Raza saw him that summer he looked diminutive in his khaki shorts and shirt, and was under the tutelage of Lallan Sahab, whose room was next to Raza and Abid's.

Ibn Dawood would be seen emerging after lessons in Urdu in his white Indian dress, flitting in to see Zahra, who was a year older. He had only two friends, Zahra and another cousin. Zahra remembers that she had a difficult time trying to get him to contribute to the price of even one bottle of coca cola. He guarded his pocket money so well that he was already being called a miser. He didn't seem to have any male friends, and spent most of his free time with his two girl cousins.

Raza did not take much notice of his cousin at this time, who was also now being referred to as Shaikhoo. There was too much of a difference in age. Raza noticed his cousin had a coquettish manner in relating to cousins older than him. His sisters were all in Iraq with his father. Zainab, the eldest of these, and her husband Hurr had also departed for Iraq in the interim. The nawab's paternal influence as a socializing figure was absent, and instead he was left open to the influence of male palace secretaries and hangers on.

To Raza, Shaikhoo was of a nervous disposition, perspiring so profusely that his kurta appeared drenched, and seemed so flustered most of the time that Raza seriously worried about his health.

"These summer holidays in other respects seemed much of a muchness to the year before. Out and about in Lucknow the effects of Hindi replacing English were visible everywhere—in signs over shops, road signs, everywhere. On the humorous side, when I and Abid had arrived in Lucknow the local newspaper had captioned a photograph of us stepping down the airplane with: 'British Schoolboys Arrive in Lucknow,' and showing a photograph of us with straw boaters in our hands. When you read the story carefully it was about the visit of some English schoolboys who had arrived on some kind of an exchange visit, and not really about us at all. It just so happened that we had arrived with our school boaters on the same plane."

In a sense though, Abid had also become a bit more anglicized after 18 months in London, and this is illustrated by what he confided to Raza one day: that he had walked to the park by the river and said "God Save the Queen" in a loud voice before a statue of Queen Victoria that stood there, and which people now wanted removed. Concurrently, something else was going on—an agitation in Hazratganj for the replacement of all English signs by Hindi ones, when an incident was reported of a respectable Indian citizen of the old school who stood his ground and facing the agitating throng he asked individuals who seemed so avid for the removal of English signs to kindly remove their wristwatches and hand them over to him, promising to return them once the English numerals had been changed on the dials. India was on the march and what the boys had known as home was beginning to change.

CHAPTER 10

THE SCHOOL REBEL

Back at school, throughout the Lent and summer terms of 1953, Raza found himself to be one of the older boys in the class, in 4th Form now, following combined Oxford and Cambridge Universities O-level course, in two compulsory subjects (English language and math) and five or six optional subjects, which in his case included geography, French, history, general science and English literature. It was a two-year course and he would sit his exams in 1954. He was the same age as one or two in the House who had already been made prefects and wore the prefect's uniform of black jackets. He didn't mind that but there was a tension between those who had been made prefects and those who had not.

"I must say that one of the boys, Michael, and one or two other friends started referring to ourselves as 'the nonexistents, a meaningless term really, but I joined them as well. The point was to flout school rules whenever we could. At the beginning, these were trivial rules like stepping over the railings and walking across the land rather than walking along the path but our ambition was to create more havoc."

In short, Raza was turning into a rebel, and started attracting attention, and he confided his woes to Abid, who observed from then on the interactions between Raza, the prefects, and Kirkhall, while keeping his head down rather than follow the example of his brother.

NAWAB HAIDAR ALI ARRIVES IN ENGLAND

Raza's behavior and his lack of progress was duly noted and included in his school annual report. The reports were usually sent to his father in India, but by summer 1953 his father, who was not far away in India, but had arrived in London by then, received the report at his London address. He was in London because he had made the decision to come for two reasons: one was that his brother's leaving for Pakistan and later to Iraq, which had left his own future uncertain, and the other reason was a need to generate income.

On that basis, he was the first member of his generation of the Amadabad family to decide on getting qualifications in order to find suitable employment in India. His distant cousin, referred to earlier as a practicing barrister in Lucknow, also came as the father's confidant. He advised Haidar Ali to register for the Bar at one of London's Inns of Court. The more Raza's father thought of the idea, the more he liked it. His wife had always tried to encourage him to become more independent. When he shared the idea of studying for the law, she agreed to it and told him that she could manage Zahra's and Jafar's upbringing on her own, and not to worry. Raza's father then decided to register at Lincoln's Inn, and through a little bit of research via his contacts, he was told to ask to be attached to the chambers of a particular Queen's Counsel.

He also found inexpensive bed-sit accommodation in Doughty Street nearby. It was a boarding house adjacent to the house Charles Dickens had once lived in. His decision seemed serendipitous when during 1953 the news of the abolition of zamindari by Nehru administration reached him. This also meant the end of "sanads" or stipends that all the heirs received. And his second reason for coming to England was that it would also be easier this way to keep an eye on the education and development of the two boys. The reports he had been receiving from school about Raza and his growing rebelliousness were disquieting.

At the age of 17, Raza found it impossible to accept the school regime. Yet the boys around Raza were annoyed and irritated rather than inspired by his humility and forgiveness. Not to be destroyed by their misdirected energies, he decided on another tact. He and his housemaster in particular weren't hitting it off. The net result of which for the father was to assess the situation and to discuss it with the school. He was gravely concerned. He had a private meeting with the headmaster, and then with the housemaster.

"Keep in mind by that time the general consensus was that the school did not feel that it could do much more for me, but they did say they were willing to give me the chance to sit for my O-levels the next summer, but beyond that I could not stay because after all I would be 18 by then, and this was the age when boys were expected to have sat for their A-levels. They pointed to the example of Abid, who was studious, and applying himself, whereas they didn't really hold out hope for me being able to attain up to six O-levels."

The father continued to hear all about Raza's general behavior throughout the summer until:

I decided to run away from the school.

He was discovered to be absent that night from the House and an alarm was raised but Raza was nowhere to be found and when Abid was questioned, he said nothing. He had promised Raza not to tell anyone and only he knew that Raza was hiding in the woods nearby. On that first evening, Abid sneaked out to deliver a bar of chocolate to his brother, who was hiding in the woods near Mr. French's home in Butterfly Lane. He intended to sleep there.

Raza's absence from the school continued for a second day, and then into a third; by this time, he had decided to move on from the woods, and even Abid no longer knew his movements. The school was embarrassed—what if the tremors of this incident went back to the parents of other boarders?

Mr. French, in his capacity as having befriended Raza as the housemaster, was also informed. There was a whole search party of people looking out for him. Then, on the third day, walking back from Edgware, he was found by Mr. French. He had spotted Raza trudging and limping wearily up the hill from Butterfly Lane. The old man stopped the car as he caught up with the recognizable figure:

"Get in, my boy." Raza got in the car without a word. He was too tired, cold, and hungry to put up any resistance and he was driven back to the school. The matron examined him. He was found to have blisters on his feet. In order to calm the situation, and the ruffled feathers of Mr. Kirkhall, it was suggested that Raza have a rest in the school sanatorium and recuperate.

Raza explained that once he'd got into trouble about his clothes further disciplinary actions had followed.

"Petty stuff. And, I found myself with a reputation that made some of the other boys avoid me. And I found the situation becoming quite unbearable so I decided to run away. I confided my intentions to Abid and knew him to be entirely dependable. We even arranged a secret meeting point. Things escalated and I didn't know a way back. Not with Mr. Kirkhall after me. I took to walking across fields and keeping away from roads and traffic. After the second night, I slept in the arch of an unfinished tube line in the middle of a field that was being used by a farmer to stack hay. On the third day, I walked all the way up to Edgware Station, scrummaging around for change in my pockets to buy a ticket into London with and finding none I was still feeling hungry from not having eaten a proper meal for two days except for a cheese roll, a mars bar, and a packet of crisps that Abid brought for me. I had found drinking water from taps and drinking fountains, but no hot drink."

"I wandered around Edgware Station. Sam Cook's the green grocer's shop outside the station caught my eye. I noticed a card advertising for an assistant, and was told that I was too young. Tired, I sat down on a bench for a while outside the station, trying to catch some warmth from the sun, watching people go in and out. I suddenly noticed from the corner of my eye a child being pushed along in its pushchair drop a piece of chocolate it had been given by its mother."

"My mouth watered. I looked this way and that and found an opportunity to grab the chocolate without being noticed, scrubbed the grit off, and put it in my mouth. Then I started walking aimlessly and found myself going back toward Butterfly Lane. It is some seven miles from Edgware Station. I was trudging by now, my feet sore from the walking, and from wearing the same pair of socks I had left in, all caked from drying sweat that had not been allowed to properly dry because I had slept in my shoes for two nights."

Meanwhile the school had informed his father, who came to the school as soon as he could and was met by the headmaster as well as Mr. Kirkhall. The father was a patient man and heard from the school side first, calmly listening to stories circulating about the reasons behind Raza's escapade, it transpired that a House prefect had been instructed to keep an eye on Raza by Mr. Kirkhall, who thought Raza to be a bad influence on the other boys.

The movie and other magazines that Raza had gotten subscriptions for like *La Vie Parisienne* had been discovered in his locker. These were seized as the source of being part of Raza's exotic charisma as a boarder. Such things were banned in school in any case, and Raza's father was left in no doubt about the matter. The father listened to it all, thanked them for the chance the school was still willing to give Raza and left, promising he would talk to his son during the coming summer holidays over time and at length.

Nawab Haidar Ali had been given ample cause for concern as a father. Back in London, during the holidays, he decided to listen to Raza's version of events, and to Abid's, as well. He was a patient and understanding father who knew that the situation had to be handled calmly, without anger. He understood both his sons well, and knew that Raza had grown into a young adult with his own independent mind. He asked Raza to tell him what happened.

"I just found it impossible to get on with the new housemaster."

His father raised an astonished brow at his son's inadequate response, "Why don't you start from the beginning? *La Vie Parisienne* or whatever the magazine is called, that's some French sort of erotica isn't it?"

A nod from Raza.

"But it's not that. You remember the two suits that you had given me? Both double-breasted suits of yours with white stripes, one is black and the other is dark brown? Well, I decided to put on the brown one when leaving for Xmas holidays and Mr. Kirkhall had a go at me."

"Surely that can't be all. I am told that you started subscribing to magazines from the pocket money I give. You know that I don't approve of you being so film crazy."

Raza said nothing.

"What were you doing with that French magazine in your locker?"

"Nothing."

"Well, it can't just be nothing. How did you come to hear of it?'

"From a friend at school."

"I have warned you before about bad company at home, and now I find that you are still prone to falling under bad influence here. Your mother and I have made sacrifices for your and Abid's education. This route that you seem to have adopted is not going to do you much good. There are other boys at the school, why don't you mix with them?"

Raza narrated his flight from school, while his father listened. His father didn't lecture him except to say that he talked to the headmaster and to other teachers and in their opinion Raza won't do as badly in his studies as previously thought and that he should:

Start having some expectations of yourself.

Raza acquiesced to his father's wish to try for his O-level examinations in the coming year, and the challenge to prove the school wrong. That summer he stayed on in England with his father while Abid, who had overtaken him academically, getting very good results in math and science, as well as excelling in English literature, was allowed home to India with all the positives going for him. All kinds of openings attracted him. His excellent results in pure math meant he could study to become an actuary. He mentioned to Raza one day that there are only a handful of actuaries in the whole country. Then there was physics and chemistry.

But it was also the end of the road between Raza and the boarding school, a parting of company and just one year more to negotiate.

"I found some respect amongst many of those in my year and made new friends. During the summer holidays that year I stayed in England, it was Abid, who went home. The school had agreed to give me one more year to stay on and finish the O-level course."

For the rest of the school year, Raza studied hard and duly sat for his examinations. By the time he came to say his goodbyes to the school, his father had negotiated an arrangement with Mr. French to take Raza on as a paying lodger. In the circumstances, he felt it to be the best arrangement for him because it would be thoroughly impractical for him to stay at his boarding rooms in Doughty Street. Raza's goodbyes were fleeting. He saw Mr. and Mrs. Schnabel and promised to keep in touch. He gave a scarf as a leaving present to the sergeant major, the PE teacher, who he had ended up making his peace with. At that it was done.

During Raza's trip home, Abid learned that Nawab Dawood Ahmad had returned briefly to Amadabad from Iraq that year. People at home told him when he returned, that his uncle's arrival was an amazing event. For a moment people believed that he was coming home for good.

"Some said that once the news had reached Amadabad and that the nawab was on his way from Lucknow that day, the scene that greeted the Nawab was truly amazing. Imagine an 18-mile-long dirt road with potholes all the way made by the monsoon rains, that cars and lorries have to weave past when the earth dries. Imagine the same road dotted either side with villages along its length. The nawab's car is spotted turning from the main road.

Villagers come out from their huts, men, women and children, with some parents holding their children, the village dogs barking, the peasants raise their hands to their foreheads. The nawab is moved and gets down from the car. He starts walking. As he gets nearer to the family estate, more crowds gather until he is totally surrounded by people. They cannot believe he has returned; they ask him to stay. That's how unbelievable it was.

Abid retold what happened, but then went on to say that no sooner had his uncle arrived than he left again. One story suggested that the nawab had gone from Lucknow to Delhi to meet Nehru, and that he had carried a carved ivory handle, silver plated Colt '45 from the Amadabad family armory with him as a present for Nehru, that Nehru had asked him to come back to India and stay. Whatever happened the nawab didn't stay but left overnight without a word of explanation. Imagine the impact of all that. It seemed that Nawab Dawood Ahmad was intent on burning all bridges behind him."

CHAPTER 11

CRAMMERS

By the time September 1954 came around, Raza found himself traveling into town on a Green Line coach to the Crammers. The Crammers was an intensive course to pass entrance examinations, and five days a week, he would commute, carrying a bag for his course, containing exercise books, notepads, and a lunch prepared by Mrs. French.

"I had secured lodgings my father negotiated with one of the Crammers who had been recommended to me, and after finding the place to my liking, registered at a Crammers in Maida Vale for me to study for two 'A' levels, one in history, and the other in English literature. I must say that the place itself was not easy to get to from the French's, all the way near Elstree by bus and underground to Warwick Avenue; even if the journey was a bit long it was something I had to do. I wasn't totally unhappy about it even though I had to travel Mondays to Fridays and back for about three hours each day."

It was not soon afterward Raza received his results and had passed in all the subjects he had taken. His father was very pleased. So pleased that he allowed his son to open a book account at Bumpus the booksellers in Oxford Street. The Crammers were based in Warwick Avenue in a large building four or five floors high.

"The Crammers were registered with an accredited Boards of Examination—Oxford and Cambridge, jointly or singly, as well as the London Examination Board. The ground floor of the building was occupied by the administration offices, the floors above were the classrooms of the contracted tutors in different subjects. The tutors were generally very skilled in getting students through a two years A-level syllabus in one year, which is what gave Crammers their reputation."

[Raza with 53 classmates (51 British classmates and Raza and one other Indian boy), 1951.]

The tutors were usually Irish, Welsh, or northerners, seeking a better wage than they could get in state schools. Classes were usually quite small, not larger than six, and sometimes no more than four or five. The students were usually taking a crash course, mostly in English, or math or languages, and in Raza's case he was registered for A-level history, and English thrown in as an extra. On the first day of term in September, Raza was ushered into the main office and, having signed the register, was introduced to his history tutor, who turned out to be of a different orientation to the teachers at his boarding school, some of whom had been majors and captains in the army, and were generally from a solid conservative middle-class background.

"My new history tutor, Mr. Peter D'Alroy-Jones, was sitting casually in his small classroom reading the copy of a newspaper that no one would have been caught dead reading at the boarding school—the *Daily Mirror*. 'Ghastly, my dear! What? A working-class newspaper, here? Never.' Not even the *Manchester Guardian* was allowed at the boarding school."

And yet, as Raza was to discover, Mr. D'Alroy-Jones read both. The double-barreled name belied his origins. He spoke with a northern accent, wore an ordinary suit, and carried a friendly smile. He had Raza's application form in front of him, from which he would have read not just Raza's personal information, but also about his education history.

"Well, Mister Khan,"—Raza was to discover in time that all the students were addressed as "Mr.," or "Miss" followed by their surnames—"I see that you want to study modern history at A-level. That covers both Modern European History and Modern English History, I take it?" Raza nodded. "Fine, I'll throw in some history of the United States as well. It'll be hard work, but I will do my best to get you through, and make sure that at the same time that you enjoy it. History can be a very enjoyable subject. The rest is down to you to discover."

Raza stood up and shook hands and was told there would be history classes for three full days a week, and given a list of essential books to buy, and a copy of the timetable. He was told there would be three other students in the class and that he will meet them soon enough. He was then told how to locate the English teacher.

"Mr. Brown, the French tutor, was also the deputy at the Crammers. He was the picture of the color brown: brown three-piece crumpled suit, tawny brown hair and mustache, and with a bespectacled look of someone in a permanent brown study. Mr. Brown looked at me as though waking up from a reverie. He enquired in a dull voice, 'Yes, you're Mr. Khan aren't you, here to study for A-level French?'"

"And I can see him now noticing me nodding in the affirmative, continued by handing him out the curriculum for the year. He would then tell me 'if you look down the list of set texts you will note the names of, Molière and Jean Anouilh. Your set texts will be "*Le bourgeois gentilhomme*" by Molière and "*Antigone*" by Anouilh. Besides that, you will also be expected at the examination to translate passages from French into English, writing a short essay in French from a choice of different themes, as well as an oral examination in spoken conversational French. Doesn't sound too bad, does it now? If you were going to sit for it at A-level, you would have four set texts, as well as having a longer oral examination."

Raza said he understood and added he would have additional help from the family he was living with, as the family was bilingual in English and French. Mr. Brown's face seemed to take it all in, but otherwise, no emotion passed across it, before he finally said that there would be classes two days per week.

"I should say thereafter the ball was set rolling, and for my first history lesson the next day, Mr. D'Alroy-Jones entered the tutorial room with a rolled-up copy of the *Daily Mirror*, which he smacked against his leg. Then, having caught everyone's attention unrolled the newspaper and held it up. The headline blared: 'Go on, Marge, do what you want.' He passed the paper around. It carried more news and pictures of the ill-fated romance between Princess Margaret and Group Captain Townsend. Despite Townsend's distinguished career, which included being an Equerry to George VI. 'Now, I would like you to understand some of the background to the story,' Mr. D'Alroy-Jones would say. 'You see, in England the social atmosphere of the times is such that divorced people are severely frowned upon. They are certainly not allowed to remarry in the Church.'"

Townsend, therefore, had no realistic chance of marrying the princess. Their relationship has caused enormous controversy, particularly in the pages of most newspapers like *The Mail* and *The Telegraph*.

"In Britain, *The Mirror* and the *Manchester Guardian*, are exceptions. They are more inclined to ask questions such as why should commoners not marry into the royal family? This was the start of Mr. D'Alroy-Jones history class that day. He asked students in turn what we thought about it and were asked to challenge the shock comments about a commoner marrying a royal and give good reason why this shouldn't be allowed to happen."

None of the four students had an answer, including Raza. As he got into the swing of things at Crammers, and being taught by a more approachable person than anyone he could recall at school, Raza had time to reflect on his new history teacher.

"Other than being a good teacher of history, providing his students with a comprehensive list of books on the curriculum—Lewis Namier, A. J. P. Taylor, Hugh Trevor-Roper, and J. M. Thompson, Elie Halévie's masterpiece, the *History of the English People in the Nineteenth Century*—he showed he knew his subject in and out, and was himself in the process of writing a book: *An Economic History of the United States since 1783*.

Not only was he very widely read, but he also introduced US history's relevance to English and European history. On his part, D'Alroy-Jones too developed a liking for Raza, and one day after class, he made him sit down for a chat.

"He looks at me with a quizzical stare and said if I like reading and want to develop a critical sense, he would prepare a list of some essential literature I ought to read." He then proceeded to ask Raza to write down the titles and names of authors in his notebook. Raza wrote them as they were called out: Aldous Huxley's *Eyeless in Gaza* and *Chrome Yellow*; Faulkner's *Intruder in the Dust*; Koestler's *Arrow in the Blue*; Hemingway's *For Whom the Bell Tolls*; Orwell's *Down and Out in London and Paris*; James Joyce's *A Portrait of the Artist as a Young Man*; Steinbeck's *The Grapes of Wrath*, and so on. When he had finished writing, the names were like manna from heaven.

Later in the week after his morning tutorials, Raza met with his father for lunch in nearby Oxford Street who wanted to be brought up to date about the Crammers.

Raza was feeling contented with the examinations and he reassured his father. Afterward was taken to a large bookshop, which his father referred humorously to as "Oh, Mr. Bumpus." Raza smiled, he was happy to see his dad in such a jovial mood and ever since childhood he remembered his dad having a penchant for playing with language. More was to follow.

As Raza produced his list of books, his father led him to the history section and asked the assistant to pick out some of the books from the list he could see already on the shelves. That was the beginning of Raza's own personal library. His father also bought for him some essential stationery and a briefcase, and then they went to the language section where Raza picked up a copy of a French/English dictionary, as well as the set texts of Molière and Anouilh.

The half dozen selected books, and the stationery just fitted his brand-new briefcase. "That's enough for the day, you don't need to be carrying more," said father to son. Raza thanked his father. "In any case, Abbajan," Raza said breaking into Urdu to his father, "I need to get some further advice from Mr. French about the grammar books before I select them."

After lunch Raza returned to the Crammers, and from there after each lesson came back to Mr. French's. This became a kind of pattern for the year. Father and son might meet once a week for lunch, otherwise it was studies and Mr. French's. Abid was still at boarding school.

When the Christmas holidays came at the end of 1953, Raza and Abid both stayed with their father in Doughty Street. Husain Bhai joined them from Oxford, but stayed elsewhere. As we have noted before, there was precious little else to do for non-Christian foreigners and visitors in London and Raza's father was still in the habit of scouring the pages of *What's On* to find places to eat. On one such occasion that Christmas, he reserved a table at the famous Savoy in the Strand. They were given a table in the middle of the large restaurant. Raza looked around and saw the other tables occupied by the rich and the famous.

While waiting for their order to be taken, a waiter approached their table with a note from another diner, sending his greetings. The note was addressed to Husain Bhai, the diner having mistaken him for Crown Prince Faisal of Iraq, who was studying at Harrow at the time. Raza's father looked back toward the table at the man who had sent the note and smiled. He sent a note back saying that regretfully Husain Bhai was not Prince Faisal.

During winters the streets of London were covered by a thick fog known as a pea-souper: a fog so dense that you couldn't see more than a few yards in front, and the headlamps on buses, cars, and taxis were barely visible until the traffic was almost on you. Usually the fog also seemed not white but a kind of yellowish green because of the mix of smoke from London's burning chimney fires. It gave London an eerie Dickensian feel. However, Raza's father seemed to enjoy walking in it, usually through places like Hyde Park.

"I listened to my father speak about these times and he would compose poetry while walking through fog and mist. For me it was all about the movie, because I would escape to see movies on my own."

We know that Raza had been writing down the names of all the movies he had seen since boarding school days, and calculates he must have seen 1,500 movies in three years. This was his escape. An escape like dreams that money could buy.

During those holidays, Raza learned that Zainab Baji gave birth to a son named Maysam, born on March 1952. There had been some teething problems though—not so much to do with the young Maysam, as to do with his grandfather. The nature of these has only recently come to light from the notebooks Zainab kept, where in one of them she writes that her father, the nawab, was not only a very tactile person—not picking up the baby, for example—but seemed frustrated by it all, and showed his impatience.

They all lived together in a house the nawab had bought, not far from his office in "Share'al–Rashīd" or Rashid Avenue, in Baghdad. The avenue was named after Haroun-al-Rashid of *The Arabian Nights* fame. This thoroughfare contained the city's financial district, many government buildings, and the copper, textile, and gold bazaars. Raza came to learn about the house and office because Abid had gone there to stay with his uncle on the way home that summer.

"During the Easter holidays the following year, my father and Abid traveled to Oxford to visit Husain Bhai at Magdalen College, with its deer park, and the Cherwell running through the grounds under Magdalen Bridge. Husain Bhai was due to graduate and had already lined up a managerial job with Imperial Tobacco in Pakistan. I started thinking more and more about the city as a place I might want to live and find a residence. With Husain leading the way it became easy to get to know the place by simply walking around and getting one's bearings from the central landmark of Carfax. Oxford was nothing in size compared to London. I also discovered Blackwell's, the famous Oxford bookshop, some eating places, and of course, the cinemas."

During term time and in between the holidays with family members, there was a set routine Raza followed: Crammers and the long journey home to the

French's. There was an early supper, followed by some polite conversation with his host's family. There was another lodger called Malcolm, who shared a room with Tim French. Ogilvie was another Old Boy from the boarding school, who had done his National Service in the RAF, and was now working as a civilian pilot at the nearby airport.

"There was only one bathroom in the house and therefore early in the morning a rota (system) had to be established for a shower and a quick shave in a basin of cold water because the French's were too penny-pinching and wary of the cost of hot water. They then rationalized their miserliness by saying that shaving and washing in cold water was better."

As the year wore on, Raza's library grew too. He used the account his father had opened for him and had got to know one of the assistants with whom he could talk about different books. The man was very knowledgeable.

By the end of the year, Raza had amassed a little library of world literature. He would follow D'Alroy-Jones's suggested list of authors and, if he liked an author, he would follow it up by purchasing and reading another book by the same author. Such was the case with Hemingway, Faulkner, Scott Fitzgerald, Steinbeck, Huxley, Dostoevsky, and so on. D'Alroy-Jones's history pupil had a broad enough base by the end of the year for thought and enlightenment. While still retaining his love for the cinema, he had dropped subscribing to movie magazines and erotica and swapped that for world literature.

After supper in the evenings, Mr. French would retire to the living room and sit in his favorite armchair. With a log fire burning, he would read or listen to classical music, and sometimes would invite Raza and anyone else who'd care to listen to Mozart's "Horn Concertos," or Haydn's "The Clock." This, apart from the jazz music he'd listened to in the Senior Common Room and the religious music and chanting he had heard in Amadabad, were Raza's introduction to music. The attitude of Mr. French, a most gracious host, was one of silent approval and encouragement since he had a collection of books himself through which Raza would browse.

During the summer, Raza sat for his exams in History and French. He had revised as well as he could. He had discovered a trait of sustained concentration in himself when writing an essay for homework or when revising, and the rest was in the lap of the gods. Prior to the exams he had said goodbye to Mr. D'Alroy-Jones, since the examinations were going to take place in examination rooms at London University.

"Well, Raza," Mr. D'Alroy-Jones had taken to calling him by his first name, "I hope you do well, you should, but do keep in touch, and I'll send you a copy of my book when it's published, and don't forget from what you have learnt that as far as US/UK relationships go, the roles have been reversed since the war, even earlier you might say, to the days of Woodrow Wilson and World War I. Britain is no longer a senior or even equal partner, despite what Churchill says. All the talk about the 'special relationship' disguises the fact that Britain is nothing more than a glorified US aircraft carrier." He smiled and waved goodbye.

This critical observation was the first time that Raza heard such a view expressed. The Cold War was at its iciest at the time. You were more liable to be called a Communist for expressing such views as D'Alroy-Jones had. Raza had learnt from reading history that its study was not a learning of facts, but a weighing of evidence. To Raza's ears the observation sounded true.

A seed of independent thinking had been planted in Raza's mind, but it was more like an incendiary device as he soon discovered, when one evening at supper, in front of the whole company, Raza blurted out at the French's that, in his opinion, Britain was a glorified American aircraft carrier. It was an injudicious remark to say the least. He realized it no sooner than he said it.

The remark was met with an absolute silence. Faces from around the table looked at him aghast. Then followed a burst of outrage from the whole household. Raza had not realized just how Tory the French household was. From that point on, he thought perhaps it's best to keep his political views to himself. The matter never came up again.

He didn't go home that summer, but stayed for part of it in London. By then, his father, forever a man for maintaining a budget, had found lodgings in Barnes, southwest London, across the river. The No. 73 bus took him all the way there. Barnes lay across Hammersmith Bridge and the lodgings consisted of a first-floor bed-sitting room, with a little kitchenette, and a shared bathroom and toilet. It belonged to an Iranian Indian doctor, who lived with his large family in an adjacent house thoroughly refurbished and furnished, unlike the house for rent, which had been bought as an additional source of income. Raza became a frequent visitor that summer until he went away to France for the remaining holidays.

Mr. and Mrs. French suggested to him earlier that he might ask his father's permission to go to France for two weeks. The matter had obviously been discussed between Tim and his parents. They had come up with the idea of a camping holiday in the south of France, and a return via Grenoble in the Alps where some of their relatives lived. Abid had decided to go home that year, and although Raza was going to be on his own, the father agreed.

"We packed our bags, including a portable tent and Tim had purchased a round trip train ticket for two that took Tim and I via Paris and Toulon to a place called Le Lavandou, near Fréjus and St. Raphael, which had been recommended as a nice camping site. The overnight journey from Paris brought us the next morning to a practically deserted sandy beach."

"We had pegged down our tent in the sand beneath some palm trees less than a 50-yard walk to the beach, where a lonely shack played music and served drinks. For the next few days, we decided to get up early and have coffee and a piece of baguette and then go and spend the rest of the morning swimming and sunbathing. This was followed by a lunch consisting of more baguette, with some cheese, plain chocolate, followed by a shared melon, and washed down with some mineral water. At times we would join in a game of volleyball on the beach with some friendly French holidaymakers. Then, when the sun was a little lower on the horizon we would return to the beach for another round of sunbathing, reading, and swimming."

Raza said there were few people around, and certainly not many girls.

"I noticed straightaway that we would normally see the same pair of girls, lying on the beach a little further down, or swimming. One of these girls caught my eye. She was bronzed with long blonde hair bleached by sea and sun, and wore a pink and grey bikini. From what I could see of her face she looked beautiful, but our problem was neither of us knew the first thing about how to pick up a girl."

By the time they left the South and traveled to the Alps, Raza's face and body had gone an almost dark brown to a black bronzed color from the sun, standing out in contrast against his bright yellow swimming trunks, and his flashing white teeth in a tanned face. They spent a day or two in Grenoble with a distant relative, an old farmer with a face lined by the sun and the wind, before eventually returning to London. The tan was still sufficiently there on his return to London, causing his smiling father to comment on his complexion.

The A-level exam results were out by now. Raza had passed in history, but not in French. His father discussed his results with him and helped him to decide on repeating the French and taking Classical Persian as his third subject. A different Crammers for French was looked for in the hope that they would have someone more sparkly than Mr. Brown. It was located down the Old Brompton Road.

MR. K'S ILLNESS

Raza's father had become known as "Mr. K," and not by his full title. In England he had dispensed with that for reasons that were unclear. But the telephone rang and one day telling Raza his father was ill. It was the Persian doctor and Raza spoke to him in Urdu. It turned out Raza's father had been acting strange since his successful completion of his studies in law a short time earlier. The doctor had meant to mention it to Raza and Abid but Abid had gone home that summer, and had not been able to get in touch with Raza until now. In any case, the doctor told him he had better come over and take charge of things.

It was midafternoon at the time when he set off, and the journey to Barnes took him almost two hours. It was early evening and just getting dark when he reached the two houses, the one his father lived in and the doctor's house. Throughout the journey, he remembered how his father had behaved just nine years earlier. All of this went through his mind as he traveled, changing buses and trains along the way. Then he was there, and suddenly very calm. He had instinctively put on the caretaker's uniform. He was now the caretaker and his father the one to be cared for. Calmly as he climbed the stairs to his father's bedside, he saw him looking down. That proud familiar face now gave a pathetic-looking smile, and speaking softly, said to his son: "You've come." "Yes, father I have come."

Raza noticed how his father looked bedraggled, not at all like the smart clothes he had always seen him wearing. The bedroom looked dreary, the bed unmade, the curtains drawn, the clothes scattered. He greeted his father respectfully enough, but now found himself speaking to him as to a child: "Father, what has happened?" The father tried to pull himself together, on hearing the word "Father," but only succeeded in looking lost and absent-minded. Then he started talking, saying things that sounded like gibberish but sometimes there was sexual innuendo: "I am a mole who lives in a hole. No, no that's a snake hole. I wish your mother were here, then I could be a mole."

On seeing the shock on his son's face, he suddenly said: "All right, be like that." Before Raza could see or do anything his father had gone out of the room, dressed only in his jacket and trousers and wearing no shoes. Raza quickly grabbed a pair of his father's shoes and decided the only course was to follow him, which he did as his father had already gone out of the house and was walking down the side of Glebe Road leading to Barnes Green Common.

The father, sensing his son was following him, turned around and looked to see his son emerging from the front gate. He decided to stop and stand there looking at his son. Raza stopped too. Then he started walking again stopping every few yards to look behind him. At this point, Raza had decided against startling his father and kept his distance. Soon the father reached Barnes Green Common and walked past a decorative round shallow pond with a small fountain in the middle, as though he meant to go on. Thankfully, for everyone, the doctor, who must have seen the father come out of the house, drew up in his car. He opened the passenger side door and leant forward looking at Raza's father smiling: "Please get in." The father grinned sheepishly and obeyed. Raza got into the back seat before they drove home.

That night the father slept soundly, while Raza spent the night watchfully in the armchair. By morning, the voice of the doctor could be heard inviting them for breakfast. Raza greeted his father, which he hadn't yet had time to do and was sounding more normal that morning.

The doctor had seen them walk up the pebbled drive and opened the door and led them to the front room where his wife had laid the breakfast table. Raza asked if he could use the telephone. He telephoned Mr. and Mrs. French to let them know that he'd be staying over another night or two. The hesitation in his voice made it clear that he couldn't talk then, but that he would probably need to spend more time with his father until things were sorted out about his treatment. The others may have heard the conversation, but at any rate, after breakfast, the doctor asked the father whether he would like to join him for a cigarette in the study.

Raza stayed talking to the wife and after what seemed to be about 15 or 20 minutes the doctor and Raza's father walked back to the living room. Whatever transpired between the two of them, the outcome was that the father had accepted going into a residential psychiatric home in Harrow-on-the-Hill. As Raza was already an adult, he would need to give his consent as next of kin, if required to do so. That decided, some other things needed to be attended to as well. Raza sent off two telegrams immediately, one to his mother and the other to his uncle, asking for advice and instructions.

Fees for the treatment were not a problem since the father had an account with McDoug's firm. The father needed to pack his clothes and essentials. Then in mid-afternoon, with everybody ready, they set off for Bowden House, the name of the residential psychiatric home in Harrow-on-the-Hill where Raza's father was to be admitted.

Bowden House was an old Victorian mansion set in its own ample grounds. It was private, of course, and Raza couldn't guess what the fees would be in such a place.

"We waited at the reception for the psychiatrist with whom my father had an appointment, and in walked a tall lean man in a dark brown suit wearing a bow tie. He nodded and smiled, then asked if he could have a private session with the patient before meeting us together. His name was Dr. Knopfman, a name I found kind of funny sounding for some odd reason. But he showed my father to the door, closing it behind him. After about 50 minutes he came and explained to me that in his assessment my father was showing a recurrence of symptoms of paranoid schizophrenia and that he would need to undergo a six weeks treatment and rehabilitation program he and my father had discussed and happy to agree to it."

Raza took serious mental note of what was said though, unsurprisingly, he did not fully understand what the terms meant. Yet, he took it seriously enough at the moment to realize his father needed to remain in doctor's car.

"I notice my father then shaking hands, embracing and saying goodbye to Dr. Knopfman and it was later back in Barnes my father phoned to thank Dr. Knopfman profusely for all his help, and went to pack his father's remaining belongings because the room would need to be vacated."

Finally, having packed then ordered a cab, Raza said a few words to the Malaysian Muslim nurse lady, who lived in the bed-sit below and stopped to explain what had happened to his father. By this time, the cab arrived to take Raza back to the French's. His father had given him some money to use as he needed. It was a few weeks before seeing the father again. His father's recuperation would more likely be back at home as he was unlikely to return to his London residence.

Six weeks elapsed with Raza visiting his father on three occasions, besides keeping otherwise in touch via the telephone. The French household was very supportive through this time and around that time received a message from his uncle in Baghdad, saying he was making arrangements to fly over and attend to his brother's help. This was of great relief to Raza since he was simply not able to carry the responsibility of his father's health on his own. He was already trying to reassure his mother and sister in Lucknow, as he had to book several phone calls and speak and console her as best he could.

"The most lasting effect on my memory at the time was the difference I noticed in my father each time I visited him; because on the first occasion he appeared to have put on a little weight and seemed happy, or at least happy enough on the surface, and he would be talking to fellow female and male patients. Yet and in spite of this I could see something was not quite right and he wasn't himself. It was like he was going through the motion, lethargic, and seemed to have aged."

His father had been only 39 at the time. Indeed, whenever he was mistaken by chance acquaintances as the older brother of Raza and Abid, he would hide a smile. When he asked about the changes in his father, one of the psychiatric nurses had told him they were the effects of 30 incidents of ECT (electroconvulsive therapy) accompanied by drug-induced therapy. Raza shivered with the thought of it, though it did make him toy with the idea of studying psychiatry. He even discussed the idea with Dr. Knopfman during one of his visits. The psychiatrist listened to him but said that a degree in medicine was a prerequisite. This ruled that idea out without totally making him lose interest in psychology, he bought some books by Jung, Freud, and William James. Occasionally, he dipped into them to try and gain an understanding of himself.

Meanwhile Raza's uncle arrived in London, shortly before his father was due to be discharged from the nursing home. His room had been booked at the Bonnington Hotel in Southampton Row. His uncle showed Raza a lot of kindness and asked him how his father was doing and was reassured by Raza somewhat. Then out of family etiquette, Raza enquired about the rest of the family in Iraq.

"Ma sha' Allah, they're all fine. Your Bari Baji now has another baby son called Jaun."

"When was he born?"

"In April last year, I think. Your other Bajis are well too, and your Baray Bhaisahab—well, he is writing poetry and composing a marsiya."

The uncle was never a man of many words. They exchanged a few words about Raza's father. Raza expressed the view that he was relieved to learn from Dr. Knopfman that his father was well and ready to be discharged. The uncle asked Raza to accompany him to the nursing home in a couple of days.

"The nawab had other affairs to sort out meanwhile—personal expenses, and settling the bill at the nursing home. Besides, he was still active in Pakistani politics behind the scenes. He kept his ears open and maintained contacts with both businessmen and politicians. There were tensions between East and West Pakistan, where the nawab's tendency was to favor the people from East Pakistan. Suhrawardy had recently become prime minister and was trying to bring in a process of reform and restructuring of the military, and its ally, the Pakistani landowners. Suhrawardy found the block between the two an obstacle to progress toward democracy.

He had Maulana Bashani's support too. The nawab found them both to be charismatic figures, but he was also aware that trying to tamper with the military carried very high risks. Through his Irani tea-exporting friends he was in touch with people like General Sikander Mirza. He met him in London. But all this he kept to himself. I should state straightaway that I had no inkling until much later."

Raza arrived at his uncle's hotel in order to accompany him to the nursing home as the two of them left by taxi for Bowden House. The uncle was nervous about meeting his younger brother, in part because he had suffered from depression himself, and remembered his brother's breakdown in 1946, when he had been equally apprehensive and wary of his brother's sudden mood turns.

Fortunately, the appointment with Knopfman coincided with the time that the residents were having lunch. Whether or not this was intentionally arranged is anyone's guess, but the meeting with the psychiatrist reassured him that his brother was near enough his normal self to be discharged. Having settled matters at the nursing home, the uncle returned to his hotel, having booked an extra room for his brother and went back to fetch him two days later. Raza after staying at the Bonnington for about a week, his uncle and father left for Iran for some alternative treatment for Raza's father.

His uncle gave him two unexpected presents: a Contax camera, and a Montblanc "Meisterstuck" fountain pen, and his father gave him his Rolex watch. Yet his father gave him a wry smile that reminded him of the way he used to smile and laugh before the recent bout with depression. Then they were gone, journeying on to Iran to consult a well-known Hakeem, who diagnosed the father's condition as a problem of the bowels; his father lacked faith in Western medicine and had prescribed a specially prepared purgative lotion.

A far more mature Raza was left to mull over what had happened as he prepared for another year at the Crammers. He put his father's experience down as a product of extreme loneliness combined with anxiety related to Western decadence, pressure about his legal studies and given his age, fidelity to his wife, where sex, alcohol, and a certain kind of tacitly accepted immorality brought on mental malaise. Even though he passed the bar exam, his resolve not to give in to these temptations must have created a conflict that caused mental collapse. After all of this, a young Raza was due for some kind of a break from his duties as caretaker of his father and the new Crammers provided the opportunity.

CHAPTER 12

SECRET LOVE

CRAMMERS: YEAR TWO

This new crop of Crammers was in the different setting of South Kensington and Gloucester Road. It was much smarter and more cosmopolitan than Maida Vale. French and Italian students flocked there—most of them to study English. The area had a large number of coffee bars and after registration at the new Crammers, Raza soon made friends with some French students.

"I found it easy to make friends and showed no hesitation in speaking French, living in a French-speaking household as I did. There was Bernard, and his friend Georges, sneaking in English girls into their rooms; and there was young Jacques, and Claude, they were all French and I often visited them in Paris. I developed a taste for jazz music by visiting clubs on the Rive Gauche, listening to music and watching movies and talking about books, philosophy, and girls. The most interesting of these was Bernard, who also had a way with girls that defied prevailing English morality in the mid-1950s."

One day, in late September 1955, while sitting at the new Crammers for his French lesson, Raza could not but help catch a glimpse between the bobbing heads of other students of a young dusky-skinned woman with short curly black hair, full lips, and almond-shaped eyes who, though silent at that moment, was not shy about expressing herself in class. From the answers she gave during the French lesson, it was evident she was armed with a quick tongue and a sharp mind. She sounded feisty and flirtatious, in an innocent, teasing kind of way. She spoke with just a hint of an anglicized Indian accent, with a slight lilt tone as the words flowed from her mouth.

At that moment he caught a glimpse of beauty, a pretty gaze that Raza couldn't help but stare. Then, all too soon, and while his mind still idled with the idea of leaning forward to take a closer look, the lesson was over and he quickly left to meet Bernard and Jacques, the two French students he'd met, and who he promised to meet after English class and walk with them toward Gloucester Road tube for lunch. They were also talking about "this, really beautiful Indian girl"—*trés belle, vraiment jolie!*—who they referred to as Shireen. Right then, Shireen herself came down the stairs and, with a turn of the head, to say *Au Revoir!* in perfect French went off in the other direction.

He rubbed his chin and thought to himself, no surely it couldn't be, but she looked like a girl he once knew. At the next French lesson, he looked around and saw that she wasn't present. With Persian classes on some days, he didn't see her again until the beginning of October. And then, when he did see her, he didn't know what to say or think, for the young woman standing there in front of him was none other than Shireen, the love he thought he had left behind in India, never to see again.

She had grown taller, as indeed had he, during the past five or six years, their sprouting teens, during which period they hadn't seen each other, but she was still as slender, as willowy, as beautiful, and as radiant as ever. What had stopped instant recognition was the situation seemed too much of a coincidence, one that you only dream of happening. It was too much like the movies. True, she had dramatically shortened her long black wavy hair. Raza had only seen her profile, which if she resembled anyone, it was a little like Dorothy Dandridge in *Carmen Jones*, a film based on Bizet's *Carmen*. That was a movie Raza had recently seen, but Shireen was real and she was his secret love back now from all these years.

After what seemed like an eternity, it was Shireen who broke the silence:

"For crying out loud! Well, don't just stand there! For goodness sake say something! Yes, it's me, Shireen."

"But, but" Raza finally managed to blurt out, "What's all this with Sherry?"

"Oh that! Don't you know that at an all-girls' English boarding school that foreign names that they can't quite get their tongue around, and for a whole lot of other reasons, they simply anglicize those names, but this is really me, Shireen. Just call me Shireen, I prefer that anyway. Only I don't know what to call you. In Amadabad where I first saw you, they all called you by your family nickname, but I found out that your real name is Raza. So, do I call you Raza, or simply my lord and master?" She said, tauntingly, disarmingly, mockingly, but also with a bit of softness.

Recovering his cool, Raza smiled back and said: "Just call me Raza, my name has also been anglicized, or shortened." This is true because he first got called Raza at boarding school.

People at the Crammers milled past going up to their classrooms or coming down. Shireen and Raza also had lessons, so they followed the rest up the steps, side by side, Raza trembling with emotions inside.

When the lesson was over and the enthusiastic, if not eccentric, Mr. Kilcoyne, the Irishman teaching French, had finished explaining what Cyrano de Bergerac, in one of the prescribed texts for the French course, had meant when he says toward the end by "c'est mon panache," as he is dying: "Panache literally signifies the white plume that cavaliers wore on their caps or hats. For Cyrano wearing the white plume has come to mean more than that. I'll leave you to discover what that means when you write your next essay. Right now, ladies and gentlemen, class dismissed, I too want my lunch." Shireen and Raza packed their books and things together and walked down, talking.

"By the way, Shireen, where do you live?"

"I live in Putney, with my parents, but don't start getting any ideas."

Unfazed, he responded: "Ideas, what ideas? Has proposing taking a coffee with me sounded a bit too hasty and suggestive to you? Or are you just playing hard to get? You know that they call you 'Miss Frigidaire' at the Crammers, don't you? And it's not because you use Colgate."

Her teeth flashed white as she smiled, slammed her two jaws together with a sharp clicking of the teeth, as though to say that all they say about Colgate were true: "Touché Monsieur Pussy Cat! But no, a coffee would be very nice, but not today, I mean that. I haven't told my parents that I might be late, that's all. I'm on a tight rein, I'll explain why. I'll have coffee with you the next week though, I promise. You still mean something to me and there's lots to talk about." With that, Shireen turned away with another smile and walked toward her bus stop.

"I'll keep you to your word," Raza shouted after her. "A Persian quatrain I had heard Dr. Haideri once recite at Cambridge, that went coursing through my mind, making me want to shout it out loud: Glide your willowy form that I may see / Turn your radiant face that I may see / I have heard that behind your lips you hide pearl, Part your ruby lips, that I may see."

Raza went his way smiling, reciting that poem in Farsi to the trees, the air, the stars, the sky, and the moon. People stared at him. He must have been gesturing. He continued to reminisce on the journey by underground, and along the long walk home. He was lost in memories of the original meeting in Amadabad and how, more recently, he had blurted out "Shireen," as the girl he wanted to marry to his shocked cousins, pleasurable memories that he was eager to rekindle.

He was acting like the nineteen-and-a-half-year-old virgin that he in fact was, but occasionally during the journey back he would stop smiling and grow thoughtful and serious, conscious of the fact that her feelings might have changed. Why was she on a tight rein? What does all that mean. And that comment about meaning something to him? Could that be true? He was in a limbo.

The next week passed with Shireen on his mind. When the week was finally over, and the appointed day came around, and he went back to the Crammers, he was not disappointed, since Shireen had kept her word. Out on Gloucester Road, there were one or two coffee houses, but they wanted to go a little further away from the Crammers. They walked side by side, trying to be casual, until they arrived at a coffee bar called Norland, one of many around South Kensington Tube Station since the London of the 1950s.

They had become a new kind of hub for meeting people, not exactly replacing the English pub, but offering an alternative. People would go there for lunch, pretheater and when pubs, cinemas, and theaters closed. Raza had chanced upon the Nordland on his way down the Old Brompton Road on his first day at the Crammers. His heart still thumped like an eager schoolboy as they walked side by side. It was their first meeting alone, and unchaperoned, unlike the last time they had met in January 1950, when her grandmother was there.

Along the way they just exchanged small talk and friendly banter. Then 50 or so yards short of the tube station he stopped, opened the door of the coffee house, followed her in and found a table in an alcove in a discreet corner. "A cappuccino please." He nodded and went to the counter to place his order. A very tall, lean Indian-looking man, long angular face with high cheekbones, an aquiline nose, sporting a beard and a mustache, looking every bit the gypsy, glanced at Raza as if he recognized him, a kind of look of recognition that a fellow Indian might make toward a fellow countryman. His name was Arvind and he was soon to get to know Raza. He was already sizing them up as Raza sat down with Shireen.

He could tell Raza was an Indian, and from his speech he knew Raza was probably a middle-class Indian student, as he thought was Shireen. Arvind, the first Indian Raza had met other than his own family members, was in fact the outcast son of the editor of an Indian film magazine in Bombay, who had come only recently to England to seek his fortune. He was extremely attractive to English women—resembling the painting by *El Greco* of Christ. Of course, Arvind played on this. Right now, he was looking toward Shireen and Raza, giving Raza a knowing leer.

But this reflection mirrored back to Raza too. What did Shireen see in him? What did he look like to her?

"At the alcove table I sat down and looked at Shireen, still the same and yet not the same look in her eyes of the girl who had stolen my heart. I took a good deep look at her face, breathing her in and wanting to keep that image forever. Shireen had meanwhile taken off her navy duffel coat, underneath she was wearing a burgundy roll neck jumper and a slim grey skirt. She also wore knee-length black leather boots. There was the mere tinge of pink lipstick, but otherwise no make-up. She didn't need any. We kept talking because we wanted to catch up."

It turned out that Raza did not call Shireen "Sherry," because that was the name of the Irish Red Setter of the Frenchs' dog that had come over with its family during the summer of 1950, just a few months after he had.

Raza remembered telling me about Shireen's background. He said that her mother was related to the Nanparas and described the situation in some detail.

"Her dark-skinned father, a relative of Ruqqaiyyah Dadi, reading the signs of independence in India, and what that might mean for Muslims like himself, had decided some years back to uproot himself, his family and business and invest his future in England. Like some other well-off Indian and Pakistani professionals they had acquired good property at an affordable rate in postwar London, and started up a business. He was a timber merchant by trade, as I recall, and so it was a more straightforward proposition to simply set up a similar timber business in London. The construction industry was booming in the postwar decade. They bought a large house with a garden, in a quiet street off Upper Richmond Road, in Putney, and sent Shireen to Cheltenham Ladies College, and her brother to Marlborough."

Shireen was in a pensive and relaxed mood talking to someone from a similar background and normally she couldn't open up like this either at the Crammers or with the English and European people she met at school. She mentioned this in relation to her younger brother who was called Firoz, but at Marlborough his name had been anglicized like hers to "Fozzie." But he did not understand Urdu or Hindustani.

She went on to say that her father had done very well in business and about her mother, she said in her lilting voice: "My Mum's been a brilliant driving force of the house, a bonne femme, managing everything from the children to taking care of the house and letting out flats and rooms in the other house in order to earn more income. She now wants to manage my life by sending me after my A-levels here to a finishing school in Switzerland, and learn to become a good hostess, and eventually get married to some wealthy, boring

Indian and breed. Dad stays out of it but would back her naturally. I love them both but [...]"

"Is that what you want from life?"

"No, not really, I'd be bored stiff. I don't really want to think about it. Why don't you be my champion and come and meet my family, and then rescue me. You would definitely be a most acceptable suitor, and take this worry off my mind by finding me a husband into the bargain. Would you, would you please do this for me? I'll give you a kiss. They already know I'm meeting you today. I had to tell them that because I would be a bit late and they had to know why."

"For a kiss? Done," said Raza, his eyes full of mischief.

The time in the coffee bar had been relaxing, but because time was of the essence, Raza noticed Shireen looking at her neat little watch. "There's so much more to talk about, but I better start my journey home. Will you walk me to the bus stop? Please remain my friend, and be patient. I need a true friend." With this they both got up. He held out her duffle coat as she turned and put out her arms behind her. He stopped at the cash desk, paid and looked toward Arvind.

"Arvind, this is Shireen. Shireen, this is Arvind," he said. They nodded toward each other, then Shireen and Raza headed off toward the No. 30 bus to Putney.

It was beginning to get dark as they waited facing each other at the bus stop. When the bus came, she gave him a quick kiss brushing the corner of his lips. She whispered: "I still owe you a proper kiss, but after you've met my mum and dad, and passed the test." She hopped on her bus and went up the stairs to the top deck. His eyes followed her up and saw her find a seat at the back and look down from the window at him waving, blowing him a kiss. He had never been kissed by anyone before, not even on the corner of his lips. He waved and smiled back before turning and making his own long journey to the French's.

During the following week, Raza and Shireen saw each other at the Crammers, but it wasn't until the week following Shireen told him on the Monday her parents had invited him around on Saturday afternoon.

"Well not my parents really, I just told them about having met you at the Crammers and asked them if I could invite you over. Seeing that you had a nice Indian Muslim name they couldn't very well refuse," she said smiling.

Raza smiled, waved back at her as she left, and shouted out "See you soon." That gave him time to tell Mr. and Mrs. French not to wait for him for lunch or dinner, but that he'd be back late. When he got back, he told them an Indian student had invited him to her home and that he'd be back late. They all looked surprised. His housemaster's eyes twinkled behind his glasses and Mrs. French murmured something like "Oh, so you have a girlfriend, that's nice for you." Tim just uttered a snort. Raza did not know whether his father kept any correspondence with the French's, but then realized he must have and, metaphorically shrugged his shoulders and thought, "Ah, well, I was going to tell him one day myself anyway, but what is awkward is that there is not that much to tell right now. It's not as though I'm getting married, just courting." To them, his hosts, he smiled sheepishly before finishing his supper and saying goodnight and going up to his room.

"When Saturday came, I went into town at about 11.00 a.m., took the usual route to South Kensington, from where I caught the 30 bus, following a route that was to become familiar. Shireen had agreed to meet me at noon at the first bus stop in Putney High Street. I had put on a navy-colored jacket, gray-worsted trousers, and striped tie. It was a bright late autumn day. Shireen was already at the bus stop as I stepped off to see her. She was wearing pink slacks, and a red coat with a hood. She also had some silver earrings twinkling on either side of her face. As usual she wore her inimitable smile, hooked her arm into mine and started walking down the street. We headed to the junction with Upper Richmond Road, past loads of Saturday shoppers out and about for the weekend shopping. She asked if I was nervous about meeting her parents."

Shireen, sounding naturally matter-of-fact: "If you are, you needn't be."

With his culture and upbringing, Raza was neither apprehensive nor nervous about meeting the parents (the Ishaqas). He had heard about her parents from Shireen herself, knew how to make polite conversation in Urdu and how to present himself as the kind of respectable suitor they wanted for their daughter. He said this was the ploy agreed between her and Raza.

"My desire to be with Shireen gave me a certain confidence, all the confidence I needed really, and also since it would give her the freedom of movement that she wanted. She had told them that I was from a well, noble family. I could sit down and talk to them in Urdu and that would be that. Once the meeting had taken place I would officially be regarded as her welcome suitor."

At the traffic lights on the high street, Shireen pointed to the road sign for Upper Richmond Road. "That's the long road we need to go down. Normally the No. 30 comes down here and I get off at the third Request Stop, but let's carry on walking, we're a little early anyway."

They crossed over still chatting, and he feeling so proud to be seen walking along with such a beautiful young woman by his side. By the time they reached the turning, they were still too early, so they just kept walking on toward the edge of Barnes Common.

Just then there was a shower of rain. Shireen, who knew the Common, led him running toward the ruins of a house, with just two walls, one with a broken window but only part of the roof standing. Here she stopped and turned toward him, hugging him for shelter. She then reached forward and, going slightly up on her toes, kissed him on the mouth. It was no ordinary kiss, but a totally unexpected full-blown kiss. He was bowled over. He had never kissed a girl like that before and didn't know what it would feel like.

"Promise fulfilled," as she nestled in his arms, "How was that?"

"Wonderful, sweet, like I don't know what." Another verse from another translation of another Persian poet, Rumi, flooded his mind:

"Came to me,"
"Who?"
"She, in the dark, afraid"
"What of?"
"Her father's anger."
"Confide!"
"I kissed her, twice."
"Where?"
"On her moist mouth."
"How was it?"
"Like cornelian, sweet."[1]

He turned her around and holding her, pressed her back against the wall and kissed her back. So they would have continued except for some passersby. The shower of rain had also passed them by on its way to Richmond. *"That's enough now,"* as she pulled her face back gurgling with laughter, "I only promised a kiss, and besides, everyone will be wondering where we have got to."

Reluctantly, Raza took her hand and intertwined their fingers and walked back in an enchanted silence. When they had reached the road she lived in, he made a slight adjustment to his tie and she to her hair.

The parents' house was as Shireen had described it: a large red brick house, with a white-painted front door with bay windows on either side, half way up the side road. As they walked up the front path toward it, a pretty fair-skinned girl, a little shorter than Shireen, and a little younger, opened the front door. It was her cousin, Zizi, who had seen them coming from an upstairs window. Zizi

---

1 Jalal-al-Din Rumi. The Essential Rumi. HarperCollins. New York. 1995.

smiled, was introduced and took his coat, while Shireen shot up to her room to make sure she looked presentable under the discreet maternal scrutiny she was bound to encounter. Meanwhile, Firoz or "Fozzie," as Shireen referred to her 15-year-old younger brother who was home for the weekend from his boarding school, came down and was introduced to Raza by Zizi.

He was a little darker than Shireen and a little shorter, though not as petite as Zizi. Shireen had told Raza in advance that people found Zizi more beautiful than her. This may have been only because she was fairer-skinned, and Shireen thought he might prefer Zizi, but Raza had eyes only for Shireen's dusky beauty.

Luckily, Shireen didn't take long upstairs and came down to usher Raza in to meet her parents, who were sitting waiting in the living room. Raza bowed in salaam, in the traditional way.

"I knew I would be sized up and they nodded and gave me a wary sort of smile, Mrs. Ishaq asked me to take a chair for a minute. As I sat, I felt their eyes on me, sizing me up, for sure, and when I looked up, I noticed that Mr. Ishaq was a man of medium height and much darker skinned than his wife, and he had a close-trimmed broad mustache, but was otherwise clean shaven. His black hair was beginning to thin a little, with bits of the grey dyed over with henna. He wore a suit and spoke hesitant English with a slight Indian accent. Mrs. Ishaq, on the other hand, was more fairer-skinned than her husband or daughter. At some time, she must have been quite petite, but now looked a little matronly. She was wearing a sari. If anything she looked more like Zizi's mother than she did Shireen's."

Following the introduction to her parents, Shireen left Raza there to talk to her parents, saying, "We'll be in the garden room." Meaning herself, Zizi and Fozzie. Raza nodded as she walked out of the living room. The parents could see Raza was well dressed and the jacket he wore fit him elegantly, attired himself like his father and they he could see he would make a fine suitor for their daughter.

Raza briefly replied in his best formal Urdu that they were all well, thank you.

Mrs. Ishaq then asked him what he was studying. Raza filled them in and said he was hoping to go to Oxford. Mr. Ishaq nodded and said little. There was an ambiguity and a silence that underlay the unasked question: "And, what are your intentions with our daughter Shireen?" They were aware that in their absence Raza and Shireen had met in Amadabad.

Raza was beginning to feel uncomfortable, despite his outward calm and courtesy, and just then, thankfully, in the other room that belonged to the children, and not entirely shut off from the living room, Raza joined the party of the youngsters. They were playing some rock'n roll, much to Mrs. Ishaq's irritation, and talking. They were having an idle conversation about what they wanted to do. Zizi wanted to be a photographic model, Shireen wasn't sure and Fozzie was noncommittal.

They all laughed, and drifted into other conversations about the music they liked, and the books they liked reading. On music they were all into the new sound of pop about to erupt, but still on the fringe—people like Little Richard, Buddy Holly, and Elvis Presley. Raza hadn't even heard of them and only caused them to laugh when he confessed to liking Frank Sinatra and Louis Armstrong, as if he was really an old foggy. They teased him and insisted he listen to Elvis, Shireen and Fozzie's favorite. Later the conversation turned to what they liked reading, but here Shireen and Raza were in some agreement: they both liked Dostoevsky. Shireen had just read *Crime and Punishment*. So the conversations would have continued, like two people getting to know each other, until Shireen looked at her watch.

"Oh, my god, look at the time! Come on, you better go and say khuda hafiz to my parents. I'll come along with you and then walk with you to the bus stop."

After he had said his farewell to the parents, Shireen walked him out to the bus stop, hooking her arm through his elbow. "I'll see you tomorrow," she said, before drawing her face away from Raza's proffered kiss. "We're friends remember. You're my bestest friend, but I'm not sure that I love you." Then noticing his sad wistful look, she added: "But I could grow to love you. See you tomorrow." He hopped on the bus and traveled back in a thoughtful mood. He was in for a long period of courtship. She was going to test him, but he also knew she was genuinely fond of him. He savored the memories of that kiss.

And, thus began a series of meetings between Raza and Shireen, sometimes with Fozzie and Zizi included, sometimes not, and these were, by agreement between them, set to continue.

Over the next few months, now that her parents knew who she was seeing, Shireen and Raza continued to meet during the week at the Crammers, but there she would often flirt and he took it to be because she didn't want to appear to be anyone's girlfriend. But most women would find him a good catch, standing tall and looking handsome, he even had a welcoming sense of humor, but he often hesitated when near her and since he often knew what to say but couldn't quite say it.

Raza realize Shireen's flirtatiousness was just Shireen being Shireen. Yet Raza appeared not to mind, because there was an unspoken understanding between them: to give her time. Inwardly he would be hurt and niggled and wait for the next time they were together alone; and these times came usually at the weekends when he went to her home, and then she'd assuage his feelings, assuring him that they would be friends again. On one occasion, Zizi saw how her cousin was behaving toward Raza and she told her cousin off for being cruel. Zizi even went so far as to say to Raza alone one day that Shireen did really love him, just give her time. Time, time, time. Perhaps Zizi's advice to him was due to some girl talk between the cousins.

What emerged was Shireen had developed a secret crush on a young lodger called Makos, a student lodger at the Ishaq's other house that was let to overseas students flocking to England. There were some Iraqi lodgers too that Raza was to meet later. Raza never met him, but when Shireen showed a photo of Makos, he saw a slight, fair-haired person, who it turned out was two years younger than she was. This can't possibly be serious, Raza thought. Shireen guessed his mood, and he recall her saying to effect that she couldn't tell him her feelings and that she would write him letters about everything.

By this time, autumn had turned into winter. It was soon going to be exams coming up in the summer. One planned event before that was scheduled to be Raza's return home to India in February. Travel arrangements were being organized in liaison with his father.

The other promised item was Shireen's letter, which she did write, in fact more than one letter, and the first letter had been written on handmade blue paper, the size of a note pad, and the handwriting hurried but neat. There were 66 pages of it. Raza was amazed and chuffed. He had never received such a long letter. Never from a girlfriend, not even when you count Jean. He felt flattered. All the pages had been sown together and made to look like a book.

Then he began to read the letter. It read almost like a diary of the inner thoughts of a troubled and uncertain teenage Asian girl who was unsure of who she really was. Her mother in particular was very strict, and the Ishaqs kept very much to themselves and only kept contact with one or two other Indian families, who they saw occasionally, and one or two other nationalities as neighbors.

The ladies in the Indian families kept on trying to match make. Mrs. Ishaq was not really aware of her daughter's feelings for Makos, and if she had suspected anything the whole place would have blown up. Raza could be such an ally if only he would put his own feelings aside. It was not her fault that she didn't want to marry the one or two young Indian men who had been introduced to her. Surely Raza could understand since he had also been sent to a boarding school where Anglicization was the implicit norm.

Raza read the letter through to the end. At first, he felt frustrated by being asked to play second fiddle because certainly the hint was there that Shireen did regard him more or less as just a friend. Or was he simply reading between the lines, and all that she wanted from him was to be a friend she could lean on, a confidant? Then toward the end he came across a much darker passage hinting at how she had been violated as a young girl in India by one of her uncles. This shook Raza as this must have been during the period when he had first set eyes on her or soon after. He was aware that family sexual abuse occurred in various Indian families and went unreported. He had heard accounts from friends. This changed his sentiment and he started feeling protective toward her and no longer niggled. He loved her more, and wrote a long letter back in response.

Then in mid-January, she wrote him another, slightly shorter letter not replying to his, but more in the same vein as the first letter.

"In the meanwhile, it was revision time for exams and meeting deadlines on written assignments, attending lessons I was still meeting with Shireen until going home time arrived. At that time, I would meet her at her home usually, but on one or two occasions I went to the movies in the West End. *The Blackboard Jungle* had just premiered in London, in which Glenn Ford plays a war veteran who turns to teaching in a high school in inner-city New York. This also starred a young Sidney Poitier who was about twenty-something. I had already sneaked off to see it by myself and I must say was electrified by the movie, not least by the musical sound track 'Rock Around the Clock,' which opens the film and recurs once in the middle and once at the end. I decided to see it again and invite Shireen to see it with me. I found myself tapping my feet and enjoying the music."

"I didn't mention Bill Haley and the Comets to her. On the next Saturday she and Zizi met to see a film showing in a small cinema next to the Empire Leicester Square. When Shireen and Zizi got there, they noticed the giant lit-up notice board above the Empire and started shrieking, 'Oh, my God! It's Elvis! Let's go and see that.' The film was *Love Me Tender*. I made them a deal: if they came to *The Blackboard Jungle*, he would go with them to see the Elvis movie the next time."

He won because the following week Fozzie would be around to see it too. The Glenn Ford movie, and the soundtrack made them change their minds about Raza. He was no longer a square in their eyes.

"The following Saturday I suffered through Elvis without showing it and pretended to enjoy it for their sake and the rounding off of movie going ended the following Saturday, for the time being at least, because I persuaded them to come and see *High Society*. When Satchmo came on with his trumpet, it was my turn to get wowed, and I think I showed it. Shireen and the others let me have my day."

Raza hadn't been home for quite some time and home time arrived at half term. He was man enough to let Shireen get on with her crush and felt that time and space would give them both a break. He had already booked his tickets with the money his father had arranged for a return trip home. He was going for six weeks from mid-February until the beginning of April and his decision to go home was also important because he had received a letter offering him a provisional place at Oxford, subject to him passing his A-levels.

His father would want to discuss that and going in mid-February also meant the weather would be pleasant and only beginning to get hot toward the end. He might also have the opportunity to revise for his examinations away from distractions of the heart, and he would be spending time with his family at home, and that would keep him busy.

The first time after the holidays that they met at the Crammers in January, Raza had already decided to tell Shireen his plans over a cup of coffee. Raza felt she had grown closer to him even if she was still half in denial of her feelings. For the next three or four weekends, Raza continued to travel to Putney; he had some urgent business and perhaps wanted to hide his emotions. I know the young have a tendency to melodramatize, as if this were unique, but there can be real torments all the same. I think for Shireen and Raza they were just plain, old-fashioned, youthful 1950s lovers, constrained by time, morality, religion, custom, and struggling to overcome it all.

CHAPTER 13

JOURNEY HOME

Raza had traveled elsewhere in Europe and was getting used to the process of negotiating borders, and so his flight home, even after four years, was uneventful. Nevertheless, his father had arranged an overnight stay in Delhi at the home of a distant relative, and an onward flight to Lucknow. Once home, with all the familiar faces, he went directly up to his parents' quarters. He found his mother in good spirits as a result of her husband's resolve to make his own independent living.

"My father had a cooler installed just outside his room. It was an Indian contraption: a box about 30 inches cubed covered with khas matting (made from the roots of a tree that is watered by jets of water that in turn is blown by a little engine inside the room) sitting on a metal-framed stand. My father was only recently back from Iran and due to start taking his purgative, and in the process of making arrangements to be attached to the legal practice of Ismaili Khojas and Bohras in Bombay. He looked well and was happy to see me."

"As for Zahra and Jafar, Zahra was now in her 14th year and still going to Loretto, while young Jafar was in his 6th year, and had just started at St. Joseph's."

In the meanwhile, his uncle had given instructions from Baghdad for Raza to stay in his own vacated personal suite of rooms on the ground floor of the palace in Hyderabad. This was because Raza had shown much maturity in handling his father's breakdown the year before. Raza felt quite pleased at being treated like an adult.

"The suite, as I remembered, consisted of a sitting room, where my uncle would receive visitors. It contained a large desk at the far end, and some modern chairs and a small settee as you entered. There was also a small four-side wooden table with a glass top. A Persian carpet partially covered the concrete slabs of paving stones. As you look left, behind the sitting room, you caught a glimpse through three arches of a large inner sanctum that also, on occasion, served as a bedroom.

Surveying it all there was good reason for me to feel chuffed. This was far nicer than staying in a single room at the French household, and, apart from missing Shireen, I reveled in it."

These holidays were also the first time Raza started eating meat at home, something he began doing in London already. However, he still abstained from tea, a practice he had started since doing special physical exercises. For his main meals though, this was the first time that he was to taste Tunday's kababs, ordered from a popular kabab shop in the old part of the city which both rich and poor frequented.

Tunday was reputed to have a special recipe, and his kababs were unlike any other Raza ever tasted. They were extremely spicy hot and tender, made from a marinated joint until the meat would literally fell off the bone as you tried to help yourself. These kababs were usually eaten with bread (sheerrmals or parathas). Raza liked them so much his mother would order them whenever he arrived home.

During the visit, his father and mother talked to him about marriage. They were concerned that he was still unmarried, and one day mentioned that they had received an enquiry from two separate lots of relatives about the possible alliance between Raza and their daughters. He listened obediently with his head bowed and in silence. He thought about his father who had married at 14 years and his mother at 17 years.

His parents, sensing his lack of reaction or response, didn't pursue the matter. One of the two relatives was too close anyway and his parents were relieved that Raza stayed silent, signifying no by his silence. As for the other more distant relatives, his parents both thought he ought to reconsider. Raza couldn't explain why. His father, who was aware that Raza was seeing Shireen, didn't bring up her name. Nor did Raza from his side mention her name, anticipating disapproval because Shireen's family was not Shi'a, but the matter remained in a limbo.[1]

---

[1] The issue of age at which males and females got married depends on whether they were from the growing cosmopolitan elite or from the agrarian aristocracy and the peasantry. Raza's eldest male cousin got married when he was 21 to his cousin who was no more than 17 years old. You should say the pressure was on if you were male and had completed your education. Girls rarely went beyond high school and that was considered normal.

A SAFARI IN THE JUNGLE

One person who was more frequently around visiting his parents was a distant cousin called Hashim Bhai, a handsome athletic-looking man about the same height as Raza, but several years older. He looked every bit like an Indian Clark Gable with a mustache exactly like Gable's. In 1953, he had married one of Raza's paternal side cousins. Hashim would sometimes announce himself in his mother's quarters, and on one of these occasions he asked Raza's parents if he could take Raza on a "shikar" or safari to Ranikhet for a week. Raza's parents looked at Raza and, discerning from his looks that he would rather like it, they gave their permission.

From that point on Hashim, or "Hashshoo" as he was referred to, visited Raza often in the ground-floor suite of Nawab Dawood Ahmad. Hashshoo Bhai was a popular man and he would sometimes arrive to see Raza with some of his chums. At that time, they included Agghan, Arshad, and Askari. The three of them were also going to go on the animal hunt for big game, and in this case it was tigers. Agghan in fact knew the jungle at Ranikhet well and excelled at tracking deer and tigers. He referred to this as "the hunt," or "shikar."

For the days before they were due to depart, they would assemble in Raza's uncle's room, spending afternoons playing Monopoly, during which Askari, who was from a nawabi Lucknow family and didn't speak English too well, was made to feel silly constantly, and he took it all in a good-natured way. "I want two hotels on my property at Mayfair," or "Mr. Raza, have you ever been to Africa?" he would say, making the assembled company roar with laughter.

By the time they came to leave for the "shikar," reservations had been made for a party of five in a bungalow. This was the first time he had stayed in a jungle bungalow. He was in another part of the country, one he had never imagined, with the noises of different birds, and the sight of monkeys jumping from tree to tree, eyeing the intruders. Ironically, the jungle bungalow was a modest affair with bedrooms, kitchen, and a porch.

Of the party of five, Raza, Askari, and Arshad had not been on a safari before and had never held a gun. They would walk out with one casually slung over their shoulders. As for Askari, he also had never held a gun, let alone knew how to hold one and fire it. Raza had owned air rifles, and practiced shooting at boarding school. As a result, he knew about holding it firmly against the shoulder to lessen the recoil, but he too was a novice at this sort of thing. This left just Hashim and Agghan as practiced hunters, with the latter being able to spot an animal's footprints from a moving jeep and know what animal it was.

"One day Agghan spotted a tiger's footprint, much to my amazement. That was the whole purpose why we had gone there—to hunt a tiger. Agghan bided his time to trap one. In the meanwhile, he shot a small four-horned deer called a 'chausingha,' a small species of a four-horned antelope. I couldn't eat its meat. I could not eat an animal that I had seen get shot and then skinned and slaughtered. Hashim teased me about it but understood. Askari meanwhile showed his prowess as a cook. On one occasion there was a rustling in the bushes and the three of us nearly jumped out of our skins. This was like being in some kind of Hemingway country, and it was not for me."

Raza quickly retreated into the bungalow as did Arshad. Askari stayed his ground, sweating profusely. "Come on, I'll show you how to fire a gun," said Agghan and Hashim Bhai in a chorus of laughter. They loaded his gun with a couple of cartridges, showed him how to hold it firmly against his shoulder, with cheek resting against the butt and the eyes looking up the barrel toward the sights, aligning with the target before gently squeezing the trigger. It didn't work. Askari fired the gun without any of the precautions and it resulted in him being twirled around by the force.

Finally, the day came when one of the "beaters" hired to make a noise and flush out the tiger reported that a tiger had been spotted in the vicinity. A bait of raw meat from a buffalo was laid on the ground, and a *machan*, a kind of canvas blind, was erected in the branches of a tree. Among the elaborate preparations, an elephant had been hired to crisscross in the elephant grass in pursuit of the tiger, to corner it and make it run out into the open. Agghan sat on the elephant together with the elephant rider or *mahout* and Raza and Hashim Bhai sat on the elephant bed carriage or howdah behind, while Arshad and Askari sat on the machan.

"Then the beating started. There was cacophony of noise as the elephant weaved its way through the grass, which stood half way tall or more as the elephant. All I can remember was that there must have been a sudden flash of orange color that only Agghan could have seen, followed by two quick shots from his rifle and the tiger was dead. We all went to examine its dead body. The two bullets from the rifle had landed scarcely two inches apart in the tiger's head. The tiger's body was still now but I was in awe. I stooped down and lifted one of its magnificent paws that were capable of slapping an animal down with one blow. I said nothing, but knew I would never go on a tiger hunt again. I reflected how during Hemingway's childhood, when they went to the hills and his father had introduced him to Jim Corbett, the legendary tracker and forest dweller, who only shot man-eating tigers and leopards and how anyone could kill such an animal made me sick to my stomach and vowed to myself never to be part of this kind of spectacle ever again."

Raza visited family members during this time, and both the Ammijans and Khalajans as well as some of their children were there. The party included Ibn Dawood (Shaikhoo). Raza met them when he made the expected rounds of visits to pay respects. On these rounds, he would come across his cousins who were the daughters of his younger maternal aunt.

As for the male members of the family, there was no Husain Bhai who was settled in Pakistan, working as a managing director for one of the multinational tobacco firms operating there. He was not yet married but Raza learnt that he had requested his maternal uncle, Nawab Dawood Ahmad, for the hand of his second daughter, and that wedding would take place in Iraq. Among the males still unmarried were his younger brother, Jafar, and, of course, "Shaikhoo" or Ibn Dawood, who got his name of Shaikhoo around this time.

Apparently, Ibn Dawood was already showing signs of acting as the natural successor. This demeanor had not passed Hashim Bhai's notice, who had teasingly referred to him as "Shaikhoo." Ibn Dawood had only just passed his 12th birthday a couple of months previously, and was still attending the Martiniére, and already giving himself these airs.

Raza didn't notice these changes. Four years had passed since he was last home, and whenever he saw his cousin what he saw was a friendly, coyly smiling, still short, slightly plump, bespectacled cousin coming back from school in his khaki shorts and shirt. At that time, Ibn Dawood was living in the first room at the top of the main staircase, and next to Raza and Abid's former room. Their paths would cross when Raza was on his way to his parents' quarters and Shaikhoo was on his way to see his mentor, Lallan Sahab.

Raza would smile at his young cousin and maybe exchange a word or two. Apart from school, his Arabic, Farsi, and Urdu lessons, specially prepared meals with strict dietary taboos, usually in his mother's quarters, and the female companionship of Zahra and one other female cousin, he had some time allocated for recreation. Shaikhoo's appointed companion for the time was a man called Hasan Sahab, from the family of Raza's old mentor. Hasan was a bit of a narcissist and liked to groom his black wavy hair with Brylcreem, and trim his pencil mustache precisely. It was his job to escort Shaikhoo to the far courtyard where they would play badminton for recreation. This would usually be in the early evening.

This was about the only exercise Shaikhoo ever seemed to have. The one other person Raza would see Shaikhoo with was a young man called Rajjoo, the son of one of the old loyal courtiers. But unlike his father, young Rajjoo also liked to groom his hair, and put masses of talcum powder all over his plump, slick body. Rajjoo was about four years older than Shaikhoo, and at the time attended Lucknow University. He hadn't been officially appointed as a companion or escort, but in the life at the palace at the time there were precious few young men, apart from servants.

On his return from Ranikhet, Raza's mother asked him to move into the *Araam Kamra*, his grandfather's room, directly above the uncle's suite, in order to make it easier to call him for meals and things. Raza obliged. This move meant that for the rest of his stay, he saw more of Shaikhoo. Raza was fond of his younger cousin and felt protective like an older brother. He would call him over whenever he could and get Shaikhoo to join him in his daily calisthenic exercises in his room. That's when Raza noticed just how unfit and soft Shaikhoo's body was, perspiring profusely every time he made any physical movement, and willing as he was, he showed signs of suffering from nerves.

During all his time in India, Raza never forgot about Shireen. Her soft image followed him everywhere. He missed her company. He managed to sneak a phone call or two just to hear her voice. The first time Shireen answered herself and told him that she was missing him terribly. He promised to send her a card on the 4th of April, her 19th birthday. Not finding any suitable birthday cards in the news agents in Lucknow, he decided to send her a birthday telegram.

He needed to exercise some care because whatever message he was going to dictate over the telephone would become known to the household secretary who dealt with the phone and telegram copies. So Raza decided on something cryptic that the secretary wouldn't understand: "Happy Birthday, Little Shireen. Hope you have a nice party. Thinking of you. Raza." But the secretary was no fool. He did guess. "Little Shireen," he said to Raza, with a knowing look in his eyes, "Now who could this little girl be?" Raza pretended to ignore the question and said nothing, but he knew that his secret was out.

Finally, the days of departure arrived, and he felt a mixture of happiness and sorrow to be leaving his mother, who wanted him to finish his studies. On the other hand, he happily looked forward to seeing Shireen.

CHAPTER 14

RETURN TO LONDON AND SHIREEN

When eventually Raza returned to London at the end of the Easter holidays, he had missed Shireen's birthday by a matter of about 10 days. He was eager to see her again and there she was at the Crammers, looking all the more radiant since he hadn't seen her for so long. She was coy at first, a little cross too about his silly telegram, and decided to tease him by saying something about whether she really remembered him or not. But Raza had a surprise for her: a beautiful, dusky pink cashmere shawl with motifs of little darker pink flowers embroidered all over. He had obtained it from his parents' extensive collection and chosen it with his sister's help. Sisters are such useful allies in keeping secrets because he had told his parents that it was for him and had it wrapped and folded it in a cloth before placing the bundle in strong brown paper parcel during the flight. On this morning he had carried the neatly wrapped parcel inside his briefcase intent on giving it to her as a belated birthday present. Looking suitably ashamed, he turned to respond to her and asked if she would join him for a coffee.

After some hesitation, mingled with coquetry at which she was an expert, Shireen agreed. They walked down to the old Norland Bar where they first met. Raza could feel his heart skip a beat. Arvind was still behind the espresso machine and smiled at them both as they walked in. They exchanged a few pleasantries before Raza and Shireen found an empty table and ordered coffee and fresh doughnuts from the new doughnut-making machine by the window.

Raza didn't produce the shawl at first, thinking it would be too much like emotional blackmail. He asked about her family, her brother and sister; she looked at the gift but told him it would not change anything. And plus he wanted a favor since she needed to find a place to stay.

Since feelings come first, Raza could see no alternative but to agree to help out. His decisiveness surprised even him. He talked to Mr. and Mrs. French, both of whom had been aware that Raza had been going steady with Shireen for about a year and they discussed matters. The French's seemed to understand

Raza might want to leave and be with Shireen. They wished him luck. Behind his back it was certain they would be conveying the news to his father and Raza was reconciled to the fact. As for helping Shireen find accommodation and a job, he had already agreed to meet Shireen the next morning at the Norland Coffee Bar. Overnight he packed just one light suitcase, leaving his other clothes and belongings to collect at a later date.

Thus, it was on that fateful morning of Friday May 25, 1956, Raza set off on the quest for love and quietness of spirit. In Raza's understanding, it implied finding his own apartment and not sharing it with anyone. He reached a moment in his life when he wanted to be an adult; yet he believed his father would continue to provide him with a reasonable trust fund to keep him comfortable. Raza was never overly concerned about money or where it came from, an allowance which he always took for granted.

It was a middling sort of day, neither spectacularly sunny and warm, nor with any sign of a threat of shower or downpour. He had already observed that sunny days usually coincided with exams time, when you look blankly outside the window and wish you were there outside and not having to write exams, but this was not the case today. The early morning drizzle had gone.

"I wore my raincoat and I had these gray trousers and a navy blazer because I needed to look smart if I was going to go room hunting with Shireen. I arrived at the coffee bar straightaway, but she was there ahead of me, wearing a roll-neck top as was her wont and a gray skirt. Shireen was perched on one of the stools at the bar and talking to Arvind. I gave her a hug around the shoulders, and nodded to Arvind. It was an ideal opportunity to find some immediate work for Shireen. I spoke to Arvind in Hindustani in order to be discreet. Shireen could follow it so there was no need to interpret and I explained to Arvind that Shireen had left home and was looking for a temporary job and a place to live."

Arvind and his crowd of largely Indian acquaintances were all a few years older and familiar with the kind of situation in which Shireen now found herself—in fact, she was told to leave her home—that is, in a gender-specific way. Looking quite the gypsy, and trading on it by claiming to be from the Banjara tribe, Arvind had developed a friendship and liking for Raza. This friendship now stretched to Shireen as well. He agreed to speak with the manager and see if there was a waitress job available.

Shireen seemed happy with that, so Arvind asked them to come back when the manager returned in the afternoon. When they returned, Arvind introduced Shireen to the manager and, sure enough, she was offered the job. Waitresses, particularly attractive and presentable ones, were much in demand.

"I looked on from the bar and was amazed at the alacrity with which Shireen picked up on things. When she had finished her trial run, she was formally offered and gladly accepted the job. Running away from home was still an adventure. She quickly said that she could start on Monday. Arvind smiled and winked. He had become like an elder brother to both of us, and my friends and acquaintances all formed a new network and provided a safety net for both of us."

Raza began to think about who these new friends were. Laxman was the oldest, a 40-year-old Malaysian Indian who had been in a Japanese prisoner of war camp, with hair-raising tales about how he and other companions had been buried up to their necks, captured and tortured, and given a reprieve just before dogs were unleashed at them. He would drop by at the coffee bar from time to time, and was trying to set up a business.

Jimmy and Homi also worked in coffee bars. Jimmy was an Indian Christian, who had been in the Indian Olympic cycling team in 1952 in Helsinki. He had stopped over in London afterwards and remained there ever since. He shared shifts at the coffee machine with Arvind. People used to laugh at his English, which was the prototype of what has become known as the "Peter Sellers accent." Arvind and others would mimic him saying, "walking the stairs in the direction of up at one o'clock in the hour of midnight, I said to my landlady, 'I like very much you sexy English ladies.'" Homi was a Parsee from East Africa, also trying to set up business. He had a kind of staccato speech when talking, as well as an eye for the ladies.

"Many more acquaintances were made at the coffee bar over the next eighteen months or so, but for now the important thing was to find rooms for Shireen, Zizi, and myself. The idea was to find something locally so as not to have to travel too far to work. The Crammers, where Shireen and I both were still studying, at least until the end of summer, were just down the road. South Kensington was very much a bed-sit land in those days, but unfortunately neither Arvind nor any of the others could suggest anything because they all lived in other parts of London. Nothing other than tramping on foot, up and down the nearby streets and looking for vacancies in windows was needed."

So tramp they did over the rest of the weekend. It wasn't easy, but it was an eye-opener for Raza at least. They saw windows with signs saying: *"VACANCIES. WHITES ONLY—NO DOGS, NO COLOUREDS"* and even where the landlord advertised a simple vacancy, they were usually politely or otherwise turned away by being told that *"Unfortunately, the room has just been let."*

"The experience was bringing us down until we decided to walk up Old Brompton Road. This was out of desperation because it led toward

Knightsbridge, a much more posh and expensive area. Eventually we walked into a wide cul-de-sac called Beaufort Gardens, with a fenced garden down the middle and tall, six-story buildings on either side, seven if you include the basement rooms, and here we found our salvation. Toward the very end of the cul-de-sac we saw two adjoining houses that had been turned into one. They were advertising vacancies. I rang the bell and when we were let in the landlady met us. She must have liked the look of us because she offered us a double and a single room. She did say that unfortunately the rooms were in the basement with not too much natural light, but we thought it was just perfect. She led the way down to the basement. We all followed."

The double room at least had the benefit of a window looking up at the street and a separate entrance. It was large but had the minimum of furniture—a carpet, two single beds, a wardrobe with a mirror, a couple of chairs and a table. The walls were totally bare with white wallpaper providing the sole decoration. The bathroom and toilet were shared with the other single room that had been squeezed into a smaller, square space with windows that looked out to nothing, not even the sky, but only concrete. Their hearts sank. The landlady read their looks and added, "It's not much I'm afraid, but you can have the first choice of moving upstairs when the next vacancy comes up."

Beggars can't be choosers, so they agreed to move in at a rent of £5.00 for the double and £3.00 per week for the single. They accepted and paid one week's rent in advance.

The next few months were like those halcyon days of yore for Raza, days that seem to stretch forever and never end; untroubled days of discovering each other, days of work and study for Shireen, days of finding some modeling work for Zizi. They were happy. Once their A-level exams were over, Raza and Shireen didn't wait for the results but went swimming at Raza's old school during the holidays. The boarders had gone home and the school was largely deserted. Ex-pupils, even those like Raza, were allowed to use facilities like the swimming pool and the tennis courts and he would go with Tim at times, the French's son.

Otherwise they would go to the movies, and at other times, they would sit and listen to records. Raza bought Shireen a pair of bright red pajamas they had seen one day when window shopping. Usually, Raza would walk with her to her work and walk back with her when she finished, her legs aching from going up and down stairs. He would sometimes sit at the bar and have coffee and talk to people while waiting for her.

They were already regarded as a handsome couple, but during late August and early September they were briefly parted when he decided to take a trip on a train to Paris to see his friends Bernard and others. He knew he would miss her and she him. "I took a trip on a train, and I thought about you" went Sinatra's refrain, singing as he looked out of the window at one or two cars parked under the stars as he thought about her. Two weeks later in mid-September, he returned to her looking bronzed from the sun. His teeth shone white. They were happy and their pattern of life continued until the beginning of 1957.

They had still not made love though he'd had what has been referred to as a wet dream. In it he had fondled and caressed her as she was standing on tiptoes rubbing her stomach against him and suddenly ejaculated inside his pajamas. He had many opportunities to attempt sexual play with her but when he approached her, she just laughed at his awkwardness. Something in Raza held him back and perhaps it was the idea of sex before marriage, honor, and so on.

Perhaps it was this diffidence that Shireen questioned in her mind—did he really love her? If so, how? Why didn't he make the first move? Perhaps this is what Shireen meant about wanting him to be more like Dmitri the carnal rather than Ivan the cerebral Karamazov. Things were left in a kind of hiatus that he hoped would end in a climax. But, for the moment, they were happy, and most people continued to look at them as a young couple in love.

Then at the beginning of 1957, while marking time before going to Oxford, he registered at the Regent Street Polytechnic, where Tim was also enrolled. Unlike Tim, Raza registered in the Science Department. When Shireen would come up to meet Raza, Tim and Shireen started flirting. Unsure whether Shireen loved him—a question mark that she had always used for real or to entice him—Raza dithered, while Tim and Shireen started seeing each other. Raza was hurt. He still didn't really imagine Tim being a rival and Shireen tried to ensure that through her genuine fondness for him, Raza would remain a friend.

During early 1957, they still lived in the same place: he still met her at work and walked home with her; they still read the same books and saw movies together. Tim continued to live with his parents at Elstree, and only saw Shireen at weekends or at the Poly during the week. Yet weeks went by and Raza saw nothing of her. It was almost but not quite a kind of *ménage à trois*, but actually a strange situation that had gone terribly wrong.

Raza recounts how he had gone to the Astoria partly to escape the cold, partly to see a new French film-noir *Rififi*, which was being double-billed with *The Quatermass Xperiment*, "a terrible, risible British science-fiction picture." Needless to say, he didn't stay for the second feature. "I must have been the only one though, alone as I was outside, standing in the snow, alone and lost in thought, deciding what to do? Whether to return home, or to have something to eat? I reached into my jacket for cigarettes but couldn't find any matches."

And there was Shireen. "She looked like and sounded like the young woman in a scene reminiscent of Ava Gardner lighting Gregory Peck's cigarette in *The Snows of Kilimanjaro*, as she struck a match, and moved its flame toward the cigarette held between his lips. There, in the glow of the flame I caught sight of her face, saw the tight curl of hair and the full lips and realized it was really her. It was as if I fell in love all over again at that moment. I wanted to hold her, kiss her, to tell her all the things I had on my mind but of course I could not, and tried to act cool and leaned over to catch the light from the quivering flame she offered in her delicate, cupped fingers, but exhaling that first cloud of smoke, I watched her then lit her own cigarette, saw the fire's glow illuminate her lovely face. I embraced her."

Raza didn't know what to say because he didn't know how to treat this chance encounter. So he didn't say much of anything, but as he told this story, said he was relieved that he had a cigarette to smoke. He had started smoking after his trip to India. As it turned out, saying nothing was the smart thing, because then she asked him if they would have a drink nearby.

That solved his earlier dilemma about whether to go home or to eat first and then go back to his dreary old room. He hadn't mentioned what was slowly becoming a resolution for him to move out. Yet it was on his mind and would eventually get around to discussing the situation.

"You must have read my mind, why don't we have something to eat with our drink?" Meeting no objection and thinking rapidly, he realized that Soho was right around the corner, and he remembered a couple of restaurants he had been to with his father. "Where would you like to eat? French or Turkish"

"French would be lovely," she smiled, "but are you sure we can afford it?"

Feeling flushed, because his pocket money allowance from home had just arrived, he replied, "I don't see any reason why not." With that he led the way, both of them engaging in small talk instead of going into the heavy stuff.

L'Épicure was a small, intimate, medium-priced French restaurant on a corner of Frith Street, just one block up from Shaftesbury Avenue. It was a romantic spot and gas torches burnt outside above the entrance. They looked at the menu outside, and Raza reassured her that it was affordable. On entering he asked for a table for two, since they were early, and after being asked for their coats and scarves, they were shown to a discreet table in the corner.

Once they had sat down, Shireen said, "I was looking for just something like a pub, but this is lovely, thanks Raza, but I want you to know that I wouldn't have accepted if you weren't an Indian like me. I would be seen as a loose woman, which I'm not. Just friendly and a little bit of a flirt."

"Suits me," Raza responded, "I've been wanting to talk to you for some time."

"I'm flattered."

"No, seriously now, even though you know I'm attracted to you, you also interest me as a person."

This kind of repartee went on, as though they were speaking as strangers who had met for the first time.

This chance meeting resulted in Raza and Shireen becoming a couple again. Gone was the *ménage à trois* since she told him during dinner that she had decided to end things with Tim and would tell him so.

"I don't know what it is with Tim but he made me feel so cheap." She spluttered out the full story. "He's still a virgin you know and he took me out in his father's car and pulled out his cock. He expected me to suck it, and when I grew embarrassed, he started calling me names. I finally wanked him off with his hankie, wiping my hands on it, afterwards I ran crying from the car. He tried to follow me but I just kept walking."

She didn't stop there. "His family is quite racist, you know. Do you know that?"

"Yes, I know that," Raza interrupted, thinking back to stories of Mrs. French's brother who was a pied noir from Algeria who belonged to the OAS and enjoyed raping, torturing, and killing Algerians.

"Well, like brother like sister. Mrs. French, with her polite little smile and hard steely blue eyes, didn't exactly approve of her son going out with a blackie. So what was I to expect from the son? I'm such a fool Raza. Tim wasn't serious about me except for wanting some pathetic schoolboy sex, and nor was I in fact. You have to believe me. You seemed to have gone off me, thinking I was cheap for flirting. Well, I feel cheap now. I wasn't aware of the black-and-white situations. Tim just wanted to show me off as a trophy." She half smiled with tears in her eyes. "Urghh [...] You know what came into my mind then? Those novels by Faulkner about plantations in the south [...] urghh!"

Raza continued to listen to the story and he felt for Shireen, putting his arm around her as they walked in silence to the 19 bus stop. They sat silently on the top deck, right at the back, all the way to Knightsbridge, with her head resting on his shoulder. All that way, he had thoughts running through his head and a welter of emotions; yet, underneath it, the thing was that he still trusted and believed her. He had been hurt, yes, and had pretended to act so stoic, so cool, but his diffidence had paid the price. If only he had acted like Dmitri! But then, he was not Dmitri. Although his love for her was overwhelming, he did not possess the power to express it in a maddening fashion. Friends like Arvind had urged him to bed her, and crudely suggested that she was asking for it. It wasn't in his nature, or could it be in his nurture, the values he had been brought up with?

In the next few weeks, Raza avoided going to the main building of the Poly where Tim was based, instead went to the Annex in Great Portland Street where he had his classes. He wasn't sure how he might react in seeing Tim. Shireen also stopped coming to the Poly when she wasn't working, feeling somehow avoidance was the best policy. They had both decided confrontation would solve nothing. Fortunately, there were no telephones in their rooms at Beaufort Gardens, only coin-operated boxes on different floors. The basement where they lived was reasonably obscure from the street. The only place that Tim could find Shireen was her work place, which was a secure spot where she was surrounded by friends and work colleagues.

Tim never did come. However, Raza received a letter from the French's. It was discreet, mentioning something about the rest of his belongings were still there and ending by expressing the hope that he would keep in touch. Raza mulled to himself wryly over the letter and a couple of days after the letter had arrived, he telephoned.

"Hello, stranger," came the response from Mr. French. "How are you, dear boy? Now listen, Tim has told me all about it, and such unfortunate things do happen. Sowing one's oats, what?"

Raza could imagine his face at the other end of the line. He hesitated and registered no reaction of any kind in his voice, but politely and calmly accepted the invitation. He told Shireen about the phone call, and said that he had agreed to go on Saturday to face the old devil and collect the rest of his belongings.

Then duly on Saturday he traveled to Butterfly Lane, and told himself that he was going to fetch his belongings, above all his precious books, his few records and the precious photographs of Shireen that had been taken by a professional photographer using the Contax camera that Raza's uncle had given him the year before.

He had been invited to eat at about lunchtime. The journey passed in quiet reflection and he soon found himself at the gates, with the familiar pebbled drive leading to the house. He noticed that the car wasn't there. Tim must have borrowed his dad's car and gone out he thought. Maybe the Frenchs had decided to be tactful and see Raza on his own. "Let's wait and see," he thought. He unlatched the gate but, before he reached the front door, Mr. French, wearing his customary tie, even when relaxing at home, opened the door before Raza could knock.

"All my things had been packed in a large old-fashioned travel trunk, originally belonging to my father and consisting of two parts: one with drawers and the other for hanging suits and trousers. I had left it behind before I moved out almost a year ago during father's illness. I lifted it and carried it out into the lobby, where I put on my scarf and duffel coat. I stood there talking to them for a few minutes, thinking about the place, my father, the room, at the same time being always courteous and a little formal. I assured them I would be keeping in touch. Thankfully the cab arrived promptly. I shook hands and said goodbye as Mrs. French shuffled to the door to see me out. I thought I saw Mr. French's eyes moist behind his glasses and for a moment I thought the old codger was a bit soft and sentimental after all as he shut the door of the cab, tapped the car window and winked. The last sight was of Mrs. French waving at me through the window, I reflected on all the years of knowing them and through my mind flashed mixed thoughts as the cab drove along the road heading to the station."

Raza knew he would never see them again and had mixed emotions: a bit of hurt, a pinch of anger, a tinge of sadness at all that had transpired over the years, but I'm sure he acted as courteous as his upbringing had taught him to do.

"When I returned with the luggage, Shireen was getting ready to work the late shift. We didn't talk much but I felt or at least I believed in my heart that everything would be right again. So we walked down to her cafe and I told her all that had transpired at the French's. She said Tim was already engaged and "That makes you his bit on the side."

Though a bit hurt and outraged, Raza had always been conscious of being the object of racism at boarding school and felt this was another example slapping him in the face. Shireen tried to appease him by saying she loved him.

He looked down at her face, one eyebrow raised for an instant, and then he smiled looking at her as if to say okay, as he put his arm around her and continued walking in silence.

At the coffee bar, Arvind looked at both of them quizzically. He didn't know about what had happened with Shireen, only that Raza had been seeing less of her recently. Whenever he had met Raza outside of work, he had his own domestic problems to ask too much about Raza. But he suspected that something had happened between the two.

In Hindustani he asked, "Everything okay?"

"Yes, fine." Raza replied, "We'll talk later, not right now."

During the summer, Shireen and Raza grew perceptibly closer. Raza was marking time to go up to Oxford, now that he had passed the required A-levels and notified the college about his results. Shireen was still undecided about her future and said nothing. Though none of this was mentioned, they would have to separate, geographically at least. The work at the coffee bar sapped all the energy to even begin to think about what she wanted from life. She was intelligent and if she wanted could make so much more of her own life.

I could argue that more of a gender and class analysis could be imagined here as we see her life unfold, but Raza suspected that more important than her inclination, it was the absence of support from her parents that had left her undecided. They both thought about each other and would occasionally daydream, connecting thoughts as if they were one.

Raza was no more certain than Shireen about what he wanted to do after university. Joining the diplomatic service had crossed his mind and he had toyed with the idea. He thought that, with his uncle and father's connections, he could get a job in some backwater tropical consulate where nothing much happened and where he could devote himself to writing. She was unsure whether she wanted a career or not. Still they daydreamed. For the moment it was just a question of whiling away time, sheer enjoyment and fantasy with their ever-expanding network of acquaintances and friends.

"I got to know another friend during this time. The way this happened was that one day, sitting at the coffee bar talking to Arvind, waiting for Shireen to finish work, a young, smart-looking man in a sports jacket sat down next to me. He started a conversation in a quiet, friendly, open kind of way, with just the hint of an American accent. Arvind looked at him suspiciously, making a comment about how he must be a pederast or something to that effect. He said this to me in Urdu."

"As our conversation rambled on as I still waited for Shireen to finish her shift, I came to know a little more about this American-sounding man, whose name I was finally told was Stephan. It turned out that Stephan was also going up to Oxford that September. We had many things in common: a love of literature and poetry, a wild sense of humor, and a healthy dislike of the establishment. Stephan had received a cosmopolitan education, and was the son of a Polish-American mother who owned an art gallery in New York, and a Polish-English father who traded as a jeweler in London. He was partly educated in New York, hence his American accent (as when he said "cawfee" when ordering at the Norland) and partly at a private school in England."

Raza often invited Stephan to the picture show, and it was through this connection that Raza and Shireen got to see French and other European movies like Andrzej Wajda's *Kanal*, but that happened later. Meanwhile, other young men like him who were living around the South Kensington area at the time were also attracted to handsome couples much like Shireen and Raza. Most were single and many without steady girlfriends. And, although they all ribbed Raza about just wanting to be a breadwinner and get married, he wasn't interested in chasing other girls as they did. His eyes were for Shireen only.

Then the time to go to Oxford was suddenly upon them. The term was due to begin in the third week of September, and on that day itself he had decided to take a coach to Oxford rather than going there by train. Shireen and Zizi decided to go with him, which made him happy because it was a 90-minute journey, and they would sit in the back row of the coach by the left-hand side window.

The coach wasn't crowded and they found themselves alone at the back. As the coach started, Shireen moved from her seat next to him and sat on his lap, smiling and kissing him and arousing him as she moved her body on his lap. This time he did not ejaculate in his trousers but responded to her. Zizi was embarrassed, she smiled but pretended not to notice and looked another way. For the first time her cousin had thrown herself at Raza. No one in front seemed to notice. Forgetting themselves as well as the time and place, Raza and Shireen went into a passionate clinch that only came to an end when the coach arrived at Oxford.

Raza was registered to live in the college for the first two terms as the rules required, so from the coach station they headed toward Exeter College in Turl Street, a narrow winding street, off the High Street. It was a white stone building, smaller than All Souls next door, where the door of the college led to a quadrangle around which the undergraduate rooms were based on several floors. The place seemed cold as they went past the Victorian Gothic chapel to the registry office, where Raza checked in and was led to his rooms by one of the monitors.

"You know that women visitors are not allowed, don't you?" The monitor told him and led the way. This led to an increase in the chill Raza felt at his separation from Shireen, who looked a little sad too. "We'll wait for you in the tea-room we passed on the High Street," she said as she and Zizi left. In the meanwhile, Raza followed the monitor to the opposite side of the quadrangle, and into a narrow, arched doorway that led to a winding stone staircase. They climbed to the second floor and he was shown to a small, wood-paneled room, with a stone floor covered with a carpet as these were to be his quarters for the next three years. He wasn't exactly enthused by his new living quarters despite the dingy basement flat he inhabited. He would have gladly at that moment changed places with a tramp or vagrant in London.

"I was given the keys and told that all undergraduates were expected to be in by 10:00 p.m. Lateness was punishable by a fine or penalty. The monitor then left and I put the luggage down, at least what luggage I had brought with me, looked at my watch, and took one more look at the room before hastening to join Shireen and Zizi.

Shireen looked at me wanly and I looked back at her looking equally sad and glum. The reality hit us, the reality of separation and being alone without each other. It was almost as intense a sensation for me as had been that first night in England seven and a half years earlier. We got up to go to the coach station to see both her and Zizi off and say goodbye. At the station, I kissed Shireen long and hard, my lips and mouth still sore from the earlier passion in the coach."

"I don't know when I'll be back in London, but soon I hope. Maybe, during the weekend after next. A whole fortnight before I see you again."

"I'll be waiting."

They kissed one last time before she boarded with Zizi. He waited until he saw them find a seat and sit down. They waved and then the coach was gone.

Raza trudged back to his room in the college and forgot all about eating. The following week passed with difficulty, and he couldn't resist going back to London at the first weekend, one week earlier than planned. Since he made up his mind at the last moment, he didn't have time to telephone Shireen to let her know.

He boarded a coach on Friday afternoon, hoping to catch Shireen at home. From the Victoria coach station, he hopped on No. 52 bus to Knightsbridge and arrived at the basement flat in Beaufort Gardens, just as it was getting dark. He went down the separate basement entrance to her flat and peeped through the window. The curtains weren't drawn and through the netting he saw the glow of the table lamp and the gas fire. Shireen was alone, lying in bed reading. Zizi must have gone out, he thought. He silently opened the door to surprise her and entered her room. Shireen looked up and saw him. She gurgled with laughter: "Oh, Raza!"

Before she could get out of bed, he eagerly rushed to the bedside and lay down half across her body and started to kiss her. She responded. As their bodies writhed, he raised himself to take off his coat. As he disengaged, he noticed that she was wearing his pajamas and that they had parted, showing her lower belly and a curly triangle of hair between her thighs. He was in awe. For the first time he had caught a glimpse of a female body. Embarrassed at himself he paused,

Shireen half blushing, half smiling, pulled him back to her as he wrestled off the rest of his clothes, and they went back to their embrace.

During earlier months, when he had lived in the adjacent room at the rear—a small windowless box—they had only embraced and kissed each other goodnight. Raza was playing the perfect gentleman. Only once while she stood on her toes and reached up to his face to kiss him, pressing her belly against his, feeling her small perfect breasts against his chest and writhing he thought about that dream and had laughed. This time it was different because, after moments of passion and kissing her body all over, he finally went inside her.

That is how Raza's virginity came to an end with the girl he had first fallen in love with at the age of 13.

Their tongues and lips sore, bodies aching, they continued their love making, rising only late the next morning from a long satisfying sleep, happy, and hungry for something to eat. He gently kissed her and after a shower they got dressed and went to El Cubano, a newly opened restaurant at the top end of the cul-de-sac on the corner of Brompton Road. They ordered a steak with pineapple, salad and fries, which all came served on a wooden platter. While waiting, they asked for two large cups of coffee, drank the coffee, ordered a carafe of red wine, a jug of water to go with their meal, and not many words were exchanged except those of ordinary pleasure, as countless couples do who are in love, with a lot of the talking being done with the eyes. Raza recalls Shireen saying "Gosh! I didn't realize how hungry I was."

Raza nodded, smiled in agreement, as he mopped up the platter juices with pieces of bread (a very French thing to do, he thought, but not very British). They didn't order dessert and Raza just asked for the bill. Shireen was due to start her afternoon shift, so they went back to the flat for her to change, do her hair and makeup. He sat and watched her move about, saw her naked body longingly as she changed clothes, noting it was not a sight he had known until yesterday. He feasted his eyes. It was perfect. When she was ready, he walked down with her to the Norland, window-shopping along the way.

Reaching the coffee bar, they were all surprised to see Raza so soon, as surprised as Shireen and Raza himself. Jimmy, who was working on the coffee machine, piped up in his drop Oxford accent mimics saying: "So vaaht is this my dear fellow? We thinking you are being at Oxford."

Raza smiled shyly: "Yes, yes, expect to see more of me."

There was a plan brewing in his mind to visit Shireen every weekend, but with the college restrictions, it was not possible for her to come up to Oxford, even if he helped with her fare. The plan developed further in his mind over the next few days though it was his decision to make, and his alone. Making a joint decision with Shireen would be unfair and out of the question. If things didn't work out, he didn't want her to feel guilty as the reason for him quitting his studies.

After telling Shireen he will come back to walk her home he left, and at the flat, he continued thinking until finally he came to a decision: he would leave Oxford.

"I rationalized the situation this way. First, if I had to wait until matriculation it was just far too long, another term and a half, or six months to be exact. And after that there was no guarantee that I would be allowed to transfer to history. On the other hand, there was Shireen and my love for her beckoning me. I sat down at the typewriter, drafting and redrafting a letter to the college. Finally, I wrote to the Rector of Exeter College, telling him that regretfully Oxford was not for me. And with that done I folded the letter, sealed it and then wrote to my father, who was aware anyway that I wanted to study history, and that being registered at Oxford, even if it was for PPE [Philosophy, Politics, Economics] might open a route to History."

His father knew of Raza's involvement with Shireen, the daughter of a family known to him, and felt uneasy with Raza's behavior. The whole situation was weighing heavily on him. He didn't feel a man with his values and class should conduct himself this way. In turn, he did not hesitate to let his son know how strongly he disapproved of the situation and indeed, deep inside, his father felt ashamed.

In his letter Raza told his father he was sorry to disappoint him, and promised to continue his studies elsewhere. He then went to post both the letters. He would tell Shireen of course, and all his friends would come to know in time. He repeated in his mind that he needed time and had no one else to blame for his actions but himself.

It was in this preoccupied frame of mind that Raza went to find her. She looked tired. Going up and down stairs, serving people, acting friendly even when she didn't feel like it, waiting at tables, all made her legs feel dead. She looked at him with that helpless look. "Take me home please Raza, I'm exhausted."

Outside they took the bus back to Beaufort Gardens, when normally they would have walked. Once at home, Shireen took off her coat and shoes and flung herself on the bed, to try and get some sleep. "Let me massage your feet," Raza said, 'I'm quite good at that." Memories of Amadabad, where they had first met, with her smiling and sitting on the floor, as Raza had his legs massaged by his Amma, his nanny, flashed through his mind.

CHAPTER 15

FAREWELL TO SHIREEN

What a different world that was. She let him massage her feet and her ankles and calves, and then gently her back. "That's nice," she murmured. He continued massaging until she fell asleep.

Life continued for the two lovers like this over the next few weeks and into late November, but over time Shireen became distracted, more tired, more worried. Running away from home and defying the family and feeling free and independent could not possibly mean this—an eternal life of drudgery in a coffee bar. Whatever she had imagined, she certainly hadn't bargained for this kind of reality. The harder reality of the situation was that on his part, Raza couldn't find any way out, any practical resolution, some way to help.

He spent the major part of his allowance on the year's fees at Oxford and realized that he might have to get some temporary job himself, let alone offer financial support to Shireen. The old Polish chef in the Norland kitchen referred to her as "princess." Raza agreed that she was a princess, but he still had ideas of finishing studies and having a career. All that would take time, before he could marry Shireen and make her happy.

Raza noticed that they made love infrequently now. She was often tetchy. One evening when he was at home and hadn't gone to find her, she came back late.

"Where've you been? It's way past midnight."

"Oh, there's this nice, shy young boy called Paul who does the washing up at the Norland, I got chatting to him, if you must know."

"Chatting?"

"No, flirting actually, making love on the milk crates if you like. What do you think Raza? Who do you think I am?"

It was just a tired, acid repartee, and Raza should have let it go at that, but the fact that he didn't was a sign of the fraying nerves at the edges of the relationship. Their relationship became very tense, until it got to the point when

Shireen took to staying away without letting him know. He felt jealous without her being present.

Then, one day, Raza found a worn copy of *The Ballad of Reading Gaol* in the room with the name of Paul inscribed inside. Raza began to imagine that Shireen was having an affair. He moved out of her room they had started sharing after Oxford and into his own small dingy room. For days they wouldn't see each other. Raza was absolutely distraught and became more distraught still when, after some days, there was no trace of her being around. He went to the Norland, and seeing no Shireen there, he confided in Arvind, who told him that he knew Paul, but didn't feel there was anything going on there. He said Arvind laughed sardonically at the thought of Paul having any connection to Shireen. Arvind told him. "He's (Paul) just, as Lawrence Durrell said somewhere, 'a pimply little catholic youth, making a bicycle saddle out of his sexual organs.'"

He told Raza that the problem lies elsewhere. When he said Shireen gave her notice two days earlier and was no longer working at the coffee shop, and his guess would be that she has gone home to her parents' house.

Raza felt something else was not being said and asked Arvind, who told Raza that he should "not get dragged into something he should not get dragged into."

"Meaning?"

"Meaning that you don't lose your self-respect. Remember the words of Mikhail Naimy—'More possessing, more possessed. Less possessing less possessed.' Be brave my heart."

Raza nodded his head: "Yes, whatever."

"To be perfectly honest inside, deep inside, in my heart, I was in turmoil. I had loved her for so very long, and despite the hurt I still loved her, but now my world has blown up in my face like a soap bubble, but more painful like a glass bubble. I couldn't try phoning because I must have been held to blame by the Ishaq family for helping their daughter abscond and then not looking after her properly."

For the next little while Raza moped in his room, sitting in the basement, shut out from any light but the naked lamp, drinking on his own and playing that album of Sinatra's *In the Wee Small Hours of the Morning* over and over, and looking a sight. But even this state, this self-indulgence, couldn't go on for too long because economic necessity snapped him out of it. Feeling unable to ask his father for help, he started job hunting. With his network of friends that wasn't too difficult, and, in fact, Arvind got him a temporary job on the coffee machine while Jimmy was on holiday for two weeks, though he would have to find something elsewhere after that.

Raza agreed and was shown the ropes of working a Gaggia espresso machine, how to prepare different kinds of coffees people might order—espresso, double espresso, cappuccino, flat white, and so on; how to prepare for the lunchtime and after theater rushes; coping with drunk or noisy customers; supporting the waitresses in awkward situations; and, so on. Raza got right into it.

He also took the time to write his father a letter. In it he said:

> My dear Abbajan, I am well, as I hope you are too. I am very sorry to have let you down with Oxford. I explained my reasons for doing so in my last letter ... You will be glad to know that I have decided to "dump" Shireen.

His father's response when it arrived was very direct. He rebuked his son for dumping his girlfriend:

> In our culture we never behave like this toward women we love, nor talk about dumping them as if they were rubbish. I am very disappointed in you. If Mr. and Mrs. Ishaq contact me I will need to apologize for my son. A day that I never thought I'd live to see.

Then, about a week or so later, Arvind told him that Fozzie, Shireen's brother, had come looking for Raza at lunchtime.

"He was with a couple of mates, looked like Arabs, I thought. I didn't like the look of things, since I had met Fozzie before with you and Shireen whenever he came around to see the two of you. Naturally I asked Freddy 'what's up?' He just glowered and said his sister was pregnant. So watch it Raza, I don't mean Fozzie, I mean being made to marry Shireen. Do you even know if it's your baby she's carrying? Believe me I've been through these kinds of situations."

This was Arvind's second caveat within a few days of each other. Raza again nodded his head and said nothing. He was shaken though.

He started running the various scenarios in his mind.

"It was true that Shireen had missed a period in November. It was now mid-December. She had also started acting different, tired and broody in the later part of November when Paul was not yet on the scene. Could her broodiness have been something to do with her knowing she may be pregnant? If that was the case, I must then be the father. What to do? I had burnt my boats with my own father, so my father could not mediate between me and Mr. Ishaq, who he felt had every right to feel dishonored. What then, if I am the father?"

Feeling that there was no way out, Raza became even more morose, and in the gloom of December nights in London, he reflected on Dostoevsky's portraits of students in St. Petersburg. It wasn't until mid- to late January 1958, when Raza had moved on from the Norland to working as a hall porter in Belgrave Square, and when going in search of a coffee and some company after work, he still dropped by at the Norland, despite memories now associated with the place. One day as he did so, Jimmy, who was on the machine at the time, handed him a note from Shireen. The note was very brief and to the point. It asked him to meet with her.

The telephone number and address of an office situated on the second floor in the block between Albemarle and Berkeley Streets was given. Raza, who wanted nothing more than to see her and to be with her again, agreed to try to talk to her, to talk to her openly and honestly, without bitterness or anger, and to clarify what had happened between them. He telephoned the very next morning. The voice at the other end sounded brusque. "I can't talk right now; I'm working here as a receptionist. Why don't you come up and see me during my lunch break." Raza couldn't but agree.

He spent the rest of the morning showering, shaving, and putting on some smart clothes. As he shaved and looked in the mirror, his feelings were torn between his love for her and his hurt and anger at the bizarre behavior. He soul searched. Why had they been unable to talk? Why didn't she feel able to tell him that she might be pregnant? Arvind's caveats, and that of Stephan, who had come back on the scene and met him again at the Norland, rang in his head at the same time as his feelings for her. It was an important meeting, perhaps the most important meeting in his young life. He was trying hard to maintain some calm and equilibrium.

Once dressed, and having taken a sip of coffee at home, Raza walked up to Knightsbridge and took the tube to Green Park, picking up the mail on the way. The January morning was not too bad, but there was a chill wind with iron in its soul and a bleak sun shone through the clouds. As he came up the stairs from the tube station on the north side, he looked back at Green Park across the busy road, stretching down from the Ritz to Hyde Park Corner. He caught sight of rows of trees with bare branches. Only the evergreen bushes still bore leaves.

He took a deep breath as he turned toward the entrance of the offices where Shireen worked. He took an old-fashioned lift with wooden paneling and a red carpet up to the second floor, as instructed. As the doors of the lift opened, he stepped out on to a black-and-white marbled floor, looked to his right, and saw Shireen at the reception desk. She looked up from the magazine she was reading behind her desk and their eyes met as he walked toward the desk. Her face was stony, hard, and expressionless, as he had never seen it before. In that instance of silence, he couldn't help looking at her well-remembered and well-loved face.

He noticed her pink lipstick, her charcoal gray pullover, and a silver necklace that was new. Still expressionless and businesslike, she said as she got up and came around from behind her desk:

What kind of sandwich would you like?

Raza's half smile, with which he had emerged from the lift, froze then vanished from his face at hearing her tone of voice and seeing her expressionless face. His best-hoped desire for openness, peace, and all that he had been rehearsing that morning when getting ready vanished, been nullified, as if being met by a stone wall. He saw a side of her that was cold and determined. All he could get out of his mouth at the moment was "a chicken sandwich please."

"And a coffee?" she queried.

"Yup, a cappuccino will do, though God knows I could do with a drink," he said, still trying to make light of things.

Still nothing doing. She merely placed an order with the boy from a local café who went around offices collecting orders for lunch. Then, still businesslike: "There's a table in what serves as a staff rest area round the back. Let's move there and wait for our lunch," she said. He followed her into a little carpeted room with three or four small table with chairs. There was no one else there at that moment.

"Raza, now I know that you don't have to marry me. Men never do, not even 'honorable' men from good families ..."

"But who said ..."

"I know what you are going to say. Don't. I feel so ashamed of having dishonored my family. Please just go."

It seemed like *parc fermé* to Raza. Try as he might, he realized he was not going to be given an opportunity to make amends or even to say he would marry her. And without finishing his sandwich, he just got up disconsolately and without looking back left Shireen, but with tears in his eyes. He wiped his eyes as he got into the lift and went down and out of the building. He crossed over to the park side, got onto a bus, went to the upper deck and sat down, crying intermittently at all the memories, their time together, the tender moments, the talk, the hugs, all that rose up until he reached home. He saw people looking at his face and averting their eyes, because sorrow is regarded by most as being such a private business.

Once home, he shut himself off. Life would continue but not for now. It was such a painfully bizarre ending that the relationship with Shireen had come to, a love story that he would look at over and over again. Raza was in a way like Prince Myshkin, in Dostoevsky's *The Idiot*, when he wrote

> The men of the eighteenth century were absolutely not the same sort of people as we are now [...] In those days they were men of one idea, but now we are more nervous, more developed, more sensitive, men of two or three ideas at once.[1]

The reason I say this is because Raza saw himself as a young man with good intentions, humanism, and sensitivity, but he was an idealist who wanted to be a man in the grip of "two or three ideas at once."

Raza seemed a divided creature, and believed that at the end there is no immunity from self-doubt, guilt, and self-contempt. In regard to the nature of moral choice, Dostoevsky believed that there did not exist a single ethical system that would provide solutions to all problems because reasoning and feeling on most fundamental issues of moral choice could not be reconciled. This impasse resulted in the divided conscience being at the center of the tormented soul of his characters.

Had he missed seeing how conventional and Indian she still remained? Had the free-spirited and independent-minded Shireen failed in an attempt to get away from convention? Was it his fault that he didn't see that for girls it was much more difficult than for boys to act and behave independently, particularly Indian girls, no matter how Westernized they seemed on the surface? What were Shireen's real feelings for him? From her parents' point of view, it had been implicit that a match with Raza would be very desirable.

Shireen had told him long ago, right at the very beginning, and she had laughed with him about how simple that would be. But then she wanted to spend some salad days, flirting and being the talk of the town, before settling down in suburbia, with a nice husband, such as Raza himself would make. And what were his feelings for her? Were they wanting in the final analysis?

It had been a question of instant attraction from the moment that he first set eyes on her in Amadabad. Then the surprise meeting at the Crammers and falling in love all over again. Yes, he thought, he did and still does love her, and besides, they were also friends and shared ideas and laughter. He had also come to trust her over time despite everything. They would probably have ended up

---

1 Dostoevsky, *The Idiot*, Dostoevskii, Polnoe Sobranie Sochinenii, Nauka, Leningradskoe Otdelenie. 1973. Vol. 8: p. 433.

getting married. And, then there was the unborn baby? Yes, he had wanted babies with her.

They would have been so perfect. But I don't think he was ready for marriage and a family because if he had he would have proposed to her. I sensed he worried what his family might say. I also think he was kidding himself now that they could had coped. Raza didn't say what happened with Shireen's pregnancy as of this date, whether she had an abortion, or it had turned out to be a phantom pregnancy.

It was clear the guilt about how Shireen was treated after their last encounter pressed heavily on his mind. After all, he had every opportunity to say at that very moment that he would marry her if she was pregnant and save her from all the "dishonor" he knew she certainly would endure.

No doubt she had many faults, but she also did not deserve to be treated this way. Raza essentially "punked out" as the slang in vogue at the time put it; that is, he acted cowardly and disgracefully as a man and as a friend.

And his father voiced similar words after Raza used the word "dump" in his letter to his father in referring to Shireen before all this came about. These were not happy moments for the couple and Raza basically thought only about himself, but he felt uneasy and the situation was frightening to him. And then there was the matter of responsibility in the sense that they both had lived privileged lives and now they faced equal dilemmas. Chekhov used to say that the past of an educated man always seemed beautiful to him, but his present situation was a state of calamity.[2]

Raza and Shireen loved to evoke Dostoevsky in their conversations and I wonder what Dostoevsky would do if he were a character in his own novel. But the main issue here is the fact that Raza had lived his whole life at that point as a privileged person, from a royal family and never having had to really take responsibility for anything and now suddenly Raza is in a situation where he suddenly had to be accountable.

In some ways, Shireen too was in a similar situation and now they both had to find a way out. Raza did think about this and had deep meditations regarding these issues as he racked his soul for ways to reconcile his behavior.

He suffered from a deep sadness as he continued to reflect on this situation. Sadness remained and, of course, memories too. As Faulkner reminds in *The Wild Palms*, without one you can't have the other, and if you'd rather not have the grief, there's no memory. But no matter how he yearned to find happiness

---

2 Anton Chekov, *Longer Stories from the Last Decade* (New York: Modern Library, 2000), xv.

again with Shireen, Raza realized that it was impossible. Were he to shed more tears he would drown; he kept his memories and his grief locked in for the time being.

For the moment, he had to accept that he was single. He'd come to a phase in his life when he has perhaps given up on studies by walking out of Oxford for love, then lost out on love, and spent all his pocket money for home, with just friends to help and advise. Abid was studying for his MB at Cambridge.

His father was practicing as a barrister in Bombay and sending his earnings to his wife and children. In order not to drown he had to grab hold of himself, find a job, and repair fences with his father by demonstrating that he was determined to complete his education. Some friends said that he just needed to have sex.

CHAPTER 16

DOWN BUT NOT OUT

Soon after Shireen's departure, the landlady informed him of a vacancy in a single room on the first floor. He went upstairs with her to take a look. It was a narrow, high-ceilinged room with self-contained washbasin, kitchenette, and a built-in wardrobe. A long window at the end looked down on to the cul-de-sac with its circled off park with shrubs and trees obscuring the houses opposite. Daylight! He immediately accepted the room, and with his little remaining cash paid the week's rent in advance and moved his stuff up from the dingy basement so full of memories.

"The next thing on my mind was to find a job. Bindo told me that the coffee bar had no vacancies, and recommended to ask at the picture-framers next door. The work didn't last long and I was asked to leave within a week of starting. I was considered straightforward inept at molding and varnishing frames. Without qualifications, which I didn't know how or where to use, I didn't have any other employable skills except manual ones. Fortunately, a fellow tenant on the same floor, a woman called Barbara something or the other, who affected a posh accent and worked as a receptionist at the Institute of Directors, asked me whether I would be interested in a hall porter's job. Public school had at least taught me how to graft.

I accepted the job and was taken along to meet the director of the place, a tall erect man, sporting a major's moustache, who looked me up and down, smiled and gruffly welcomed me to the job. I was fitted out with a new uniform in black chosen by Barbara for this newly created post under the Commissionaire who wore a sergeant major's uniform."

"I couldn't really help being patronizing without realizing it. I again found myself as the sole 'darkie' in the place. This was still 1958. Although there had been mass migration from the West Indies throughout the postwar period and into the 1950s, migration from the Indian subcontinent, though still unfettered, was on a much smaller scale. Race and class structures as observed and experienced firsthand were firmly in place. Outwardly, I put up with the patronizing attitudes without showing insult or resentment. I held on to this job for the next few months of 1958."

Any thought of further studies was deferred for the moment, and for Raza, history remained the most likely option. He marked time deciding which branch of history and where, or whether something else, like languages, became of interest. It wasn't so much a question of marking time as an unresolved tension between his different belongings: Indian, Islamic, and now the seminal one inherited by living in England for eight years.

He certainly made it clear that he didn't want to study English literature. What else could there be other than Chaucer, Milton, Shakespeare, Byron, Keats, Shelley, Dickens, and Austen, when he showed more interest in Dostoevsky, Tolstoy, Stendhal, Balzac, Pound, Hemingway, Faulkner, Scott Fitzgerald, Emerson, and Thoreau? Though he read voraciously, the reason why I call him an autodidact, he was demonstrating a jejune aversion to the British contribution to world literature. Sometimes friends recommended books and authors to him.

Reading all those incredible books had made him want to become a writer, though he had still not given up the idea of becoming a film actor, because he still went to movies when he could afford to, though not as often as earlier. He even wrote to his father about going into the movie business, although, as was to be expected, his father's reaction was not very supportive. "People from respectable families don't enter these vulgar professions." Yet, he did offer to introduce Raza to Marie Seton, the biographer of Eisenstein, who was living in Bombay, and helped set up the University Film Society at Nehru's invitation. The father reasoned that if his son was serious then there was no better person to advise him, but that would wait until Raza returned to India.

Though Raza procrastinated, he always made friends easily. These days he met people mostly at the coffee bar, where a crowd of people of all sorts would gather after work, and most of them would happen to be Indians. There was Bindo of course, the center of attraction, forever holding fort and proselytizing, what Raza regarded as his strange blend of theosophy, Hindu mysticism, and Ouspenskii. Others were attracted by Hindu philosophy. Here is an excerpt from Ouspenskii's reading aloud *In Search of the Miraculous*.

> "The miraculous" is very difficult to define. But for me this word had a quite definite meaning. I had come to the conclusion a long time ago that there was no escape from the labyrinth of contradictions in which we live except

by an entirely new road, unlike anything hitherto known or used by us. But where this new or forgotten road began, I was unable to say. I already knew then as an undoubted fact that beyond the thin film of false reality there existed another reality from which, for some reason, something separated us. The "miraculous" was a penetration into this unknown reality. And it seemed to me that the way to the unknown could be found in the East.

Though Raza did not say it at the time, he did feel beckoned to the East and found Ouspenskii's philosophy fascinating. People sitting at the counter would listen to Bindo, who could be amusing. Raza noticed Bindo was a bit of a lady's man too, like some Indian version of Elmer Gantry. He carried around a photograph of himself posing as Junior Mr. Bombay. One evening as he walked with Raza up the Brompton Road and past a Chinese Restaurant called Shangri-La, he peered through the window and spotted his next prey, one of the waitresses, wearing a short Chinese-embroidered top. He suggested to Raza that they go in for a coffee.

Raza knew the manager of the place, Mr. Chang, because he had accompanied Shireen to find a waitress's position there. After ordering drinks at the bar, Bindo lost no time in chatting her up and getting her name, which was Jenny, and offering to meet her after her shift. Jenny was a white South African with blue eyes, black hair, and finely arched eyebrows. Soon the two grew into a trio, with Raza being invited around frequently to taste Jenny's cooking.

They both liked Raza to be around, and enjoyed his iconoclastic intelligence as one who would deflect from any questions or comments about faith, as in Raza tries to oppose religious images through his humor. Bindo tried to turn him into an ally and for a while Raza began to show interest in Sufism, the Islamic counterpart to Hindu mysticism. He had been introduced by Bindo to Gibran's *The Prophet*, read some Rumi, Persian poetry and, of course, Omar Khayyam.

However, his taste for irony and humor led him to making friends with a young man called Michael whose girlfriend, Annie, had started working at the coffee bar as a waitress. Both turned out to have an Indian connection. Annie was obviously an Anglo-Indian, whereas Michael was a Cambridge graduate who had studied literature and whose father had been a British official, responsible for administering an Indian estate. Michael's father had been made ward of court, because of the youthfulness of the heir. His friendship with the couple continued, and since they lived round the corner in Thurloe Square, he was invited to have a meal with them now and then. It turned out that Michael had made an overland trip by land over to Iran, and was busy writing a book about his adventure. Michael, who was prone to stammering, explained:

> Well, actually what happened was quite funny really, you might say. My tutor at Cambridge was none other than E. M. Forster. When one of my friends mentioned to him that I was writing a book on Iran, he asked how long I had spent there, and when informed that I had been in Iran for three months, Forster is alleged to have remarked that, in that case, the book wouldn't be that good. Now, I know that Forster had spent a much longer time in India than I had in Iran, but I wrote to him in any case saying what I'd heard him as allegedly to have said about my book. Forster wrote back to me and said: "The geese have been cackling. I know precisely where they are and I will deal with them, but I do wish you the best of luck."

Michael chuckled recounting the incident to Raza, and thinking of the friendship both he, Michael, and Annie shared so naturally. Raza got introduced to Durrell's *The Alexandria Quartet*, so evocative of the decaying city, moving, exotic, droll, and obscene at the same time. Then there was Cavafy, followed by Kazantzakis's *Zorba the Greek*. A character like Zorba, with his larger-than-life personality and his simple philosophy, were an instant hit with many of Raza's friends. I think what Raza liked about Michael was the broader horizon from which he saw things that were much more than narrow Englishness.

Then during Easter 1958, Steve came back from Oxford. Raza says:

> Steve had also decided to give up on studying there and decided to become a playwright under the tutelage of Robert Bolt. Quite suddenly he appeared at the coffee bar one day and he and I picked up our friendship from before. Steve or Stephan as he was also sometimes called, had a wild sense of humor and was up for all kinds of pranks.
>
> On one occasion when I was with him, we went walking near Knightsbridge, where the upper classes largely live, and ended up serenading people having a party in a flat in Montpellier Square, declaiming lines from Romeo and Juliet's balcony scene. The people having a party encouraged them with "More, More," while the residents on the floor below asked for all the noise to stop. At another time we found ourselves hitchhiking to Oxford from the middle of Park Lane, with Stephan wearing a sombrero and a borrowed shawl from a woman friend draped as a serape. Steve started stopping people with "Say man, have you seen my horse? I lost my horse, he's called Pegasus."

On the back of such antics, someone in a van did stop and gave them a ride to a party at Oxford. The funniest and weirdest episode occurred when Steve took Raza to Soho to look for some hashish. Steve had got to know a man going by the name of Ted Hakim, a strange-looking figure even in London, frequently to be seen walking around in bare feet, his jeans rolled up to his knees, a long scarf appearing to hang underneath a small V-necked sweater like a loincloth, but most of all his unkempt African hair and beard poking out in all directions. Ted was nowhere to be found but Steve left a note telling that he was looking for him.

During Easter 1958, Stephan decided to join a demonstration against the use of potential US nuclear strikes from Brize Norton (Royal Air Force Station) in Oxfordshire. The demonstration was organized by the Campaign for Nuclear Disarmament. He was persuaded by the reasons for the demonstration and invited Raza to come along. Raza was open to the ideas that had convinced Steve, but was unable to join the march because he was working. This shouldn't have been an excuse, because relatively speaking Raza was more open politically to the winds of change because of his own family's history. His anti-imperialist feelings against Britain and France had been given further impetus by the British and French invasion of Egypt, which had nationalized the Suez Canal in 1956, even though its failure led to the resignation of Prime Minister Anthony Eden.

At around this time, Raza also heard of the military coup in Iraq, and the overthrow of King Faisal and his Prime Minister Nuri-al Said. Nawab Dawood Ahmad left Iraq for Pakistan again, together with all his family, except for his wife and Ibn Dawood, who remained with his mother. Two further grandchildren had been born by then—Qais, Zainab's third son, was born in 1957, and Buddhoo, the eldest born of his second daughter, was born in 1958. Some of his retainers stayed behind in Iraq, not fancying a future back in the subcontinent, and having established successful businesses in Iraq. Not so with Nawab Dawood Ahmad who had maintained regular contacts with senior figures in politics and business. The political climate there was not stable, but the nawab bit the bullet and left Iraq for Pakistan.

All these pieces of news were relayed to him at a time during early summer when he decided to quit his job.

"I had had enough of working at the rich man's club when someone mentioned to me about working as a railway porter at Waterloo Station. Wages would be the same but I'd earn more in tips. I went along to enquire and taken on as a temporary alongside a permanent porter. There would be eight-hour shift work involved and the early shift was between 6 a.m. and 2 p.m. The middle shift started at 10 a.m. and ended at 6 p.m. Then the last shift was from

4 p.m. to midnight. No uniform was required. The job was a little like my first job over Christmas at the post office. I was happy wearing khaki trousers, a T-shirt, a pair of plimsolls, jacket, and sailor's cap."

"I would walk through Harrods, looking all the world as though I owned a yacht, and take the tube for Waterloo."

"On the first morning, when I was to start at ten, I reported to the station master's office and was introduced to an Irishman called Gordon who was to be my mate. Gordon led me across the immense concourse containing 19 platforms, toward platforms 1 and 2."

"This would be my patch, and besides helping passengers with their luggage, his job was to go through the carriages before the train turned around and sweep out the carriages, picking up articles left behind and taking them to the lost property office. Soon I was a familiar site in my khaki trousers, navy jacket, and plimsolls, so much so that other porters would shout out 'Where's yer yacht mate?'"

"One day I spied this red-haired young man with a face resembling Kirk Douglas, wearing jeans and a Jimmy Dean-type bomber jacket. For a day or so we just eyed each other. Then one day we found ourselves on the same night shift. We said hello when we clocked off at six in the morning, and decided to walk together across Charing Cross Bridge. The sun was just coming up over the horizon, so I paused on the bridge and stood looking at it for a moment in silence. I broke the silence by talking about God. He was quite into Dostoevsky. 'They say that the sun gives life to us, but it is quite dead. Everything is dead, save man.' My newfound friend called himself Jack and confessed he hadn't read much lately. 'Thinking is dangerous, once you start you can't stop,' I said half-jokingly; Jack looked at me with a wry smile. We talked and mused, as we walked along across the river to Charing Cross underground, and that was the beginning of what turned out to be quite a long friendship."

Raza discovered Jack had come over from Canada to enroll in art studies at the Regent Street Polytechnic, in order to be able to draw and paint live models, because he couldn't afford to pay for one himself. He was quite clear about this and didn't want the teachers there to teach him how to draw or paint. As a matter of fact, he'd recounted an incident when he was drawing a nude model, seated on a dais. When he finished, he decided to draw a decorative flowered sheet under her seated figure. The instructor came over and said, "You can't draw like that." To which Jack responded, "I think I can draw any way I like."

To put it into context, Raza didn't profess to know much about art and painting, even though he'd had art lessons at boarding school. Sure, there were reproductions and paintings in the family homes in Lucknow and Amadabad, and sure he had been to the Louvre, but what he was to learn through knowing Jack was the meaning of art. For the young didactic Jack, in order to paint you have first to learn how to draw; you have to know exactly where to put the line, without need of shading, so that it would suggest curves and roundness. His ideals at the time were Botticelli, Modigliani, Picasso—to be able to draw like them!

"At that moment of time, Jack was living in a shared apartment in Netherhall Gardens, near Finchley Road Tube. He shared it with Al Grant, who wrote poetry, and Gerry Braham, who also painted, but had a kitsch taste for the nude drawings of Russell Flint, which Jack found quite vulgar. Anyway, we all began seeing each other and I introduced Jack and Al to friends like Bindo, Jenny, Michael, and Stephan. Usually what Jack and I would do after work was to go and catch the movies. They liked Westerns, musicals, comedies, thrillers, all kinds of movies. It was at this time that I first came across films of Ingmar Bergman: *The Seventh Seal*, *Summer with Monika*, *Wild Strawberries*, and *Smiles of a Summer Night*. They opened a whole new dimension of filmmaking to my visual imagination. As a rule, the conversation between Jack and I after work would usually go something like:

'Well, what are we going to do this evening?'

'I don't know. What do you want to do?'

Upon which we would look each other in the eye, smile and go chasing a movie we wanted to see, wherever it was showing. We met up in Ealing Broadway or The Elephant & Castle."

Raza had already developed a knack for this habit during his first years in London. Since shows were still continuous at the time, he and Jack would sometimes go from one movie to another, and some time end up by seeing two double features in the same day. With Jack, being a recent arrival and not knowing London well, it was usually Raza who made the decision. At other times, they would sit listening to jazz music in Raza's room, drink freshly ground coffee and talk, but it was Jack who broadened Raza's mind around modern jazz, to the likes of MJQ (Modern Jazz Quartet), Miles Davis, Errol Garner, Ben Webster, and Art Tatum. When Al was around, they would discuss poetry they liked, particularly that of ee cummings, Cavafy, and the French surrealists.

CHAPTER 17

THE GARRET

Jack was easy company for Raza who had a wry sense of humor, loved poetry, and normally used to knock the English for one reason or another. Ezra Pound's poem "The Garret" particularly symbolized their life at the time, but they also liked Rilke as well as ee cummings, who Raza introduced Jack to with one of his favorite sonnets and became one of Raza's favorites since: "I find it such a modern day rendering of a Shakespearean style." Jack had a west coast Canadian twang, a trait of knocking the English both shared with others in their group from the former colonies. His mocking description of English art was: "It's all full of pea greens and shit browns."

At other times Jack would scoff at the English and their jeans, because at that time blue jeans were not being imported from the States or Canada, but made in England and the denim was usually lightweight and the cut was such that the jeans didn't sit on the hips but were tailored to wear at the waist.

"You couldn't swagger in them like cowboys without looking funny." Raza hadn't observed this until Jack pointed it out by showing up someone wearing English jeans by strutting past in his own GWG (Great Western Garment) Canadian jeans and saying, "Watch it cowboy."

Oddly, with his dry sense of humor, Jack was also quite gullible and trusting of friends. There are several occasions when Raza and Al played jokes on him, which he usually ended up by taking good-naturedly. One particularly intricate prank was when Jack, Al, and Raza happened to be quite broke, and hadn't eaten a proper meal for a few days. Talking about ways of easing their hunger, they started earnestly enough with Jack and Raza agreeing to go to their respective High Commissions. In those days, it was possible to show your passport and borrow £10.00 on the strength of that. Al scratched his head and came up with the idea of borrowing from a friend.

"What happened was with that settled, they agreed to meet by the fountains in Trafalgar Square at noon, following our hopefully successful expeditions. I was successful in borrowing £10 from the Indian High Commission in Aldwych by surrendering my passport. Al had been unsuccessful in his mission and was already waiting in Trafalgar Square." They exchanged news and Al was relieved to learn that Raza at least had been successful, but there was no sign of Jack. "Time ticked on as we waited and waited. Patience turned into impatience and in an act of revenge for his lateness, we decided to play a joke on Jack by telling him when he arrived that we'd had no luck in getting any money either."

If Jack had also been unsuccessful they would concoct some ploy for feeding their hunger, by pretending to get away without paying.

"I have a better idea. I know a small Indian restaurant in a quiet side street in Soho that I've been to before. The restaurant is small and darkly lit. There just seems to be a chef in the kitchen and just one waiter, the manager is generally not around, and the waiter happens to be cross-eyed. The food's quite nice." Raza continued as Jack's eyes opened wide in anticipation. "If we were to eat there and then run out, the waiter may not be able to chase and catch us that easily." Raza was amazed at the audacity of his idea. This charade would be easier to carry out than the previous one. All that needed to be worked out was how to pay without being seen by Jack, while keeping up the pretense. Jack made the solution easier for them. After arriving at the restaurant, and ordering a generous-sized meal with a bottle of wine, they waited hungrily for it to arrive.

Raza and Al glanced at each other and smiled knowingly, because Jack had swallowed the bait. The evidence was that no sooner had the food and drink arrived that Jack started wolfing the food and drink down and wiped his plate clean, leaving Raza and Al to eat at a more leisurely pace. Spotting their opportunity to keep Jack in the dark they suggested to Jack that he could help by getting up and leaving. This way only two would have to run the waiter's gauntlet. They said they would catch up with him further down Berwick Market after they had finished. About 20 minutes after he had gone, Raza and Al finished their meal and asked the waiter for the Steve. Raza put the brand-new note he'd obtained from the Indian High Commission on the table before walking out of the restaurant with Al.

Little did they realize that Jack would be waiting at the crossroads watching out for them. But as soon as he saw them come out of the restaurant he started running, not even noticing that the two had been calmly walking, showing no panic. So Raza and Al decided to keep up the pretense and started running too, all the way down Berwick Market and into Shaftesbury Avenue. A number 14 bus was just coming down the road that would take them straight back to South

Kensington. They jumped on, out of breath, and clambered upstairs, sitting down at the rear.

They all laughed with relief.

Raza says: "Jack laughed at the relief that we had got away with it, and Al and I at the relief that we had successfully tricked him. Getting our breath back we decided to continue with the pretense." "You know that there's racial prejudice in this country. How do you imagine that a cross-eyed Indian waiter would get a job again?" Jack squirmed and said, "Gee guys, let me try and find another source for some money, so I can go back and pay him." Al made him squirm some more by reminding him that it was he and Raza who had taken the risk by letting him walk out of there first.

But when Raza produced a 10 shilling note, Jack realized he had been taken for a ride and roundly cussed them both. As he himself acknowledged, he had loads to learn about the ways of the big city. Without telling him, his friends admired a lot about Jack, mostly his openness and generosity, honesty and integrity, his amazing visual sense, his sense of humor and a whole load of other things, because the story of his friendship with Raza has only just begun.

As 1958 drew to a close, Jack and Raza found themselves needing something to do, so early in 1959, they decided to hitchhike overland to India. Jack was enthusiastic because of all the Indian friends he had got to know, and especially excited because of a petite Indian female student who had recently taken his fancy at the drawing class. He declared to Raza one day, "Aw man, you have to see her. She's so delicate, and I feel like a clumsy ogre standing next to her. Tell you one thing though, I've begun to take oriental art more seriously. I couldn't see any dimension in it before, until I realized that it was all there in the flatness. It was that question of line again, so perfect, so nuanced, so suggestive. Besides, I'm excited about visiting India. And by the way, did you say you had a younger sister?" Raza smiled and said, "You'd just be asking for trouble."

They started counting down the weeks and the months, and making initial preparations. Raza agreed to subsidize Jack's expenses from the money he was still receiving from his father. Jack promised to pay him back later as he planned to go back to Canada, and work and save enough for repaying the loan while having money to live on. Into this mix came Steve, who had decided to leave Oxford, and asked to join them.

The envisaged journey to India took on a purpose for all three as the time drew nearer. Jack and Steve were in a bit of awe at visiting Raza's family homes. In conversations with Raza, they had discovered a little about their friend's family and where and how they lived. They would stay in Lucknow and Amadabad of course, but they also wondered: would they also be able to go and live with villagers in their huts? Raza said something like that could be arranged. He told them about amazing accounts of fearless monkeys everywhere, and kept them amused. Steve, who had recently heard Allen Ginsberg recite from "Howl" at Oxford, and came across Maharishi Mahesh Yogi talking about transcendental meditation in London, was curious to go to Rishikesh on the Brahma trail and explore for himself. Raza assured him that there was no problem in putting him on the right tracks when they eventually reached Lucknow, since Rishikesh lay to the northeast of Lucknow in the Himalayan foothills. Raza was not into this mysticism lark.

For Raza, it was the beginning of a search since it was three years since he had last been home. Three years in which much had changed in him. His parents had grown older, and he had become a stranger to his youngest brother. How would he feel about returning there permanently one day to settle? Since they would largely be traveling through Turkey and the Middle East, he was interested in finding out about his feelings of Islamic belonging. He had traveled before to Iraq and Iran as an adolescent and was aware of customs and traditions, as well as having a smattering of useful words and phrases in Farsi, Arabic, and, of course, Urdu.

Whether it was the impending journey or not, these musings were a contributory factor to Raza applying for registration at the School of Oriental and African Studies (SOAS) to study Arabic. Why Arabic? He had walked out of Oxford. He may be good at French, but Arabic belonged to a different group of languages, where he was familiar with the script, although not much more.

The explanation lies partly because Islam and the Middle East was where Raza felt some of the family's core religious roots lay. The other part lay in Abid having drawn his attention to Arberry's translation of the Quran, *The Koran Interpreted*. He bought a two-volume copy immediately, which I have seen in his personal library on my last visit. Although he had not regularly said prayers five times a day, nor fasted for some time, when he set to reading verses from it, he felt that the translation captured the amazing rhythms and cadences of the original Arabic, without losing out on meaning. The irony was that Abid had found love for his special academic subject, had recently been sent down from Cambridge, which was the reason he found himself in London. Abid confided to Raza that the master of Trinity had written to their father about his divided attention between his medical studies and, what the master described as "his other worthy but unfortunately distracting activities" in Arabic poetry. The master added to his opinion of Abid by stating, "he is temperamentally unsuited to the subject of his choice." Abid ruefully said to Raza: "You had been wiser in changing your subject much earlier. I was still in pursuit of proving the master of Trinity by successfully completing my medical studies elsewhere."

Abid spoke Arabic far more fluently and had been in fact fond of reciting Arabic poetry, even more so than he was fond of Persian poetry. The reciting of poetry on occasions was something the brothers shared in common. They would burst into it in Urdu or Farsi just as easily as they would into English or even French poetry. This was the first time Abid shared some of his love of Arabic poetry with Raza, drawing attention to Arberry's *Seven Golden Odes of Pagan Arabia* as well as other bilingual editions of Arabic and Persian verse.

So there it was, this is how Raza decided to compensate his parents for all the faith they had placed in him and the sacrifices they had made for his education, by studying at a university for a degree and to obtain a qualification. He was honoring his parents by deciding to return to school. When Raza wrote to his father about his planned journey, he also mentioned the fact of having been accepted at SOAS for a course in Arabic.

"We set the departure date for some time after Easter, which was early that year and fell at the end of March and that meant leaving some time during April. Although we had no idea how long a trip there and back would take, there was a consensus that we wanted to be back in six months and not much longer. This period would include time that I would be expected to spend at home, leaving Jack and Steve to explore India for themselves, meeting up with me when our itineraries coincided.

Let's say the stay in India was for about six weeks, this left 20 weeks for stopping en route at places, and in countries we had never seen before, and may not get the chance to see again—Florence, Rome, Athens, and beyond. If a bus route to India was supposed to take two weeks, our mode of travel— hitchhiking and staying in youth hostels for the night or with contacts for two or three days—we calculated that could take 12 weeks or more for the entire trip.

Steve had contacts from Oxford who would help the group with places to stay during their travels: I know this Greek girl student, quite pretty but unfortunately now married, but I'm sure she would find somewhere for us to stay while we saw as much of the remains of Ancient Athens as we could. And in Izmir we could stay in the family home of one of my Turkish friends."

Raza too had been given names of people in Iran who were friends of his father, and of course in Karachi they would stay with his uncle, the nawab who was now living with his daughters and grandchildren. The news of their adventure would reach members of the family everywhere soon enough.

In the meanwhile, preparations and enquires had to be made. Between them they had an Indian, a Canadian, and a US passport. The Canadian passport turned out to be the one most hassle free and not requiring many visas. The US was the next in terms of visas, while Raza's Indian passport would require visas practically everywhere. They decided that the best approach to adopt was for Raza to apply for some visas beforehand as they were likely to take time, and then to apply for others when leaving the previous country. Next came the issue of checking out vaccinations and inoculations. Visa and travel requirements of different countries showed the range of immunizations they would need. Finally, there were the dietary safety precautions of charcoal tablets and mosquito repellents. They each made sure to carry their own medications and ointments.

"About a month before departure, we all went to Millett's, a camping shop in Oxford Street. Steve already had a rucksack. Jack and I bought an army duffle bag in the shape of a cylinder made from strong khaki canvas, and meant to be carried over the shoulder. Jack already had a sleeping bag, but Steve and I chose lightweight sleeping bags made for arctic wear, containing fun things like sleeves and a hood, and which folded up nice and small. Apart from these, I decided to take two pairs of jeans, two or three shirts, spare underwear, boots and socks. I decided also to pack a heavy sweater and a toilet bag with essential toiletries, medication and insect repellent, and right on top, a towel."

THE FIRST ALDERMASTON MARCH

The year before, Raza had not been able to go on the march from Aldermaston. This year it was again going to take place over the four days of Easter and travel from Aldermaston to London, to the seat of power, as it were, and thereby attract more national attention. It was expected to be a larger and more national affair. The program was organized by CND (Campaign for Nuclear Disarmament) with clear objectives, printed on leaflets and distributed during the march. These were:

> The unconditional renunciation of the use, production of or dependence upon nuclear weapons by Britain and the bringing about of a general disarmament convention. In the meantime, Britain should halt the flight of planes armed with nuclear weapons, end nuclear testing, not proceed with missile bases and not provide nuclear weapons to any other country.

Raza was determined not to miss it because the Gandhian-Tolstoyan strategy of passive civil disobedience had come in his purview and he was simply carrying on with the traditions in his own way. By now his hair and beard had grown quite long, his hair almost down to his shoulders.

"One day, a few months earlier, after I had first started to grow a beard and not cutting my hair, I happened to be walking down Brompton Road with Al when a man stopped me and asked for a cigarette, he proceeded to walk along beside us for a few paces. The man wore a striking-looking black beard and started speaking to me very seriously, almost earnestly and asked me why I wore a beard and I told him for no particular reason, to which he told me that he'd grown his because of the revolution in his country, which was Cuba."

There was a revelation in these words for Raza because he had heard the news in January of the success of the Cuban Revolution in overthrowing Batista's regime. Few in Britain had supported the revolution, but Raza felt a personal warmth for it, and he knew the United States was supporting Batista. Before the man left, he said:

> When I arrived in your country, I was greeted at the airport by senior members of your Foreign Office staff. I shook their hands but did not bow down to them, nor did I expect them to bow down to me. We are equal in my country.

Al and Raza mused about their encounter, but couldn't decide what to make of it. However, by Easter 1959, Raza had become a Fidelista of sorts who admired what he read and heard and was not going to be fazed by the distorted coverage in the British press on Cuba. Raza was beginning to politically define himself as left of center.

Raza was thus determined to link up with Steve and participate in the march from Aldermaston. Raza marched along his friends from Oxford and with Steve, who was carrying a banner bearing the name of Steve's college, St. Edmund's Hall, shouting slogans, carrying the by-now-familiar and ubiquitous symbol "CND" on a lollipop, and singing songs. There must have been a thousand people there of all ages, male and female, families and friends, and different beliefs: pacifists, priests, and socialists alike.

By the time they had reached Reading at the end of the first day, Raza's feet were feeling pretty sore. He felt as if he was getting blisters, and so he decided to return home for the night, bathe his feet and join the march again from Reading before it started. Many people had brought sleeping bags and made arrangements to stay at friends' places overnight, but many more had returned to their homes like Raza had. He didn't know what Steve had decided to do, but he knew they would find each other along the march somewhere. He would look out for the college banner.

"I had tried to encourage (Bindo) another friend to join me the next day, but without success, and the next morning I set off early for Reading, catching the train from Paddington, because I knew the march was due to set off again at 10:00 a.m. the next morning, and was bound to get there in time. I also knew there would be other demonstrators on the train, so I would just follow them off the train and find the assembly point."

"The weather on the Saturday was squally and unsettled, but reasonably warm for all that. I couldn't see the Oxford banner anywhere. Many more people seemed to have joined at Reading. I walked along the side of the march to try and spot a banner I could fall in behind until I spotted an international section, consisting of people holding placards or lollipop signs bearing names of different countries—Canada, Australia, New Zealand, India, Jamaica, Pakistan, Kenya and so on."

Raza fell in behind a group of Canadians singing songs. He joined the singing by quickly learning the words of "Alouette, gentille alouette, Alouette, je te plumerai." Other songs were sung too, just to keep the spirits up during the distances when they saw nothing but fields with cattle or sheep grazing in the meadows, and caught sight of the occasional newly born lamb. Occasionally, there would be shouts of "Ban the Bomb" in defiance when passing vehicles hooted them. There was a *Daily Express* reporter trying to interview people. The aims of papers like *The Express* and the *Daily Mail* was to try and expose the march as being organized by communists, anarchists, and loony pacifists.

The reporter had heard there was a Cuban on the march and tried to locate him in the international section. Spotting Raza with his long hair and beard, he stopped Raza and said: "Excuse me, but are you from Cuba?" "No, I'm from India," Raza replied.

The reporter lost interest. People laughed. There was a general feeling of camaraderie. It was here that Raza met his first West Indian friend, a Jamaican man.

"He was a short man dressed in a checked red-and-grey lumber jacket, with a kind of felt Red Indian hat, and had a beard and the day I met him he was carrying a placard with the word 'Kenya' written on it. When he spoke, it was in a low, deep voice. There were placards representing different countries. After the incident involving the man from the *Daily Express*, I was handed a placard bearing the name 'CUBA.' Finding ourselves marching next to each other we broke into conversation."

It turned out that the man's name was Fergie and he had a sharp political sense of humor. When an Englishman came up to him on the march and said, "So you're from Kenya? I've been there myself," Fergie's immediate retort was: "Go ahead man, confess your sins, it's good for the soul." Raza couldn't help laughing when the meaning dawned on him. Like him, Raza was also from a former colony. The map of the world in geography books studied since childhood had largely been colored red, so even when English people weren't being patronizing, there was always going to be an edge to any relationship with them. Fergie and Raza became friends and exchanged telephone numbers during the march.

By the early afternoon of Easter Monday, the march finally arrived in Trafalgar Square and was packed with an estimated crowd of sixty thousand people. "The police and Press, as usual, underestimated the numbers," says Raza, adding, "That demonstration was my initiation into progressive politics."

In April, it was time for them to leave on their trip to India. They held a farewell party with all their friends, packed the next morning and off they went, trying to reach India before the onset of the hot winds blowing across Lucknow. This was when the orchards of Amadabad would ripen, transforming the green into orange, red and yellow mangos into sweet delicious fruit.

Raza has dealt with a number of questions at this point of his life. It is clear he is an example of the profound transformations India is undergoing and he sense this but unable to fully comprehend what it means for him and his family as of yet. He is in a prophetic state in his thinking and this trip is allowing him to perhaps recapture, or, better still, recover something that he feels is being lost to time. He is getting older and beginning to see how the male privilege expressed throughout his life has provided him with comfort and rewards others do not have. He needs to provide some kind of protracted reflections as essential before he moves on with his life and he is having difficulty expressing what needs to be said. He envisions the trip to be exactly what Cavafy poetized it would be, "full of adventure, full of discovery."

PART TWO

ITHAKA

As you set out for Ithaka
hope the voyage is a long one,
full of adventure, full of discovery.
           C. P. Cavafy, translated by John Mavrogordato, London (1951)

CHAPTER 18

AN INDIAN ODYSSEY

It was a morning of dark dull gray clouds interspersed with sudden flashes from a bright April sun hanging over London when the three travelers met at South Kensington Station to take the tube and travel to the Elephant & Castle, from where they would take the bus to New Cross and start hitchhiking. They all carried A4 size cards bearing the name of the next major town they were headed for. Here, on the Old Kent Road, their cards simply read "DOVER" as they stood a few paces apart from each other holding their cards up. If someone stopped, they would ask how much room there was. If there was only room for one or two, they would split, otherwise travel together.

It was just beginning to rain, but fortunately they didn't have to wait long. A small secondhand blue van driven by a young man about their age pulled over. The driver rolled down his window and asked where they were heading and then reading the destination on their cards, offered them a lift all the way to the port.

He said he could only take two of them. Jack got in the front and said thanks to the driver, and offered him a cigarette. It turned out that the driver was a novice priest and once again the van was on the road:

> We passed the time chatting, smoking cigarettes, telling the driver about our ultimate destination and being wished good luck, sharing chocolates we had brought along; Steve and I looked out of the rear window at the traffic, stopping at a filling up station, and using the time to go to the toilet, and within a couple of hours the three of us found ourselves near the ferry port.

They thanked the driver again and walked to the ticket office to find out when the next ferry was due to leave. Having bought their tickets for £2.50 each to Calais with the American Express traveler's cheques Steve was carrying, and Raza with £300 he was carrying for the journey for himself and Jack. Boarding the ferry, they waved goodbye to the white cliffs of Dover and were soon en route for La Belle France. Once at Calais, they walked out to the main road to look for a signpost to Amiens. The road to Amiens leads through Boulogne and often the cars would only be going as far as Boulogne. They waited in vain for anything going to Amiens or Beauvais or Paris. The French drivers didn't seem to be so keen on stopping for hitchhikers, and just passed by without even looking. Raza says:

> So what we did was put our cards away and tried to just thumb a lift to wherever the car was going. We split up after a while and stood about fifty yards apart along the road to give ourselves a better chance. If the plan succeeded, we would follow this pattern the rest of the way to India, with the next major city marked on the card. We did make one concession, namely, that as far as Jack was concerned, Steve and I would try to get Jack a ride with one of us because he spoke little French. The plan did take time to work but all three of us eventually got to Paris by late afternoon.

Paris was familiar to them from previous travels, as was much of France, but this was Paris in the spring, and it was decided they stay there for a couple of days at least. For this part of the journey, they used the youth hostel map they carried with them covering youth hostels for most of France and Italy. They had joined the IYHA in London and selected one in Paris by the Gare du Nord, which turned out to be clean, pleasant, and cheap.

While in Paris, they spent most of their time going to the Louvre and the Jeu de Paume, browsing in bookshops—especially Shakespeare and Company, famous for having published *Ulysses* and *Lady Chatterley's Lover* when both books were banned in England, and wandered through a Paris made famous by the likes of Hemingway, Scott Fitzgerald, and Gertrude Stein in the 1920s, all of whom Raza and Steve had read.

Raza also made a point of going to Brentano's in avenue de L'Opéra, which stocked American editions of some books, unavailable for copyright reasons in England, and it was there amid some of Faulkner's novels that he found an out-of-print copy of *Absalom, Absalom*, a Random House edition. He also picked up a copy of the epic novel by Romain Roland *Jean Christophe*, a large, 900-page tome chronicling the life story of a musician.

He wanted something to read along the way and fortunately it fitted in his rucksack. And, of course, they ate in bistros on the rive gauche where people their age congregated, and sauntered on Ile St Louis looking at the Notre Dame, but eventually they had to take leave, so they went out of Paris the way they had left London, out to the southern suburbs, looking for the main roads going south and stood by the signpost for the road to Versailles.

The plan was to head towards Nice, and so they had written "NICE" on their cards. Lifts proved hard to get: by midmorning, they only managed to get as far as Versailles itself. They decided to split up and agreed on a rendezvous point in the youth hostel in Nice in a couple of days' time. They stationed themselves separately on the main road but within seeing distance.

"As it turned out Steve and Jack got into the first car that stopped, but I had to wait a bit. Then, luckily a sports saloon car stopped. It was a Frenchman who was going all the way to Nice. He had been in Canada and was back in his own country after a few years. He reminisced all the way, while I listened and counted myself lucky. By the evening, having reached Aix-en-Provence, the man decided to stop for the night. He said that he would pick me up the next morning by the bridge. It was too good to be true, or so it turned out."

After eating cheaply, Raza went to the local youth hostel to sleep, and the next morning waited at the appointed place, but there was no sign of the guy or his car. Raza evidently decided to move on. The day proved to be long and he didn't know whether he would make it to Nice by the evening, even though he was more than half way there from Paris.

Getting only short lifts via Marseilles and Toulon, he had to trudge his way on foot wherever people dropped him off along the road to Nice. Then out of Toulon, which was largely a naval base with little through traffic and quite dreary, his luck turned when he spotted Jack by the roadside. The two of them smiled, glad to see the sight of each other. Steve had apparently gone ahead all the way to Nice. So Jack and Raza trudged some more with their rucksacks, which were by now getting too heavy to carry. Along the way, Jack asked to stop for a drink. "Sure," said Raza reaching for the back pocket of his jeans. He panicked because his wallet was gone. It turned out to be payback time for Jack for all the jokes Raza had played on him before.

Jack wore a broad grin on his face. He had been walking behind and had noticed the wallet fall out of his friend's pocket, decided to pick it up and say nothing. Shame-faced and relieved, Raza just had to buy him a drink before finally making it to Nice where they eventually met up with Steve and spent a couple of days in a huge and lovely youth hostel, complete with rooms fitted with little balconies.

Steve wanted to visit where D. H. Lawrence once stayed, and Jack to see the Chapelle du Rosaire de Vence, north of Nice, which Matisse had designed in his old age, not just the stained-glass windows but the entire chapel and its contents. Jack had read his life story and told them, as they gazed at the stained-glass windows, that in 1941, Matisse, who had been living in Nice at the time, developed intestinal cancer and underwent surgery. During the long recovery, he advertised for a pretty young nurse, named Monique Bourgeois, who answered the call and took care of Matisse.

Later that evening in Nice, they went in search of a meal. The three of them wandered inside the chapel in silence, taking in what they could and vowing to return some day.

Raza, who had learnt from an earlier trip that the trick was to go three or four parallel streets behind the main seafront, the Promenade des Anglais, which was prohibitively expensive, suggested the idea and they followed him as he led them to a small family-run bistro called La Cigale, where one could eat cheaply and well, which of course they proceeded to do, ordering a steak with ratatouille and boiled potatoes, washed down with a glass of house red, after which they walked along the Promenade des Anglais, so named since Edward VII, as Prince of Wales, spent his time there in the gambling casinos. Even a coffee at the Negresco would cost them a wad of French francs. Beggars can't be choosers; Raza, Jack, and Steve decided to turn the other way and look at the sunset instead, which at least was free.

"Then Jack and Steve started to horse around on the pier, trying to make one of us lose balance and fall off down to the beach a few feet below, while I stayed my distance and watched, not wanting to getting caught up, until a tweed-suited old Englishman came up and stood next to me. 'What's the matter with those two? Are they friends of yours?' 'Yes. They are,' I told him. 'Subterfuge them or something, will you. They might do themselves some damage.' Upon hearing this bloke use of the word 'subterfuge' in this context, I thought it was rather funny."

Nice was the last place still familiar to them from previous travels since they had all been to France before. Further afoot on their planned route, none of them had visited Italy, Greece, or Turkey. Sated by the experience of Nice and its surroundings, they headed for Menton and the Italian frontier. They carried cards now reading "ROMA." Jack and Raza got a lift in a little Goggomobile from a couple of Italian priests who reminded them of Don Camillo (*The Little World of Don Camillo*)[1] and they really had to stop themselves from laughing.

"But the priests were jolly fellows and sang songs along the way like 'Ciao, ciao, bambino,' and 'Arrideverci Roma' all the way, which wasn't very far, but

---

1 Giovannino Guareschi. *The Little World of Don Camillo* (London: Penguin Books, 1970).

that was okay. We were dropped off just beyond San Marino. The day was advancing and we all had wanted to reach Pisa by the evening, but again, as in France, hitchhiking didn't prove easy. By evening, Jack and I just managed to reach the outskirts of Pisa and decided to stop for the night. We would catch up with Steve the next day because we were too tired by now and could go no further. We found a field, unpacked the sleeping bags and lay down for the night under the stars."

They must have slept well because early in the morning they were awoken by the voices and faces of some kids who were looking down on them. They were from a local little farm and with signals and gestures they invited the two back to the farm where the parents gave them some simple breakfast and a welcome cup of coffee. After thanking them, and with a warm full belly, Raza and Jack set off to catch up with Steve. He was waiting in Pisa just in time to look at the town with its famous leaning tower.

"It was at that point Jack had got a bout of diarrhea, presumably from drinking tap water, and all plans to go to Florence had to be abandoned, but somehow we got on to the autostrada for Rome. Steve had used his humor to locate it by asking passersby for the direction to 'Via Aurelia, la strada per Roma?' It worked, and by the time of the second evening in Italy, we had reached Rome. The regret remained that we had missed out seeing Florence—'shitting all the way to Rome,' as he wrote on a card to Al. Fortunately, Steve had the charcoal tablets, and there were no further problems, at least not for the moment."

Rome, the Eternal City, was a place they could not afford to miss. They stayed three nights in a youth hostel and let Steve be the guide. They needed to watch the money, so Raza remembers little except the Via Veneto where they ate ice cream and sneered at the Italian males, strutting like "peacocks," saw the Spanish Steps, and caught a mere glimpse of the Coliseum and St. Peter's before they agreed to return another day. From Rome they headed south and east towards Bari and then on to Brindisi, from where they would try to get deck passage on a ferry to Piraeus, the port of Athens. The lift all three of them got together in the same car was straight to Brindisi, avoiding the need to go via Bari.

"But I must say that this proved to be a hair-raising affair because the car was a beaten up old Italian saloon, whose driver looked like a member of the Italian Mafiosi. He was big and burly and swarthy, smoked incessantly, and talked in what sounded like Italian patois to his sidekick in the front. They stopped and asked us where we were going and Steve explained in broken Italian as best he could. 'Bene, a Brindisi,' the driver asked us to squeeze into the back seat, where it felt fairly cramped, with our rucksacks squeezed between us and wedged under our legs.

I felt awkward and nervous all the way. The man drove the car at speed and it careened along the winding road, as the two men in front laughed and talked to one another in that patois that we hitchhikers couldn't understand. At one point, the car swerved so violently that I holding a lit cigarette by the side, ended up by stubbing it inside my boot. I looked at Jack and Steve but didn't let out a sound. Finally, the driver dropped us at the port of Brindisi."

They thanked the two men and left them with a packet of Pall Malls. They carried Pall Malls all the time and found that continental people really appreciated American cigarettes. They felt okay after their ride, except for their nerves, and thought that their benefactors had probably not been gangsters but ordinary folk. It was evening and they discovered that a boat was leaving for Piraeus during the night.

"Steve negotiated deck passage, which was truculently and reluctantly agreed by the stuck-up, officious sounding purser, a short stocky man with two pips on his uniform and a black mustache. You could see how much those two little pips meant to him, and with Steve's sense of outrageous humor that could get them an easier passage than in the deck passage class, we knew we were in for an adventurous overnight trip."

The boat was a small passenger ship regularly ferrying people between Italy and Greece; most of the passengers appeared to be Greek people going home.

"We were the only English-speaking people on board, and the deck passage was very cramped with passengers. Since it was going to be an all-night journey, we scouted around for food and drink, but it appeared that the bar and restaurant were closed to deck passengers, and were reserved for first- and second-class passengers. Those traveling by deck passage were expected to have brought along their own provisions, as many regular travelers had. However, Steve insisted on going to the bar to get some food and drink."

"We can pay, so I don't see what the problem is. Look, we are hungry and thirsty and we've come a long way. We didn't buy anything at the port because we thought we could buy things on board but we didn't know they operate such a rigid class system for passengers," Steve was saying to the barman when the purser appeared from somewhere and showed us the two pips on his uniform and banned the barman from selling us anything.

"Steve mocked the man with the two pips while the barman shrugged. We hung around on that part of the boat because it was less cramped, when one of the passengers redeemed the day by buying some snacks and beers for the three of us once the purser was out of sight."

The next morning, they arrived in Piraeus and headed for Athens where Steve knew a girl from his Oxford days and partying contacts. She was engaged now and living on Mavromateon Street with her parents. Steve called her from a phone booth at the port. After the conversation, he told the other two: "Yeah, she was cool and it was okay to call around for tea and that she'd sort out some cheap accommodation for us in the meanwhile."

When they arrived at her posh apartment in a modern block on Mavromateon Street, she opened the door and kissed Steve on the cheek, shook hands with Raza and Jack. Steve was asked how he was doing and if he was still writing. He was introduced. "These are my parents."

The trio turned around and responded courteously and respectfully but couldn't help noticing the iciness of the parents.

Their daughter was engaged to a nice young Greek man and didn't want people from her Oxford past reappearing. It wasn't the thing to do. Steve's friend came to the rescue and told them there was a cheap room available for two or three days. She wrote the address down for Steve. After finishing their tea, the trio politely said goodbye and left in search of the room.

Their plan was to stay for two or three days in Athens before finding another deck passage to Izmir, where Steve had some other contacts. Directions would dictate that they should go via Thessaloniki or Salonica, and then across the Bosphorus to Istanbul. Yet, this was not an option because hitchhiking across would be virtually impossible.

It was the middle of May and they had been traveling already for about two weeks. Athens was beautiful though blanched and hot. The room they had been told about was on the second floor of an apartment block looking on to a courtyard and across to adjacent apartments. They checked in and eased their rucksacks on to the floor by their beds and started to take off their shoes, socks, and jackets. They all wanted a cold shower and agreed to take turns.

Steve had meanwhile got into his Lawrencian mode and was walking around in his T-shirt and underpants by the window looking down across a courtyard to the windows of other apartments. Raza and Jack had all passed the window and looked admiringly at the sexy-looking red-haired woman at the window opposite, smoking a cigarette and looking back coolly. Now it was Steve's turn to parade in front of the window. She just kept looking back without the flicker of any expression.

At this point there was a knock at the door. The young caretaker said that the woman opposite had asked to see one of them. All three, with Raza now out of the shower, gathered at the window again, but she pointed to Steve. Steve smiled smugly back. Jack said: "You lucky bugger," as Steve traipsed out of the room for his tryst. No one knew how long Steve would be, and they had an appointment to see Steve's friend later. Raza and Jack used the time to wash their jeans, socks, T-shirts, and underpants because they had run out of clean ones, and hung their clothes out to dry.

"There was still no sign of Steve and I started to get a bit impatient. More from the desire to explore Athens than any envy of Steve sowing his wild oats, though that did come into it, and eventually, early in the evening Steve returned to the room, showing off the scratches and love bites on his body."

Jack was more easygoing about his lateness than was Raza, and instead of going with the flow, what bugged him didn't entirely leave him but stuck in his craw, so he turned into his polite and formal mode. He wasn't being his convivial self. It certainly affected Jack. Sure he accompanied them to the Acropolis and the Parthenon, heard Jack and Steve discuss the ionic columns and how sections of columns were placed one on top of another to form a perfect column, ate ice creams in the baking sun, but Raza didn't snap out of whatever it was until they left Athens and reached Izmir. Jack even remarked about the gray cloud hanging over Athens.

Raza felt partly responsible, and realized that there was going to have to be some give and take on all sides for the rest of the journey. There was a long journey ahead, and three different individuals embarked on it together.

After three or four day, they took a deck passage on a boat to Izmir. It was a shorter and more pleasant journey than the one from Brindisi to Pitaeus. Once in Izmir, they went straight to the home of another of Steve's friend, but this time it was in a villa, surrounded by a wall with a garden all around. There were fig trees in the garden, reminding Raza what, among other things, Izmir was famous for its figs, but unfortunately, it was not the fig season.

They sat in the shade of the trees in the garden and talked and had tea with Steve's friend and the friend's father, who helped plan the route to Ankara. Then, following a welcome day of rest, they headed off for Ankara about 300 miles away to the northeast. It took a couple of days to get there. When they arrived at Ankara, there wasn't much to see, but they visited a local market and bought some very cheap sheepskin kaftans. Jack's and Raza' were sleeveless, but Steve bought a full length one with long sleeves.

"We knew that altogether the journey across Turkey was nearly a thousand miles, and that we had so far only skirted the folding mountains from Izmir to Ankara, from where our journey would descend to the Anatolian Plateau before reaching Erzurum, from where onwards we stretched a controlled military area of NATO and CENTO, circling the Soviet Union, to which Turkey belonged as an ally. Hitchhiking would be difficult. Fortunately for us three brand new sports cars, each driven by a young German, were being driven all the way to Tehran, to sell the cars there and return having made a handy profit."

They stopped and offered to give Raza, Steve, and Jack a lift all the way, which was a godsend because it was more than 1,200 kilometers to Erzurum (750 miles), the Germans said, and this would help the three to cover the distance in one go. So they settled back, one in each car. Raza was in the middle of the three cars. His young blond-haired companion didn't talk much, but Raza looked around watching the scenery, and towards early evening he could see the Anatolian Plateau open up in front of his eyes stretching, it seems, for hundreds of miles like some gigantic flat green polo pitch. As they drove on, the plateau narrowed, becoming hemmed in by mountains to the north, south, and east.

As the cars approached Erzurum, they encountered a whole line of assorted vehicles ahead of them, mostly lorries, all heading for the Iranian border. Their cars were made to stop by the military. An armed soldier in each vehicle would accompany them from here onwards. As night fell, it started to feel very cold and they were glad to have purchased their kaftans in Ankara.

A night watchman in a long black leather coat almost down to his ankles blew a whistle at intervals, steam rising from mouth after each whistle. It was that cold. There were few lights to be seen in the village. When they caught up with Steve, he started talking about how similar the scene was to one of Tolstoy's stories about the Caucuses. After passing through this village, somehow the convoy got split into two, and Steve went on in the convoy ahead.

Finally, late at night, Jack and Raza got to Erzurum. They were pointed to a dormitory where they could sleep. Steve was there, again in his T-shirt and underpants, but he wasn't laughing this time. He recounted to Jack and Raza how a lorry driver had jumped through one of the open windows and tried to sexually assault him. They all had a bit of a laugh together about his Lawrencian ways going awry this time, before closing their windows and bedding down for the night.

The next morning the Germans had gone, but then they had already informed us that they would be making an early start. The three of us decided to leave it to luck and get at least a bit of sleep. Nevertheless, we woke early, got washed, dressed, packed, and strolled out into the brilliant morning sun.

The journey across Turkey had been memorable and for another day it still promised to be eventful since this passage through Turkey where traffic flows East and West lies at a crucial geographical confluence. Raza noted the area has witnessed more than a few historical conflicts and has been ruled by Persians, Romans, Byzantines, Sassanids, Arabs, Seljuks, Mongols, Safavids, and the Turks themselves. He said this is the world he would now be traveling through and Cavify's eloquence rang in his consciousness. Alexander the Great would have gone across this area on his way East, as must have Tamerlaine traveling West.

To the north lies the eastern coast of the Black Sea with the Caucuses to the northeast. Lake Van, which Raza had read about when he had looked for species of cats, lies due south. To the northeast is Mt. Ararat, of biblical lore, where Noah's Ark is supposed to have landed.

So now the three of them stood staring in awe, and felt it a shame they didn't have time or the permission of the military authorities to stay and explore more. They only had time to appreciate the large city of Erzurum, and catch a glimpse of the mosques and architecture as they reconnoitered their way through the city with the hope of catching a lift into Iran, with the first stage being as far as Tabriz.

Eventually, they managed to find a couple of Iranian lorry drivers who agreed to take them to Tabriz. Steve went with one and Jack and Raza followed in the second lorry. They were careful to pinpoint a rendezvous location which would be near the central bus depot, where one of them would leave a message with the booking office, whichever one of them got there first.

The journey to Tabriz through the steep valleys and ravines was every bit as picturesque as the journey to Erzurum. There was only one main road winding down the mountains and valleys, first going due east before turning south. For the first time, they had an advantage since leaving France in that Raza could speak a little Farsi since he had been to Iran as a child, and understood the ways of ordinary people, who seemed friendly towards foreigners. Yet, and despite this, there was the residual anti-American and anti-British imperialism sentiments, still widespread among the masses ever since the United States/Britain instigated a coup against the Iranian government in 1953.

"I recalled Hurr Bhai talking about Dr. Mosaddegh, the prime minister, who had tried to nationalize the Iranian oil industry then owned and operated by the British. Hurr Bhai would laugh at the sheer audacity of the West. Since the coup a military dictatorship had ruled Iran, with the Shah as its figurehead."

They had entered Iran moved across Italy, Greece, and Turkey and they had to manage with a few words and simple phrases, a sign language mixed with simple English, and did this with minimal problems.

"The lorry driver who gave us a lift seemed friendly enough, and as usual we offered cigarettes and soft drinks or water along the way, in exchange for the lift. We also shared food we had purchased in Erzurum—bread, local cheese, tomatoes, and as we progressed there were passages of shade and light in the mountains and valleys."

"Then suddenly it got quite dark and we found ourselves in a deep ravine that went down and down it seemed, hidden from the sun's rays. After some time in darkness, we just as suddenly emerged into a brightly lit valley and just as suddenly had entered Iran without realizing it because the frontier checks on the Iranian side were more relaxed. Across from the sunlit valley, we looked up and high above saw ancient abandoned habitations carved in to the mountainsides, also some statues.

The driver seemed to know a little bit about them, and I could ask him questions. It was only later that we read that what we had been through were historical archaeological sites dating back to ancient Persia, and that much had been destroyed by earthquakes and conquests. I could imagine how they could be hewn into the rock faces."

It was later at night now and it was time to stop. The lorry driver took them as far as the garage. "Late. No hotel, no inn open," he explained. Raza noticed that the lorry driver was laying down his mattress by the side of the lorry. He motioned that they should do likewise. At this point, something about Steve's experience the night before alerted Raza and made him wary. He unrolled his sleeping bag a little away from the lorry driver's mattress. Unfortunately, that left Jack with no option but to unroll his sleeping bag in the only available space.

Raza must have gone easily to sleep because by the time he opened his eyes again Jack and the lorry driver were already awake. There seemed to be an awkward silence before Jack broke it by saying, "C'mon let's go," whereupon they decided to say goodbye to the lorry driver who was close by.

Raza and Jack set out in search of tea, Iranian style, which they'd both tasted across Turkey, where of course it isn't referred to as "Iranian style," any more than Turkish coffee is referred to as "Turkish coffee" in other parts of the Middle East—it's just plain tea served with sugar in small glasses, and they had grown to like it, finding it refreshing. The teahouse also served some warm bread. They both sipped on their hot tea and in between Jack began to recount his misadventures during the night.

"Well, Mr. Khan, let me tell you what a clever bastard you really are choosing your space. Man, no sooner than I had dropped off to sleep than I felt a hand groping inside my sleeping bag. I really felt awkward and didn't want to make a fuss, so I just curled up to avoid the driver's groping hand going any further." Raza smiled kindly but felt hurt on hearing his friend's predicament. He was aware from childhood that homosexual activities are quite common in male-dominated societies. He had not meant to play another prank on his friend this time. "Sorry Jack, I was just trying to avoid any Steve-like situation developing," Raza replied. After another cup of tea, they decided to keep their date with Steve and took a bus for Tabriz.

They had read the guidebook according to which Tabriz, the regional capital of Iranian Azerbaijan was the fourth largest city in Iran, after Tehran, Mashhad, and Isfahan. It had once served as the capital. Located in a valley, it is famous for its huge covered historic bazaar, which they explored after meeting up with Steve at the central bus depot. As in most Iranian cities, the bazaar is famous for carpets and carpet houses intersperse with shops displaying brass and silver ornaments and decorations. The three started to feel hungry.

"In my halting Farsi, I searched for a cheap restaurant to eat in and catch up with Steve. Along the way, it turned out that unlike Jack and Steve I had a fairly uneventful journey through the bazaar, and was mightily relieved to see them. Soon they arrived at the small restaurant, located in a corner of the bazaar. I had to become an interpreter and a translator. Realizing they needed to eat substantially but economically, I dug into early memories of previous sojourns I had in Iran, and ordered some plain rice, kofteh (lamb) kebabs, grilled tomatoes, and bread.

In my father's opinion, and he ought to know, Iranians were the best cooks of rice. According to him, the test for perfectly cooked rice is that when you place a small saucer on top of the rice, and then lift it off, the mound of rice would rise up again. Another idea was to order some butter and a raw egg with the rice. Their mouths watered in anticipation the more I described to them what my father had said."

"I often get carried away with talking about recipes. Eventually the steaming rice and the grilled tomatoes and the kofteh and the butter and the raw egg in its shell all arrived just as they had been ordered. Watching as I put a knob of butter on top of the rice, break the egg on top and then proceed to mix it all together with a fork and spoon, Jack and Steve followed suit. For many of the poorer ordinary Iranians that is a meal sufficient unto itself, but we had the added luxury of the grilled tomatoes, the kofteh, and the bread. With it we drank some 'doogh' what can only be described as savory buttermilk. It was the first full meal we had in a long while. Our usual fare had been snacks since entering Turkey."

Then in the afternoon Raza set off for Tehran where a friend of Raza's father, who his father had introduced him to in London, was now living in Tehran, serving as the regional director of UNFAO (Food and Agriculture Organization of the United Nations). As promised, his father had already alerted his friends that his son and two friends were traveling through Tehran to India, and might call.

They couldn't decide on the best way to get to the sprawling city of Tehran. First they thought of sharing a taxi, which was supposed to work out to be really cheap, according to the guide, because of the price of petrol in Iran. Then, thinking about the distance to Tehran, they decided they would prefer to travel second class by train, which would allow them to stretch their legs a little. The overnight train would get them to Tehran the next morning, and this would avoid the hassle of trying to find somewhere to sleep for the night.

Accordingly, they arrived in Tehran in the early morning and decided to head for the house of Raza's father's friends, Agha and Begum Mohammad Mustafa. Tehran was an even larger city. The train station was in the southwestern part and since Raza couldn't remember much of the city they decided to hail a taxi, and headed for the house of their hosts. Threading through the traffic in the bustling parts of the city, the taxi arrived in one of the wide tree-lined boulevards in the wealthier part of Tehran.

The taxi knew where he was going, and arrived at a gated villa and handed Raza's passport to the gatekeeper, who phoned the villa from his cabin and let the taxi through. A servant opened the door to let Raza and his companions out, before swiftly collecting their rucksacks and leading them into the villa, where he handed them over to another bowing and saluting servant who led them to where their hosts were sitting.

Raza bowed to Agha and Begum Mustafa, who turned their heads in acknowledgement, before doing the same with Steve and Jack who shook their hands. "We have been expecting you. How has your journey been? I must say this is a very brave and adventurous thing you're doing. You must tell me and my husband all about it," said Begum Mustafa, "but I expect you must be hungry." "Actually, we would like to clean up and get changed first," Raza said. Agha Mustafa looked older to Raza than when he last saw him, but obviously not ready for retirement.

His regime was to get up early in the summer months and go to the office. His diary was generally full. "Well, Raza, you may not see much of me but my wife will advise on anything that you and your friends might want to do," said Agha Mustafa as he picked up his papers from the table and disappeared through the main door and into his chauffeur-driven limo. The three were then shown to their room, where they went through the routine of unpacking, showering, and getting dressed. When they came down for breakfast, they had a polite conversation with Begum Mustafa who sat with them at the table.

There were fresh fruit, cereals, toast and boiled eggs laid out for breakfast, followed by freshly made coffee. After Raza had recounted some of their adventures, Begum Mustafa helped plan the rest of their journey through Iran and on to Karachi. The route Raza once followed with his family in Iran had taken them back to India via Zahedan in the southeast corner of the country and into the northwest corner of Pakistan, but he did not want to go that way because it would be lengthy and difficult. Unfortunately, they would miss Isfahan because it would be slightly off the route as well. It seemed the best route would be to take a train to Khorramshahr in the Persian Gulf. This was the route suggested by his host Begum Mustafa: "The train journey will take about ten hours, so you'd better go prepared. I will get the servants to pack a bottle of drinking water, some fruit and nuts. The train will take you to the port of Khorramshahr at the border with Iraq. Otherwise it doesn't pass through anything but the flat countryside with villages and small towns, mixed with patches of desert. At Khorramshahr you can catch a P&O ship going to Karachi."

"After we had finished our breakfast, she asked whether we wanted to see or do anything in Tehran. 'We just want to take it easy and see things,' said Raza, 'Maybe browse around and look at shops.' 'Well, I'm going shortly so I can give you a lift,' offered Begum Mustafa, 'you can find your own way back to the house, and join us for supper,' she suggested. 'And, since Steve wants to drop in at the American School, I could drop you all there first.'"

While Steve went off to the American School to ask about the job for which he had previously applied, Jack and Raza wandered around central bazaar looking at bookshops. suggested by their hosts. They had agreed to meet Steve later in the Park-e-Mellat another recommended spot.

After lunch, they took a further stroll in the park. There were a lot of young Iranians, boys and girls, flirting and showing off. They watched the scene in the afternoon sun for a while and then decided to go back and rest before dinner.

CHAPTER 19

NAWAB DAWOOD AHMAD IN PAKISTAN

The next day, after thanking their hosts, they left for the Tehran railway station once again and bought three second-class tickets to Khorramshahr. Raza enquired about times of departure. They didn't want to arrive late in the evening because then they would have the problem of going to find somewhere to sleep, so they decided one that left in the midafternoon, a slower train that would arrive round about 7:30 the next morning. They whiled away the remaining time by buying some additional provisions, a copy of *TIME* magazine and a dated English newspaper, having a bite to eat and chatting and laughing, until the train pulled in and they went to board it early to try and find themselves some seats together.

By the time the train left there weren't too many passengers. Noticing that they were foreigners, most of those with families went to look for other carriages. Only one person, an old man, sat in their carriage. It was a long and uneventful journey with not much to see. They read, chatted, played cards, and napped.

"Disembarking from the train at Khorramshahr, we searched out the port and bought deck passage on the ship that was bound for Karachi. Most of the deck passengers were Indian and Pakistani workers returning home from the Gulf. The boat was overcrowded, with people lying everywhere on sacks and bundles of clothing, and grabbing whatever space that was still available. Flies were everywhere, landing on bowls of rice that some of the passengers were eating."

The boys from London managed to squeeze themselves into what was going to be their transport for a whole day and a night. The boat seemed to be at anchor for a long time. Steve was feeling hot and decided to jump into the waters of the Gulf for a swim. Raza said it was like swimming in soup. People on board looked on at this madness, and one of the officers started getting annoyed. To preempt things, Jack pointed at the water and shouted "Shark!" That did it, even though he knew it to be untrue.

Eventually they were off. Feeling cramped, Steve strolled up to the main deck and spied the Scottish captain at his table with invited guests. He tried reasoning with him to get himself and his companions invited. "We can pay for our meal," he told the Scottish captain to no avail. They were stuck with eating fly-infested boiled rice and daal and vegetables that the deck passengers were given. A photograph that Steve took shows that Raza had lost a lot of weight since leaving London, his beard had grown again and his hair was longer.

They mixed with their fellow passengers, Pakistani mostly, who recognized that Raza was from the subcontinent, and spoke Urdu. By his accent, they could tell he wasn't a commoner and showed him and his friends some respect, making room for them to stretch. Most of the passengers were people who had traveled to Iraq or Iran to make money. Before they eventually got off the ship at Karachi, one of the passengers asked if Raza would mind going through customs with one of the gold watches he had bought, to help him to avoid paying a customs duty.

He agreed. His uncle had sent a car to meet them at Karachi harbor. The passenger whose extra watch Raza was carrying realized what family he came from when it was announced by the immigration officer that a car sent by the nawab of Amadabad was waiting for him. Raza gave the watch back to the passenger once he had come through customs, and waved back to him as he, Jack, and Steve walked to the car. He didn't recognize the driver, but soon he realized they were nearly at Raza's home.

They were driven in one of his uncle's cars across Clifton Bridge, where his uncle's two familiar adjacent houses were located. These two houses, Raza explained, were the houses his uncle had purchased from money generated by Amadabad Estate before partition, the same two houses that he was later going to give to his daughters. They were both two-storied, one slightly larger than the other. It would be the larger one to be used for his two daughters and sons-in-law. Apparently, they had been living there ever since leaving Iraq. By now there were several grandchildren too, nephews mostly, whose births Raza had heard about but whom he had never met.

"The oldest of these, Maysam, was 8. He and Jaun, the two older sons of Zainab Baji and Hurr Bhai, were attending Clifton Nursery, while their youngest, Qais, as well as Shabbir, Husain Bhai's son, were only toddlers, to be found either with their mothers or with servants outside. I didn't have too many memories of any of them. My stay in Karachi, in any case, was brief—just four days. Jack and Steve now followed the familiar ritual they had learnt to follow in Tehran: after greeting us, my uncle suggested we go and take a shower. We certainly felt filthy and sweaty enough from the boat passage, and were relieved to have the luxury of a shower and clean clothes."

After they had been shown to their room by one of the old servants from Amadabad, who Raza remembered, they unpacked, showered, changed, and emerged into the seating area to find Raza's two older cousins, Hurr and Husain. Raza wasn't sure what they would make of him and his friends, but Raza did take note that his older cousins showed respect for his maturity and the spirit of adventure the friends had shown. He took some reassurances from the fact that he didn't need to feel like a prodigal son returning home, albeit one who wasted years and had not yet completed his education.

"In all we spent a few days in Karachi and I stayed mostly in the house with the family, while Jack and Steve, respecting the little time I had, discreetly found things to explore in Karachi. In any case, my female cousins kept strict *purdah*, and at meal times I would be expected to eat with the family, though this did not mean that Jack and Steve would be made to feel left out. A separate table in the male quarter was laid for them where one of my male cousins sat and ate with them but they had their own spirit of adventure, including the need for a drink of beer, which they hadn't touched since leaving Izmir."

When Raza, and his friends were not otherwise busy, Hurr and Husain engaged them in conversation. Hurr Bhai, who had studied under Bertrand Russell, was quite a logical positivist at the time. He was intrigued by Raza's friends and asked them what ideas they were interested in. Jack, who had been picking up ideas about mysticism, started to talk about a blade of grass, and how the water rises up inside of it, or something abstruse like that, leading to a lot of banter. On another occasion, Husain Bhai also made sure of showing them around Karachi in his car, which enabled Jack and Steve to get an idea of the lay of the land.

It was only later, after they had left Karachi, that they told Raza what they had got up to. Going to look for dope in the streets of Karachi, they had come across this man sitting selling hashish. "Man, it was the size of a golf ball. We bought it and got stoned," Jack was eager to note. Steve was much more in control of himself, and smiling, added: "Yeah, Jack was so stoned that he thought that a dry leaf rustling along the pavement was a frog and tried to follow it." He went on to describe how Jack would suddenly sit down and started saying: "I'm going to draw a Mountie. I'm going to give him a hat and gun." Then, picking up a piece of coal he found on the pavement, he proceeded to draw and had to be restrained by Steve and led to a tea shop to sober up.

Raza's uncle asked Raza to recite a salaam at a majlis in Karachi on the same day when Hurr Bhai was going to recite from one of the marsiyas that he had been composing. Raza knew it would please his uncle, who had suggested Raza recite a salaam that his father had written, so he readily agreed. But he was nervous at the same time; he hadn't recited for so long, at least not in front of a gathering. In 1950, he had brought along a two-volume edition of the marsiyas of Mir Anis to London when he arrived.

There they stood as Raza pointed them to me. He had gone on to explain that during the days of mourning he would open and read one of the appropriate marsiyas to himself each year, and so he was familiar with them. Then, during visits home for holidays, he had brought back notebooks of handwritten Salaams, Rubaiyat and Nauhas, some of them by his father, to read and remember the days of mourning, what they meant and signified. There still seemed no conflict within him between his increasingly progressive politics and religion.

"No, that came later with my reading of Lenin on socialism and pan-Islamism," Raza talked about this when he and I had a discussion in New York. "I hadn't recited marsiyas for some time," Raza continued, "and so I spent a few occasions learning and reciting it in front of my uncle and cousins. On the day itself, I somehow managed to recite at the majlis. My uncle and Hurr Bhai seemed pleased with my recital, and that I had used my voice and eyes to emote, rather than the flailing gestures with arms as more prosaic performers recite." In fact, he demonstrated what he meant by reciting a few couplets in London.

NAWAB DAWOOD AHMAD

Raza didn't see much of his uncle during his stay, because most of his time was taken up with meeting politicians and important businessmen, keeping in touch with current affairs in East and West Pakistan—there was no Bangladesh at the time—and specifically, paying attention to the shifts in balance between civilian and military rule.

"The military has always been a dominant force in politics, unlike in India. Although the Awami League had swept to power during the legislative elections of 1954, when the nawab was still in Iraq, and its leader, Husain Suhrawarfy, had gone on to become the country's first Bengali prime minister, two years later, the promulgation of the Constitution declaring Pakistan to be an Islamic Republic, and making Sikandar Mirza its first president. Sikandar Mirza soon went on to stall the republic and impose military rule, appointing General Ayub Khan as its enforcer.

As irony would have it, only two weeks later, Ayub Khan declared martial law, and ousted Sikandar Mirza. This was the furnace in which the nawab found himself and it was a furnace that he had inadvertently help create by his rash speech in 1942, which he had regretted ever since, while continuing to financially support the Muslim League from the immense wealth of Amadabad."

"As the last remaining member of the triumvirate that had led to the foundation of Pakistan, he was well recognized and respected, even though he had ruled out any political position. Jinnah, who had adopted him more or less as a son, had died barely 13 months after independence."

"Liaquat Ali Khan, the first Pakistani prime minister, had been assassinated three years later in 1951, very shortly after the nawab had left India for Pakistan. This had been a hammer blow, and the uncertainties about things to come had led him to leave for Iraq. Ever since his return from Iraq, following a military takeover there, he was careful not to ruffle any feathers among the new rulers of Pakistan. He remained on good terms with Sikandar Mirza."

In turn the generals still needed to keep civilian leaders including the nawab, as well as businessmen, the Iranis, on side. He was in a game of chess where any move could be decisive. Simultaneously, his brother, Raza's dad, kept him informed about the affairs of Amadabad. The people excluded from these concerns were the younger generation. Hurr Bhai must have sensed something, and though he could be outspoken, he mentioned nothing significant to Raza, who treated his uncle's being preoccupied as a normal phenomenon, as something he'd been used to from childhood. Now, older and more politically aware, he was nevertheless none the wiser about it.

As a result of his uncle being frequently occupied with visiting friends, politicians, contacts, and visitors in his office, Raza saw more of Hurr Bhai. At times Hurr confided to Raza that he had found it impossible to work at the university because of conditions of work, the nepotism and the "promotion of stupidity." He laughed. "You know Raza, I would be so happy to find work at an English university, but what can I do? My father-in-law would never tolerate his daughter living in London. I couldn't and wouldn't go without my wife and children."

Then, suddenly, the travelers' time in Karachi was over. Raza said his farewells to the Pakistani side of his family who in turn asked him to convey their love and respects to the Indian side of the family. The parting was quite emotional because the family was split between two countries that used to be one and the same.

"But my uncle never showed his emotions. There was just a slight change in the voice or look in the eye, which said everything. I had already said goodbye to my female cousins, and as is the custom, they had tied an *imam zamin* on my right arm. When I came from the zanana, I explained to Jack and Steve that the ribbon contained a small coin which was supposed to be given to poor people or servants in the household after one had arrived safely at journey's end. Then it was Jack and Steve's turn to thank them all, and then off we went by train to Lahore, where my uncle had arranged for them to be met by a family member who was one of the former Amadabad *tahsildars* [tax officer]."

They boarded the train at Karachi Cantonment. Raza's uncle had made first-class reservations for them on the Karachi Express due to leave in the late afternoon, arriving at Lahore Junction early the next morning. Along the way it was scheduled to make a number of stops, the first being Hyderabad, still in Sindh. After that they saw nothing, as the sunsets are so much quicker near the equator than in northern countries. They saw little of the rest of the countryside because they slept soon afterwards.

"A funny thing happened when getting off at Lahore Junction, because we were met on the platform by a man who recognized me but whom I had difficulty in remembering. He had come to drive us to his house, a small villa in one of the leafier suburbs of the city."

They were all treated very nicely, but the man felt uncomfortable about speaking English. He largely addressed himself to Raza in Urdu. He knew that Raza would translate for his companions. "Raza Mian, I don't think you remember me but I used to live in Amadabad. I am so pleased to see you. I know that you're not staying long because Nawab Sahab has asked me to make a reservation on the train to Delhi and buy your tickets. Don't worry, he has sent me the money. The travel time will be about the same as between Karachi and here.

The train will leave Lahore in the evening and go via Amritsar to Delhi. In the meanwhile, you have a whole day to rest. Please treat this as your own home." With that he left, asking a servant along the way to make sure their room was clean and provided with cold drinking water and towels.

At noon there was a knock on their door; a servant had come to ask whether they would like to eat. His master had gone to the office and would be back at five. Raza said to the effect, "We don't want to cause any inconvenience, but we'll have anything that can be prepared." The meal was simple but tasty and since they were all hungry, they helped themselves to chana daal and rice, dug into the kababs and parathas, and washed it down with homemade lemonade.

"*Shukria*," attempted Steve and Jack, smiling. The master of the house returned and knocked at their door. "Everything alright? I am just going to clean up a bit and then take you to the station."

"What could we all say but thank you?" Raza gave the servant 10 Pakistani Rupees for his troubles as he helped place their rucksacks in the boot of the car before the master of the house, whose name Raza is still unable to remember, drove them to the station and made sure that a *quli* (an unskilled worker) would lead them to their reserved seats. He then tied an *imam zamin* on to Raza's right arm and embraced him before waving goodbye to Jack and Steve.

They were on the final leg of their odyssey and due to arrive at Delhi the next morning, before going on to Lucknow. It was just as well that reservations had been made all the way since the journey from Lahore to Amritsar was crowded with relatives, old friends, and neighbors crossing and recrossing the 17 miles that separate the people from the two Punjabs.

Relations between the two countries that occasionally flare up were fairly stable at the time. At the border and before reaching Amritsar, immigration officials from both sides boarded the train and asked for passports to be examined. Jack and Steve's passports were just looked at and passed back to them without much fuss. Raza's passport was scrutinized on both sides since he was carrying an Indian passport but bore a Muslim name.

This was followed by another experience of top-heavy bureaucracy in the subcontinent when it came to their rucksack's being examined by customs. It is a fact of life, and the only way to hasten the process is if you know someone high up in officialdom, and they can ease your passage through.

This time, as it happens, they were rescued just as they began to think they might miss their connection. The people in Lahore must have sent out a message to people they knew on both the Indian and the Pakistani side, which in itself shows an interesting dimension to the matter of partition. Punjab was one unified province before independence and partition, speaking the same language and Hindus, Muslims, and Sikhs mingling quite amicably as one people. Many of these relations were maintained and continued.

Just as Raza was beginning to unpack all the contents of his rucksack, someone came over and spoke to the official dealing with him and Raza was told it was alright and that he could go right through. This happened on both sides of the border control. Raza thanked his lucky stars, or rather his family's contacts.

Jack and Steve took in the experience of traveling by train in the subcontinent with yawns and a look at the watch. Raza could share their frustration and anger at the frequent delays and sudden stops, having experienced it before himself. However, on this occasion, they could experience it from the comfort of first-class conditions, while Raza regaled them with stories about Indian trains and their notorious lateness.

"One story goes," he said, turning to Jack and Steve, that during the British Raj an English officer traveling to Bombay was compelled to call for the conductor to explain why the train had stopped in the middle of nowhere? "Sorry Sahib, but there is a cow on the line," came the reply. The officer harrumphed and sat back. After a delay of about 15 minutes, the train got going again. Then after another few minutes, the train suddenly came to a juddering stop. Exasperated, the English officer called for the conductor and asked why the train had stopped this time? "Surely, not another cow?" "No, Sahib," came the reply, "it is the same cow."

"Fortunately, on this occasion the train was reasonably on time, arriving at the grand building of Charbagh Station, Lucknow. My father had sent a car with my youngest brother [Jafar], now in his ninth year, accompanied by a secretary and a driver to fetch them. *Qulis* milled around, shouting 'Sahib' and jostling to grab people's luggage to earn a tip. They had to be shooed away by the secretary because we all were only carrying rucksacks, which were then grabbed from their hands by Jafar, the secretary, and the driver, to the waiting car, as we followed them through the vast dark hall, milling with people, before emerging into the harsh light of the sun to where the car was parked."

The car followed a route familiar to Raza: from the station, in the old part of Lucknow, down a straight road leading to the center of town. "There was Hazratganj, full of cars, busses, lorries, tongas, rickshaws, pedestrians and the ubiquitous cattle, and then turning into a narrower road to the left, and going down toward Aminabad Circus, and turning left into Kaiserbagh. Not much seemed to have changed over the years since I'd first left for London, as I tried to explain to my startled companions. In the heat of the mid-July sun, the driver honked the car horn all the way."

As the car turned into Kaiserbagh, Raza pointed out the library, named after his great-grandfather, before the car turned left at the next turning by the Baradari and entered the gate of Raza's childhood home, still guarded by a sentry, the last remaining Gurkha sepoy from the battalion that had been based by the side of the palace at Amadabad during the war. He had never wanted to return to Nepal and now saluted the people in the car as it went down the drive and parked by the front porch under which some of the family cars were usually parked to keep them from baking in the sun. The palace was a long, two-storied, yellow-painted mansion, with green-painted window frames. It stretched for about a hundred meters.

"As the car came to a halt, several servants and retainers dressed in white stood up and bowed in salaams, staring at the two Westerners, one of them with red hair. They weren't used to seeing foreigners with white faces, and certainly not ones with red hair, not since the Brits left. I knew Jack's red hair and beard would be a particular magnet for their gaze. One of the secretaries told them to stop staring and go forward and lend a hand."

With Raza showing the way and accompanied by Jafar and the father's secretary, they entered the cool marble hall. They went up the wide staircase of white marble to the first floor where Jafar informed them that accommodation had been prepared for them. Raza's father had arranged for Jack and Steve to stay in the large *Araam* chamber, and for Raza to stay in the semicircular porch room at the side. Both rooms had their own bathrooms. From Jack and Steve's reactions, Raza could tell that they were suitably impressed.

While the luggage, such as it was, was being taken to their respective rooms, Raza took his friends to meet his father, who had emerged from his room on hearing that they had arrived. Raza bowed and rushed to embrace his father. Then, as Jack and Steve approached, he introduced his friends to them. "Oh, so you are Jack, and you are Steve. How nice to meet you. Do sit down." Jack and Steve leant forward and shook hands before sitting down around the table in the verandah.

"Should I order some tea? Or, would you like something cold? Something like our version of lemonade perhaps?" "Some lemonade would be very nice," said Steve gallantly. So lemonade was ordered and some small conversation ensued. Jafar, in the meanwhile, had disappeared into his room out of shyness about speaking English, and Raza had rushed off to greet his mother and sister.

Raza's father was always polite, courteous, and finely attired. He looked with restrained curiosity at Raza's friends. They drank their lemonade, and answered questions about what they did in England. "Oh my," or "How interesting," came the response from the father. "You must visit the amazing maze in the Jama Masjid. There's a museum nearby too with a collection of ancient statues. Of course, I can arrange for you to stay in a village. Raza, as you call him, has already told me about it.

You can still buy good quality drawing paper in Hazratganj because of our art school here in Lucknow, and Raza knew an Indian artist. You must excuse me now. I see that you have finished your drinks. We'll talk again later," he said, rising from his chair. Steve and Jack got up at the same time and bowed before an attendant showed them to their room.

The room had a very high ceiling to keep it dark and cool. It was also very large with a bay window at one end, looking down onto a courtyard, and meshed doors at the other end, to keep out insects and mosquitoes. These doors led out to a seating area from where you could see across to a park and the mansions occupied by other members of the nobility. This was altogether another world compared to anything they'd seen before.

It was now mid-July and very hot, with the monsoons soon to come. Rather than being in Lucknow at the beginning of the mango season, as Raza had originally planned, it was now the end of the mango season, and they planned to stay in India for about four weeks. They were well aware that poverty tourism is all the rage in global India.

"Steve wanted to go to Rishikesh, the City of Temples, in Uttarkhand, where Allen Ginsberg and the beatniks had been recently. Jack and Steve also wanted to experience the life of a villager. And, then, of course there was Amadabad, which meant there was still quite a lot to take in, which meant I had to organize itineraries before my father left for Bombay and attend to his law practice. I remembered my father was in the habit of taking breaks, particularly during Moharram, and of course he had to keep an eye on things and keep the family tradition going."

But for now, Raza, Steve, and Jack were going to take some much-needed rest before giving serious thought to their future plans. Those present at the time among the immediate members of the family, besides his parents, sister, and Jafar, included his paternal and maternal aunts, Qasim Bhai, and the teenage Shaikhoo, among other male relatives, and three female cousins. All the women observed strict purdah, which involved some practical arrangements as far as eating was concerned.

The father had taken care of these arrangements while he was still there by organizing some meal times when he would eat with Jack and Steve in the large dining room downstairs. At other times, Jack and Steve would go out to see and do things, and later eat on their own. They expected Raza to spend time with his mother and sister since he hadn't seen them for some time. Jafar wasn't yet 9 years old and, as mentioned, was very shy about his English. Qasim Bhai was studying medicine at Lucknow University and Shaikhoo, who was in his 16th year, was still at the Martiniere, and spent his time at home with assorted friends. He came to say his *adaabs* to his elder cousin, of course, and was also introduced to his foreign friends.

"Even though Shaikhoo smiled nicely but behind the mask he had already come under the influence of one of the secretaries. This hypocrisy was always going to be the case given the absence of his father. To tell the truth, it was not as though the nawab spent much quality time with his family. As a matter of fact,

Shaikhoo was much more in awe of his uncle, and would have been shattered if anyone had advised that he receive adult guidance from anyone else.

Apart from the obligatory round of paying respects to adult members of the family, Shaikhoo kept away from my side of the family. My mother said as much to me one day: 'But your father still maintains his loyalty to his brother and his brother's family. You mark my words. Why do you think I agreed to let you go away that far? Just finish your education, come back and find a job, get married, buy a nice house, and I will come and stay with you.'"

The relationship between Raza and his mother had become closer and of course she always found him gentle and tender. But to get back to Shaikhoo, according to Abid, he had heard that the said secretary was rumored to have warned Shaikhoo against consorting and getting too friendly with Raza and Abid. Shaikhoo's own tutor had told Abid this, describing Ibn Dawood to be a young man who wore even more masks than his own father. [COMP: insert chart names of family]

The only other person who would enjoy meeting Jack and Steve would be his distant cousin Hashim Bhai, who lived in another part of the city, across the Gomti River, in a suburb called "New Hyderabad." Raza thought of him because he was so urbane and relaxed. Raza decided to telephone and let him know that they were already in Lucknow.

"On the first day, after Jack and Steve had settled in, I dropped in to see them on the way back from mother's quarters. Jack and Steve had meanwhile undressed into their T-shirts and shorts and were obviously enjoying themselves. Seeing them, I suddenly got a mad idea: to have my head shaved, as I did in childhood. I mentioned this to Jack and Steve, and Steve jumped at the idea. We would all have our heads shaved. The visit to the barber was fixed for the next day. I mentioned this to my father as we sat down for lunch, and my father just laughed and thought it all a bit peculiar."

Raza knew, as he showed Jack and Steve to the main dining room, that lunch would be good though not particularly special because it was Moharram. Certain dishes associated with 'Eid or weddings could not be prepared. The dining room was on the ground floor behind the front porch. It was cool and dark and restful to eyes dazzled by the blazing hot outdoors. It had a black marble floor, and a long dining table on which the soft light from the chandeliers shone down. The table was meant to seat 16 people, but that day it had been laid for eight people, just half the number. The father had invited one or two English speakers, unknown to them, while

Shaikhoo had gone to Amadabad for Moharram, accompanying his mother and Qasim to his paternal family's estate.

The father introduced everyone before he ordered the lunch: "*Koi Hai*," he said in a loud voice, and a servant attending in the background stepped forward bowed and said, "*Ji Sarkar.*" "*Khana lao*," meaning "bring the food." Shortly, afterwards, Kalloo, the chef who had prepared European cuisine for Raza's family ever since being retained by the father as his personal chef, appeared holding a tray, accompanied by another tray-bearing attendant. The European course would be served first. Kalloo had prepared on this occasion some goujons of freshly caught river fish, tartare sauce, mixed salad, and fries.

"The Indian course that followed included shami kebabs, chicken pulao, saada saalan (a kind of beef curry in a rich gravy), masoor daal, plain rice, fried potato bhujia and of course chapatis and accompaniment of chutneys. There were jugs of iced water and freshly made lemonade. For dessert, fresh ripe mangoes that were still in season had been placed in a large silver fruit bowl and packed with ice cubes at one end of the table. I could tell from the conversation that Jack and Steve had really appreciated the food. They had certainly never tasted Indian food like this in England."

Raza was happy for his friends but toward the end of the meal he couldn't quite resist playing one of his silly pranks on Jack. It went something like this: he had told Jack along the way about manners and customs in India, and that, in order to express one's appreciation, one was expected to belch aloud, rub one's belly and say "*bakra hazam*," which literally translates as "the goat has been digested." So when he thought it was the appropriate time, Jack looked all around, smiled, patted his belly, belched loudly, and uttered the mantra he had been taught by Raza: "*bakra hazam*." Raza's father's reaction was to look askance at Raza, as if to say, "What kind of a simple-minded friend have you brought along with you?" Hashim Bhai laughed. He had looked forward to meeting his young cousin Raza and his companions tomorrow after they had returned from Amadabad.

In the morning, they all went into a barber's shop in Hazratganj, the main European-style high street in Lucknow, in order to have their heads shaved. They must have stood out as odd foreigners—Jack in particular, with his red hair. Even Raza who had not been seen around for some time stood out. After the three emerged from the barber's, one can imagine they stood out even more. Back at the palace people tried to look away and not notice. Perhaps they laughed. Raza's parents dismissed it as eccentricity. The fun really began when Jack and Steve returned to their room. When Raza, having been to his mother's quarter, went to see Jack and Steve, he found Steve miming to a servant that a wasp had bitten him on his shaven head.

The servant spoke no English and Steve started making the sound of a buzzing bee, while miming with his finger the actions of its circular descent, bang onto the center of his head and "ping" went the finger. Raza intervened and told the dumbstruck servant to go find some medication to daub on to the spot.

After a couple more days in Lucknow, they left for Amadabad by car. Along the gravel road to Amadabad, the length of which is straddled here and there with villages, the father had arranged for Jack and Steve to stay in the house of a village elder, while Raza went on to join the family for the most important days of religious mourning and to participate in the rites and rituals that went with them.

Jack and Steve stayed in the village for three or four days, trying to observe the daily life of the villagers, as Gauguin might have done in Tahiti, or Lawrence in New Mexico. Jack had taken along drawing paper and pencils purchased in Lucknow, and made some pencil drawings of village life. There was a down side to life in an Indian village: apart from flies and not being able to speak the language, they didn't mind going to the toilets in the field so much as the simple lack of personal privacy. Whether they were washing and shaving, or Jack doing his drawings or whatever, dozens of pairs of eyes always seemed to be watching. The curiosity was understandable. The villagers had never seen foreigners before, but in the end the stay was as long as they could take, and they were glad to be moving on.

"Arrangements had been made for Jack and Steve to be picked upon the 10th of Moharram, Ashura, and brought to the palace. I had already told them about the significance of the day for my family: it was the day of the Martyrdom of Imam Husain and almost all of his male relatives and followers. On this particular day of Ashura, a room opening out on to the famed red verandah had been prepared for Jack and Steve. They arrived late in the afternoon, the car driving through the arch of the front gate and parking under the porch by my father's rooms.

From there they were escorted across the marble floor where the billiards table stood, up a red-colored staircase overlooked by a large mirror, and out into the late rays of the sun which was making patterns across the red floor. There was silence across the male section of the palace. This was the time of the burial of the coffins, and my father and Shaikhoo, together with retainers, attendants, and servants had all gone to the replica shrines, built by the family's ancestors."

"The only sounds were emerging from the women's section, wailing and crying, and the pandemonium of the parrots gathering to roost in the tree branches. Jack and Steve walked on to the verandah to survey the scene. The verandah was open on three sides to the breeze that kept it cool and was a marvel of invention. At any rate, Jack and Steve had stationed themselves on the red verandah to survey on this occasion the scene of the family cars arriving just before dark."

"I, dressed in a black kurta and white Indian pyjamas, carrying an unbuckled sword now sheathed, emerge from one of the cars and acknowledged them. A message had been sent that I would come and see them soon, after I had broken the ritual fast and drunk some water. On the day of Ashura, one is not supposed to drink any water from the moment one awakes until the burial. It is a ritual among Shi'as in recognition of what befell the camp of Imam Husain: it was deprived of water for three days."

Raza came to see them briefly to make sure that they were being looked after as well as to explain to them what was going to happen that night. The night of Ashura, a short majlis takes place in the zenana in the dark, without any lights except the moon and stars. Women loosen their hair and follow a plain coffin or *taboot*, draped in a plain black cloth, overlaid by a wreath of white flowers. It is then carried out of the zenana by male members of the family carrying a naked sword in one hand, and is taken up the steps of the Baradari.

The "Alam," or standard of Tamerlaine, which has been in the possession of the family and occupies a central place in their home, is then brought forward and leads the coffin; as it goes down the steps, it winds its way via the porch toward the front gate and back to the replica shrine of Imam Husain at Karbala. Strangers must find the whole occasion dramatic, as mourners walk behind the coffin chanting and beating their breasts in rhythm. Raza could see from amid the procession as it went pass the porch that Jack and Steve were standing on the red verandah watching and beating their breasts in harmony.

They stayed on in the palace for a couple of days, spending their time looking around the huge family library and browsing rows of shelves, stacked neatly with books in English. The English literature section was what interested them most. Here books by Chaucer, Milton, and Shakespeare through to books published in the 1950s could be found. Jack and Steve were again impressed. After lunch the next day, seated in the red verandah, Jack and Steve related their experiences to Raza.

The downside of it—the lack of privacy and being treated as objects of curiosity—was soon forgotten. Jack produced some pencil drawings of life in the village, the cattle lying around near the mud houses, peasant women washing clothes in a small pond, an old man standing and washing down his body with a bucket of water. Sitting there, Jack then proceeded to draw a pencil portrait of Raza, which Raza had kept until a few years ago, when it got left behind with some other stuff during his last move.

They said farewell to the palace and returned to Lucknow. Jack and Steve witnessed at firsthand what Raza's life must have been like, but to them their friend remained the same person in Amadabad as the one they had got to know in London, only with another dimension to him.

CHAPTER 20

BOMBAY ITINERARY

Raza's father then left for Bombay to return to his practice, with an understanding that his son would come and stay with him for a few days. Meanwhile, Raza discovered that he had a tapeworm living in his guts. That he had lost weight on the boat to Karachi was true, something his parents remarked on several times, but no matter how much he ate he couldn't put on any weight.

He noticed that when he went to the toilet, he could feel the wriggly sections of the parasite emerge. The family doctor called and prescribed a few drops of medicine to be taken regularly. It was essential for the head of the tapeworm to come out, otherwise the segments would continue to grow. Steve meanwhile had decided to go to Rishikesh for about a week, while Jack stayed behind with Raza and to do some drawings at the museum.

Raza found time to finish the tome by Romain Roland and Jack asked to borrow it. One day Raza got quite fed up with the tapeworm and took a double dose of the medicine to finally get rid of the persistent parasite, and thought no more about it and went with Jack to a bookshop in Hazratganj. Suddenly, he felt his body seized by a gripping pain and knew that he had to find a toilet. He called Jack who hurriedly called the chauffeur and rushed Raza back, climbed the stairs and back to the bathroom. He was suffering from acute diarrhea and realized he had finally got rid of the tapeworm's head; the double dose had done the trick.

In the meantime, another calamity struck the travelers. Jack had been complaining about not feeling well, and the whites of his eyes had gone yellow. The symptoms were classic. He was soon diagnosed with jaundice. The doctor prescribed medication and advised only a plain diet with no oily substance. For the next few days, Jack went on a diet of plain boiled rice, which he began to like so much that he started adding sugar to it.

"Soon after that, I had to leave for Bombay, leaving Jack in the care of the family until he had recovered. Zahra could at least communicate with Jack in

English, and even though she was in purdah she could speak to him through the curtain. Unfortunately, there were no adventures for the girls. Jack was able to contact his parents in Canada and they were forever grateful to my family, and for as long as they were alive, they sent my parents a New Year card every year as a way of saying thanks for looking after their son."

In the following itinerary notes given to me by Raza, I was struck by the material itself, too worn and yellowish in color but folded in a manila packet. He said it was in one of his nephews Maysam's old desk drawers.

Bombay Itinerary Notes

Day One

Overnight train to Bombay.

Day Two

Arrival at Seaview Hotel where Abbajan greets. Father seems to be a totally different person than in Lucknow, happy in his work at the Bombay High Court. Checking in to room on fourth floor of the hotel adjacent to father. Join father for afternoon tea in the restaurant, surveying the crowds that have suddenly emerged from nowhere, older people taking their constitutional along the seafront drive, married couples out with their children, young men looking at chaperoned young women, the crowd walking up and down seems endless. It begins to get dark, lights come on along Marine Drive and it turns into what is known as "The Queen's Necklace." Had dinner with Abbajan in a European restaurant behind the hotel. Ate fried pomfret, one of Abbajan's favourite fish, with chips and peas. Enjoyed it. Returned to hotel and went back to bed.

Day Three

Woke up and had breakfast with father. He had kept his word and made appointment with Marie Seton, the famed biographer of Eisenstein and lover of India. Met her in her hotel suite that also served as her office. Short old lady wearing black-rimmed glasses. Was very kindly but direct. Told me that a career as film actor was fraught with problems beyond normal ones: roles limited and I would be typecast; couldn't even be cast as a Frenchman or northern European. Forced to look at myself—no Gregory Peck. Thanked her, returned to hotel and sobered up. Later accompanied Abbajan to visit his friends living walking distance in the Byculla area of Bombay. The old man was a prosperous Persian gentleman whose ancestors had traded across the Arabian Sea and eventually settled there. He was a widower looked after by daughters and granddaughters. On this day some friends of his granddaughter were there, all giggling teenagers in awe of walking around with such a handsome and interesting young man.

Day Four

More of the same. Walking around the park with the girls. I see a beautiful, statuesque young Indian woman. Probably a starlet in the film studios. Made a note to write about her to Steve. Buy postcards, write and post.

Have dinner with Abbajan who tells me that he has received a letter from my uncle asking him to look after Amadabad, but feels reluctant to give up his practice. It sounds like a dilemma and I feel concerned about my Abbajan. He seems to get so much personal satisfaction from advising Muslim clients who come seeking divorce.

Day Five

Day of return to Lucknow. Again overnight. Good thing I've brought the Faulkner along. Spend day saying goodbye to Abbajan's friends. Have light snackthere'll be food on the train—and say goodbye to father.

Day Six

Woken up by attendant in coupe I've been sharing with a businessman. Tea, toast and fried egg are on offer. Unable to finish breakfast after seeing businessman pick up greasy fried egg and dunk it in his tea. Fortunately, he gets off at the next stop, Arrive at Charbagh Station. Car there to meet me and drive me back home.

Raza told me the itinerary notes were important and to include them in the other letters and memorabilia he had given to me because "it may prove necessary later on." I felt it was significant as all written documents are, so I included it here.

Raza returned home from Bombay to find Jack improving and Steve back from his adventures. They spent a bit more time in Lucknow. On one occasion, the three met Hashim Bhai in the late afternoon.

"The reason for this meeting was that Jack and Steve had heard about *bhang*, a cold drink, usually iced coffee served with cannabis resin particularly during Hindu festival times. They were eager to repeat their experience in Karachi but to be honest, I was a bit hesitant and decided not to try it. Despite it being around in London at the time I hadn't felt like trying it, but I decided to mention it to Hashim Bhai, being the tolerant and broad-minded person that he is. I made it clear that I wasn't going to try any myself, and on that condition Hashim Bhai decided to take them to a coffee and soft drink place in Aminabad.

I had a quiet word with the man who ran the place, and soon the drinks appeared. I just had a coke. He looked at Jack and Steve's glass, which seemed to contain a coffee milkshake with little black bits floating near the top. Jack said, 'Those bits taste like rose petals,' and Steve agreed. They waited for a hit but felt no immediate sensation."

Thinking it was a hoax, Steve and Jack finished their drink and returned in the car to Hashim Bhai's house across the river and in a different part of town. This was a precaution in case Jack and Steve were to seem stoned or intoxicated if they returned to the palace. Along the route they stopped by the river to take a little stroll. Jack and Steve still didn't seem affected. The experiment seemed like a disappointment. The next minute, it hit them. Suddenly Jack started to climb up a statue by the riverbank, while Steve carried a wide-knowing grin on his face. The precautionary step of going to Hashim Bhai's house had turned out to be wise. Their tripping on *bhang* had only just kicked in.

"At his house, Hashim Bhai had organized beds for the three to sleep on across the lawn, complete with mosquito nets. When the car pulled in to the drive, Hashim Bhai got out and showed them to the lawn. Fortunately, it was late and no one seemed to be around. On seeing his bed, Jack mistook the netting for a bunk bed and decided to climb up it, causing the netting to collapse. Without adding any further words, the joint mirth of the others, it was to continue into the next morning when the beds were cleared from the lawn and a giant "degh" or cooking pot placed in the middle. It was full of little mangoes covered in cold water to keep them chilled and cool.

These little mangoes are a variety that are grown from seed, and are usually sucked rather than eaten sliced. The four of us went at it, but whereas Hashim Bhai and I were accustomed to doing this, you can imagine the mess a novice can make, not used to sucking mangos, and covering shirts and trousers in mango juice."

Soon it was time for them to leave. Jack and Steve asked Raza to convey their appreciation and thanks for everything when Raza went to say his sad farewells to his mother and Zahra, hugging Jafar on the way out. Then, off they went to the railway station. Luckily, Raza's father had paid his fare to Bombay and Steve and Jack, not wanting to borrow any money, decided to jump on a different carriage just as the train pulled out. Raza traveled first class. Approaching Bombay the next morning, the train slows down through the burgeoning suburbs. Here Jack and Steve jumped off to avoid the ticket collector and caught up with Raza hours later at the hotel.

This was the first leg of their return journey to England and they stayed in Bombay for three days, spending time with Raza's dad and meeting the same friends of the father and their teenage kids, did the things Raza had already done and at the end of it all Raza said goodbye to his father, promising to complete his university education, while Jack and Steve thanked him profusely. They left for Teheran, this time by plane. This was a luxury, courtesy of Raza's father, as he had heard from their tales of the journey to India, hitchhiking was not a usual way to travel even across much of Europe, let alone across Turkey and Iran.

"Jack and I left Steve in Iran to teach at the American School, he had already fixed himself a six months' stint there. After catching a bus from Tehran to Tabriz and then another from Tabriz to Erzurum, they decided to take the train to Istanbul. Along the way they struck up a conversation with an Australian who was in the same carriage. The journey was long and lasted 36 hours, and we slept sitting upright on the carriage seats. After the train had left Ankara, we went to the restaurant car for a drink and a snack."

While there, a passing ticket collector asked them to produce their tickets for inspection. Raza fumbled in his shirt to look for them, but they were not there, and unfortunately he was carrying Jack's ticket as well. The burly, red-faced conductor did not believe Raza's story told by gestures and monosyllabic English words and, amid all declarations of innocence by Raza as well as Jack, demanded their passports. There was no way that Jack and Raza were going to surrender their passports. An ugly altercation followed. They had learnt the Turkish for "no." "*Yok passport*," said Jack. "*Passport*," insisted the ticket collector. "*Gestapo*," said Jack. The man understood the word. Flushing bright red, he made a lunge for Jack.

Finally, they had no alternative but to surrender their passports, still seething with rage inside. Matters were made worse when they returned to their carriage and discovered the tickets lying on the floor of the carriage where they must have slipped from Raza's shirt pocket when he took out his packet of cigarettes. They took the tickets to show them to the collector and retrieve their passports. The conductor was in no mood for it and accused them of stealing the tickets. His parting words were that he would be handing the passports to the station master at Istanbul.

At the grand station of Istanbul, the two headed for the station master's office, but whatever the conductor had told the station master, he refused to give the passports back. Raza and Jack were going to be stranded without them. This was too much and, remembering lines from British comedies, Raza said to the station master: "Okay, we're off to report the matter to the British Embassy."

"That did it, just as in the movies, and we got our passports back," Raza remarked. To their eternal regret they didn't spend enough time in Istanbul to look at all the historical and cultural sites. They were simply running out of time and money; however, they did visit the Blue Mosque and the great covered bazaar. Then they caught a glimpse of the Bosphorus, and promised themselves to return one day before heading across the border to Thessalonica, then through Yugoslavia to Venice, where they stayed for a short time.

"There was St. Mark's of course, Venice was another must and the Rialto, the canals and the gondolas, the Ducal Palace—the whole place just buzzed with excitement. Back in London, we had listened to the MJQ recording of 'No Sun in Venice,' and marveled at Turner's painting on the record cover. We now heard the vibes and the piano tingling the mind and sat in one of the expensive cafes and sipped hot coffee, watching the pigeons in the giant square flock for food and fly off at every passing footstep before swooping back again to pick at whatever was being thrown their way. It was reminiscent of Francoise Arnoul walking across St. Mark's Square in the film for which the soundtrack was specially composed, *Sait-on Jamais*."

By now, Raza's hair, which had been shaved off in Lucknow, had grown to a few inches. As kids followed them, they pointed at Raza in his blue-and-white striped sailor's T-shirt, shortish head of hair, and drooping mustache, and shouted "*Il Cinese, il Cinese!*" Raza and Jack took it in good humor, and as the Venetian street urchins followed them, Raza turned around and pointing to himself said, "*Si, Cinese.*" That stopped the kids, who just mumbled and muttered and trailed off in another direction.

From Venice, they took the route through the Veneto region, where they wanted to stop in Verona but didn't, and followed the route through Piacenza, Genoa, and Nice. By the time they reached Paris, they were nearly at their "provisional" home. The journey from Paris via Calais and Dover to London has remained a much-traversed route by Raza. Every time he had left Paris, he had felt sadness at leaving, and an equal sadness about going back to dreary old London. This time it contained memories for Raza and Jack that would be with them forever, and an acceptance of returning to London. Soon they would be back, and when they did get back, they were met by showers of rain.

The journey had taken them about twenty-five weeks in total: thirteen weeks to get to India, about four or five weeks in India, and eight weeks to get back. In terms of money, it had cost Raza and Jack about £250 between them, which means that the weekly expenditure for the journey part worked out at an unbelievable £6.00 per person per week.

The journey with the three of them as unbelievable. With acknowledgment to Cavafy: as the trio set out for Ithaka, "the voyage proved a long one, full of adventure, full of discovery." A rare excitement often stirred their minds and bodies. There were many a summer morning when, with pleasure and joy, they came for the first time into ports and harbors and trading stations and markets and bazaars, where they saw fine things, mother of pearl and coral, amber and ebony, smelling sensual perfumes, aromas and odors of every kind.

They savored tastes and flavors of many blends and varieties, even the forbidden ones. Arriving at Ithaka, "they were wealthy with all they have gained on the way; staying there made them wealthier still, not so much in riches, but as a glimpse into what remains of an amazing past in the present. Thankful for what they learnt from her, and not expecting Ithaka to make them rich. The reward had been in the journey itself."

CHAPTER 21

THE RETURN

Back in London in the autumn of 1959, Raza looked for digs again. Jack, meanwhile, had decided to write home to ask his parents to wire him some money to go back to Canada in order to earn enough to return to England to paint. Steve, as we know, was in Tehran and wouldn't return for another six months, after which his plans were uncertain. He would return to London and presumably continue to try to write, while earning money doing other things, such as teaching.

We will have to wait and see. As for Raza, he was in London to continue his academic education, yet his place in SOAS was not set until the following academic year. He had twin needs: to find a job and a place to live until he went to university. His personal belongings, books, clothes, gramophone records and so on had been stored with some of his other friends, Bindo and Jenny, so he and Jack decided to catch up with them and other friends, Al, Michael, and Angie.

It wasn't going to be easy to find housing. Bindo and Jenny and their gang welcomed them back. They were regaled by Jack and Raza about their travels and adventures. In turn, they said they'd ask around about housing. Eventually after two or three weeks, Raza found something through Bindo.

"The place I found was a large five-storeyed house with a terrace in Onslow Gardens, with a semibasement, which is where my room was going to be. The house turned out to be owned by an absentee landlord, not unusual even in the London of those days. The landlords turned out in this case to be an Indian couple, which again was not unusual. I had known Asian landlords before, like my father's landlord in Barnes. I took it upon myself to phone the number I had been given and spoke to an Indian woman with an obvious hint of a familiar-sounding Indian accent. Landlords are no different, whatever their nationality. She told me about the rent, payable in advance, the rules about visitors and noise, and so on. She then told me to contact the Maltese caretaker and his English wife, who lived in a flat in the basement, adjacent to the vacant room.

I rang the doorbell, and the caretaker, a medium height, middle-aged, stocky man with a head of thick black hair opened the door. When he spoke, his voice was surprisingly gentle; he gave me his name, Tony, and showed me the room."

ZABELITA

Each time Raza went in and out of the house to work or back, he would see a young woman seated by the window of a rather large room playing the piano. She noticed him looking and looked back without saying a word, not smiling but not standoffish either. Usually they were expressionless exchanges of looks.

"Then one day, I thought, why the hell not smile? And, so, I smiled back. That's how I got invited to her room. I introduced myself and she said her name was Zabelita. And that I could call her Zab for short."

Raza got on very well with Zab with her joshing, self-deprecating sense of humor, much like Raza who had a similar style of joking, and she had a hearty laugh to go with her Spanish American accent.

"And this is my friend Norma, who shares the flat with me," Zab said to Raza, who turned to see a young, blonde-haired woman who, it turned out, was studying to be a photographic model. Zab, however, was from Venezuela and was studying music at the Royal Academy of Music. Her mother, Adela, worked at the Venezuelan Consulate in Knightsbridge.

Zab herself had a disciplined upbringing living with one of her mother's English friends in Weybridge. Raza felt she suffered from low self-esteem, so he somehow took it upon himself to shake her out of it. Whenever she said she was ugly, Raza would say, "Yes, you're quite ugggly," until she saw the humor in it. She got on with Al too. All this is mentioned because, as circumstances turned out, Zab, Al, and Raza ended up sharing a house together, but away from SW7 (South Kensington Gloucester Road), far away in Brondesbury Park, near Willesden.

"What happened was this, that for six or eight months, I had a succession of jobs—in coffee bars, as a picture framer, and so on. All of it helped keep me in pocket money, but that's about all. My only intellectual and cultural activity was with books and, you guessed it, movies. There were three or four films that I saw at that time that had a dramatic, intense, and revelatory impact on me. Two of these were by Ingmar Bergman—*The Seventh Seal*, and *Wild Strawberries*, and two by Satyajit Ray: *Pather Panchali* and *Aparajito*.

I had seen them with Bindo and Al, and had talked about them. Zab was too busy with her music studies: practice, practice and more practice, but my friends and I couldn't stop talking about two such contrasting directors—one from northern Europe, and the other from India. Here were Indian films that could dazzle anyone at the international stage. I remember the impact of the scene where Apu is at the railway station leaving home, and waiting for the train that would take him to the big city, intercut with a shot of his mother leaning against the door of her simple clay hut, just as he boards the train, which pulls out of the station leaving a trail of billowing steam to block out everything. It was heartbreaking to experience the arbitrary disruption of relationships by monolithic machines. I identified in that scene with my recent parting from my mother. I still love my mother but I know that I have changed."

As for Ingmar Bergman, Raza, Al, and Bindo found resonances of a different kind—of bleakness and Armageddon, of the game of chess between the knight and death, with the mocking down-to-earth squire introducing humor to the ongoings with lines like: "The trouble with women is that like your backside they are always behind you."

There were books too, like Durrell's *Alexandria Quartet*, a book he found stunning in the use of language, and at times ribald and funny, acute with observations about the lives of British ex-colonials in a decaying Alexandria. He was right about D. H. Lawrence too, who Steve much admired: "Lawrence you are great, but why do you have to make a Taj Mahal out of every simple fuck?" This was Steve who made the comment, which made him chuckle, but it was Durrell who led Raza on to Cavafy, and then to Kazantzakis's *Zorba, the Greek*.

But there was no output. It was all a question of taking in—words, words, words and no action. This was until Bindo, who had published in PEN International, introduced Raza to an editor working there. She interviewed Raza, who as Bindo had told her, knew a lot about Urdu poetry, particularly the religious poetry of Mir Anis. Raza admitted to knowing a little and explained briefly what Mir Anis wrote about and when.

The editor was impressed and explained that the role of PEN was "in emphasizing the role of literature in the development of mutual understanding and world culture." She then asked Raza to write a brief article of no more than 1,500 words, and gave him a strict deadline. Now writing was one of the things Raza had wanted to do, and here was his chance. He could now test himself on what he was capable of producing, and whether it would be good enough. He thanked her and agreed to write the article.

"I spent the first few days thinking about the subject I had grown up with since childhood, but knew it would be difficult to compress its meaning adequately for the reader to comprehend."

He started to put things down on paper, reflecting about essays he had written; but the important thing, he thought, was the opening paragraph, which should serve as an invitation to the reader, introducing him or her to the gist of it. The conclusion or finale was equally important, and to not peter out into nothing. He found himself writing and rewriting the first paragraph and not getting much beyond that. He was aware he was working to a deadline and seemed to be getting nowhere.

"Michael and Bindo kept giving me every encouragement. Finally, when the deadline was on me and I wasn't sure of making it, they stayed up all night to make sure I'd submit it the next morning by post, transcribing from rewritten pages on to Michael's typewriter, being plied with cups of coffee and being promised by Michael that he would take me out to dinner the next evening after I had finished the article and had a good sleep. Finally, the article was finished. I read it through but wasn't totally happy. Hopefully, the editor would polish it up. I typed out just over the 1,500 words required and made two carbon copies in the early hours of the morning, placed them inside the envelope to post the first thing."

Within a week he heard that his article on Mir Anis had been accepted for publication. The magazine was due for publication during the next six weeks and eventually he received three copies of the magazine and sent copies to his uncle and father. He later learned they were very proud of his ability to write clearly and translate one of his father's couplets: "Would'st thou know the meaning of fidelity to faith? Then ask Shabbeer: It is to be willing to lay down your life for those words you once uttered."

This was Raza's start in publishing that took place during January 1960. There was still a wait until September when he would next receive his allowance for going to the School of Oriental and African Studies. Round about then, Raza, Zab, and Norma encountered landlord trouble at Onslow Gardens. Late one night, the Maltese caretaker had got drunk and beaten up his wife. The police were called, and the repercussions of it made Raza and Zab decide to move to a cheaper area and cut costs. Norma decided to move in with her German boyfriend, but Al decided to join them in the hunt.

I understand during the period up to 1965, there was no race-relations legislation in the United Kingdom. What was known as "casual" discrimination in public life, in areas such as housing and jobs, was still common in public law and went unchallenged by the law.

Raza and his Indian friends had long experience, as we know, of stickers in windows saying: "No Coloured; No Irish; No Dogs." They had tried to shrug it off, turning it into a joke, and rely on their network for finding places. White friends like Michael understood, but could do nothing to open doors. Raza's other acquaintances internalized the experience and became bitter and resentful. He recounts that one or two Indians he met in those days were ashamed of their Indian-ness and tried to pass themselves off as Iranians, as though that might save them, little realizing that racism was there, rooted in English society and entangled with notions of empire and white superiority.

"Of course Indians knew but only the half of it and beneath the horizon there was a whole hidden population of black people from the former West Indian colonies who had arrived in boatloads after the war, at the invitation of the UK government. This population had been already ghettoized and concentrated in some inner-city areas. There had been recent riots in Notting Hill when a gang of white youths had attacked black people going about their daily lives."

Raza had only known two black people: Ted and Ferdie. Of these, Ferdie had come to be a friend, though Raza wasn't sure what his other friends, Indian and others, thought of Ferdie, apart from Zab who had also experienced racism. Her grandmother had migrated from Morocco to Venezuela, and although Adela, Zab's mother, was in denial of her North African heritage and the crinkly hair, Zab, with her full lips and brown skin, was not in denial of her mixed heritage.

And here they were, Raza and Zab, escapees to an exclusion zone, before they eventually found a place to stay in Brondesbury. After a great deal of searching, the three of them found a large two-story bungalow with an attic bedroom above. The whole of the top floor and the attic were for rent for £10 per week.

They had three bedrooms, a large living-dining room, a kitchen, and a bathroom. This kind of place would have been unaffordable and, in any case, unavailable to them in areas like South Kensington. They were happy to share, and it was the first such experience for Raza since splitting up with Shireen in late 1957.

"We stayed in Brondesbury Park for the winter," Raza notes. A photograph shows Zab, Raza, and Al posing in front of the local church in Christchurch Avenue on the way to the tube station.

Meanwhile, while still in Brondesbury Park, Jack had sent Raza some parcels of clothes containing GWG jeans and a beautiful light gray jacket with a pocket along the bottom of the back, which was used by fishermen or poachers for stowing away their catch. This was also in part pay for what Jack owed him from the Indian trip. There was no pressure from Raza on Jack, since he was just keeping his word, but that made the gift all the nicer. This was concrete proof for Zab that Jack, about whom she had heard so much, from both Al and Raza, actually existed.

JACK AND ZAB

Jack himself returned to London in early 1960. As chance would have it, one of his Indian friends, Homi, had invited Raza to a party in his flat in Gloucester Road, so when Jack phoned Raza to announce his return, Raza invited him to Homi's party. Homi was someone Jack knew, so he accepted. Zab and Al came along too, and that's how Jack and Zab met. Someone had put on some *cha-cha-cha* dance music, and Jack had always fancied himself as a dancer.

He regarded the English as prissy dancers, stiff at the hips, as Raza had heard Jack say in the early days, when they were in the Place de la Bastille on July 14, and all the squares and narrow connecting lanes on the "rive gauche" were full of music and crowds and dancing. He took to the steps very easily, and liked the way the Latins danced.

Now at Homi's party, Jack just went up to Zab and asked her to dance, and Zab could dance too. Smiles just vanished, as they squared up to each other, looking into each other's eyes, the eyes locked in an embrace. That was it. They were inseparable. "I can't remember how we all got back to Brondesbury Park, but Jack and Zab did not leave Zab's room until half way through the next afternoon."

And so, the months rolled on. Raza and his friends moved out of Brondesbury Park during early 1960. It was proving to be too remote to travel to and fro and they went their own ways, though still seeing each other from time to time and maintaining contact. Bindo was moving out of his bed-sit in the attic of a house in Manson Place. This is the flat Raza had been to for many dinners over time. For an attic room it was pretty large, large enough to accommodate all of Bindo's books, and his and Jenny's belongings. The window looked down on a skyline of houses stretching toward the Natural History Museum.

There was a simple gas ring for cooking and paraffin heaters for warmth, which also served for cooking rice. Now Bindo and Jenny had decided to split. He had decided to visit his mother in India, while Jenny, with her passion for flamenco, had gone to Spain and on to Tangiers. Bindo had a word with the caretaker, who had seen Raza go in and out of the place, and he agreed to pass Bindo's tenancy on to Raza. Raza moved in soon after, and that's where Raza was to be found during his first year at School of Oriental and African Studies, right up to the end of 1961, but that's a continuing story.

Jack, meanwhile, moved out of London to Essex, where he found a little cottage to share with Zab and, of course, to paint. By complete coincidence, the village they moved to was named "Ugley." Raza chortled to Zab and joshed her about the name. Steve was also now back from Iran, and had moved to a neighboring cottage that he was sharing with someone. Meanwhile, Adela had not approved of her daughter settling down with "an artist, a man without prospects," as she saw things, and she let Zab know her feelings.

She had wanted someone better for her daughter, a professional with a career, but Jack and Zab were deeply in love and, though poor, they were happy. Raza still has a painting of Jack's from this period that Jack gave him.

The Registry Office in Kensington Town Hall, in the fall of 1961, was the next time Raza saw Jack and Zab. They were getting married and Zab was expecting a baby the following summer. When the baby boy was born, they named him John-Paul Fraser, and asked Raza to become his godfather. They had moved back to London by then and lived in a flat in Adelaide Road, Swiss Cottage, round the corner from where Raza found himself coincidentally living at the start of 1962.

CHAPTER 22

RAZA'S SECOND ALDERMASTON MARCH

This was the third annual Easter March from the Atomic Weapons Research Establishment at Aldermaston, Berkshire to the capital, organized by the campaign for nuclear disarmament and founded by Canon John Collins and Bertrand Russell in 1958. The second march from Aldermaston to London was a much bigger affair than the previous year. It started on Friday, April 17, at Aldermaston, and by the time it arrived in Trafalgar Square, there was an estimated crowd of 100,000 people—the biggest march the country had seen that century.

This massive participation was because over the previous year it had gathered enormous support from scientists, religious leaders, academics, journalists, writers, actors, and musicians. Its sponsors included the likes of Benjamin Britten, Dame Edith Evans, Michael's former tutor E. M. Forster, the sculptors Barbara Hepworth and Henry Moore, Bertrand Russell—a major influence on Raza's cousin Hurr at the time—and many others, all of whom were signatories to the Campaign for Nuclear Disarmament's (CND) founding principles.

Raza decided from the outset to join the international section, and again with his friend and comrade-in-arms Ferdie. Raza had found in him a kindred spirit despite the disparity in their ages. It was difficult to guess, but Ferdie must have been in his forties. A man of few words, Raza often found them to be like bullets going to the heart of racism when he heard Ferdie say anything.

By the time the march reached Trafalgar Square on the fourth day, Raza had been interviewed by a *Daily Express* reporter, to whom he was very curt and blunt, having been mistaken for a Cuban, an identity he chose to adopt because he was carrying a lollipop reading FIDEL. Ferdie's read "LUMUMBA," and a petite Latin American came to his rescue by offering to act as an interpreter.

At Hyde Park Corner, as the march climbed its way up Piccadilly, there were shouts of "Ban the Bomb, ban Gillette," from some wag. Shortly following the

March, Ferdie invited Raza to his place in Willesden, northwest London, one day for a meal. He lived in one of those small houses that could be seen in many of London's inner-city suburbs, row houses that had become a sanctuary, cheap housing that whites had abandoned when the blacks started arriving and buying houses.

The value of property began to fall in those neighborhoods as the white flight to the suburbs began. Those neighborhoods started to became ghettos, out of which blacks couldn't move. West Indian immigration to England after the war, known as the "Windrush generation" of 1948, had started before Raza's arrival in London. We are talking about a period of more than a decade.

"Ferdie and his partner Rose had rented a flat from a West Indian landlord. Ferdie, a quietly spoken but spirited sort of person, and I met at Willesden Station and [walked] to his flat on the top floor. I could detect Rose's hand behind some of the comfort in the room. She knew Ferdie well and acted as a bulwark for him against the outside world, working to bring in money when Ferdie, who was a skilled carpenter and joiner, couldn't find work. On entering their small apartment, I saw a picture of a gorilla, under which Ferdie had inscribed: 'This is my grandfather, and he is also yours.'"

This poster encapsulated everything for Raza about a common human origin and belonging. In Ferdie's flat, he had his first taste of rice and peas and curried goat. For some reason, Ferdie had developed a liking for Raza, who felt privileged about being counted a friend by Ferdie. After the visit they became even closer friends, and would spend quite a lot of time around at Raza's place in South Kensington.

On one of these occasions, they had been at a party together when Ferdie had suddenly vanished. When Raza went looking for him, he eventually found him sitting on a bench outside the local church. There was a small carved figure of Christ on a cross looking down on the bench. As Raza came up to him, he could hear Ferdie mumbling in his beard: "take away your fucking Christian idols." He later explained to Raza that he had felt alone at the party and had gone out to be by himself. Raza persuaded him to come back and spend the night at his place.

Ferdie and Raza quickly forged a lasting friendship. Soon afterwards, Ferdie left London for Nkrumah's Ghana, but still they kept up correspondence. Ferdie's letters to Raza were about the changing situation in Ghana, and they were always signed, "the Burning Spear." Sometime in the mid-1960s, these letters tailed off, and Raza doesn't know what happened to him. However, I did find out that he had been a friend of West Indian writers like Manning Marable and Edward Braithwaite, who had been living in London at the time.

The other friends Raza continued to see were Michael and Annie. Michael was taking lessons by now in sailing a yacht, somewhere near Chichester. Michael had inherited £5,000.00 worth of prewar stocks, and had decided to have a 30-foot clinker shell yacht, designed like a Greek caique, built in Cornwall. Once Michael had got his mariners' certificate, he decided to go for a trial run up across the Channel, the Seine to Paris. In a spirit of conviviality, he invited Raza to join him, Annie, and another friend. Raza, though a landlubber, was game for it.

"The four of us traveled to Chichester for the crossing. Michael had studied the tidal chart for the crossing, and this was the day he decided to sail across; he took his companions along to show them his pride and joy. The yacht was called *Astarte*. It looked brand new and had only sailed from Plymouth, where it had been built and designed in Devon where pilgrims set off for North America. It had a 30' mast and an engine. As he stepped down from the polished deck with its neatly stowed ropes and riggings into the cabin, he realized how neatly and compactly everything had been designed.

The main cabin contained a double stowaway bed. During the day, the cabin served as a living room with a small gas-fired kitchenette, and a table where Michael could study the charts. Beyond there was a toilet and washroom, and then at the narrow end of the bow, two bunk beds for other passengers, separated by the mast coming down to the bottom of the boat, where it was fixed."

The four set sail in the afternoon. It was going to be an eight- or ten-hour crossing. Raza tells how:

> Mike started the engine, and sat at the stern end of the boat, holding the rudder. The rest were ready to rig the sail as we neared the opening of the harbor. Annie was a dab hand at playing the skipper's first mate. Raza, who had just about gotten used to the movement of the boat, did what he was told to do. You learn that on a boat there can only be one skipper.
>
> The fun began when the yacht emerged from the relatively calm waters of the harbor into the choppier waters of the Channel. It required all hands on deck, as they say, to stay the sails. Looking back, you could see the coast of England slowly disappearing until there was no land in sight. For a while they all took turns to get a bit of rest. Annie had prepared sandwiches and some soup. Suddenly, the yacht started being tossed more violently by the

waves. There seemed to be a storm brewing. All hands were called for once more. The sails were quickly let down and furled to the mast, so the mast itself would not snap. Then, I lost it. I got violently sick over the side of the boat and, told to go below deck. It was dark when Michael came down to see how I was, and told me that Le Havre harbor was in sight.

The Seine is a tidal river upstream as far as Rouen. So Michael needed to catch the flood tide as it travels up river, providing a 12-hour "window." By the time they had entered the harbor and anchored the boat, had all the papers and passports checked, and boarded the yacht again, it was nighttime.

The Seine estuary is well known for severe mists and fogs. When under way, Michael knew the boat would be rocked, possibly significantly, by the wash from passing ships. This meant that *Astarte*'s mast must be well supported and lashed fore and aft as well as side to side.

He gave everyone the instructions, but at least they were only going to use the tiller from now on. Michael kept a VHF radio watch on the frequency that commercial traffic uses—so you can listen in and get prior notice of big things ahead or behind and catching you up. By the next morning, they had reached Rouen and the nontidal part of the Seine. Everyone on board stretched as they saw the morning sun. They looked around and saw several places to stop. By now Raza was beginning to feel better after being so seasick.

He volunteered to hold the tiller, while Michael had some well-earned rest, and Annie made breakfast. By midmorning, Raza's shoulders were beginning to feel stiff, a sure sign that they were sunburnt. He covered his bare shoulders with a T-shirt as he watched the wide river and the scenery go by. After Rouen, the Seine has been "canalized," so to speak. The contrast between either side of the first recluse at Poses is striking. One immediately enters a "Middle Earth" of leafy side channels and islands.

There are multiple options of channels to choose and explore. Michael remained alert to the different depths, and gave Raza directions for the use of the tiller. There are a number of places that were busy with dinghies, rowing and sculling boats, and canoes. Large barges and small ships continue to use the main channels and need to be given a wide berth.

Finally they arrived in Paris, where they anchored the boat at one of its bridges. Raza thanked Michael and Annie and took the train and ferry back to London. Michael and Annie were to continue from there, sailing canals down to the Rhone, right into the Mediterranean at Marseilles. From there they would sail around Sicily and head for the northern Sporades to make it their base for sailing and exploring other Aegean islands. Raza would keep in touch with him.

KAZANTZAKIS AND THE MODERN ODYSSEY

Earlier I touched on the issue of the interlocutor immersion in the life, both in practice and in thought. Through my participation and observation, I have become part of a new world of ways of doing and thinking, and indeed become a sojourner in a strange land. And in some ways, this reflection has caused me to think more profoundly and to gather a deeper understanding of the literary and perhaps fictional character of the ethnographic writing.

Sarah Daynes and I wrote in our book *On Ethnography*, and made note as we reflect on "the centrality of interpretation at every level of this narrative from the way in which we approach and construct the field, to what we hear and see, to how we understand it and frame it in fieldnotes and ultimately, is essentially in the stories we tell and the books we write." (See Daynes and Williams. *On Ethnography*. London: Polity Press, 2018.]

Some of that literary interpretation comes from books we read and study. When Raza talked to me about Dostoevsky, he describes this as one of the transformative books he has ever read. Originally published in Modern Greek in 1938, the book was translated by a Greek American scholar in close collaboration with Nikos Kazantzakis himself. The original and the translation are both in verse. It is about four times longer than Homer's *Odyssey*. When Raza caught sight of a copy of the large tome in the window of a bookshop in Charing Cross, he just had to buy it. He had already read several of Kazantzakis's books after *Zorba the Greek*, but *The Modern Odyssey* was totally different since it was an epic poem.

Raza finished reading the text, which is over 850 pages long, before he entered university to study Arabic. It had been an odyssey in itself. "Look, it may sound crazy Terry, but I couldn't let go of the book. I don't know what the readership has been or how many have read it all. It doesn't really matter." Then he adds: "There's a synopsis only a few pages long at the back. No less an authority than W. B. Stanford has compared Kazantzakis to James Joyce as the only two authors who have extended Homer's *Odyssey*: one in a centrifugal sense, within one square mile of Dublin, and the other in a centripetal sense, taking Ulysses down the Nile to the tip of Africa, and beyond to the South Pole.

Others like Dante, Shakespeare, Tennyson; no doubt countless other Ulysses have fascinated other writers as he is in Homer, but none have done what Joyce and Kazantzakis have. Joyce's *Ulysses* will be my next port of call. I have seen a copy in the family library, and made a note of borrowing it on my next visit home."

CHAPTER 23

TESS AND RAZA

As we head into the millennium, Raza's decision to marry Tess is the only surprise, and nothing much happens on the Amadabad front during this time except for further pilfering and looting. He and Tess had lived together for 17 years, had three grown daughters between them. But still the old romantic, Raza asked Tess a second time to marry him. After a lot of hesitation and persuasion from her own daughters, Tess agreed. Jack commented wryly on the phone when Raza told him: "You're getting to be just like the United States. Always rushing into things."

Raza and Tess had a civil ceremony at Finsbury Town Hall on September 22, 1977, where Gil and Peter came along with the family to act as best man and sign as witness, and through Abid he had purchased an emerald that he had mounted on a ring made by a jeweler working locally in his studio, which Raza presented her. The ceremony was followed by an all-day wedding party with friends.

The afternoon was sunny and warm, and friends spilled out on to the pavement, drinking and chatting. There was enough varied food for 100 people—the curried goat and rice went down particularly well. Then there were speeches. The groom stuttered and was saved by his daughter saying how relieved she was that someone had taken her dad off her hands. He didn't realize that it was one of the last occasions that he would see his friend Paul, the wonder kid, alive.

Hurr and Zainab didn't attend but Maysam and Qais came around to meet their new auntie at her home, knowing there would be a lot of alcohol at the party. Later when Raza and Tess went around for Raza to formally present his bride, they gave her a silver platter. Cards arrived from all his siblings and other relatives but, unsurprisingly, no word of recognition from Ibn Dawood.

"If marriage had changed anything in my life and our life, more specifically, it was the effect it had on the grandchildren—Shelley's and Ana-Livia's children.

They felt that they could now refer to me as Grandad, their natural grandparents having both passed away. For example, one evening in his kitchen, one of his adoptive grandsons, thinking that I always seemed to know everything whenever he got into conversation, had taken it upon himself to dial the number for a quiz show on TV where you could win £1 million if a certain question was answered."

The grandchild (named "C") calls Raza over and hands him the phone, saying, "It's that quiz show you all watch, just answer the question. Is the answer A, B, or C?" Raza was a bit bemused but listens to the phone and then gives an answer. The special edition of the show selected couples who had newly married that year, which was coincidentally the case for Raza and Tess. Having answered the question, the woman on the other end of the phone soon established this by talking to Raza.

By now everyone in the living room was getting excited. To his surprise, the voice said that he and Tess had been selected, subject to checking out their public records. She noted down his mobile number and says that he will be telephoned the next day around midday. It turns out to be no joke. Tess was both nervous and excited.

The following day, they decide to accompany another grandson to Oxford Street to buy some trainers. It's early in the afternoon, and Raza has forgotten about the phone call when his mobile rings just as they're outside a shop selling trainers. Because of the traffic he can't hear clearly. He steps into a side street and he hears that their selection to appear on the show had been confirmed. They're given an option whether to appear on the Wednesday or the Friday show. Raza opts for the midweek show.

The next stage is that he must telephone the day before the recording of the show that a limousine would arrive early in the morning to avoid the rush hour and drive them to the recording studios in Elstree. On the journey Raza stays calm and laidback, while Tess is excited and nervous. At the studios, they are met by a member of the quiz show staff, escorted to a caravan to be made up, briefed on the format of the show, and led to a bar where other contestants, most of them much younger than them, have gathered.

Later they are led into the darkened hall of the recording studio and seated with the other contestants in the front two rows, the remaining rows being occupied by the audience. Outwardly, Raza is still laid-back. During the second round, with a starter question on Latin American countries, he is very quick on the buzzer, and he and Tess find themselves in the hot seat. They get through the first few rounds. Tess is good on a music question, and identifies the Russian tennis player too.

They continue and reach the point when £16,000 is assured. The next question would bank them double that. The questions was, where was the Royal Mint located? Raza has a hunch but unsure they decided to use the option of phoning a friend. The friend too does not know the correct answer. They accept the $16,000 and decide to split it and go to Cuba for three weeks. They had already been on a honeymoon in Turkey, but why not a holiday in Cuba, about which Raza had talked so much about.

HOMAGE TO CUBA

In some ways I follow Raza's reflections of his life where his family history and the survival of their stories are paramount; but here I start with his homage to Cuba. These are reminisces Raza felt toward the Cuban people and Cuba itself. It is both a recall and a travelogue of a Cuba he loved and felt solidarity with, both for the people and the country, much like his emotional connection to Lucknow and India proper. And at times didactic it is overall a deep love and respect for Cuba he is expressing.

I should note that the same Cuban consulate that Jack and Stefan had visited at the time of the Bay of Pigs, still located in the same place, provides them with helpful information about visiting the island country, that had been under a US imposed trade embargo. Medicine and vitamin pills are in much demand, as well as pencils and notebooks for young people.

Raza also gets the idea of telling Jack that he's going to be in Cuba, and asking him to connect up with them, in part because of their long-standing comradeship and mutual interest. He agreed and ask them to phone once they get there. They set off on an Air Jamaica flight for a three-week holiday-cum-pilgrimage. On board the plane, Tess buys Raza a duty-free watch, the kind he liked—neat, rectangular, stainless steel, with a leather strap. He still wears it.

The flight is to drop them in Havana before going on to Kingston, Jamaica, the southwest of Cuba from the window, this looks like a small appendage as the plane circles to land in Havana. When I first heard the story about Cuba from Raza and Tess, during one of the times I was staying with them in London, it had made me want to visit Cuba.

Raza has been a self-declared Fidelista since the late 1950s and followed events there ever since. He knew Cuba's economy had been severely tested after the fall of Gorbachev, and the collapse of the Soviet Union in 1991. Soviet aid had been worth up to $6 billion, and its ending had led to severe shortages in fuel and food. Apparently, it was now on the way up again. He would wait to see for himself.

"A small group of passengers got off landing at Jose Marti Airport, us among them and we found ourselves filtered through immigration and customs fairly quickly. The weather was sunny and hot as we emerged and boarded a coach that would take us to central Havana, dropping us off for a prebooked three-night stay at a small, simple, modern-looking hotel. There was a bar on the ground floor where one could also purchase coffee. The polite manager, who also served at the bar, took our passport details and showed us to our room. It was an average size room with a small balcony and bathroom. Extra charges were paid for use of the air-conditioning."

The first thing Tess decided to do was to find out where they could drop off the boxes of vitamins and pencils, crayons and notepads, and other items they had brought along. It would make their luggage so much easier to carry. After a shower and change of clothes they decided to ask the manager who told them that the medical items could be disposed of at the medical center nearby. As for the other items, they could try schools, or to spread them out and take some along with them on their journeys. The advice sounded good.

Leaving the tasks until tomorrow because it was too late in the day, they came out of the hotel and went to the main avenue heading toward Old Havana, making their plans for the day as they went along. About three blocks away still in central Havana, they came across the famous Hotel Nacional, in prerevolutionary times a casino owned by American gangster Mayer Lansky and frequented by rich and glamorous Americans. It was a gigantic, imposing building in art-deco style, with several floors of stone-colored façade facing them. They paused at the gates and looked down the long driveway leading to the entrance. Leaving it to explore another day, they kept walking, ignoring the taxis, and using their street guide.

"But Havana seemed endless. We finally gave up and hailed a taxi, I negotiated the fare using US dollars, as the rate against the Cuban dollar was the best. The taxi driver looked at the dollars and took us to be Italian because in trying to speak Spanish he would lapse into Italian and agreed to a flat fare. Two things they had heard about were an anti-corruption drive, and a monitoring of such situations by the public."

Tess looked like a Cuban woman, and Raza had been given odd stares and looked like he could be just another foreigner here to exploit tourists.

Anyway, the taxi eventually took them into Old Havana where the architecture had changed into neoclassical and colonial Spanish styles. Eventually, it dropped them off at the seafront.

"Soon we were approached by two girls asking what we were looking for. On hearing that it was for a bar, they naturally offered to suggest one."

The two girls, who were twin sisters, took them down narrow alleys where mostly the poor lived, and where you would expect the bars and cantinas to give the real flavor of Cuba, and they found a small bar. The girls were known in the bar and over the next few days began a friendship and became guides to places in Old Havana.

Since Jack and Rosa weren't due for another week, plans changed. First, they moved to a guesthouse, situated on the third floor of an old colonial house, facing the seafront. The apartment belonged to an elderly middle-class lady reduced to renting because of the shortage of housing. As chance would have it, the twins and her family lived in the smaller house next door. They exchanged mobile numbers, and for two more days they explored Old Havana with its narrow streets and overhanging balconies.

Entertainment was everywhere, with Cuban women dancing in their traditional clothes, some serenading outside the windows of small restaurants. The narrow streets would suddenly open up in to plazas, one of them Havana Cathedral that dominated the Plaza de la Catedral.

The urge to see more of Cuba before the holiday came to an end beckoned and Raza phoned Jack to tell him that they were off to Trinidad de Cuba for about a week and would be back in time to meet them.

Raza asked, why Trinidad de Cuba? There simply wasn't enough time to explore further and travel to somewhere like Cienfuegos near Guantanamo at the eastern tip of the island, but they could go to Trinidad de Cuba, referred to as Trinidad locally because it lies midway along the southern coast of Cuba.

"We made travel enquiries and, saying goodbye to the girls, boarded a bus, crowded with ordinary Cubans, and one or two tourists as well. It was a four-hour journey with the bus stopping two or three times to allow people to stretch their legs and use the toilets. The driver pointed out the Isla do los Ingenios (the nature reserve) to the right, as they neared Trinidad. It was midafternoon when the bus piled up in a road outside the town and let the passengers off. No traffic was allowed in Trinidad.

We thank the driver, pulled suitcases out of the baggage hold, and enquiring how to find the address of the casa they were booked in to, we lugged the baggage down over and across the plaza before walking down a narrow road with pink-colored houses all the way down. Tess noticed along the way two adjacent streets, with identical-looking houses, but painted in different colors. This formed the residential area for young married couples as part of its huge public housing program. Ordinary tourists could be boarded with a family as a handy way for both lodger and tenant to find cheap accommodation and earn a little extra respectively."

The young hosts, with their teenage boy, were extremely friendly and showed them the small room they would have for the next few days. The cramped conditions made little room for privacy, but it was reasonable. They would see how it work out.

As the afternoon drew on, Raza used his limited Spanish and sign language to communicate, trying to locate food and water. He wanted his hosts to take them to the historic center where they could see the red roofs and tiny bricked streets of Trinidad de Cuba.

They ended up in a white-walled bar and restaurant in Canchancharra, near the central plaza and not far from the sea. Tess and Raza stopped at a small bar and asked the proprietor for a Cuba Libre and menu. After eating they walked down winding streets of a town that seemed to be suspended in time. The absence of cars contributed to the timelessness.

Only a few square blocks in size, the historic plaza area had cobbled streets, and houses in pastel colors with wrought-iron grilles, and colonial-era edifices such as the *Santísima Trinidad Cathedral* and *Convento de San Francisco*. Tess and Raza walked back as it was getting dark and the *casas de musica* were beginning to open, including one next to the cathedral in Plaza Major to the sounds and rhythms of Cuban music before returning to their room.

During the next few days, Tess and Raza became familiar with Trinidad de Cuba and people saw them as "sympatico." They were English-speaking tourists who mixed up Italian and Spanish words with advantage.

"Our day would start with a visit to the Canchancharra, where we invariably ate fried eggs with grilled bread, swallowed down with hot coffee. Tess had bought tea bags with her and asked for some hot water and milk. If they felt tempted, they might order a drink. Which is how they first tasted the speciality of the house, a warm drink called Canchancharra made with honey, rum and lime, a subtly lethal mixture bound to creep up on you and catch you unawares. One minute they were talking and laughing politely, and the next they were singing songs. Within a day or two the presence of the people from England spread through the town. Anyway, the guide took a party of about twenty people, mostly from Spain, but also from Sweden, Italy, and France, along one of the narrow, winding cobbled streets to the edge of town. There I could see this lone white building stood on the hillside, looking across to the north to the mountains of the Sierra Maestra, where Fidel and his band of guerillas won the victory against the corrupt dictator Batista, before marching on to Havana."

Raza reflected back to those memories before turning to join the party of tourists. Every word he uttered was a reflection on his life and times. It was as if he was living a life he would not ever see again.

"The Museum of History was based in a long narrow room with windows on both sides, and containing landmarks in Trinidad's history from before the Spaniards came. About halfway down they came across pictorial and written history of the enslavement of largely Yoruba-speaking people from western Africa brought there to work on sugar plantations. Here, Tess stopped, and broke down in tears. This was because having decided on first going on a guided tour that departed each morning from the square, Tess was insistent on going to see the historical museum that also charted the role that slavery played in the establishment of the sugar mills by wealthy Spanish owners."

"The Vallee de los Ingenios nearby, which they had passed on their way to Trinidad is supposed to contain several historic sugarcane mills. Most of the guided tours out of the way, they explored more of the town in the company of some young Cuban professionals studying either medicine or law. They had got talking one day in Chanchancharra after word had got around of two people from England who were not English. After meeting these Cuban professionals, Tess and I got invited to their houses, where they lived with their parents, had lots of friendly arguments and discussions about Cuba. They were impressed with how much I knew about Cuban history, and by the innocent vivaciousness of Tess, who would always stop me from going too far, in case it offended anyone."

Yet here was a clear example of freedom of speech that is not supposed to exist in Cuba. One of the young Cubans, who appeared to take the lead, was openly arguing in favor of the Swedish model of economy. Their friendship grew and Tess and Raza exchanged addresses and telephone numbers, promising to keep in touch. All these names and addresses, he tells me, are still in one of Raza's old address books.

Their remaining time in Trinidad de Cuba included attending a wedding party of one of the young friends, attending an open air fiesta in the grand plaza at night, and many more eating and drinking sessions, before saying farewell to Trinidad and returning to Havana, and their meeting with Jack and his new partner, Rosa, who they hadn't met.

At the bus garage in Trinidad de Cuba, there are lots of people wanting to travel to Havana and there are also long delays. A few taxis are available, but they have a system of picking up multiple passengers, dropping them where they want to go, picking up other passengers along the road and, thereby, make more money. Even here there were lines of people waiting. Eventually, a middle-aged man, who turned out to be a Cuban filmmaker, and a critic of the Cuban government, took pity on them and dropped them on the Malecon or seafront of Havana.

"It was evening and we had booked in a guesthouse in central Havana. I telephoned Jack whose voice came through clearly saying he would meet us at the bar of the hotel where Tess and I had originally stayed. We hail a taxi to the guesthouse, which turns out to belong to two old ladies. Jack, who I haven't seen since Venezuela in 1992, is standing up straight, with a glass in his hand and propping up the bar. He nods and raises his glass. Tess runs up and gives him a big hug."

They were to return to the hotel but not for the next couple of days when they went to see an exhibition of modern Cuban art by painters Jack knew about.

"Then Jack's time in Cuba was almost over. On the last day we went into the Hotel Nacional again. That day a whole lot of people, couples and families, seemed to be going into the hotel. Something seemed to be going on. We followed people through the shadows of the lobby at the rear of the hotel. Here the hotel revealed its true dimensions. They were standing under a wide arched walkway in white stone that led to function and administration rooms on both sides of the central section of the hotel, beyond which the two wings, containing several floors of guest rooms. Down the steps there lay a large marble courtyard with a blue-and-white art-deco fountain."

"We spotted some trolleys with food and drinks were also available. Some people who had paid already were helping themselves. Jack enquired and discovered that vouchers were available inside." Jack went and bought four vouchers while Raza bought two bottles of wine. We selected a plate of food and, maneuvering with the plates, glasses of wine and bottles, they slowly started to walk around and mix. It turned out that once every so often the hotel was turned over to the public. Some people brought their own hampers, but most ate the hotel's food, which helped bring in extra income.

Having finished eating and put away their plates on the trolleys, they decided to follow where many of the people seemed to be going and headed down past statues strewn on the grass along the way to where the lawn cascaded down almost to the water front. The sheer scale and design looked magnificent as they turned back to look at the hotel, and speculated about the kinds of people it must have been built for, and what they did for a living. Now it was in public hands.

"That evening was our last evening together, and we decided to make the most of it by walking along the road that runs alongside the Malecon, the long sea wall on the northern coast of Havana, and where 50s American cars, repainted and repaired would drive up and down. The beautiful old buildings were in a state of decay and abandonment, due for restoration under the huge reconstruction program.

We went over to the sea wall, looked across the deep blue waters and smoked a cigarette, before turning back toward the Hotel Havana Libre built the year before the revolution as the Havana Hilton. It was an appropriate place to have a few drinks, so we walked across the vast marble floor to the bar on the ground floor. Tess and Rosa were both disconsolate because of the imminent end of their holiday. As a result, I ordered a concoction of campari, vodka, and rum for myself and Jack, and we sat sipping cocktail after cocktail without feeling drunk, talking politics, until Rosa and Tess headed back to their hotel. The next day we said farewell to Jack and Rosa, embraced warmly, and promised to meet again."

During the evening, Tess and Raza said a long and slow farewell to Cuba. Everywhere there was music and serenades, as if meant for them. Havana had been a heady mix of eclectic architecture, ranging from neoclassical, baroque, old colonial and even Moorish to art deco and modern. Here they were sitting in the modernist building and saying farewell to Cuba.

The next morning, they packed their bags and memories and went to Jose Marti Airport, Raza humming "Guantanamera." During the time that has elapsed since the visit, he has heard how much Cuba has changed. He wonders whether the road and transportation between Havana and Trinidad de Cuba has improved.

NADIA GETS MARRIED AND EMIGRATES TO THE UNITED STATES

By the time Raza finished his latest project on drugs, race, and social exclusion at Middlesex Institute for Drug Dependence, his daughter Nadia was 32. She had had two or three boyfriends before, who Raza had met. Largely he stayed out of the way of expressing any opinion, leaving it to his daughter to tell him if there was anything serious. But Tess would be more to the point and find out for herself. For the last 18 months she had been going out with a young American who was also doing classical studies. Where Nadia had been specializing in Greek language and literature, Will has chosen classical history. The two seem happy and well suited. Tess and Raza speculated whether this was it. Then suddenly, they decided to get married that summer.

The wedding was to be on the shores of Lake Como. As it turned out, both Will's dad and Raza had long loved Stendhal's *Charterhouse of Parma*, which contains some haunting scenes around Lake Como. That's where the wedding is to be, in a small chapel on the shores of Lake Como. Raza congratulates the couple and writes to Zahra to send him the last shawl in his share, hoping it will arrive in time.

The wedding day in June approaches and the shawl hasn't arrived in time. Raza and Nadia meanwhile receive a shock. Paul H., who had been looking forward to attending Nadia's wedding, suddenly dies. He was only 57. Raza learns this from Penny. It is of great personal loss to Raza. Paul had been so much part of his intellectual formation. His books, some of them personally inscribed, beckon to him from the shelves as he listens to Penny giving him the news. There is a cremation ceremony attended by all his friends and colleagues. Raza recognizes many of them from one of the pews he is standing in. Different people get up and speak. Paul has left behind an intellectual void for many of his friends and colleagues.

Things have to move on, and they do. While Nadia goes ahead to Como with her husband-to-be and her in-laws, Raza invites Ana-Livia and her two boys, aged 13 and 12 respectively, to come with him and Tess to the little resort at one end of Lake Como, about 10 miles from Milan by train. Ana-Livia is delighted they arrive at Como in the afternoon. It's only a small place, a few blocks of Alpine houses and chalets, used as a resort by locals. Nadia and Will were staying in a small hotel in an inlet by the waterfront. Since it was full, Raza and Tess find another hotel that can accommodate all of them a couple of blocks away.

They are there for three or four days, and although Raza doesn't get to see Villa Carlotta, he does take outings in the ferries, double-decker affairs that crisscross across the lake, stopping to let people off and on at various towns, like Bellagio. I once visited the area while attending a conference in Bellagio, the 50-acre center located on Lake Como.

On the day of the wedding, Ana-Livia takes the boys with Tess to Milan, just 20 minutes away by train. They buy some shoes and clothes. The days are sunny. Raza and Tess eat together with Nadia and the in-laws in a restaurant you can walk to along the water's edge, on the other side of the inlet. They talk and get to know each other. Steve's siblings and their partners are there too, taking turns to look after their ailing mother.

The wedding day approaches. Raza is taken to the small chapel further up the lake by the water's edge. It's a simple little chapel. After previous triangular discussions about the arrangements between Alan, Nadia, and himself, a program of the ceremony has been printed and Raza and Tess are handed a copy each. Raza is to recite a verse from the Koran, while Alan will recite from the Bible. Raza has decided to use the A. J. Arberry translation and recite from the Surah called Mary. He has a copy belonging to his father, with his notes written in margins.

The day arrives when Raza has to give his daughter away. Thirty-three years and now a parting, would it be forever? He tries to control his feelings as best as he can and be happy for his daughter. Tess feels his burden and tries to soothe him and make him happy. They travel by ferry, all fifteen or sixteen of them, to the chapel. Raza has bought a new suit for the wedding, with matching shirt tie and pocket-handkerchief. After Alan, he climbs the pulpit and, unable to control his feelings, cries while trying to recite.

On returning to London, there is a large wedding party, organized and largely paid for, by Alan. Raza has tried to match it by getting a loan from his bank. The venue is at a hotel near Victoria Station, where Alan and his party are staying. There are seating arrangements for lunch, and Nadia has invited John B, Bev, Steph, Susanne, and Penny to the party from among her dad's friends, and Hurr Bhai and Zainab Baji's children. Abid, Zahra, and Jafar have sent messages wishing happiness and success from Lucknow. The wedding party is a success. After lunch Raza goes around to find Maysam, Qais, and their sisters. They are in a group apart from where the alcohol is circulating.

For the next few months, Nadia and Will try to meet their academic commitments and complete their doctorates. Nadia will be based at King's while William will be based at Bristol, teaching as well as writing.

In the post-9/11 era that is to radically change the face of things. Will mentions to Raza that he is teaching Tony Blair's son at Bristol University. The irony doesn't escape Raza, who has been aware since that fateful day—9/11— of his vulnerability as a nominal Muslim. Raza detested Blair for the illegal invasion of Iraq that had only succeeded in destroying civil society in Iraq.

As newlyweds, Nadia and Will only get to spend weekends together. Conscious of the cutbacks in the teaching of Classics, they reluctantly have to look for jobs in the United States. Raza is aware of this and tries to get accustomed to the coming wrench of separation. During January, Will has the offer of two jobs and accepts the one at MIT. For Nadia, there's nothing certain yet. She mentions to her dad that she is applying to various universities in Boston.

The day of parting arrives as Will and Nadia come to say goodbye. Nadia comes and sits on the couch by Raza's side in the living room. She rubs his shoulder as he looks away with emotion. Tess has thoughtfully brought out some glasses of wine. She and Will try to act natural. Finally, Raza pulls himself together and they all drink a toast, before they all walk down the stairs to the waiting taxi, Nadia supporting Raza down the stairs. Outside in the street there is a final embrace between father and daughter before the door of the taxi shuts.

"It won't be forever, Dad. I'll be back soon," shouts Nadia.

But she won't, she won't, Raza knows. He has brought her up to be independent. He is happy that the shawl arrived in time, and that she has his mother's emerald earrings that had been so carefully kept by Zahra for just such an occasion.

As we move from the odysseys and transformation in Raza's life, back to a concern for the family legacy; the one thing that marred the occasion for Raza and should have been a signal to him about crisscross familial alliances was that Zahra had entrusted them to Hashim Bhai's daughter who was traveling back to England. Raza had known her since she was a child, and Abid had not so long ago stayed with her and brought back some delicious raan-kabaab.

When she met Raza at the airport transfer lounge, she was very abrupt, insulting almost, shoving the packet containing the emerald earrings into his hands before abruptly walking away. Since then things had dramatically changed. Her husband was a firm believer in primogeniture, being the eldest son himself. The couple began to take sides and were to reveal their allegiance to Begum and Ibn Dawood when the husband was fatally entrusted by Zahra to send him an important document of his father, one that contained information about the qualified reasons for Nawab Haidar reluctantly signing away his legitimate claim to Amadabad.

Unsurprisingly, no word of congratulations had been received from Ibn Dawood or Begum to their niece. None were expected. Raza was aware how partisan the couple was in favoring some nieces over others. Only formal relations and communications still remained because Raza was constantly being pulled backwards and forwards between his Indian, Muslim, and European belongings.

PART THREE

Nobody quite prepares you for the first sight of Lucknow. Even today, the third courtyard of the Great Imambara is one of the world's greatest spaces. In front of you is the *Imambara* itself—the dwelling place of the Imam—with its endless sequence of crinkled arches and pepper-pot domes sheltering what was in its time the largest unsupported vaulted hall in the world. To the right, splayed at an angle so that it faces Mecca, is the Asafi Mosque with its three onion domes and tall minarets and a great swirl of shallow steps leading up to it like a fan sweeping the ground in homage, and behind you a precession of huge three-arched gateways, all adorned with the leaping fish, the emblem of the Nawab who built these extraordinary buildings, perhaps the most under-sung architectural marvels anywhere.

Ferdinand Mount

CHAPTER 24

THE DECLINE

Raza thought by following this thread and trying to understand that which united the family he would discover what, if any, future awaited the Amadabad family after what had turned out to be a betrayal of all that had bound the family together for so long; and whether it would now simply fade away into history, as so many families do. Since the passing away of members of the older generation, Raza had little time or money to travel to his ancestral home where he would find signs and clues about the future of the Amadabad family.

Raza writes a journal entry nearly 20 years after graduating from his London boarding school, recalling all the events that led to his present situation. He still lives in London and sits contemplating what to do about his double cousin, Ibn Dawood or "Shaikhoo," who has promised to provide all family members with a share of the family estate, an inheritance he would like as much as everyone else. However, these shares are not forthcoming and several years have passed and no shares. Raza's thinking about his life and the circumstances that he now faces reading his letters and notes and comes across one from his father.

November 1990, somewhere in the Middle East.

Raza, my son,

I'm old, we both know that. I can no longer walk, eat or sleep as I used to. I can't even read anymore! My whole body is decaying and there's nothing I can do about that. But my mind seems to be still working. All I have is my memories to entertain me during many dull days and nights. I've been immersed in them for so long now I can no longer tell what is real and what is not. That's never stopped me from saying what I think, anyways. So I will say it to you! Because I think that you need to hear it as much as I need to get it out of my system. God knows how you're going to take it. Hopefully it will make you some good. Nevertheless, there's a chance that our already troubled relationship will never be healed.

You know I spent much time "on the couch" trying to recover from my supposed schizophrenia under the guidance of this eccentric doctor, Alfred Adler. As it turned out, there was nothing actually wrong with me; I mean, at least it wasn't something I could control. Go figure! (perhaps not a phrase he would use) Some homeopathic purgative took away what many hours into the depths of my physique could not.

This should tell you something about life. Things could be so much simpler if we just allow them to be that way. I now realize you didn't have it easy. Neither did I. But we both were brave in our own ways, and stupid, also in our very own ways. Adler's therapy is not all losses after all. He has his theories and one of them seems to me appropriate for our cases. You must excuse me for applying the results of my therapy on your own life, but I just can't help looking at your life through the lenses of my own experience.

I'm sure you won't mind my digressing a little on theoretical issues. After all, you are an accomplished intellectual and this is the kind of stuff with which you feel at home. Here you've found your new home away from the fields of Pakistan and I'm intruding in your terrains hoping to find the right voice for you to listen.

Adler's theory goes like this, and I quote since I'm no psychiatrist:

"Childhood is a foundational stage in the formation of our personality. The best way to inoculate against what are now termed 'personality disorders' (what Adler had called the 'neurotic character'), or a tendency to various neurotic conditions (depression, anxiety, etc.), is to train a child to be and feel an equal part of the family.

This entails developing a democratic character and the ability to exercise power reasonably rather than through compensation. Hence Adler proselytized against corporal punishment and cautioned parents to refrain from the twin evils of pampering and neglect. The responsibility to the optimal development of the child is not limited to the Mother or Father but to teachers and society more broadly. Adler argued therefore that teachers, nurses, social workers, and so on require training in parent education in order to complement the work of the family in fostering a democratic character.

When a child does not feel equal and is enacted upon (abused through pampering or neglect) they are likely to develop inferiority or superiority complexes and various accompanying compensation strategies."

Just think about the way you and I were raised and draw your own conclusions. It is more than evident that in a family such as ours there's no room for such pretty concepts as "democratic character" or "reasonable exercise of power." We are part of the royalty, for God's sake! There are no such things in a royalty. On top of that, we are supposed to be obedient Muslims. Everything around us was there to work as a straitjacket. Each one of us were denied individuality, we were just part of a machine that works for a given end but never stops to question what all that efforts are for.

And so it goes. Our family name, you are aware of its burden. Our houses, our political influences, our damn reputation! There's hardly a way out for us. No wonder our lives are now such a mess. We never had an opportunity to choose so we ended up living our lives with no control over them. We were two airplanes that sooner or later would have to crash. And we did crash.

You know better, Raza! You left us when you were just a child really and you decided never to come back. You indulged in all the pleasures of life that are denied to the members of our family.

You looked down on our way of life and ended up embracing ideologies that, no doubt, came handy as justifications. To put in pathological terms, you developed an inferiority complex caused by the constraints imposed upon you by your unlucky place of upbringing. This situation led you to break away from all that seems arbitrary and irrational in your life. Hence, today you feel superior. You are above us, above your past, about your culture, above material interests, above your father. You and I, son, we are just a repetition of history, in case you haven't noticed.

We exemplify some kind of ideal type: the perennial struggle between fathers and sons. Today it is easier for me to understand your decisions and your attitude. Who would want to live as I did? There's one word that characterizes my days in this world: sacrifice. I gave my life to our family's inheritance; I gave my life to the independence of our country and to the fight against British rule; I made the life of your mother a living hell; but I also gave my life to you.

As a father you act irrationally most of the time. You are led by passions stronger than yourself. [I tell you this because you had no sons.] There's no substitute for experience when it comes to learning about life. I always envisioned you in Amadabad without even considering if that was something you would like. No one asked me what I wanted to do as a child so I didn't ask you. It turns out my fight was not to your advantage, but I thought it was. It was tradition that was guiding me in my stubbornness.

And, of course, you saw that and reacted. You rejected my life. You stepped away from the path that was being cleared for you, as if it would be the path that would lead you to a life of misery. That was not my case. I surrendered to the forces of tradition. I allowed myself to be possessed by the greatness of our history, our name and our wealth. And here I'm, a neurotic old man driven away from his family and land. You may think that I must regret my decisions, but, thanks to you, I don't. You're no better than I am, even though we took totally opposite paths. We are both embarked in a quest for meaning and we followed different leads. I put all my money on what I could see; yours went somewhere else. I tried to play safe; you took risks.

I thought I could stay in our golden cage and grow numb, so I wouldn't have to listen to all the noise that comes from outside to criticize our way of life; you though, could go afar to be carried away by this outside noise and, in that way, forget about your origins. It now seems to me that we were both wrong. There's no winning in this world. Either you suffer in one place or you suffer in another.

The closing chapters of our lives seem to prove me right. As I write you a letter from the Middle East, away from Amadabad, hoping that it will find you in London, your chosen home, I fear that it won't reach your hands. The repressed always returns. News has come that you've decided, after all these years in exile, to go back to Pakistan to fight your cousin Ibn Dawood. What is that for? Since when have you become so interested in all these earthly matters? Wealth, family honor, the will of your ancestors, is that important to you now? If you still keep me in some esteem take my advice: drop it! I've already wasted my life on it and it's not worth it.

Some years ago I would've told you that it is easier to make sense of one's life if you just follow the path you have inherited. I wanted to believe that, in part to prove you wrong. But that didn't make my life any easier, so I took off. I'm now pretending to make a life the way you did, away from everything. However, deep down I know it won't work. At least it is peaceful and new. I don't want to deal with all the crap that I found in my past. But you, you are taking, again, the opposite way. You are going back home who knows with what in mind. I'm skeptical but wish you well. It's never late to learn a new lesson. The only consolation I have is to know that you didn't have any sons or daughters. It was about time someone broke this vicious cycle of eternal suffering.

Your father,

Haidar Ali Mohammed

I believe in reflecting on this letter, I opine about how several royal families have met a similar fate. If truth be told that nobody cares about these old families, especially Muslim ones, I'm not sure how many would feel any pity for any royal family.

The first opportunity following the passing away of the older generation came about with his trip to India in the 1990s. Tess had fallen in love with India, on a previous visit at the time (1990s) and had coaxed Raza to go there for a holiday again. That decided, they flew to Delhi, followed by a trip to the south, to the parts of India he had not yet explored. They left the visit to Lucknow and Amadabad, which Raza felt he had to make, to the last, as a final adieu. Raza wasn't sure when, if ever, he'd be back again.

> Tess and Raza left for India that year (1993) during the month of August following the monsoon period, when the weather would still be warm, and flew as they had usually done to Delhi. On this occasion they were to spend three or four days in Delhi with Judge Suneet and Bal to acclimatize themselves, culturally speaking. Since Tess had wanted to see the south, Raza talked with Suneet. Being the head of the All India Agricultural Workers' Union, and on the Central Committee of CPI (M), it was no problem for Suneet to contact the Speaker of the Kerala Assembly, a fellow member of CPI (M), and gave them his card to introduce themselves, telling them: "Do go and see him. He'll take care of everything about your stay."

At the same time, Raza had met up with his niece Masuma, now also living in Delhi. She had married someone of her own choice, a man some years older than herself, in defiance of the wishes of her father Solly. He was a medium-ranking civil servant, working for the Indian Revenue Service, a position rare for Indian Muslims to hold, let alone for Shi'a Muslims, who were a minority in an already discriminated against minority.

Raza met Jack (husband) and immediately took a liking to his straightforward but respectful attitude. Zahra, who had given the nod to Masuma's marriage to Jack, had mentioned to Raza before he left for India that Jack would appreciate a tweed jacket as a wedding present, and Raza had bought one in the suggested size from Selfridge: slightly shorter in the arms than Raza was, and a little stouter. Jack really appreciated the present.

What came to Raza as an interesting piece of information was that Jack was aware of all the goings-on in the Amadabad family from the points of view of his wife Masuma and his mother-in-law Zahra. He had also come to know something about the affairs of BK, Begum's older brother, who was the chief executive of an oil company in Bombay and whose tax papers had landed on Jack's desk at the IRS. Being the straightforward, ethical kind of man he was, Jack had passed the papers back to his superiors to be sent elsewhere, saying there would be a conflict of interests. Raza tucked this piece of information away in his mind because he had heard from his own father how much influence BK had on Ibn Dawood.

Later that day, Tess and Raza met Jack in one of the upmarket hotels springing up by then in Delhi. Gone were the two Delhis of his youth, easily recognizable as old Delhi and New Delhi. Delhi had become a sprawling megalopolis. Jack was more familiar with this modern Delhi. He seemed to be known to the hotel manager, another Muslim, whom Jack introduced Raza to as someone working in drug treatment and rehabilitation. The man said that he would like to set up a charity for the treatment of drug addicts whose population was rife throughout India, with few treatment or rehabilitation options.

The idea interested both Raza and Tess and he said that he would like to think it over. The meeting with Jack was proving very interesting. He appeared to have a lot of contacts all over the place, and was sometimes given perks as part of the job. He offered to get Tess and Raza a flight to Cochin, from where they could travel by train to Trivandrum, the state capitol. Nothing could have suited them better.

To give an idea of the size of India, Raza explained to an excited Tess that Cochin was a distance of about 1,100 miles south of Delhi, a journey of about three hours by a domestic flight. The plane eventually circled over Cochin airport on the edge of the Arabian Sea, showing a coastline of an endless beach with rows of coconut palm trees. Looking through the window by his seat, it reminded him of Venezuela, but on a much larger scale. Kerala is almost the same degrees of latitude above the equator, a subtropical paradise.

By the time they arrived it was getting dark. A coach took the passengers who were traveling on by train the next morning to a modern hotel near the airport, all done in a local style of décor. Fish swam in large tanks around the main reception area and bar where they sat and sipped cocktails, chose and ordered fish picked from one of the tanks, and felt guilty. The next morning, after a good night's sleep, they left by train along the long winding track to Trivandrum, a three-hour journey in a crowded train, the faces of the local passengers only occasionally staring and then looking away. They seemed to be kind, and many of them could understand English, which is the first thing Raza noticed because he only spoke Urdu or Hindustani.

He had learnt about Kerala of course from Ces and Annie, when Ces was doing his fieldwork for his masters at the School of Oriental and African Studies (SOAS). Yet that was a long time ago. More recently, he had learnt from Suneet that Kerala had the highest degree of literacy in India, and that while the majority of people were Hindus, there were also Muslims, Christians, and even some Jewish people, the so-called lost tribe of Israel. It also had a progressive government and a relative lack of corruption. It all remained to be seen, and Tess was particularly in her element, excited and wanting Raza to translate everything for her.

The train that took them from Cochin to Trivandrum the next morning was a local that took four and half to six hours. Express trains took two and half to three hours. It was early afternoon by the time they arrived in Trivandrum in the huge bustling city, in the sullen heat.

"We found a cab to take us to the Secretariat Building where we had the appointment with the Speaker of the Assembly. The building was a colonial-style building in pale-colored stone, ornamental columns supporting the covered portico above a flight of stairs that led to the entrance through wide wooden doors into a dark-paneled interior and marble floor. From there, after presenting ourselves at the enquiries and reception desk, we were ushered into the Speaker's office.

The Speaker was very courteous and asked how long we wanted to stay and where. Since we wanted to be by the sea, he asked his secretary to reserve a room for two at the government-managed hotel in Kovalam, 10 miles to the west of Trivandrum. A taxi was ordered. We thanked the Speaker before heading off along a partly paved road with tropical trees along the side until we reached the hotel. The hotel did not disappoint, perched as it was on a hilltop overlooking the sea, nor did the friendly local people, who hovered around the entrance to tout for scooter-taxis that could take them shopping. We were able to converse in English and Hindi so we could come to an agreement over fares."

Raza and Tess spent a week at the hotel, walking down to the beach hidden in an escapement between the rocky coves over which Kovalam is situated, and watching the fishermen bring in the day's catch—one day they even asked one of the fishermen to grill some fish for them over the fire they had lit. They paid even less here for fish just out of the water. Trips by boat on other days took them to the "spice islands" that the Dutch, Portuguese, French, and English had fought over. Raza was surprised to find mosques that had been built by Arab merchants and traders, and sniffed and inhaled the aromas of spices arising from sacks—turmeric, saffron, peppers, cloves, and cardamoms, the same spices that had attracted people there from ancient times. There was also a boat trip along the backwaters. Before leaving Kovalam, Raza thought that this was the place he's like to build a house one day to spend the northern winters.

To cap it all, toward the end of their stay, Raza and Tess were invited to a Cuban food festival, hosted by the Cuban Consulate in alliance with the ruling CPI (M) government of Kerala. Here they tasted Cuban food for the first time, and Raza broke down with emotion when he was presented to the female consul. Such was still his adherence to the principles of the Cuban Revolution. He kept the card she gave him in his wallet, thinking of using it at some later date.

The return to Delhi was a long train ride from Trivandrum, taking them two days and one night in a first-class sleeper car. After such a long journey it was time for a break, and they stayed in one of the new four-star posh hotels that Jack had booked for them at a concessionary price. He did not join them because he knew Tess drank, and he did not find it acceptable to sit with a relative who drank, but he did recommend the food in the Italian-style restaurant.

It also served some home-produced bottles of wine. Yes, to Raza's surprise, India was now producing wine with the help and advice on viniculture of a French wine producer. During dinner the devil got into them when Raza suggested that he had Ibn Dawood's phone number, though he didn't know where he lived, but could phone him and arrange to meet.

The next morning Raza did telephone. Ibn Dawood answered and could not refuse a meeting, though he did say that unfortunately it would only be a short meeting because he had to meet someone "terribly important." Raza was familiar with this trait of Ibn Dawood, a move he had always made in setting up meetings.

"Bhai Sahab, we'll meet you at the back entrance to your hotel, it's not too difficult to pull up and park there. We'll be arriving in half an hour."

Ibn Dawood's car, a four-door SUV with a removable top, and fitted with all mod cons, drove up promptly as soon as Raza and Tess came down the steps of the hotel.

Neither Raza nor any of his brothers had ever been invited to Begum and Ibn Dawood's Delhi apartment, obtained one assumes through her family connections, nor known what had been taken there from the family estate like precious manuscripts, carpets, furniture, and chandeliers. Though the fact that some of the things had gone was in no doubt, as his brothers and sisters had hinted. Raza's curiosity would have to wait for another day to find things out for himself.

Ibn Dawood, Begum, and the driver, whose face Raza recognized from Lucknow, got out of the car. "Adab Bhaisahab," said both Begum and Ibn Dawood, while the driver, who recognized him, said salaams. Raza bent forward and, in mock gallantry, kissed Begum's hand. Both Begum and Ibn Dawood seemed somewhat discomfited. Tess they barely made an effort to acknowledge.

"Let's all get in, and then we can talk along the way. When the driver has dropped us off, he will bring you back to the hotel."

Ibn Dawood sat in the front, alongside the driver, while the other three fitted comfortably in the spacious rear. Not mentioning anything about Kerala—the less his cousin knew about his plans the better—Raza told Ibn Dawood that he and Tess would be going to Lucknow and Amadabad.

"It's been almost two years nearly since the passing away of Abbajan and Bajia Amma, and for obvious reasons I want to go there, as well as seeing my brothers and sister."

I should mention here that Raza said this by way of information. He was not seeking permission. Relations had not deteriorated between them to that extent, at least not on the surface. Ibn Dawood wanted to keep Raza on his side, at least for the moment.

Raza, behind the scenes, could clearly be discerned the hand of the Mishra family, who had long been Ibn Dawood's closest advisors. One would have thought that in the middle of all this he could not afford to risk any Pakistani ties. Yet, according to Maysam, he and Begum, both Indian citizens, were in Karachi together and proceeding with the sale of the remaining apartments in the area. How could they have done so except with high connections? Yet here they were intent on selling the apartments that belonged to his sisters, for which, according to Maysam, no receipt was to be produced, and no money from the sale handed over to the rightful owners.

"Maysam told us that both Begum and Ibn Dawood visited Karachi at this time, whether the Indian government was aware of or not is another matter. High-level contacts that they both had—as evidenced by Begum's affair with Jingo—must have been used."

At any rate, in the here and now, Ibn Dawood displayed no anxiety or concern about Raza's visit. He still had hopes of keeping me on his side. If he was wary of anyone it was of Abid. And, rightly so, because Abid knew more about his comings and goings than I did. So for the moment, I simply hung back taking it all in trying to pick up on the nuances as his car drove to his appointment."

Along the way, Tess developed a migraine. There was a polished wooden box between the driver and passenger seat at the front, not like the old wooden box there had been in Jack's battered old Jeep, but a polished and inlaid one. Ibn Dawood opened it and offered Tess a diazepam pill from one of a whole compendium of assorted pillboxes. Tess said nothing, expressed no surprise, but kept it until later to tell Raza that his cousin was a raving drug addict and not her, as they (Ibn Dawood and Begum) had been insinuating.

Raza and Tess said goodbye as the car dropped Ibn Dawood and Begum off at their destination; then took Raza and Tess back to their hotel. The chauffeur said salaams to Raza as they got out, adding, "Mian, I am from Lucknow." Raza couldn't remember his face, but returned his salaams anyway.

On arrival at Lucknow airport, Raza and Tess were met by his brothers, who had both come all the way to the airport in a car to greet him and Tess before driving them back home along the long familiar roads, laughing and chatting all the way, mostly in English because of Tess, but sometimes naturally breaking into Urdu, their mother tongue.

Arriving at the gates, the exterior of the palace showed no obvious signs of deterioration. The whole length of the frontal façade had been repainted in keeping with the new raja and rani's status. Money for all this was coming from somewhere, though Ibn Dawood would always say that he was relying on his wife for money whenever he spoke to Raza or any family member about such things, just in order to pretend poverty and avoid being asked for a handout as part of their shares.

Further signs of his new self-importance revealed themselves in there being two sentries now, one at the gates, and the other in front of the palace. Until then, during Raza's parents' time, there had been the solitary Nepalese Gurkha who had arrived in the 1940s and had never wanted to return home. The Nepalese Gurkha spend his nights on duty, drinking homemade liquor to keep him warm, smoking biris, and walking up and down, looking at the silhouette of the palace in the moonlight and imagining he was seeing *perees* or angels in the *Araam Kamra*.

As was to be expected, Ibn Dawood had installed himself in his father's suite of rooms and made further encroachments in the palace for his personal space toward the room at the rear, the entrance to which lay in the corner of the courtyard beyond, and whose other door lay in the courtyard below Jafar's room. If this sounds like a Byzantine layout, rife for plots and secret trysts and imbroglios, the reader would not be mistaken. This room had previously been occupied by one of the estate managers during Nawab Dawood Ahmad's time, and innuendos among the servants had been exchanged aplenty.

"Begum still occupied the suite of rooms overlooking the porch that she had since her wedding, and the sons, still at school in England, had been allocated rooms above, alongside the *Araam Kamra*, that could be reached on the way to the Imambara, where long-unused rooms had been opened up around a courtyard at the end of the palace next to the southern gate to Kaiserbagh. To the left of Ibn Dawood's domain, and below the balcony room, there was another suite of rooms that had been used by various people at different times, most recently by Abid and Jafar's Arab and Iranian friends."

These friends had been guests of Abid and Jafar while Nawab Haidar Ali was still alive. They were serious young scholars and students, just like the ones who used to arrive during previous years and who were largely studying Shi'a Islam in India. Because of this association between his two sons and the young Middle Eastern visitors, Nawab Haidar Ali had referred to Abid and Jafar, along with Raza as his "three musketeers," among whom Raza was obviously meant to be the secular Marxist one. Ibn Dawood was trying to make much more of this situation than of the Iraqi and Iranian students, and after his uncle's death he started putting it about that his cousin Abid was associating with dangerous Middle- Eastern radicals. On one occasion, on a visit to London, he had even mentioned his concern to Raza, playing on the latter's egalitarian left-wing tendencies and hoping to sow divisions.

"After a hasty look around at the familiar façade of the old palace, acknowledging the salaams of the house servants and the other sentry who had been seated by the porch but now came to by the main entrance, I went along the familiar marble hall with old family photographs hanging on both sides, and up the marble staircase down whose wooden balustrades I used to slide down as a boy, until I finally came up under the verandah of the inner courtyard and looked around at my parents and brother's quarters I saw things much in need of refurbishment, and the walls needing a good coat of plaster and paint. In the old days, the grandfather had taken responsibility for the upkeep of the entire palace."

"It was he who had added an extension to the palace in depth toward the rear, adding the inner courtyard in 1932. After him, Nawab Dawood Ahmad had continued with the renovations and upkeep up to a point, and when the occasion demanded, as it had done just prior to his eldest daughter Zainab's wedding in 1950 to Hurr, as the reader might recall from an earlier account, having to borrow the money from his wife, his own having been spent on the Muslim League."

"But he had then gone to Pakistan. There followed a period of gradual decay, as costs grew. There was no income from the estate. Family units within the Amadabad clan, like that of Nawab Haidar Ali, became responsible for the renovation and upkeep of their own quarters. After him the new edict issued by Ibn Dawood was that the remaining family units would have to pay their own other charges, such as for electricity. So here I was now, looking at all the familiar places and rooms in my parents' quarters, wondering how my brothers would actually be managing it all."

He was soon to find out. Abid had kept possession of the *Araam Kamra*, that room had historically been his grandfather's room, the high ceilings providing a natural coolness during the summer. It was from here that he would descend the marble staircase for meetings. Later, ever since Raza's uncle had seen the ghost of his father when sleeping there, and decided to have his own suite of rooms built downstairs, the room was used as a guest room. Raza remembers one of Hurr Bhai's uncles, Taqi Chacha, a giant of a man, hirsute and with a big laugh. Taqi Chacha, like his brothers, had stayed in England, unable to bear the heat of Lucknow. One summer he had taken a shower in the magnificent adjoining bathroom, fully clothed in his kurta and pajamas, and emerged feeling much refreshed to everyone's amusement.

Even before Raza's uncle had left for Pakistan, the *Araam Kamra* was regarded as being part of Raza's father's domain where, during holidays, Raza would stay. It thus had a historical significance. Abid occupied it while his parents were still alive, and this prevented Ibn Dawood and Begum from taking it over, as they had done with other parts of the palace, extending their reach everywhere. One could get the sense that they were now the main attraction, the center of everything, and that others were tolerated as poor relatives.

So there was Abid explaining his reasons for the occupation of the *Araam Kamra* to his brother, but he told Raza that in reality he slept in Jafar's room in the middle because the *Araam Kamra* was too far to send any of the few remaining servants to. Meanwhile, Jafar had taken to sleeping in Bajya Amma's room. Zahra's room was unavailable because she was due there shortly herself. Accordingly, Raza and Tess were accommodated in the *Araam Kamra*, and during their stay, Raza and Tess volunteered to contribute to the daily food and groceries, as well as for their laundry. Tess insisted on this and insisted on giving a £10 note, which was an inordinate amount of money by Indian standards. Everyone laughed.

"Munnay having passed away, there was only one man servant to do the fetching and carrying, or else Jawaid Sahab on his motorbike. I discerned an impish look in Abid's eyes one day. It was a look I recognized from childhood, and it denoted that I knew something that others didn't. I would try and find out, but the opportunity would often pass by. Abid was very good at teasing and prolonging the telling. Knowing this I knew that eventually Abid would tell me. On the surface, Abid seemed to be doing all right financially, having invested wisely. Jafar, who was totally unlike Abid, who was taller and more blunt speaking when he needed to be.

Their mother had told me that Abid was unable to lose his temper with his younger brother because Jafar was not afraid of responding in kind. Jafar was trying to earn money as a property developer, having invested his inheritance in a business partnership with someone, and would often be out during the days on his motorbike, asking others not to wait for him for lunch. On some days, he would come home and eat lunch at three in the afternoon."

During the few days he and Tess spent with his brothers and sister—Zahra had arrived from Kanpur to see him for the time he was there—Abid told them, in more so many words, that their cousin was up to no good, and that he was aware that Ibn Dawood was after their father's papers and documents on some pretext or the other. Abid had kept on stalling him and had meanwhile photocopied the documents and secreted them away. He also mentioned of the several steel book cupboards from the Amadabad Library, full of precious Arabic and Persian manuscripts that had been moved by his father to Kaiserbagh during the period the palace in Amadabad had been sealed, and that had stood there to the right of the anteroom at the top of the marble staircase ever since.

"I remember passing them on my path whenever I left mother's quarters to go down the marble staircase," Abid was now saying, shaking his head, "and that the keys to those steel book cupboards had been given by father to Ibn Dawood, and I suspect that some manuscripts had already been smuggled out in his own or Begum's luggage, and once via a niece visiting from London, who moreover had been given a sweetener in the form of other books from the library."

While waiting for the property to be released, Begum and Ibn Dawood were evidently not wasting any time in cashing in what they could. The value of the contents of the steel bookcases alone must have been tens of millions of pounds, all of them standing in such a tempting place.

"Abid knows because he had once managed to take one of the manuscripts, a small copy of an ancient Quran and sold it to an antique dealer, but the dealer had returned it [to Abid's father], and the matter was hushed up. Now that Ibn Dawood had the keys, it was clear that he was going to appropriate the whole lot for himself. Equal shares for everyone? Forget it."

Now we can reveal the mystery of that impish look that Raza had discerned in his brother when he had arrived. It was about a bottle of scotch that Abid had secreted away in the *Araam Kamra* to take a snifter from now and then. The truth is that most of his generation drank alcohol, even Ibn Dawood. Hurr Bhai would joke about it to his wife and say that he wouldn't mind taking alcohol, and Raza recalled the incident in London when Hurr had dared himself to eat a liqueur chocolate and said afterwards that he had felt funny. Raza had smiled to himself. Hurr Bhai did not know what being inebriated feels like.

The point is that Abid still liked to drink, and from his recent London visit he had realized that Tess was a bit partial to it as well, so for her to partake of his scotch he would invite Tess and Raza when they talked freely about Ibn Dawood and Begum. This was the locale where all that was to be revealed was revealed, although one suspects that Abid knew much more than he was willing to let on.

"After a stay in Lucknow of two or three days, the time had come for Tess and I to go for a day and a night to Amadabad, the place of my birth. We went by car, driven by Ibn Dawood's favorite and most trusted chauffeur, the one whom I had met in Delhi. The plan was to visit the graves of my parents, spend a day in the palace, and then eat dinner in mother's quarters. A lady chef and kitchen maids had already been alerted."

"When we arrived in Amadabad, I sensed that the signs for the future of the Amadabad family were not good. The palace in Amadabad was largely deserted, the grass of abandonment growing on the walls of the Qila, the halls and empty rooms were cobwebbed and un-dusted for years. Bats had made their home at the top of the winding wooden staircase in the corner of the red verandah, where in my young years I would hide with friends and smoke our first cigarettes. Now, if you open the door the acrid stench of bat droppings filled the entire staircase."

Raza said at one time there were crowds of people milling about the palace, from the garage at one end to the large kitchen at the other, but now if you were to keep a daily attendance where once there were hundreds of people, the only person who kept up regular visits he knew for sure was his sister Zahra. He knew that while she could and while still able to travel from Kanpur, she would steadfastly travel to Amadabad in order to observe all the family birthdays according to the Muslim calendar, all the days of commemoration of ancestors past, lighting incense and candles.

"Zahra knew because she would write to tell me so: 'My dear Bhaisahab, I am in Amadabad today for Abbajan's birthday...' or some similar news, is what she would write to say. Others, like Abid, also continued to go to Amadabad but not as regularly as Zahra. Jafar rarely goes. Begum and the eldest son also show their face during Moharram, but Ibn Dawood rarely does; he has made himself as unpopular with the Amadabad public as he has with the public of Lucknow.

He largely prefers to live in Delhi, in Begum's apartment, if you believe—a place, which, apart from his wife and sons and some trusted managers and servants, no member of the family has ever been invited to. On the whole, he prefers to conduct the affairs of Amadabad from afar, through his highly paid and trusted personal secretary, the execrable Saggoo, whom we have met before when he used to be my father's secretary. Saggoo had been dismissed for malingering, and then immediately re-employed by Ibn Dawood, traveling as a first-class passenger to meetings with his master in Delhi. The day-to-day management of Amadabad is delegated to three or four chosen people, loyal to their paymaster. Wages of ordinary servants—the ones who fetched their tea and cigarettes, their bread and food, from the bazaar because no cooks inhabit the male kitchen in the palace any more, only those who keep a lone vigil during wintry nights, crouched over smoldering braziers, the wages of these and other menial laborers are often unpaid for months."

Raza tells me how beyond the main lawn, the walled garden with the swimming pool lies wild and deserted, and the "kamrakh" or starfruit tree his mother had tended for so long to produce sweet is now withered. No groups of gardeners work there. Only one is employed to keep the main lawn in trim, but the giant tree planted by his great-grandfather has fallen. Beyond, where the main kitchen and the stables used to be, is a total wilderness.

"You could say a wilderness of another kind hangs in the air of the female quarters. No kites, no eagles, no crows fly over the barren courtyard looking to snatch some food. Even during Moharram few women gather, many of the "nauhakhans" are dead or have moved away. The palace feels dead because it's too big to manage. Why should anyone want to keep it all to themselves? It should be turned over to the local people whose ancestors built it. Turned into a space for co-operatives. Ibn Dawood and Begum won't do that. They'll want to milk the last out of it if the estates are not released by turning it into a hotel perhaps, or hiring it out to film companies. Only they know. There was talk of turning it into a heritage site also."

As he walks from his room to his mother's quarters, Raza talks to Puttoo, his loyal manservant, Amma's son-in-law, who gets to hear what people are saying outside. He confides: "Miyan, things are very bad. What can I tell you? People outside don't respect Raja Mian. He has made himself very unpopular with his meanness. People remember your father's time here not so long ago. They remember his modesty, his forthrightness, and honesty. Managers couldn't pull the wool over his eyes. Now I only come here when you or Abid Bhaiyya or Nadia Bitya come here. Will you be staying long?"

"No, we have to go back in the morning."

"You should come for longer, and bring Nadia Bitya with you."

"Yes, I will try to do that."

Then as they reached the door, Puttoo held the screen away. With Puttoo's words ringing in his ears, Raza entered the *zanana* through the side door where his mother used to live. He knew what they meant. How could he explain that he had made his home somewhere else? Tess and Zahra were waiting for him. Dinner was ready. Abid had specifically requested Nargis, the daughter of one of the former chefs de cuisine, to come and cook something special. Finally, Abid appeared, and seeing that everyone was at the table, washed his hands and sat down to eat with everyone. "Bhaisahab, try these," he said, pointing to some round kofta kababs in a rich sauce, "I have asked them to be made specifically for you." They were good, very good, melting in the mouth with the hot taste of chillis and spices coming through later and hitting the palate. "It's the spicing and the marinade. She learnt the skills from her father, I have often said that she should go with you to London where it's crying out for good Indian food."

The next day Raza went to visit his parent's grave with Zahra, leaving Tess to be shown around the male section of the palace. At their tombs, he wept once more and was then gone, not knowing, in spite of his caution to Puttoo, when he'd be back again.

CHAPTER 25

IBN DAWOOD'S CLAIM

That winter Raza's organization was facing a funding crisis regarding monies for drug services, treatment, and rehab services. It had been a campaign in which Raza had assisted by being the organization's representative in the NCVO's Community Care Alliance consortium.

"I should just tell you that the Department of Health was forced at the last minute to agree to the amendment because it was facing a rebellion in the government's own ranks, but when it came to it the department took its revenge by agreeing to give conditional funding to the coordinating organization, provided the director left and the remaining staff posts were put under review under a department-appointed consultant."

Real politics can be very brutal and wasteful of human resources, so during 1994, Raza was going to have to be watchful of his job.

However, as we shall see, 1994 was to be eventful in many other ways too.

On October 21, 2005, the Lucknow Supreme Court gave the final verdict directing the government to hand over vacant possession of the nawab's estates to his "legal" heir. However, the news Raza received of the release of the family property was not from Ibn Dawood and Begum on this occasion, as it had been in 1994, but from his own brothers. According to them, Ibn Dawood was strutting about after the Lucknow Court's decision, calling himself "a born fighter."

"Jafar said Shaikhoo was more like a bloody fool and this is what he said in an email I sent to him. But keep in mind, however, that the whole thing turned out to be short-lived. One month Begum had been rewarded by her husband for all her efforts by being given the bungalow in Nainital, behind the hotel Nawab Dawood Ahmad had bought during my childhood when there was every sign of permanence, and then leased out to a professional hotel manager for rent. At the back of the hotel, there had been a bungalow with its own garden and according to reports, this was refurnished and, during the summer months, she would invite special guests, those who would praise her lavish hospitality and write about it."

"The next minute, Ibn Dawood was reported in the Lucknow newspapers for using the police to evict leaseholders from the property owned by the family. Now, these leaseholders had legal and binding 99-year leases, and had sublet units to shopkeepers. This led to counter demonstrations by shopkeepers against the self-styled raja of Amadabad. What compounded the situation, I heard from Abid, was the situation was made worse because their cousin had behaved so naïvely and with such arrogance with the lawyer representing the shopkeepers."

"The lawyer was not going to forget it, and in the coming national elections, the lawyer stood as a BJP candidate and was elected to the central government. The Centre soon brought in an ordinance to maintain the custodian's hold over the properties."

The long-awaited release of the family estate had turned into a farce before blowing up in Ibn Dawood's face. In a fit of bravado, he had tried to evict the shopkeepers and tenants, even though they were offering to negotiate higher rents. He sent his son to tell the tenants and leaseholders the evictions would go ahead. His attempt failed and there were chants of "Down with Amadabad" as victorious shopkeepers marched through Hazratganj when the order was rescinded.

Early in January, Raza received the news from Ibn Dawood that he had finally launched his claim for the release of the estate with the central government, and that, Insha Allah, he was hopeful for the release of all the property, and that everyone would receive their share as soon as this happened.

The phone conversations:

"Congratulations," (Raza)

"No, Raza Bhaisahab, believe me, everyone will get their share," Begum said, as she came on the phone before the conversation between Raza and his cousin ended.

"Do you believe that Raza?" asked Tess, listening in at the other end.

"Let's wait and see." Raza then spoke, "£80,000 would do nicely. He can't buy us out that cheap. There's more at stake than money."

Raza spoke with Abid, who agreed with his brother and doubted whether anything would come of it, even if the case was successful. "Bhaisahab, he'll never share," Abid had said shaking his head wisely.

Maysam, when Raza spoke to him, felt the same. His mother Zainab had already received the news from her brother, but based on his experiences, Maysam doubted his uncle's words and advised caution to his mother: "Amma, why do you continue to listen to him, or believe him?"

"I know, but what can I do, he is my younger brother."

The question arises: Why was Ibn Dawood so eager to inform everybody about his case when he knew that it would take years? If he really wanted to share with members of his family, he could have right then and there. He had lots of money and could have given everyone a share at that moment. The one simple unnoticed fact glaring everyone in the face was that there were millions of pounds worth of fortune in family fixed assets alone that was available for the entire family to share.

Presumably, he had promised Begum that everything was for them and their children alone because, as far as it is known, no one else had ever been offered anything, unlike his father, who from exile had said that everything should be shared by those who continued to live there. He had given the keys to the storerooms in Lucknow and Amadabad to his brother, Raza's father, in 1965. Even Raza, who didn't live there, was given permission to take some books.

As for Abid, who did live there, he had asked his uncle for the mango orchard in Amadabad to which the nawab had agreed, as well as the Austin car that used to take him and Raza to school. Things were now different. Not only was Abid denied the mango orchard, but Ibn Dawood awarded the contract to someone else and reaped the profits for himself, because he regarded all these assets as his and his alone, "as if by divine right," Qais says.

> Now here's the interesting thing. Unnoticed by anyone, except by Abid and Jafar, Ibn Dawood and Begum had already started to help themselves to it, while everyone was being asked to wait for the sale of property that may take years to materialize. This ill-gotten wealth was being stashed away in the same Swiss bank account, and invested in real estate in Europe and the United States, as future security should things not work out in India. They really had no loyalty to India. The language of capital, as Lenin has noted, is international, transcending national boundaries.

While this was happening in India, the next twist of fate facing Raza in London was that he was about to be made redundant. Things had not worked out under the Consultant, who had his own agenda and had decided to get rid of the permanent staff and install some new recruits to carry out his agenda. Raza didn't like the man, who seemed to him to have all the mannerisms of a sergeant major barking orders, and Raza told him so to his face. He and the two other members of staff involved decided that they would take their case to the Industrial Tribunal for having been made constructively redundant. Their Union Rep told them that the process could take months, and they would need to look for other jobs. In Raza's case, this was not going to be easy since he was approaching his 59th birthday.

"Fortunately for me, two things came to my rescue. The new director had written to the two European networks the old director had committed to organizationally as a partner, that he did not have the human resources to devote to it. The French and other Europeans of course took this as an insulting rebuff. Secondly, Jean Pierre head of T3E, on hearing this piece of news, and needing an English-speaking UK coordinator, who was essential for pan-EU work, offered to pay Raza an honorarium to continue coordinating for T3E in the United Kingdom. Financially this came to his rescue, and he was kept busy in being involved in the submission for the next funding program to the European Commission."

Raza, not wanting to be beholden, proposed that, apart from the coordination of the network, he would also like to contribute by carrying out his own action research in four European countries—England, France, Portugal, and Belgium. They were selected for having been four of the leading colonizing powers with large settled black and ethnic minority populations from their former colonies. Raza's research would focus on accessing the hidden needs of drug users and their families from these communities.

Jean Pierre had initially looked askance at Raza's proposal because in France everyone was regarded as equal—*Liberté, Ègalité, Fraternité*. Jean Pierre felt that Raza's approach was too Anglo-Saxon, but anyway he proposed that Raza come and explain his research to a group of directors from French drug services at a meeting in Paris. While waiting for the official start date of the contract that summer, Raza started sharpening his research skills by working on small contracts in London for service commissioners with N.A. The European Commission finally agreed to fund J-P's project for a 15-month period, with a start date of June 1, 1994. There were toasts all around in London and Beauvais. During that summer, his case before the Industrial Tribunal against his previous employers was also settled out of court. It amounted to over £8,000 and there was reason for more joy. He shared some of it with Tess. At any rate, for the moment, he wasn't short of money.

ABID IN FORCED EXILE

Yet another twist in the family saga was about to take place during 1996. Raza had completed the Dutch and Portuguese legs of his research, and was about to begin the English version, and was also about to celebrate his 60th birthday during February. Abid had written to him the previous December and wanted to spend some time with his brother in London. Sometimes he missed his brother, remembering their times together in Britain, after all, he had spent some happy years in Scotland as well as England and now had saved enough money to get away.

"He wrote to me in late December '95 and, on being informed that it was okay with me and Tess, that he would be welcome, Abid arrived during January and was to stay for an indefinite period, enough time to get away from the intrigues at home. Abid stayed for some time with us, since during the day, both Tess and I worked, he had time to visit various friends we both knew and had in common. Conscious of the lack of privacy he would eat out at old haunts, but at any rate he was no bother to us nor us to him."

When they were all together and sitting down, Raza and Tess would find it difficult to discuss things with Abid. Somehow in the English environment he seemed to have quaintly reverted to a younger brother. Away from there, Raza and Tess heard stories from friends of how charming and interesting he had been. His friends would get to hear stories about his family that Raza had never mentioned or talked about. Abid's stay became prolonged and for a few weeks he went away to stay with friends, as well as making trips to Scotland and, surprisingly, to France, where he intimates about a love affair he had with a young woman.

"This piece of information slipped out inadvertently one day when he came back to stay with us for a few days prior to his return to Lucknow. He was going to be there for his brother's birthday dinner party that Tess had organized in a friend's restaurant in South London. The party had gone well, and Abid had enjoyed himself by getting drunk. On the way back, Abid shared a cab with a friend (Duncan) because there was not enough room in my car. But I hadn't notice he was drunk. It was Duncan's kindness toward an honorary Scotsman that brought Abid safely back home. Abid's return flight was two days later. On the day of his flight, he had packed his bags and ordered a taxi before hugging us and saying goodbye."

A few hours later Raza was to receive a telephone call. It was from Abid saying that he had been refused permission to land in Delhi—he carried a British passport you see, and required a visa and permission to stay—and that's how he had been forced to land and put back aboard the plane returning to Dubai from Delhi. Now he had no option but to stay with a relative, while trying to find a solution to his predicament.

Abid was there for a few weeks, living in a state of anxiety which did his nervous nature no good, not knowing why he had been prevented from entering India. On what grounds? He had his suspicions and kept Raza informed.

Finally, he received news that it was on very high orders received by the Indian immigration police that his reentry had been prevented. The grounds given were that he was someone whose presence in India was considered undesirable. The finger pointed clearly at Ibn Dawood and Begum, since she would certainly have the connections, and then there were the stories being spread of Abid's association with dissident Arabs and Iranians, and the security risks that he posed by associating with them. Fortunately for Abid, his own contacts got him his re-entry visa, but Abid was much more careful of Ibn Dawood and of Begum's clear influence on him from then on.

"It seemed as if Ibn Dawood had managed to silence the one critical member of the family who lived in India, and who could see at first hand the game they were up to. But underneath it all, on his return, Abid was more determined to see how much further Ibn Dawood would go, and how much longer he could go on to tolerate living under the same roof. In reality, he loathed to leave the ancestral home, but, while having come to an accommodation with his cousin, he kept a watchful eye on the latter's further stratagems."

Whenever Raza telephoned or sent him an email, Abid would reply that he hadn't really seen Ibn Dawood and that would be to only occasionally show his face when he was in Lucknow, which was not often. As for Begum, who he would sometimes refer to as "that woman," she never came around. For the real news he would pick it up from the gossip among servants and employees, and would then record them as notes and later use them for a critical analysis on Jafar's computer. It was from these notes that he would send emails to his brother whenever Raza asked.

As for Jafar, he had no time for Ibn Dawood, no more than Ibn Dawood had for him. Jafar never had an interest in Amadabad affairs beyond those he had in keeping alive his deceased parents' maxims, and the affection for his own siblings, even though Zahra only came some times, and Raza even less often, so whenever Raza asked him for any news it was more in the way of a factual nature. Zahra too was bitterly critical of Ibn Dawood and Begum about the betrayal of the family legacy and she would also write to Raza about any news she had.

Here is what Qais says in an email about the Karachi apartments, bringing Abid's commentary into it:

> The land and property at No. 2 was sold in the fall of 1993 or early 1994 and no official receipt given to the owners (Amma and Khalajan) as arranged by uncle—who else? Not only is the exact sale price of No. 2 not known to us

till this day, the people involved have been given hefty "sweeteners" (bribes) to shut them up.

—What happened with the sale proceeds of No. 2 was a re-run of what happened with the sale of the textile mill. Again, it was uncle who organized everything in collusion with Mr. Ibadi. Honour amongst thieves!

—Officially, Raja Mian had no right to any property since being an Indian national he was a declared enemy!

—But Raja Mian's "philosophy" is that all that ever existed in Pakistan, he (Raja mian) had an inalienable right to under Muslim property law. However, whatever exists elsewhere (be it India or Europe, esp., Switzerland) is his and his alone or else his greedy wife and sons. Pseudo-shariah when it comes to any property in his sisters' names and law of primogeniture (more accurately the Law of the Primate!) when it comes to any property where he wishes to keep them out and claim sole possession.

"No. 2 was sold to one vey greedy developer after 1993—a much later period. Talks were going on about the sale of No. 2 when I visited the house with Amma between Dec. 1992 and Feb. 1993. Amma and Khalajan's then secretary was involved in negotiations throughout. On more than one occasion he personally criticized uncle to—whom he referred to as Raja mian—for his behaviour toward his sisters in terms of what he saw as an injustice and how "he (Raja mian) was usurping what rightfully belonged to his sisters." It was known to him that both the sisters were completely "helpless" when confronting Raja mian. In fact, they knew not how to confront him. He would run rings round them. Well, he ran rings round Amma because she being the elder of the two was always pushed forward to deal with the greedy brother and his even greedier wife.

After the sale of No. 2, uncle shut Mr. S's big mouth by a large cash payment to him, as well as facilitating that sale for uncle, S was able to buy an apartment or two (actually I heard he indeed got 2 apartments) at a heavily subsidized price in the new development at No. 2. I was also told by Amma that the place continued to be called Amadabad House (it might still be but I don't know) well after all the flats had been built and sold to buyers or tenants. This too might be significant since there might have been a deal between the buyer and uncle that the place may still be called Amadabad House (perhaps for a given period of time) as long as the buyer is prepared to pay a little extra. I have a strong suspicion about this though no proof of course. Obviously, it could not be easily confirmed of because the deal was done under the table.

According to Abid, mamujan, it was No. 1 which was supposedly for uncle, as insurance, I believe, for any mishaps that might happen to the family property in India."

Raza says here that "it was no wonder that first Maysam, and then Qais wanted some justice for their mother. No such help was available to the other sister—two of her sons lived in Karachi and the other, the youngest, was still studying, and her position with regard to the family was more ambiguous toward her brother, for the purposes of maintaining family unity. I had once argued by asking the obvious question of unity on what basis?"

By this time Maysam had also become understandably and implacably opposed to his maternal uncle for reasons we can understand, this was because of his personal experience of being arrested and imprisoned. He felt betrayed by Ibn Dawood who, he says, could have cleared him. Ibn Dawood was conveniently out of the country. Maysam was now out to expose his uncle for continuing to rob his own sisters. Qais, who tried to help his parents financially when he could, turned out to be a born archivist, when Raza approached him for information. Being stuck away from his family in Rotterdam, this was his reflexive response to keeping the family legacy alive—collecting family photographs and keeping a diary of events. Both of them, Maysam and Qais, had ranged themselves against Ibn Dawood and Begum.

This does not mean that Ibn Dawood and Begum did not have any allies, since it is obvious that wealth and a little bit of largesse work wonders some times. It was that, taken together, with mistaken sympathy for being perceived underdogs because most others criticized them. Raza came to learn that not only did Ibn Dawood rely on the whole Mishra clan with all its high-level connections, but being the runt of the family, and unable to count on the support of older cousins and the siblings he had betrayed, he and Begum turned to inviting those who were in Lucknow around to dinner, and making a point of taking gifts for the ones in London.

"Begum and Ibn Dawood's two sons, now at a boarding school, were also instructed to keep in touch with their cousins in London, which they did, except with Maysam, though of course they couldn't help bumping into him when he was at home. To me it didn't seem odd that at least Ibn Dawood did not ask his sons to keep in touch with me. I felt that it was a deliberate act on the part of his cousin and Begum, because they were trying to keep their sons deliberately ignorant of family history, feeding them all the time a revisionist history of the family, just like the ones from cloud cuckoo land he was fond of telling Begum, like the one that his father would have liked and approved of her."

"The portrait he wanted to project of himself was as the 'sole legitimate heir,' following this up with the vanity of according to himself all the titles his great-grandfather and grandfather had been given. Abid and Jafar had laughed about this piece of narcissistic affectation when they wrote to me about it, saying quite categorically that these titles were not hereditary but awarded for services rendered. However, for Ibn Dawood, all these titles also served to adorn his claim to the estate, then before the government. All these titles were displayed on the website."

Daddhoo and Buddhoo—the two spoilt dullards, as Maysam referred to his cousins—were two young princes who lived and toured around without ever really feeling any material sense of want. They had been placed in a public school, and went home for their holidays during winter and spring traveling first class, living as only the privileged do. During the summer, Ibn Dawood and Begum would arrive, escaping the heat in India, and take their children away to Europe or the States for holidays. Their names were already down for automatic entry to Cambridge, whatever their grades.

Nothing much seemed to be moving on the legal front for Ibn Dawood, despite lakhs of rupees being spent on lobbying and lawyers' fees. Abid kept Raza updated about all these happenings and the Amadabad story during this period of time resembles the theme of parallel lives: Ibn Dawood and Begum continuing to live a life of ill-gotten luxury with the rest continuing to work and struggle.

Raza's work did not allow him to visit his cousins on a regular basis though he still kept in regular touch by phone. He gathered from his conversations that nothing much had changed, Zainab Baji would still say that she hadn't heard anymore from Ibn Dawood about her share, but that he did usually at least reply to her telephone calls, even if it was about other things. There would always be a sad tone to her voice, as if to say: what can I do? At home it would make Raza's blood boil with rage, since he knew what a renegade Ibn Dawood had turned out to be. Not keeping his word to anyone, not only not keeping his word to Raza's father, but also defrauding his sisters. He exchanged letters with Ibn Dawood to no good avail.

All the while Raza and Tess continued to work, Tess as a practitioner and counselor, and Raza as a researcher for T3E. The first study containing the report on England, France, the Netherlands, and Portugal had been submitted to the European Union after drafts sent to the partners for consultation had been received. Later it was published as a *Cahier T3E*, a copy of which sits on his bookshelves. I had already met him by then as the only US correspondent for T3E.

The circumstances and what I thought about Raza until his life story began to be revealed are mentioned at the beginning of this book. He followed the work up by extending his research to Belgium, Germany, Italy, and Spain, which brings us to 1997 when, based on the recommendations for each country based on the findings, Raza proposed (he admits that it was partly to eke out a living until retirement and after for him and Tess) to do a pilot project with partners in order to provide training and evaluation in issues of race equality.

CHAPTER 26

IBN DAWOOD'S VICTORY

"I heard about this whole tragi-comic episode from Abid and finally decided on getting off his backside and taking joint action with Maysam, and whoever else wanted to join them against Ibn Dawood. His first step was more an act of pretense and provocation. Even though the idea of a return to Lucknow and Amadabad had turned sour in his stomach, nevertheless he decided to invite Ralph, his former head teacher and his wife to come to India with him and see the places he had grown up in. The idea was to get away for three winter weeks from mid-January onwards. Ralph and his wife were quite excited, as was Tess. Tess had also suggested they go to Kerala.

The next thing I did was to write to Abid, informing him. Then he decided to write to Ibn Dawood and wheedle some travel expenses to and from Lucknow. I thought this was the least he could do. Ibn Dawood and Begum were none too pleased to be put upon in this way, but grudgingly agreed. The next step was to make the bookings for all four of us, and to meet up at Heathrow. We were going to travel by Air India to Delhi, where Ibn Dawood would meet us. The flight was due to leave early in the morning and scheduled to arrive Delhi local time towards six in the evening."

Ralph and Kris were seasoned travelers but they hadn't been as far East as India. Remembering that during January and early February nights, North India could still be cold, and that even in Kerala, although it was the start of the tourist season, the sun would still be a pale imitation of itself, Raza had advised that it was best to take a range of clothing. During the flight Raza enlightened his friends about the family situation.

Ralph knew that Raza had been to public school but little about his family and its history. Ralph had struck up a contact in Shoreham with a man who collected books about India and had seen the marvelous collection of nineteenth-century photographs showing India during British rule, and could relate to what Raza was telling him.

It was Tess, who had already met Ibn Dawood, who directed the flow of the conversation towards Raza's cousin and Begum, his wife. "You'll be able to see for yourself," was all that Raza said, leaving his friends intrigued.

They didn't have to wait long before their first encounter with Raza's cousin and his wife. Not expecting to be met at the airport, or for even a driver being sent to fetch them by car, Raza telephoned his cousin who, knowing that Raza was bound to contact Suneet, asked for the address and said that he would leave the tickets and some money in an envelope in Suneet's office.

From then on, the whole trip turned into an embarrassing scenario. It was dark and an ill wind blew through the street when the four of them arrived at Suneet's office, but Suneet had assured Raza that someone would still be working there. No sooner had they arrived at the office than Ibn Dawood, Begum by his side to give him some backbone, came into the compound and headed towards the office. There, Ibn Dawood quite unceremoniously, and without even so much as a salaam, collected the train tickets and an envelope and muttered something about the plans being changed. He then took the party to a fancy restaurant where the manager seemed to know him and quickly found a table for four.

Evidently, Ibn Dawood and Begum weren't going to join them for dinner. At the table, Ibn Dawood ordered a pint of lager for all four and then slammed an envelope containing a wad of Indian rupees on the table and departed. Ralph and his wife looked uncomfortable about the affront Raza had just received from his cousin. As for Tess, she knew all about Ibn Dawood and Begum, and she just held Raza's hand under the table. There'd be time to explain the family situation to Ralph and Kris later.

Ibn Dawood and Begum then departed. The matter didn't end there. Before they had time to take more than one gulp of the welcome pint of ice-cold lager, Ibn Dawood and wife were back again, with Ibn Dawood saying: "Please hurry. There is an earlier train to Lucknow, and we may be in time to get you on board."

Everyone felt even more uncomfortable. Not wanting to make a fuss in a public place, the party got up and followed Ibn Dawood into a waiting car, which hastened through the traffic to the railway station and was a few minutes early before the arrival of the express train for Lucknow. The driver and a coolie rushed down the stairs to the platform carrying the luggage, with Raza and his party following. No goodbyes were said to Ibn Dawood and Begum. Once on board the train, Raza and his friends finally relaxed.

He felt a chump for having asked Ibn Dawood for anything and wanted to make the rest of the journey more enjoyable for his friends. He didn't regret what he had done, and felt that he was seeing Ibn Dawood and Begum in their true colors. Family meant nothing to Ibn Dawood, his allegiances were to Begum, and they both worshipped Mammon.

"After we got to Lucknow, we were put up in the palace adjacent rooms for three days, which was all the time the visit was going to last. Ralph and Kris stayed in the balcony room, while Tess and I stayed in the room that had been allocated to Ibn Dawood's eldest son. It was lined with a collection of college books." There was bedding at least. In the balcony room his friends were in, there was no bedding, mattresses, or mosquito nets.

"Abid had to make arrangements for all these to be provided from Zahra's room. I had met up with my brothers and introduced them to Ralph and Kris. For the time that they were there, they ate with my brothers the simple good food of home. Later they excused themselves while I showed friends some of Lucknow. Needless to say, Tess was thirsty for some cold lager and asked me to take them to a bar. We hailed a couple of rickshaws; one of the servants got the rickshaw drivers to give a reasonable price. Then they proceeded to Hazratganj and the bar at the Capoor Hotel Tess and I had been to before."

The bar largely had young people, those on a tryst. Raza ordered four lagers, ones that they could at last enjoy and finish, unlike their experience in Delhi. When the time had arrived to return for dinner with Raza's brothers and they hailed down a couple of rickshaws, they thought it a good idea to pick up a few bottles of lager to take back for drinking in their rooms. The rickshaws weaved through the back streets where the liquor stores were and Raza, as the only Hindustani-speaking-person, negotiated the prices and paid with the wad of rupees that Ibn Dawood had given.

It was a starry night as they reached home. They knew they had to be discreet with the bottles of lager. Abid had consumed alcohol in the house, and that as we know was done discretely. Why offend the customs and traditions? Even during Nawab Dawood Ahmad's time, odd, anglicized individuals were known to imbibe their glass of scotch discretely, and that was okay too.

Hence Raza advised discretion now as he dismounted, not allowing any servant to carry the black plastic bag containing the lager. Instead, he carried the bag up to their room to drink later, after dinner. The first night Raza managed to find a trusted servant to dispose of the bottles. On the second night, the bottles were not disposed of in time, and Raza hoped that somehow the bottles would be cleared away.

On their last day, they were all driven in one of Ibn Dawood's cars left in Lucknow for a brief visit to the palace in Amadabad. The chauffeur took the short route to Amadabad and the car arrived at the newly painted gate of the palace, where he had been born and spent his childhood, just before lunch.

The interior of the palace had also received a new coat of paint, but the palace was otherwise deserted. Ibn Dawood's eldest son had been instructed to meet them and to order some food for the visitors. Raza noted that the son's living arrangements had been made in the oldest part of the palace, where the lower level, with the library above, the young Nadia had once referred to as "Granddad's shop," had been opened up, and dusted and cleaned. The son occupied the rooms looking out towards the eastern side of the town. He was obviously being groomed as the eldest to succeed his father. It was a case of sticking to the rules of primogeniture.

"I had not seen the boy Maysam referred to as 'Daddhoo,' someone who despite his education and collection of books still remained a dullard, and by Abid's account someone being pushed to study Indian history. I was still to meet him. The son was under instructions to be present and to provide them with a hasty lunch and a little bit of tour before sending the party packing home. Tess suspects that he was under instructions to be there in case I took something, as if there was still anything valuable to take. The son was quite short, and wore a beard and mustache, and had obviously inherited his parents' stature. He behaved very respectfully, though, towards his uncle."

"I wasn't sure what Daddhoo might have heard from his parents, but he showed no rudeness. He was respectful, formal, and polite. On the tour Ralph and his wife were taken to the Baradari to see the marvelous red crystal glass Venetian-style chandelier with its 100 lights. As earlier mentioned, there are only two such chandeliers in existence. The other is reputed to be green. The one in Amadabad, which had a special beam installed to bear its weight when it had been purchased, was always seen and admired by members of the public when it was lit up during Moharram. Later we were taken to see the huge red verandah columns to look across the vast lawn towards the walls of the phulwari."

On the return down the corridor, Raza pointed out who was who in the photographs that hung on the side on the walls. Daddhoo went ahead to make sure lunch was ready, while Raza and his party sat down on some chairs under the portico across the courtyard. Suddenly Munnay, who used to be in the employ of Raza's father, appeared. He had heard somehow of Raza's arrival, though the visit had not been announced because otherwise Putto would surely have arrived.

With Raza's and Ralph's agreement, Munnay proceeded to massage their heads before lunch was ready. The lunch, which was served under the portico opposite, tasted quite awful, nothing like even the plain dishes Raza's friends had tasted in Lucknow. Immediately afterwards, before the January sun was low on the horizon, they were driven back to Lucknow, from where they caught the train back to Delhi, and from there a long train ride to Kerala to sweeten the taste of the trip. Raza did not anticipate returning to Lucknow and Amadabad ever again, though he knew that his brothers had no such choice, and in the case of Abid, no desire or stamina to leave the ancestral home and go elsewhere.

CHAPTER 27

RAZA AND MAYSAM

It was also during this time that relations between Raza and Maysam became closer. They became allies and Maysam started sharing information with Raza and when Raza first had the notion of writing a book, similar to Giuseppe di Lampedusa's *The Leopard*, only his version would be much darker. Since an early spat three years earlier, relations between Abid and Ibn Dawood seemed on the surface to have normalized. The latter would have denied that he ever knew anything about Abid's forced deportation from Delhi, and Abid on his part had long since realized that they both had to live under the same roof. Raza mentioned the book to him, and thus he too became a source of information. Maysam also wrote to his uncle telling him that a book was being written about him in which all would be revealed, and Ibn Dawood had threatened that he would take Raza to court. Nothing came of the book immediately, since Raza was still working on his research, but as the eldest son, the necessity of redeeming his father's life from oblivion played on his mind.

"I had heard from my sister in 2006 or 2007 about the sale of the famous cut-glass red chandelier that had hung in the Baradari ever since grandfather had purchased it. I had been told about its history by my father, and how it could be disassembled into hundreds of wooden boxes and packed, and how it had come in those boxes. It was the centerpiece, and now it was gone. Golu had sent me a photograph of it hanging in a palace in Gwalior. When I had looked at it, it had looked smaller than the one he remembered. I wrote back to my sister, who confirmed that yes, it was the one from Amadabad, but that it probably looked smaller from the angle it had been taken, and that her son had found a photograph in a travel brochure."

The matter didn't stop there. He made further enquiries and learnt from Rizzoo that Ibn Dawood had given the public excuse that it had been sent for cleaning, as well as for the beams to be strengthened on the roof. Several years later, and it is still not back. That chandelier alone would have attracted any Texan oil billionaire's wish list and paid enough to at least pay off the mortgages on Ibn Dawood's sisters' apartments, but there was none of that, Raza assures me, from Ibn Dawood.

What gave him further impetus were the visits to his cousins in London, mostly Hurr Bhai and Zainab Baji. Usually, he would agree these arrangements over the telephone. Hurr Bhai, who would normally be watching some science program on BBC, and thinking that Raza wanted to speak to Zainab Baji, would call her. He could hear his voice calling from the semibasement where the television was—"Bibi, it's your brother Mohammad. Pick up the phone upstairs," before Raza had the chance to say that he also wanted to speak to him, which he did.

He carried fond memories of his eldest cousin, and respected and admired him. "Then I would hear the voice of Zainab Baji saying—'All right, I am just going to pick up the phone and speak to him,' and then her voice would come on the phone, and she would accept his salaams and ask him whether he was okay, always making a point of asking about Nadia and Tess. It was then that I would ask if he could come over and pay his respects."

Raza's journey would take him to Hendon Underground. If it was on a weekend, Maysam would come and pick him up by car, otherwise he would walk around the Hendon roundabout and go one stop by bus before walking to the turning in which their house was based. The house, when he came to it, was deceptively large, large enough to house all the family even though Qais had a job in Rotterdam.

He would ring the bell, and the door would normally be opened by one of his nephews or nieces, who would say adaab, as Raza took of his shoes and left them where the family's shoes were left. Then Raza would walk across the carpeted hall, ignoring the white-painted staircase that led to the family bedrooms upstairs, and walk towards the living room to the right. Everything was kept spotless, and there was a notice saying "No Smoking," because Raza knew from his younger days just how anti-tobacco Hurr Bhai was. As a consequence, none of the children smoked either.

One of his nieces or nephews—there were four of them, including Maysam, who lived there with their parents, Qais working in Rotterdam, and dear Jaun in the unsold portion of the apartments—would escort him towards the comfortably furnished living room that overlooked the garden at the rear, where he would see his Baji and Bhaisahab sitting down. He would bow in respect before taking a seat.

A general conversation would follow and Raza would be offered a choice of cold water or a fruit drink, which one of the nieces would bring before returning to prepare food in the kitchen. When the lunch was ready, it would be announced and Zainab Baji would say—"Come, bhaiyya, let us go and eat,"— and they would troop into the adjacent dining room with its long oak dining table and eight or ten chairs and an oak sideboard, and sit down to eat. Zainab Baji no longer cooked the food, but left it to her two daughters, both of whom were very adept.

Raza was made to sit at the head of the table, despite his protestations. Dishes and casseroles consisting of daal, rice, green vegetables, and only a small dish of meat were laid on the table. Hurr Bhai, since his heart bypass operation several years before at the Royal Free Hospital, where Raza had been to visit him, now ate simple food. When the freshly baked chapatis began arriving, wrapped in serviettes to keep them warm, Raza would be asked to help himself, and conversations would continue.

These conversations were no longer animated as before, when Hurr Bhai was younger and full of optimism for his family. They would exchange news. Zainab Baji and Hurr Bhai had always known what Raza was doing from the days he had been a councilor. Zainab Baji had asked him once or twice for assistance and advice regarding her children. They also admired him for having single-handedly raised Nadia, and were pleased for him that he was now with Tess.

It was now, on his last visit, that he began to perceive at first hand just what was happening to most members of the Amadabad family, and understand the ferociousness with which Maysam—who had seen right through his uncle, and why he had to come to his mother's defense with such alacrity—challenged his uncle Ibn Dawood.

Raza could see greater signs of hardship and need. The grown-up children were all contributing towards the monthly mortgage payments from their salaries. Knowing that Raza already knew about Ibn Dawood from all that he had heard from her son, Zainab Baji made no secret of the fact that her brother was not helping. She bore all this with stoicism, reflecting on her life and disappointments. She wished she had never come to England, lured there on false grounds by her brother and Ibadi to get mortgages on flats, whose monthly payments they were now having to meet out of their own savings, for fear of being dispossessed, while the money from the sale of their Karachi flats remained a mystery. It was a life in suspension.

All the while Ibn Dawood and Begum fiddled. Raza came to learn from Abid that Ibn Dawood had bought shares in Jordan Airways, which Maysam thinks must have been through the royal connection through Bitlan. This meant that they and their sons could fly first class between India and Europe and that they were frequently doing that. When in India, they rarely showed their faces in Lucknow, preferring the luxury of their apartment in Delhi. Nothing it seemed would interrupt their narcissistic saunter through life. Whether in Delhi, London, New York, or Paris—Ibn Dawood was now reputed to be the owner of a small chateau and able to speak French—stories were printed of how and where they entertained literary celebrities and selected journalists, the kinds of people who would inform the wider elite who form an invisible union about this scion of an aristocratic family, his life and travails for the benefit of those living in similar luxury. And, of course, there was some jealously in all the doings.

Initially Raza worried because he did not want to act against Zainab Baji's brother. Maysam reassured him: "Don't worry Mamujan. You know that both Amma and Khalajan have always been blind to their brother's ways, always too soft despite his blatant acts of daylight robbery, but Amma has now come around to seeing things in their proper light. I have told her about you and she understands. She trusts you. And, if she knows that you are going with me to consult any solicitors, she will agree."

This phone conversation took place in 2009 when Raza was on the final leg of his research project that was going to culminate the following summer, though the project was finding itself in difficulties surrounding visits to prisons in different countries and the hurdles to overcome before prison governors might approve. The Summer University to be held in London had already been postponed because the report's findings would not be ready for presentation.

During this period, Raza and Maysam started getting the documents to take to some solicitors who Maysam had been informed about by a financial investigator who had already been on the track of the financial misdeeds at CBCD, and written about the scandal. The idea was to launch a joint legal challenge between Zainab Baji and Raza, plus whoever else would agree to sign against Ibn Dawood for his false claim to be the sole legitimate heir.

"I should mention now that NK, the investigative financial journalist, and I met Maysam and took them along to the solicitor's office in Doughty Street, near the Inns of Court, where my father had briefly lived. The solicitor, who was of Indian descent, had obviously been briefed by NK about the nature of the advice, and had already agreed to provide pro bono services."

To cut the story short, a series of meetings followed, which convinced the solicitor that there was a case to answer, and that, provided they got the right high court judge in India, they could get the judgment reversed. He contacted the Delhi office to do some initial research and reported her findings to London, including showing a family tree going back to Raza's grandfather; a list of properties belonging to Amadabad Estate, spread through urban as well as rural areas of Awadh; a list of previous cases where equal rights had been awarded, that is, primogeniture; and, of course, much of the documentation that Raza already had.

There was enough to start with, but then came the problem of fees for the Delhi office. While the London office would be willing to work pro bono, the Delhi office could not provide these services. An amount of £7K would be required for more research to be carried out in UP courts where the properties were registered. Maysam and Raza looked at each other. There was no way this amount of money could be raised, even as a loan from the bank, unless it was a certainty. The legal route was no longer possible, and it would take too long anyway. That's when it was decided to name and shame.

Raza's working life as a paid employee continued until September that year.

The choices for Raza's continued employment right upon his return in 2005 had become restricted, both by virtue of age, and because of the diminishing opportunities for trans-EU work. The European Commission had ended the era of encouraging different networks and was beginning to encourage the growth of consortia. Jean Pierre and Raza had been invited to a meeting of different drug networks in Europe. They were there to listen before jumping in. The convenor of the meeting, who had also been an EU consultant, appeared to have a project in mind. It was around drugs, criminal justice, and HIV/AIDS across several EU countries in a much-expanded EU. The meeting was to take all day and at the end potential partners had to present their research topics.

During the interval, Jean Pierre (J-P) had taken Raza to one side to discuss matters. He did not see any options for the French half, but encouraged Raza to keep a foot in and see whether it would open up other opportunities. Necessity kicked in. Raza needed and wanted to go on working for as long as he could without heeding the arbitrary notions of a retirement age. After lunch Raza spoke eloquently about the dimension of racism and equality.

It was an obvious dimension that no one else had picked up. He also had the recognized experiences. From there things had rolled on. He had been asked to complete a long application for funding, including the title of the project, aims and objectives, a theoretical description, a costed budget, as well as all the other detail such funding applications require. During March, funding for the consortium was agreed with the lead and all the added bureaucracy going to a university partner.

It was to be a three-year project, and to start in September 2005 that year. Raza alerted NA, his research partner. They met and agreed to a division of labor. They'd both be working from home, thus cutting overheads. Raza, as an associate research fellow, could still use Middlesex for some things, including their guidance and approval of the project's research ethical guidelines, as well as mailing and photocopying.

The project occupied the next three years of Raza's life: arranging interviews in prisons in different countries that took him on fieldwork trips to Italy, Portugal, Slovenia, France, and Spain. Raza kept me updated with his work, but at this time I still knew little about his background or personal life apart from having met Tess and Ana-Livia.

Following his return from India in 2007, Raza wrote a letter to Ibn Dawood in February, telling him that he wanted to retire and live back at home, since to impose himself and Tess on Nadia and her young family—Samir Eaza, Raza's grandson, had been born in March 2006—was out of the question. On consideration, he would have more than enough money from his pensions that would provide more than enough rupees for him and Tess to live on.

He received no response until June, when finally his cousin told him in so many words, although the letter goes on to ramble for three whole pages, that unfortunately the space in Hyderbad was so badly organized that there was no room. Then he ends with a homily about the imbibing of alcohol in the house, referring to his visit when he and his friends had brought bottles of lager to drink in their rooms, and the bottles had been discovered.

Raza was cross with himself for seeming to grovel to his younger cousin. In reality, he had no such intention, and wouldn't want to live under the same roof. He tells me that he was simply testing his cousin's sincerity and good faith. Begum must have had a role in the decision, because soon after that she declared to Zainab Baji that she had decided not to see Razabhai again. Correspondence between Raza and Ibn Dawood also came to a stop.

But what did not stop were Maysam's letters, sent via email, to his uncle. He sent copies of these to Raza for information and these had started in 2006. Then more recently he wrote a long letter to his uncle that is full of the historical sins of omission with which the reader is already familiar. It begins:

Dear Mamoojan,

I write to inform that your game is over. The game of stratagems and deception you have been playing at least since 1973, as predicted by me years ago. Fortunately, you are entirely predictable. The only unfortunate outcome has been that my mother, who supported you has suffered all these years. She has been most patient, and now realises that the man whom she looked after when he was a child and cared for has grown up to be ungrateful and iniquitous. You have told too many lies. The world, including the Indian Government, would be more appreciative if you spoke the truth. You should not be, as I am not, un-inclined to help the world in uncovering the truth.

Before listing the trickery and robbery of his sisters, luring them to London in connivance with Ibadi, Maysam outlines all of Ibn Dawood's deeds: how he saved his uncle's skin from the liquidators at CBCD; misappropriating the funds left behind by his father—sufficient for all the grandchildren's education, including that of Nadia's— and then lying about it; destroying his father's will and lying about that to Raza's father by saying that he had dreamt that his father had asked him that he wanted to be buried in Mashhad when that was in the Will; and, the following year, spending the ill-gotten money and living for months in the Hilton Hotel in Park Lane, London.

The reader will be familiar with most of this, though the account is concise and thorough—we have not seen it in this form before, even though it serves as a suitable reminder; Maysam then introduces a new element and a new dimension to his uncle's character. He refers to the jewels in the Habib Bank in Karachi that Zainab Baji had been contacted about, and which had been mentioned by Zainab Baji to her brother, who had no knowledge of these jewels previously. Following that Zainab Baji had asked Hurr Bhai to hand the briefcase with the jewels to Ibadi, who had later handed the briefcase back to Ibn Dawood in 1977. Maysam then provides a shocking revelation:

> In 1996 you told me that you had taken possession of the jewels, changed the briefcase, and misappropriated the sale proceeds. You lied to CBCDs liquidators, including Dave Walter, and falsely accused Raju Abba for illegally taking the jewels to Pakistan. The jewels were taken by Raju Abba to Karachi in 1946, well over a year before India became independent and Pakistan was created. Your statement to CBCD's liquidators, including Dave, was false and known by you to be false.

> In 1990, you began destroying the CBCD and LCLC documents evidencing your and your wife's accounts. (I do have copies of the documents signed by you and by your wife). Evidence that you had accumulated around US$10 million came, when you were in Qais's car driving through Cool

Oak Lane in 1992–93, and made a critical remark. How else could you have done that except by dispossessing your sisters?

Confirming Qais's earlier revelations about the Karachi apartments, Maysam concludes:

> Under pressure from your wife, you visited Islamabad, Pakistan, in 1990s in connection with the sale of the apartments in Karachi, which belonged to my mother and my aunt. You interrupted Qais's meeting with Nawaz Shareef (Pakistan's former prime minister), and you lied to him in my brother's presence when you said that you wanted to discuss with Nawaz Shareef, matters concerning the Muslims of India. You are not a political leader, and your intentions were simply to subvert Qais's attempts at meeting Nawaz Shareef, and to steal from your sisters in which you succeeded.
>
> My days are numbered, as indeed are yours. Whereas I am prepared to leave this world when I am summoned, you on the other hand, would not like to let go this world. In this matter, however, you have little choice and you cannot lie to the Warner who will hold you accountable for your transgressions against our family. In a way, I do feel sorry for you. You were a product and part of a corrupt system—a system that had been condemned by all the Prophets and by the Law. You were a lonely child who felt insecure and grew up to use his knowledge, with comparatively poor academic record, not to serve the community, but for the sole purpose of procuring for yourself by whatever means, moral or otherwise, the worldly possessions, whether they belonged to you or not.
>
> I believe it was your temperament and personality that caused you to search for a wife whom you would find compatible. And the Mishras proved to be most suited to you in every way. Your mother-in-law had reportedly impoverished her father-in-law to the state of penury. Thankfully, Raju Abba is no longer here to face such a treatment. (Equally, had he been alive, you would never have been able to marry amongst the Mishras.) But sadly, I believe that his daughters have been given the same treatment by your wife, as her mother had extended to her father-in-law. My mother, her sister and her cousins have also suffered due to your actions; either of your own volition and/or advised by minds more powerful than yours.
>
> My mother and all my aunts deserved to be recompensed with present value of the cost of university education; as that cost ended up as a saving for Raju Abba. And this Raju Abba knew and had agreed with me on one occasion. But your wife had the audacity to tell my mother that daughters

did not inherit anything from their fathers. With respect, this is 21st century and a civilised part of the globe; these are not Ayyam-ul Jahiliyya when the daughters were buried alive or sacrificed at the altar of some minor deity, as is still done in some backward regions of the world today.

During or around 1994, you were given the original copy of the Mughal Album by my maternal aunt, to be sold so as to alleviate the hardship which she and my mother were facing. You stooped to steal the item and have the same in your possession today.

In 1996–97 you collected Tafseer-ul Qur'an from my mother and purportedly sold it. I have reasons to believe that the original Tafseer-ul Qur'an is still with you, and you only paid a nominal sum to my mother and my maternal aunt, to avert temporarily financial impediments; and that too from the assets of their late father. The actual price is considerably more than the nominal sum you paid. Significantly, you involved your wife in that transaction, when to your full knowledge she was totally irrelevant.

Finally, the metamorphosis of Amadabad, initiated by your actions, both unwise and dishonest, has begun and is irreversible. Your sons neither have the strength of character nor the personality to stand up to or check the conspiracy underway. Within ten years, the metamorphosis of Amadabad to Mishrabad would be complete, and your brother-in-law would emerge as the victor; and he would bring to fruition the ideas he developed while sitting idle in your flat in Belsize Park in 1980's.

May the Lord God protect us, and may He protect you from your corrupt practices, your character and your schemes and stratagems; and may He deliver us from the Mishras. For your salvation, fear God and be content with your morsel of bread, and give to your sisters and cousins what rightfully belongs to them.

    With respects,

    your concerned nephew

    So oft it chances in particular men,

    That, for some vicious mole of nature in them,

    Carrying, I say, the stamp of one defect,

    Shall in the general censure take corruption

    From that particular fault.

Maysam signs off with the same penchant for quoting verse that Raza and other family members seem to have.

CHAPTER 28

THE UGLY PORTRAITS OF IBN DAWOOD AND BEGUM

The portraits of Ibn Dawood and Begum are almost complete. They will be further supplemented by Abid's messages to Raza: "The news is that mistur *(sic)* I-D is due to arrive this afternoon, Thursday, 27 October 2011. He still has a case filed by him against gvt for contempt of court regarding actions taken following the presidential ordinance, which had lapsed and the bill to replace it has now been rejected. It's all a legal jigsaw."

It is in a sense the picture of a man not content with all the wealth he possesses and forever thirsty for more. Raza, meanwhile, continuing to write his story, is kept aware by messages from Abid or Maysam that Ibn Dawood and Begum were frequent visitors to England, together with their sons, but that they rarely visited Zainab Baji, preferring to speak to her on the phone, and offer excuses of a kind that Zainab Baji had by now lost faith in—excuses for not visiting by claiming for example to be at important conferences. All hogwash. Maysam accuses him in July 2011:

Dear Ibn Dawood,

Imperial College denies all knowledge of your false and fraudulent claim of being an occasional professor of Astrophysics; or for that matter temperamental professor, or professor of any kind. Have you ever worked? Do you have a tax code with the Inland Revenue of UK? Do you have NI number? I think not.

Remember that you are not an astrophysicist as you have never worked as one. Do you remember that you failed to understand why helium exists in a solid state on a neutron star? Or, how the inclination of the earth's axis causes seasonal changes? When I asked you in Strathmore Court what a wave function was, you could not explain. Astrophysicist, my foot. You are foremost a "raja", a "vadera", a "zameendar", a Mafia don—the Don of Amadabad. So don't spew statements about yourself which are patently false, and known by you to be false, and thus avoid becoming a laughing stock in the circle of my fellow mathematicians/physicists.

Maysam then makes another mind-blowing revelation about Nawab Dawood Ahmad's Will:

> Do you think a man who was punctual with his fasting and his prayers, would omit writing his will? Ask your son whether or not the Quran stipulates the writing of one's will in the same Sura where the Book stipulates fasting. It is not surprising that you began to portray the negative side of Raju Abba's character after his death. Until recently, Khalajan wanted to protect the memory of Raju Abba and mentioned on more than one occasion that she had seen a hand written document in Raju Abba's hand, describing the apportionment of the estate. Knowing Khalajan, I suspect she must have consulted Z (Begum's close friend), and was probably advised not to repeat her statements. Khalajan, being your sister, has started to distort the truth too, and now says she has misplaced the document.

This revelation came as a shock to Raza. He had respected both his female cousins equally, but no one had suspected the concealment of a document that was tantamount to a written Will in Islam. His own father had left such a note.

Maysam's accusations against his uncle continued through email messages on a regular basis, sometimes repetitious, and sometimes bringing new revelations:

> You are surrounded by some petty ulemas in Lucknow whom you keep feeding food and lies, while penny pinching from what Raju Abba had left behind. *The Grand Ayatullah Sistani has declared that all relations of Raju Abba are entitled to their share in Raju Abba's global assets.* But you do not believe in any code except the Mishra Code as tutored to you by Begum.
>
> In so far as Begum is concerned, I believe Chee's depiction of her to me and independently to my parents in 1993 was very accurate, and her detailed account of her past, as well as that given by Jingo, is consistent with later events. Members of our extended family have given me.
>
> In the spring of 2011 you exchanged e-mail communications with my mother concerning Raju Abba's assets in UBS Geneva. Not a single e-mail from you ever mentioned what you had said about five years ago. During

or around 2005 you had said to my mother that Raju Abba had transferred his assets in UBS Geneva into a trust by employing some Islamic rules. That was a lie and known by you to be a lie. For if it was true, you would have mentioned that again in one of your several e-mails.

Did your parents not teach you never to lie? Or did Begum, who lied to my paternal and maternal grandmothers about her antecedents and her globe-trotting escapades with men known to you, teach you to lie? If so she is a very poor teacher of teaching how to tell lies. She wrote letters purporting to care for Nadia, once she was married to you. She, of course, turned away from Nadia soon after her marriage. Like mother, like daughter.

Begum lied to my mother about David Walter, with whom I am still in contact. I cannot even begin to describe what people in India, Pakistan and England think of you and your wife, and your and her dishonesty. I am reliably informed that she has now set up a company ostensibly of clothes and handicraft, but allegedly to launder the ill-gotten funds originating from Raju Abba's assets in UBS Geneva.

You can hide away here in this world but not for long. My days are numbered, and so are yours. We are bound to meet elsewhere, but I as a victim of your lies, deceit and petty stratagems, and truth will be revealed then.

Maysam

Raza confirms the story about the company for clothes since he had heard a story from his siblings: during the early years of her marriage, Begum had tried to impress members of the family with the notion that she wanted to take an active interest in preserving the local crafts in Lucknow was famous for, such as "chikan wear"—a traditional embroidery style from Lucknow. Literally translated, the word means "embroidery." It is one of Lucknow's best-known textile decoration styles, and widely available, as well as "jamdani," flowers and designs woven on garments of the finest muslin that Raza remembers his father wearing.

Later she was said to have set up a cooperative of skilled women to produce the garments. Raza was informed that the cooperative Begum set up was registered under the name of "Ranisaaz." All credit to her one might think. Nadia and Tess had both been presented with a "chikan" garment and Raza thought nothing further until the charity was brought to his notice by one of the social networks for professionals. To make a long story short, when he looked at the charity it appeared as registered under the name of its executive director,

Begum Khan, with Ibn Dawood's name alongside, which was later for some reason removed.

He probed further and found that it had outlets in London, New York, and Paris. Only the very rich and wealthy could afford the prices. Raza and Maysam suspect that it also served as a front for money and asset laundering, a fact with which both Abid and Jafar separately concurred.

There has been no acknowledgement or response to Maysam's letters from his uncle, only complaints about them to his sister Zainab about her son, warning him through her that he will take his nephew to court unless he desists from such charges. In London, Raza is still kept in the loop by his siblings about Ibn Dawood's nefarious activities. They know he is determined to tell the story, washing dirty linen in public, because that is the only way left to right wrongs.

I am sent blind carbon copies of many of these exchanges. Raza meanwhile has not seen Hurr Bhai and Zainab Baji for some years, when his sister Zahra arrives in London and spends a couple of days with Raza and Tess. She seems well and happy to be with her brother for whom she had acted as a confidante when young. Happy to see Tess as well.

This is when she also meets Molly, Raza's cat. She's surprised and a little bit nervous until she sees Molly lying on her brother's lap and him stroking her. Before moving on to stay with Chhoti Baji, she observes how her brother and Tess live—a simple, happy life with their pet cat. She doesn't say much. What has stirred her are the worries she has at home. She won't say much because of shame, but from what Raza can gather, she is worried about Golu's insatiable demands for money, and more money. Her family situation is not a happy one.

She and Solly are estranged though still living in the house in Kanpur. Solly has never readjusted to returning from Ajman. He has been unhappy that his daughter made her own decision to choose her husband, without going through the traditional channels. The fact that Zahra accepted the marriage added to the estrangement. Raza sympathizes with his sister. It seems that Zahra has just come away for a bit of peace, a bit of distance and getting her bearings back to the values and virtues taught by their parents.

Sometime before her arrival, she had told Raza over the telephone that her son-in-law wanted to invest £80,000 in an apartment in London and was willing to transmit it to Raza. Raza thought about it for a little while, but then declined by saying that he couldn't accept the responsibility. On this visit, she brought the subject up with Zainab Baji. One of her daughters remembers the occasion, according to Maysam, as Raza discovers later.

Then she was gone, returning to her regular travels between Kanpur, Lucknow, and Amadabad. Moharram was approaching. Leaving Raza with some unanswered questions, one of them being about Zahra's son-in-law. The man had avoided Tess and Raza the last time they were in Delhi.

Soon after Zahra's visit another rumor broke. Abid wrote to Raza that Ibn Dawood's favorite chauffeur and confidant, [R], who was privy to all his master's secrets, had been fired by him at Begum's behest. He had been a long-term employee of the Amadabad family. Begum, mystified by her husband's daily movements, had decided to follow him with their eldest son to the corner room in the courtyard below; peering through the curtains they both saw Ibn Dawood *in flagrante diletto* with the chauffeur.

The chauffeur went running to Abid and confessed the full story about the acts of pederasty Raja Sahib would want performed. The chauffeur was in fear of his life because of the long arm of the Mishras and had no option but to run away to Saudi Arabia with his wife and baby. He had been asked to clear his belongings on the spot, and of course had not been paid any wages.

Abid felt sorry for him and helped him out, and the chauffeur promised to keep in touch. Raza thought to himself that this had really put a cat among the pigeons, and ironically enough, Begum now held the upper hand. Metaphorically speaking, she had him by the balls, and that will no doubt change the dynamics for the future of Amadabad. Raza kept the news to himself and did not even mention it to Maysam at the time. He did not know what effect the knowledge would have on the remaining sister and other members of the family.

Zahra's visit prompted Raza to telephone Hurr Bhai and Zainab Baji. Zahra had stayed with them for a couple of days as well, while he felt guilty about not dropping in on them. It was easier when he had a car and still drove. The public transport journey, involving buses and the underground, more buses and on foot were beginning to prove a bit daunting, and cab prices prohibitive. They understood all that, and were happy to hear from him. They had taken a liking to Will and always asked about Nadia when Raza phoned.

They knew that Raza had been to the States to stay with his daughter and that in 2006 she had given birth to a baby son called Samir Azim, but about themselves they were more reticent, saying very little. Hurr Bhai was still in the process of completing his epic Musaddas, a long philosophical treatise, written in Urdu of the purest form, extolling social justice as epitomized by the martyrdom of Imam Husain, and by its very epitome condemning the abuse of power and the worship of Mammon. This was not directed at his cousin Ibn Dawood, because he was not important enough, but it should be taken as covering people like him.

Raza said nothing to his cousin about the book he was writing. That was between him and Maysam. But every year Raza would remember Hurr Bhai's birthday at the end of January, and he would say in a cheery reply, "Well, I am ready to meet my Maker."

CHAPTER 29

THE SAD AND TRAGIC DEATHS OF HURR BHAI AND ZAINAB BAJI

I would like to take the reader many years ahead in time, when at the beginning of the year, on January 27, 2012, Raza telephoned Hurr Bhai at the usual time to see how he was doing. Since he was now 86 years old, he was beginning to sound weaker, and Zainab Baji, not in good health herself, worried about him constantly. Raza could only listen in silence to Zainab Baji. It was a moment of grief and anger since he knew that what had ailed them both was estrangement and betrayal—estrangement from home, since England would never be their proper home, and betrayal by Ibn Dawood and his wife Begum. They had married during that fateful year of 1950 when, following his wedding to Zainab, his father-in-law had made that political error and had split the Amadabad family into two separate countries forever.

Despite protestations to the contrary, it suited Shaikhoo and Begum's purposes to have the palaces to themselves. The presence of elders would hamper their designs. Abid had just written to tell him that a plot of land belonging to Khalajan's estate had just been sold for the equivalent of £8,500.

By rights, there should have been a share for Zainab Baji and Chhoti Baji as well, but Abid told him that it had been signed over to Daddhoo, the elder son, and heir apparent.

That summer, a number of years back, Ibn Dawood and Begum came to England again when the tourist season for rich Indians coming to England had begun. Raza remembers because Rizzoo had come too and had made a point of phoning him and meeting him for lunch at the Commonwealth Club. Rizzoo brought with him his eldest son and a parcel of homemade sheermaals, wrapped in foil that had been kept in a deep freeze on the airplane. Yes, Rizzoo had heard that Ibn Dawood was here. He was surprised when he heard that Ibn Dawood had not been to see his eldest sister, but he did encourage Raza to come back to Lucknow and Amadabad: "Mian, ghar ajaiye." That, after all this time he should hear these words, touched him.

After Ibn Dawood and Begum returned home from their summer holidays, that autumn, Abid told Raza that their cousin had sold another plot of land from the estate left behind by Khalajan. This one sold for the equivalent of £6,500, and again it was signed over to his eldest son. Not a penny from these latest transactions was shared with his two sisters. The month of Moharram began on November 3 that year. Hurr Bhai, approaching his birthday in January, had become increasingly weak, and increasingly worried about his wife of 63 years. Then there was the insult of the ever-present shortage of money.

His daughters and their husbands, one already in Pakistan, felt compelled to live with him, Hurr Bhai, because he didn't want to put Zainab Baji under pressure. He reluctantly stayed in Karachi though he was never really happy there. Later he had followed his father-in-law to Baghdad, and then back to Karachi again.

Raza had known Hurr Bhai and idealized him when he had been young. He was intelligent and tall and handsome, with a quick wit and an iconoclastic sense of humor, and above all outspoken.

"I considered him mature enough by my father, and already at Cambridge when I was sent to England, Abid and I had spent many holiday times with him in Cambridge and London until 1952 when Hurr Bhai completed his studies. At Cambridge he had studied for the Moral Sciences Tripos (philosophy, logic and psychology), before turning to the Oriental Sciences Tripos (Classical Arabic and Persian) under the tutelage of Professor Arthur Arberry." Hurr Bhai's tutor in philosophy had been Professor John Wisdom, a name that has stuck in Raza's mind ever since—what can be the origin of that family name?

Raza had always felt what a loss of talent Hurr Bhai's life had been in his forced exile, and often told him so. From his side, Hurr Bhai had grown to respect Raza, who had matured into an independent-minded individual in the 1960s, talking socialism and Marxism and denouncing wealth and the abuse of power. The two had not met for some time when more than a decade later one day in November Raza received a phone call from Maysam:

"Mamujan, I just wanted to let you know that Abba fell down the stairs and is being taken to the hospital by ambulance. I will be following in my car."

"How serious is it?"

"It looks serious, but I can't talk right now Mamujan. I'll phone you if I get the opportunity."

Raza sat on the sofa, pushing his back against the chair, stretching his neck further until the back of his head touched the wall; he banged his head hard against it once. Tess got worried and turned around. She knew that something had happened. He told her, and for the next two days Raza was on edge because Hurr Bhai had not recovered consciousness; he had been pronounced dead on arrival. Qais, Raza's trusted nephew had also come over from Rotterdam to commemorate Moharram with his parents when this happened and together the brothers and sisters had not quite decided when and if to tell their mother. They didn't believe that Zainab Baji would survive the news, since she was ailing herself and unable to walk. A nurse was attending her daily to give physio, but she was bound to ask and look for her husband. This was also one of the reasons that Raza was not invited to come around.

"Mamujan, I will phone you as soon as we feel it is feasible, and I will come over in my car and drive you back."

The cold November day arrived. Raza stepped out of the car, approached the white door of the house, and rang the familiar bell. There was not long to wait. Qais opened the door as Raza fumbled to undo his laces and take his shoes off. Qais looked solemn as he said salaam and embraced his uncle. Raza was dazed by the events, so dazed that he was treating it as a normal visit. Maysam joined them and led his uncle up the staircase on which Hurr Bhai had fallen and hit his head, his face taking the full impact.

Still in a daze, Raza went upstairs to the white-painted passage, with bedrooms on both sides, and a bathroom leading to the door of a bedroom on the left that was Hurr Bhai and Zainab Baji's bedroom. Raza had never been upstairs; as he entered the carpeted room, with windows looking down to the street below, he saw his Baji's face who had by now turned around on hearing Maysam. "Amma, Mamujan is here to see you."

"It is a face and a smile that I saw that I feel I will never forget. That Hurr Bhai smile was the same smile that I first saw on my cousin's face when she must have been about eight years old, walking along the path bordered by the henna bushes. I must have been a toddler then. Suddenly back to reality, I came in and was asked to sit down on the edge of the bed. Zainab Baji uttered no words. The nurse entered, and soon after, my visit was over. Proud pathos filled the house, as nieces and nephews gathered to see me off. It was also to be the last time I saw Zainab Baji alive. Her face and kind demeanor still haunt me."

Soon after hearing of Hurr Bhai's passing,* Ibn Dawood and Begum arrived in London. They had also been informed, as family etiquette demanded, and had responded by observing the same etiquette. According to Maysam, they had sat there looking stony faced, then went away. They offered nothing, and nothing would have been accepted. Maysam had also observed the etiquette and sobriety the situation demanded.

Within 40 days of her husband's death, Zainab Baji also passed away. She was buried in a grave next to her husband's. Maysam promised to take Raza there one day.

When Raza heard the news, it reminded him eerily of his parents' marriage: how they had also married for love, had several children, and lived happily; how they embraced every circumstance that came their way, bearing things with dignity, and handing on a legacy and tradition to be plucked from the air. Zainab Baji and Hurr Bhai had been married for 63 years, had six children, and treated them equally. Hurr Bhai had been writing a Musaddas in the purest form of Urdu with its main philosophical theme focusing on social justice and equality. Qais has now taken responsibility for getting it published.

During January of the following year, scarcely two months after the death of his sister Zainab, Ibn Dawood had agreed with his brother-in-law for a wedding between his younger son and the brother-in-law's daughter. Both Abid and nephew Golu, the latter playing his own game of being loyal to none, sent photographs of the bride and groom. When Abid had casually mentioned the wedding to Ibn Dawood, his explanation about it being held so soon after his sister's death was that unfortunately the date had already been arranged. The wedding was kept a secret, and no one from the family was invited. Qais also got to hear of it and wrote the following email:

---

* It still remains unclear, at times, what kind of presence Ibn Dawood has in this narrative: he seems to move in and out, with little sense of his motivations or purpose but it should be clear that he is to be regarded by readers with distrust, and each episode in which he plays a role, the point of origin of that distrust should be clear. My sense is that he might be less important to the overall narrative than his introduction at the beginning of the manuscript suggests. That being said, his role could be clarified and emphasized were he treated with a bit less foreshadowing in the earlier chapters: I realize too that it would be more interesting to have him develop alongside his deceit, but I have chosen instead to express his villany in selected locations in the narrative instead.

Of course, if two consenting adults want to be together then it is fine, but I guess the ground was prepared by others to maximize the chances of this outcome.

All this reminds me of a conversation I had with Mamujan back in the 80s at Khalajan's flat in Kensington. He was huffing and puffing about the state of family affairs and how in India we are maligned because of what Raju Abba did, namely work for the Pakistan movement.

He then openly said that to remain in India and prove one's loyalty, people like us (meaning himself) have to show loyalty not just to the Indian state but also to its cultural and religious heritage, adding that to be fully accepted one has to almost become a Hindu!

The current development is a step in that direction. How right was Perry Anderson about India and Indian ideology. Our family is well on its way to proving him right once again!

—Qais

Raza explains the reference to Perry Anderson as being part of an exchange between him and his nephew about Anderson's coruscating critique of Gandhi's role in the history of the Indian independence movement. For Anderson, Gandhi gave birth to the notion of an imagined unitary India that never existed.

Soon afterwards, Raza received another message from Abid. Dated February 12, 2014, showing a rare temper. It reads:

Rajasthani woman left with second son, as i am told on Monday afternoon. I-D is here trying to arrange sale of more land in B.

As I said on phone, R had phoned to tell about sale of lands. Land here is measured in bighas, which in rural areas here is: 4.8 bighas =1 acre. He had already sold 25 bighas for Rs 1,750,000, now he is wanting to sell the remaining 150 bighas. He is seeking 600,000 per bigha, while the offer so far has been of 450,000. The people at B are not happy at the sale of lands there.

R had worked for cousin for 19 or so years and had been close to him in matters, to the extent that even at the Supreme Court appearances the man had stood beside him holding the files and papers. Then he was summarily dismissed and given just 24 hours to leave the house, which had been particularly harsh as the man's wife was due to give birth in one week, I have mentioned the story to you before.

On the very mention of Begum he starts cursing her etc. Over the phone he said that they call her rani when she is not worthy of being so called etc. He went on and on saying that she was a loose woman, staying out for long hours, not returning 2.30 or 3.00 past midnight. This seems to support what Maysam has already told you. I note that this too, is part of Abid's message.

CHAPTER 30

RAZA VISITS HIS AILING SISTER

For the next few months in 2014, Raza collected documents and other court-related materials together. He was once again pulled towards Lucknow, where he hadn't been since 2007. He often thought about the place, and indeed had often been forced to do so because of the nature of the story he was writing. In October 2014, he had a dream that his sister was calling him to come to see her. He mentioned the dream to Tess then forgot about it, putting it down to the fact that they were both excited to have a holiday there, and this dream was perhaps a sign.

It turned out to be no dream. He received an email message, followed by a phone call from Abid, telling him that Zahra was critically ill and was asking to see him. Abid was willing to help out with the fare as was Tess who says of Raza:

> You must go darling. It's your sister. Imagine if something happened to her and you weren't there. And, don't worry about me, I'll be alright.

Raza agreed that he had to go, yet many thoughts held him back: What was holding him back was whether to take his laptop with him or not and the writing, and the decisions he might be required to make. One of them he was being required to make was whether Zahra should come to the family home to be treated or whether she should remain at her married home? Abid and Jafar felt that she should come to her family home. For one, the hospitals were better in Lucknow.

"I went along with Abid's and Jafar's counsel. They lived there and would know better. In the end I felt obliged, mostly because I have always been close to her. She was Abbajan's Bitya, my little girl, and I remembered how she had been my confidante and had protected me from being bullied by Abid. This was mid-November and it was Diwali time, the annual festival of lights; banks and businesses would be closed, flights would be filled with thousands of British Indians, followed by the New Year and yet more demand for travel to India."

Abid and Raza kept checking at their ends, while Raza went for immunizations and a visa. Raza discovered that the Indian High Commission had outsourced its visa service because of the demand, and was now based nearby in Goswell Road. Getting a visa involved long queues, but once the application was in, the service was fairly quick and your passport with the visa would be returned within two days. Raza got a message on his cell phone from the passport agency that his passport would be ready the next day.

"I felt no justification though for the exorbitant fee I had to pay—£97.80, a perverse disincentive for countries wanting to encourage tourism, and countries playing tit-for-tat over visa fees, but there it was. Then the search began in earnest for a return flight. I got in touch with an Indian travel agent who could offer me a return flight for a reasonable price. I informed Abid and Tess that my flight would be leaving London on Thursday January 15 in the evening and arriving at Lucknow the following evening, after a change of planes at Delhi. All being well, I would be returning home on February 9."

Raza spent the next three weeks writing when he could, and wondering how he would find things when he got to Lucknow. He let me know that he was going when he sent me a piece of writing, with a message telling me what had happened. I encouraged him by saying that he would find it a rewarding experience.

Finally the night before his departure, Tess had been asking him what clothes he was taking, and sorting them out to be packed. She had bought him a wool cardigan for Christmas. Altogether he was taking one suitcase, his laptop, and a small piece of hand baggage.

"The winters can be cold in Lucknow and so I took my thermals and a warm coat. The flight was pretty full with a mixture of English and Indian travelers and I had a seat between two Indians who were constantly talking to each other. Eventually they had the good sense to move by offering me the window seat. I started to reminisce, wondering how I would find my brothers, and whether Ibn Dawood and Begum would be around."

Raza had offered to stay in a guesthouse because of the last bit of *contre-temps* he had with them eight years earlier regarding the drinking of alcohol. Abid had responded with "if you wish, but you can stay in the *Araam Kamra*." In the end he decided to stay in Kaiserbagh. This time he was going back to the ancestral home unannounced in order to see his sister. He carried no alcohol on this occasion, and should he feel the need, he could always go to a hotel or bar. Abid had made arrangements for Raza to stay in the *Araam Kamra*. Ibn Dawood was bound to know of this either from the servants or from Abid, since Abid was a pretty straightforward person with nothing to hide, and quite capable of being frank. What could Ibn Dawood do about it if his cousin was going to stay there?

Raza wondered too how he would find Zahra. The brothers had insisted that she come to the ancestral home to be treated. He wondered how his brothers would look, and how the place itself would look.

When he arrived at Delhi, it was evening. The new modernized airport meant that you could now walk from the international terminal through to the domestic ones without having to take a coach or taxi. People were smartly dressed, wearing winter clothes. Air travel between cities in India had become more popular; new airlines offered ongoing connections everywhere.

There was a lot of walking up and down the escalators to search for one's flight and terminal. Two or three English people had flown to go to an Ashram in Madras and Pondicherry. Having passed through Immigration and Customs—there had been no scrutiny of the name on his passport, as Raza had expected. He was waved on towards the domestic flights terminal, and Raza eventually found the flight to Lucknow and noticed that even Lucknow attracted tourists these days. On board there was an elderly English woman about his age, though he resisted the impulse to ask her why she was going to Lucknow. The flight was only an hour long and it was a little late, but somehow he saw in this woman's face the new India, the new face that India wanted to present to visitors.

"Lucknow airport had also changed and been modernized since the last time I was there. The single runway for flights, and the small white colonial terminal building I had departed that cold January day 65 years ago, when my uncle and everyone had been allowed to walk through the departures and see me off. I was a bit sad but impressed. Emerging through the Arrivals gate I didn't see Jafar for a moment, until the driver of the car that had come to fetch me, tapped me politely on the shoulder. I turned and suddenly saw my brother, embraced him tightly and looked at him. He didn't seem to have changed at all."

The Lucknow night was chilly. He remembered to bring warm clothes. Thank god for that. He sat muffled in the back seat of the car as they drove home from the hugely expanded airport terminal along the road via Amausi, with Jafar pointing out along the way where a subway from the airport to central Lucknow was under construction, causing long traffic delays. He felt tired by the time the car reached the palace gates. The sentry at the gates let the car in. The car had not been for Ibn Dawood, but borrowed from a stepbrother. The brothers knew perhaps that to ask Shaikhoo for a car to go and get Raza from the airport was not tactful or appropriate. I wanted to know who was now left in the palace. *This was important because if Raza gave that information it would serve as an opportunity to provide the reader with an overview and a refresher on everyone who will appear in the narrative that follows.

Meanwhile, upstairs at home, Abid had already eaten, but was waiting up to greet his brother. Jafar's nanny's daughter Zam was still there after so many years and she prepared a small dinner for Raza, something the brothers knew he would like. A small table was laid in Jafar's room. Abid now occupied it because of the treatment he had been receiving for two years for his neurological ailment. This was news to Raza: no one had written to him about this, so they sat and talked, bringing him up to speed about their sister, while Raza ate in a room now crammed with his brother's book cupboards to one side and Abid's bed in the middle. A brazier was brought in to provide additional heating besides that provided by a small electric heater. It was still cold.

"Bhai Sahab, we didn't want to tell you the full story about Zahra because we wanted you to see things for yourself. We didn't want you to be influenced by what we feel."

Raza didn't say much at that moment. After dinner, while his big room was being heated by a brazier and a hot water bottle was prepared, he went indoors to his parents' quarters to see his sister who had always had a room of her own.

"The light was on as I peeped through the door and saw she was asleep, with servants sitting by her bed, and also a young plump woman he hadn't seen before. Then Solly and Golu emerged from the room. Solly spoke in his usual loud voice:

Adaab Raza Bhai, Going home now. Just came to see my sweet wife. I must introduce you to my son's new wife. This is Deba, who's also my cousin.

"Then he was off to Kanpur since he too was ailing and unwell. He rushed back to Kanpur just as I went to the cold *Araam Kamra*, hoping I would sleep that night."

During the remainder of his time Raza fitted into his brothers' routines and visited his sister every day religiously. There was a lot to catch up with and he noted that Abid would usually get up later than Raza; Jafar would be up early on most days, reading English and Urdu newspapers delivered daily. He'd sit at the small low table outside the room on the verandah, hoping to catch the sun. Other days he'd be asleep in Bajia Amma's old room when Raza had breakfast.

The winter was on the cusp of change, and a brazier was placed under the dining table during breakfast to keep the legs warm where Raza would sit wearing his cardigan. Abid sometime joined him for breakfast, but was fussy about his food. He usually ate Weetabix with milk and honey, with almond nuts on the side. After his expensive porridge breakfast, Raza would go along to see his sister again.

By then a nurse would be in attendance trying to feed Zahra and Dubya. Golu and Dubya apparently slept in the same room on a mattress offered by Begum, which was somehow suspect since it was rumored to be a kind of spying situation. As it turned out later, Begum had offered that room to the couple. The fact that Dubya didn't sleep there but slept on a mattress next to Zahra's bed was soon to lead to ructions. The brothers were uncomfortable with these arrangements and wanted them to do something as the eldest members of the family.

ENTER IBN DAWOOD AND BEGUM

One morning soon after his arrival, Raza was sitting with Abid and Jafar when, in his impulsive way, Abid phoned his cousin and informed Ibn Dawood that Raza was there.

"I hadn't asked to see him, but so be it. After a few moments Ibn Dawood had arrived with his eldest son. It was the first time I had come face-to-face with him in years."

Raza found himself surprisingly calm and in control of himself. He looked at Ibn Dawood and could see he had not changed much. He only seemed to have lost a bit of weight, which he had been asked to do by his doctors because of his extremely rich diet. He had lost even more hair.

"He never looked directly at me, not making any eye contact apart from a cursory acknowledgement, and addressed himself to Abid and Jafar, talking a load of waffle, which the brothers responded to with more waffle as I watched and listened."

Another time Raza felt he would have also engaged in this kind of vapid conversation. Ibn Dawood hadn't changed in that respect either. Whatever the news there was about him, Raza was only to discover it through Abid and Jafar, plus one or two other mutual acquaintances he was to meet during his stay. The first piece of gossip Raza learned was that Ibn Dawood now slept in the room that was in one corner of the ground floor of the courtyard that had been the site of a homosexual tryst some years before, and where he had been spied upon *in flagrante diletto* with his trusted chauffeur by his wife and eldest son. That same room had now become his bedroom, where he was rumored to see other homosexual lovers. This rumor could not be confirmed and it remains just that, gossip, perhaps the result of a disgruntled employee attempting to extract revenge.

As for Begum, aware of her husband's behavior, and apparently accepting it as a *modus vivendi*, she now slept apart in the room that Raza's Khalajan had always lived in. It had become known as Begum Saheba's room. The front room on the ground floor that Nawab Dawood Ahmad used to stay in, where Raza had also spent his holidays on two occasions with his uncle's blessings, was now only used by Ibn Dawood to receive people who came to see him. "He is afraid for his life and he no longer have government-appointed sentries for protection," explained Jafar and Abid almost in unison. More revelations were to emerge during Raza's stay.

Meanwhile, Raza's account returns to his sister and her condition, the primary reason for his visit. Raza met his nephew Golu for the first time on his second day in Lucknow. He had gone to have his breakfast, when Golu had appeared, looking for something in the kitchen, and not finding it. He was in the process of asking a servant where to find some food when Raza was at the table. He bowed very respectfully to his uncle, and said he'd like to see him and went away. Golu hadn't changed much either, chubby in appearance, and apparently still ate heartily whatever he could find. This had apparently been a scavenging visit, looking for food in the kitchen.

Raza recounted the story to his brothers, who told him that Golu normally shouts at servants, and had even shouted at Jafar's maidservant, Kaneez, from childhood. Raza realized then that his help was also needed to keep Golu and his wife in order because the brothers had given up on it, and to find out for himself that Golu and Dubya were not there to help Zahra with her illness. Raza had always managed to get on with Golu, who in his own fashion showed his respect and affection. From the countless email messages that Golu sent around to almost everyone, Raza had begun to understand that he pretended to be a straightforward Shi'a Muslim. He could perhaps even be trusted as far as Ibn Dawood and Begum were concerned. At the same time, he could be playing his own game because there were indications that Begum and Ibn Dawood were siding with him behind the scenes, waiting and watching.

Raza decided to confront Golu and tell him that he must stop shouting at servants because that was not the custom of the house. Well, of course, Golu denied that he shouted at servants, but Raza contradicted him and said that he had heard otherwise. The next thing he learnt was that Golu's wife slept in Zahra's room, and that she could be heard talking all over the place on her mobile while her mother-in-law was trying to sleep, and could be heard by the servants since Jafar slept next door. Raza asked Golu to raise the issue with his wife and to tell her not to sleep there but instead in the balcony room where he stayed.

Yet the problem didn't stop there. Raza was still paying daily visits to his sister's room, often twice daily, around the times that the nurse and physician were both there, trying to give Zahra her medication. He talked to the two women, who in turn spoke to his sister:

"Bitya, your brother has come to see you from London."

Then Raza would hold both his hands under the covers, reaching for hers. He held it, and gave it a gentle squeeze. He felt no response. They would hold her eyes open to look at him, but to no avail. A disconsolate Raza was assured by the physician that his sister knew he was there. Up until this time Zahra had apparently not been given any food, and she was also being given some dubious Ayurvedic medicine that Golu and Dubya had ordered. The nurse and physio were glad for his support. Oddly enough it also aroused the attention of Ibn Dawood and Begum, who arrived one day out of the blue and asked to see Raza.

"They were sitting at the dining table in the verandah and we all started speaking, interrupting each other as they did so. I finally got a word in implying that Zahra was being given some Ayurvedic medicine that had been made for general purposes and was surely doing no good. The implication was that it was being done with by the family's approval. By implication though, fingers were being pointed at Abid and Jafar for not ensuring the right treatment for Zahra. I roundly disabused them of their misconception, and told them the medication, supplied via Golu and Dubya, had been stopped. They went away to their own quarters leaving a trail of intrigue behind them. I mentioned the story to my brothers. They picked up on the slur that was being cast on them and told me there was more to it."

Raza felt as though he was Hercules Poirot or some other fictional sleuth, trying to discover another crime that was about to be committed and he was somehow in the palace to prevent it from happening. The most likely informants other than his brothers were going to be the sister and the nurse, neither of them with anything to gain. The sister had also provided physio treatment for Abid over a period of two years. Kaneez also was loyal and would speak her mind, as would one or two older employees. However, Raza was told to be wary of another woman, a tall one, who would come daily to Zahra's room because she was from "the other side," and regarded as an informant.

"I had by now developed a daily routine by getting up early in the morning with a hot water bottle still warm, but the body would feel cold as I got up, and I would quickly turn on the electric heater to get dressed and washed. The process of warming up the water by turning the boiler switch on would normally take twenty minutes. And for this period I sat huddled, sitting at the desk in the corner and trying to get my laptop to connect with Jafar's erratic modem connection to see what messages I had received, and to send daily bulletins about Zahra to Tess, my daughter Nadia, and Maysam.

By now the water was hot and I would wash or shower. Some days I would stay in my thermals and pajamas, and when I thought Kaneez might be up and awake, would go to my deceased parents' quarters and ask for some tea and toast. On some days there would be a heavy urban mist from all the uncontrolled emissions in the city and on other days the sun could be seen trying to break through. My brothers said that after the 27th the sun would get hotter, though it would still be low on the horizon and throw its warmth out for a few hours only."

The sister and nurse arrived daily, the nurse in the morning at about 10:30 and during the afternoons from 2:30 to 4:30, and the sister just during the afternoons. Raza formed the impression that they were both pleased to see him and when he had finished breakfast in the verandah he would return to his room to reflect and write down his thoughts, leaving Jafar to read his newspapers. On occasion, he would ask for Immy, the grandson of his nanny and one of the young men now employed by his brother Abid, who drove a motorbike, and whose education in computing sciences Abid was paying for, to do the food shopping. Otherwise, he would go himself. Abid meanwhile might be up or still lying in bed.

When the time would come for the arrival of the nurse, usually Kaneez would knock on his door and let him know. He would then trundle out from his room, occasionally bumping into Golu on his way to or from the balcony room to his mother. He would bow respectfully to his uncle, and Raza would respond in kind, still treating him as his sister's son.

When Raza arrived in his sister's room, he'd see her upper body raised, her eyes shut, and the nurse trying to give her some medication and water.

"Why wasn't she being given any food?

"She was refusing to eat anything."

The sister confirmed to Raza one afternoon, early in Raza's visit, that his sister was getting very weak, too weak in fact to put up any resistance to the tumors lodged in her brain, and the breast cancer that had gone too long undetected.

Picking up the thread of his sister's diet, Raza discussed the matter with his brothers. He was informed that Masuma's husband had undertaken all the financial responsibilities for his mother-in-law's treatment and welfare, and that Golu received the money for the food and welfare side of things, including his wife's and his own. The brothers felt that, therefore, the responsibility was with Golu and his portly wife.

Not wanting to take his brothers' side, Raza says that his brothers were not in well-off circumstances, and having to budget for the maintenance and upkeep of the family quarters—one geyser and one boiler had to be replaced while Raza was there, as well as the curfew on keeping the boiler in the bathroom off during the night in Raza's bathroom. However, when Abid and Jafar heard the story they at once volunteered to order either fresh fish or chicken for their sister on a daily basis, that it would be prepared by Kaneez and put in a blender to make soup. Zahra would take some soup from that day on, and the sister assured him that he would see her strength increase daily.

In one of Raza's bulletins to Tess, dated January 31, 2014, he writes:

Hi—today Jafar's modem to which my laptop is connected is working, so here goes:

1. Sister: her condition seems to have stabilized thanks to the daily attendance of the nurse, a lovely woman called R, and S, the physio. Sister is gaining energy and appears to be fighting her condition. She is given liquidated food of different kinds—twice a day—fish, bone marrow, chicken, mixed veg, etc. Before my arrival she had only been given biscuits, toast, etc. Also I have had some quiet but direct words with Golu and told him in no uncertain terms that I don't want his wife to sleep in Timmy's room and disturb her with phone calls. She has also been found fumbling around amongst my sister's belongings and the servants have told her to desist. This morning Yasir slept there and not the wife, who we have taken to calling "Dubya" after the Disney cartoon. It's a relief for us because it seems that my words have had an effect.

2. We, that is to say all three brothers, had a meeting with Ibn Dawood and Begum to inform them of our decision to ask Dubya to be gone. Dubya is Begum's protégé, which is the way she operates, planting her people here and there. What an evil woman! Ibn Dawood said nothing much. Having fulfilled his role in providing her with two heirs, she

has now discarded him. They sleep apart in separate rooms. Rumors and gossip abound in Amadabad and Lucknow about his homosexual activities, which seem to have continued.

3. Today I am due to meet Comrade Suneet, whom Abid telephoned to tell him that I am here, and tomorrow I have a rendezvous with my stepbrother who is pursuing his own legal case against Ibn Dawood. He is the one I've met before in London. This July he is due to arrive in London, when he has promised to point out Ibn Dawood's and Begum's luxury apartment in Regent's Park.

In this message we find Raza confirming some issues concerning his sister's health while, at the same time, introducing other facets to the story of his visit. The first of these is the emergence of the intrigue over his sister's inheritance. The fumbling about in the bedroom, his brothers had told him, was because Golu and Dubya were both very greedy and intended to take all of Zahra's wealth, without apparently giving a hoot for Masuma, his sister. Golu had also turned out to inherit all his father's property too. For a moment the idea crossed Raza's mind that perhaps Golu and Dubya were trying to poison his sister, but then the idea was dismissed. Attention returned to Zahra's health.

On February 3, Raza notes:

The nurse who attends sister daily slept over in the room last night because Zahra had vomited the night before. Her dinner the night before had been served too late due to interference by the nasty couple. I called Golu to one side and told him in no uncertain terms that this must not happen again.

This morning, after a small breakfast of tea and toast in the morning sun—what a luxury not to have to make it—I went to Zahra's room. The nurse was feeding her. I enquired how my sister had passed the night? "Fine," was her response. I sat and looked at Timmy's face as she took her food from the spoon with closed eyes. For the first time she looked serene, with no furrows in her brow.

Did this signify some hope for his sister? But soon Raza was disabused of this false hope when Abid sent for the family doctor for consultation. Dr. Bhatya brought along all of Zahra's medical records and revealed the worst. Zahra had been very anti-medicine and hidden things for far too long, and now it was a matter of weeks or at most of months for her to live. The only thing to do was to keep her comfortable and alive for the moment.

But things were not going to go that way. Masuma was telephoned and it was found that she could not come from Delhi because her teenage son had severe asthma, but she did confirm that her mother had suffered a fall and injured her head eight years back and refused to consult a doctor. Things were to get worse. Instead of speculating about why, why their sister had felt compelled to hide things, the atmosphere was made harder to bear, given Golu's recalcitrance in sending Dubya away to get some peace, Golu, getting wind of the fact that his mother was to be moved to Delhi, where there were better medical facilities, and where his brother-in-law, still paying for everything, had decided one morning to drive away to Kanpur in one of his two cars parked at the front, one of which was ostensibly supposed to be for his mother.

The same evening Golu returned with his ailing father at his side, in order to take his mother to Kanpur, where there were worse medical facilities than there were in Lucknow. Father and son were there for two nights, packing Zahra's bags and what they could, leaving the rest for later, and at the request of the brothers locking the room. To Raza's knowledge, his brothers had decided to put another lock on Zahra's room in order to prevent Golu from raiding and getting away with the spoils. The storeroom next to Bajia Amaa's was where Zahra kept all her more precious belongings. This was also locked. The two rooms were only to be opened when Golu and Masuma, brother and sister, were present together. Zahra had been a very careful person and the brothers were sure that she had labeled everything with initials. Father and son avoided the brothers.

Solly slept for those two nights in his wife's room, unaware of his wife's condition, talking loudly and kissing her on her cheeks while she was asleep. Golu pouted and kept to himself. One doesn't know what Golu had told him. Dubya had gone, but Masuma had arrived, summoned by her father to help him pack. She came to see her uncles for a few minutes during the night she was there, and then went back to Delhi to see to her son. She was sweet and understanding, but unable to distance herself emotionally from her father and brother.

That evening Raza told her that among her mother's belongings she would also find an *Itr-daan* or ornate perfume container that had been given to him by his uncle when he had come of age, and which subsequently Bajia Amma had given to Zahra on Raza's behalf as a wedding present. Now, he said that he wanted her to have it. Early the next morning she had flown back to Delhi.

"A few hours later the ambulance that had been ordered to transport Zahra by road to Kanpur arrived. Abid and Jafar sat with me in Jafar's room, waiting to hear when the ambulance men would appear carrying Zahra on a stretcher unconscious. What words would she have said to me or my brothers if she could speak to us? I went outside and sat under the verandah, until finally the stretcher carrying my sister arrived from the side door of mother's quarters with Solly ahead of the ambulance men when, suddenly seeing my brothers and me he dived back indoors and took another route, the same one Golu had taken. My brothers advanced slowly together to follow their sister down the marble staircase and out to the waiting ambulance below. For a moment in that house that had witnessed so much history, all the people living there had assembled at the front in a show of unity. Ibn Dawood and Begum weren't around."

The three brothers kept their composure as they saw their sister's stretcher being carefully laden on the ambulance, and saw Solly sitting in one of the cars looking away. Surprisingly Golu came and bowed low before his uncles. Abid responded, but Raza did not, looking across to his sister and saying farewell. Then the ambulance carrying his sister was gone, followed by Golu's car.

It was Raza's farewell to his sister. The three brothers returned upstairs. Zahra's unforeseen departure for Kanpur meant that Raza had three or four more days to spend in Lucknow. He had already been to dinner with Rizzoo and his brothers but still needed to get some things from his stepbrother's shop. While his brothers did their own thing, Raza went on the back of a motorbike to Hazratganj. The atmosphere was somehow lighter now.

On February 5, his brothers hired a taxi to take them to Amadabad and back to commemorate their mother's passing. Something in the conversation between his brothers seemed to imply that it was something only they were doing. He didn't go, but when his brothers returned, they said he should have gone with them, and that a lot of people in Amadabad were asking about him.

"I felt like an outsider, the prodigal son. My two brothers had become very close after my parents' death. I lived in London and our sister lived with her husband's home. That's why I didn't go: because they seemed to be talking to each other. It was force of habit, not meant to exclude me. And so it turned out."

When they returned, they had another story to relate. Daddhoo, the eldest son of Ibn Dawood, who Raza had seen earlier, and who had appeared to be a polite young man, had spent one night in the Bara Banki police station for having knocked the wall of their compound down while trying to be the country gentleman and use a tractor to till some land. He had apparently also been beaten up. Abid and Jafar had come to hear the story in Amadabad and now one can surmise that the district constabulary, well known for taking the law into its own hand and respecting no status, had been rough and ready with the response.

However, Raza's brothers pointed out how the eldest son had also behaved like a raja's son towards the shopkeepers of Hazratganj, which is why the sentry provided by the police had been removed and why, because of this and in fear of his life, Ibn Dawood slept in the courtyard room down below. Raza said Ibn Dawood had no idea how to govern, nor does it seem did his son. They were behaving like the cosmopolitan elite, out of touch with agrarian realities, and incapable of ruling as his ancestors had until partition and independence. It could be argued that there is nothing to rule.

Prior to his arrival, Raza had one day asked Maysam: "Look, I have been writing the story of our family, as you know, but it occurred to me to ask whether Hurr Bhai and Zainab Baji had ever mentioned in conversation who they thought would have been the best successor to his uncle?" There is more on this issue perhaps.

Without hesitation, Maysam's response had been: "Yes Mamujan, they did mention it once that they think that your father, Nana Abba, would have been fair and equal." This indeed has been the theme of our story—redemption of his father, Nawab Haidar Ali Mohammed's life and work, and the fatal consequences of its usurpation by primogeniture.

Raza's stay was almost over. His sister had been taken to Kanpur. At home, Tess was due to have a knee operation. His brothers understood the situation and Raza says that the remaining time with his brothers was very rewarding. The weather had grown warmer, and they would start the day by having breakfast in the sun, sitting in the open air, one door away from the kitchen. For lunch and dinner, they would ask him what he would like to eat, to make their brother's remaining time more enjoyable. Kaneez plagued him for European recipes and loved watching TV programs on cookery. Raza would go to his computer, Google the recipe, and send it to Jafar's computer to translate for her. Suneet also arrived one day, accompanied by a young comrade he was training. He had parked the car outside and telephoned when Raza was in his room.

"Abid had already ordered some freshly made jalebi, a sweet popular in India, by deep-frying a wheat flour (white flour) batter in pretzel or circular shapes, which are then soaked in sugar syrup. Abid himself went to the top of the stairs to receive him, while I asked Kaneez to prepare some tea and send it with the jalebis. There were going to be five people. I stood up and they gave each other an affectionate hug before Suneet introduced his young comrade, who had been accompanying him around in adjoining rural areas, learning how to support poor peasants in their struggle against landlords occupying land illegally, and eventually to get them legally evicted. An enjoyable conversation about his retirement from the central committee, and his desire to train up younger people to take over followed."

Raza talked about the person downstairs, and whether he had bumped into Ibn Dawood, who Suneet had the unfortunate experience of meeting the last time Raza was here. Then Suneet was gone.

Raza promised to meet him in Delhi the next time he came, and by now just a couple more days remained when Raza, sitting under the verandah by Jafar's room, heard the staccato sounds of two pairs of shoes coming from his side of his parents' quarters. He looked up and saw the two young sons of Ibn Dawood and Begum coming towards him.

"They bowed politely before I asked them to take a seat, and sat there while I sensed them weighing me up. I hadn't seen the younger one, the one who had been married the year before, but I could see he had also inherited his parents' stature. Very few words were spoken. After a few minutes I told them I was going to do some work on the computer, and excused myself. I had no explanation for that encounter, except that they had arrived from the direction of mother's quarters. Early in the morning two days later, I muffled up for departure, had breakfast with my brothers, gave the remaining cash to Kaneez and the others who had served me, and was gone out the back entrance in a stepbrother's car, because none of the brothers wanted Ibn Dawood and Begum to know about my movements."

During March 2014, Raza heard the expected news that his sister had died in Kanpur, and that her body had been taken for burial next to their parents' graves in the mosque of Karbala in Amadabad.

CHAPTER 31

TRAGIC ENDS

The passing away of the remaining family members of his generation was inevitable now. There had been fourteen of them at one time and now only seven, including Raza, remained. During summer of 2015, Abid carried on communicating with Raza who seemed to be chirpy and in good spirits. His first few communications were about a conference that had been held in Lucknow to which Abid says that both Ibn Dawood and Daddhoo had been invited. The conference was on Lucknow Shi'as and was attended by Saudi and Israeli diplomats and military personnel. Ibn Dawood's participation made Abid's blood boil.

Later in the summer, Abid had written to Raza that he was planning to invest in repairing the Austin Minor he had been given by his uncle—the same car that had been used during their school days when it took them to Loretto Convent. Seventy years later, it would now have the status of a vintage car. The tires were the only problem. Abid had researched online and found in England some suppliers of vintage car tires and other accessories unavailable in India. He notified Raza in London and asked him if he would mind purchasing them with the money he was asking Suneet to have transferred. Raza had agreed and waited for another communication from Abid.

Abid also had an honorary position in Professor Irfan Habib's History Department at Aligarh University, the same Irfan Habib who had written an agrarian history of India during the Mughal period that Raza had read in the School of Oriental and African Studies in 1968—a riposte to Weberian theory that the growth of capitalism was an endowment of the West.

Then out of the blue, shock hit him when Jafar phoned him to say that Abid had passed away on September 26, 2015.

"What happened? He sounded so well?"

"Bhai Sahab, he was physically very weak. He collapsed one day in the bathroom and hit his head against the bath."

The news shook Raza to the core. The death of a younger brother is harder to take. They had been brothers for 79 years, behaving sometimes like Tweedle-Dee and Tweedle-Dum, but always inseparable. They communicated in a universal language and shared the same values, raging against all the deceits and lies that Ibn Dawood and Begum had heaped upon the rest of the family.

Tess had known Abid well, and told him that he must go to India again. But he was going to be too late for the burial. Also, since Muharram was due to begin on October 11, Jafar had hurried the chaleeswan ceremonies. He was the one who was bearing the hardest blow of all, writing to Raza and saying that he had lost a companion of 45 years.

Raza sat feeling morose. Jafar was the only sibling he had left. He went through the motions of being alive, as he sent messages of the bereavement to the remaining members of the Amadabad family—Nadia, Maysam, Qais, Qasim Bhai, Chhoti Baji—as well as to friends in England that Abid had known in London. While messages of condolence poured in, and were sent on to Jafar, Jafar, going through Abid's computer archives, had discovered an old letter from their father to Zahra. Raza knew that letter, and immediately sent it on to his relatives. The letter, which the reader may recall from an earlier chapter, simply reads as follows:

Lucknow   20.1.1990

My dear Bitya, Your husband came, as expected on 1st January and brought all the breakfast foods and cash in instalments of Rs 3000 and Rs 1000. 5 had come out of Dr. Hansraj's nursing home after the cataract operation and the drops of medicine have been continuing. Dr. has not yet given me power lenses yet, and will give me the prescription in February so your money was very helpful, not only in meeting some of the expenses of the operation as part of it was used by me. I-D is too full of his political ambitions to care about you or myself or Raza, although I have stepped down in accordance with the family custom of primogeniture, so the Custodian has stopped all my income. Now I am selling my assets to meet my expenses here. This is the world! I-D's attitude towards me is merely superficial and not substantial! He is a "man of the world" and his in-laws have put him under their thumb. How long can I go on tolerating this state of affairs and on living in "his house"? God only knows! Your mother's health is much better. The winter was severe, but she has got over her cough and plans to go to Ajman after Ramzan, i.e., April. So, keep your hands crossed. She will be with all of you after Spring and up to Aug. when you will all come to Lucknow again 'Insha Allah for Moharram, which will start about 24th July this year.

Look after your health and your husband's happiness,

With best wishes

Yours lovingly

Abbajan

This was a personal letter to a daughter from a very private man who seldom expressed his feelings and emotions publicly, willing to undertake all sacrifices to avoid bringing shame onto the family. His nephews, nieces, and their children knew nothing really about it, even if they had their suspicions. The receipt of this message was a universal expression of shock.

Maysam responded:

Dear Mamoojan,

I am shocked as mamoojan had US$ 1.2 million credit facility from LCLC (Grand Cayman), which he never paid back, and I had to answer questions concerning that. I later arranged for the liquidators to write off that sum in return for Mamoojan cooperating with them against Ibadi's wife. [I did this expecting him to extend help towards his sisters and cousins]. He and his wife tried to push me aside, but as I was a consultant to the liquidators at the time, I came to know that he signed a false affidavit. When I questioned him in December 2000, he and his wife became hostile towards me and they stopped meeting my parents!

It reminded me of what I have read about Banu Omayya and their stratagems to uphold falsity and injustice.

With respects

Maysam

Maysam is stunned by the amount of money Shaikhoo has been involved in and yet has constantly refused to share any of it with the family other than his own inner circle. Spontaneous messages and letters, all expressing shock, followed and of course why should they not? Raza was particularly caught by the response of Qasim Bhai, who had made his own life in Pakistan, was happily married, and normally kept out of family affairs. Only recently, when the two had last spoken after Hurr Bhai and Zainab Baji's passing away, Qasim Bhai had fulminated at Ibn Dawood's claim to be the "sole legitimate heir," a claim that he had also read about. This time Qasim Bhai had raged in his sorrow again. The reassurance such responses gave him was that his side of the family were not alone and that other members of the family also felt deceived and cheated.

The hardest blow has been borne by Jafar who, as we know, has only stayed in that house after the death of the parents solely because of Abid, for whom it had become too late to move elsewhere, just as it had been for their father.

"Jafar, now living in isolation, has kept me updated on daily events, knowing that I couldn't get there in time for the burial and *chaleeswan* [days of mourning] which followed within ten days. I knew that a lot of people had gathered in Amadabad for the chaleeswan. Abid had been very well known and respected, just like his father. Jafar says that people had gathered in the baradari, now naked and stripped of the fabled red chandelier. No one asks questions about it anymore. They know. They also know so much more—the changes that had occurred over a lifetime, and the faces of those members of the family that had always been there to share their lives through thick and thin."

Rizzoo was present, as well as people like Puttoo and his sons, and others Abid had financially supported. Of course Ibn Dawood and his son were present too. They had to show their faces. Nothing less would have done. However, Ibn Dawood also used that occasion to approach Jafar and asked him if the two rooms across the courtyard from Begum's new abode could be cleared for refurbishment. The rooms referred to had been used as storerooms by Bajia Amma and Zahra, and Jafar intended to clear them anyway, as part of the overall clearance of Nawab Haidar Ali's side of the family from Amadabad and Lucknow.

Abid too was buried next to his parents, sister, and other ancestors. Jafar tells his brother that he had made all the arrangements, including having the gravestones inscribed with their names. On leaving Amadabad, Jafar sent another message to his brother in London: "The people of Amadabad love me." Thinking of his parents, and their relationship to the common people of Amadabad, of the glue that had always bound the family to the inhabitants, he responded: "Of course they do."

"Back in Lucknow, Jafar had to clear out all the wanted and unwanted things with only servants to help him. Abid had left money for various people, but most of it to Jafar. It must be a lonely job because he keeps sending messages and photos to me of items I don't know what to do with. Recently it was photos of two marble tables from the White Palace North that their father had transported there after 1946. From a distance all I can advise is to consult friends like Rizzoo, Suneet, and his step-cousins in Lucknow. In anticipation of being asked to clear the *Araam Kamra* of Abid's belongings, including Abid's considerable collection of books, manuscripts and family documents, Jafar is currently doing so."

The speculation is that the refurbished storerooms will be used as a bridal suite for the younger son and his wife, while the *Araam Kamra*, that magnificent room with its memories, will be there for the brother-in-law's use whenever he wants to take a break from Delhi and dream of being a prince. The fact that the brother-in-law's wife, a known alcoholic, will probably accompany him, and face no objections from Ibn Dawood, is an irony not lost on the reader.

"By the time all this happens the transformation of Amadabad into Mishrabad, so long ago predicted by Hashim Bhai, will be complete, and their combined business acumen will turn the palaces in Lucknow and Amadabad into moneymaking cows. The latest report from TNN announces that the palace and other 'historic sites,' including the White Palace, are to be opened to the public, and, why not? The same happens in England."

"A guided tour for members of the public is also proposed, conducted by the eldest son, the heir apparent—yes, primogeniture does stay intact. What the public will not know is that they are being fed a fabricated history by someone who has been fed on myths by his father, who never lived in some of the historical sites like the White Palace. Someone should ask him."

EPILOGUE

For the present our story is almost finished. The evidence is there for readers to weigh up and judge for themselves. At the beginning of this story, Raza had likened his family's history to a tapestry, because when he looked back at all the stories that he heard from his father and others during his childhood, the story had evoked for him some striking ancestral figures, ancestors with their symbols adorned with decorative features, a little like Persian or Mughal miniatures from a dim and distant past, all linked by a common thread that united them, through thick and thin, for so long, the living proof of which lay in its continuity.

This has been a tale about a legacy and a live tradition about some universal human values of love and honor, compassion and pity and sacrifice, a legacy betrayed by envy and covetousness and greed, but still unbowed. The story needed to be written, and all the dirty linen washed in public because to have remained silent would have been a disservice. The story of Maysam and Qais, Jafar and surviving members of that generation and what they make of their own lives in foreign lands, still following the values bestowed upon them by their parents is yet to be known, and whether Raza ever returns to his Ithaca, and what he finds there is another story someone else will have to tell.

Maysam, who often uses social networking for posting various things including his passion for maths and Shi'ism, posted the following:

Following is Maysam's post on Facebook:

An article by Dudhoo Amadabad, lamenting about himself being a stranger in his own land. Well, had he been schooled in India, and not in Winchester, England, and he had gone, to an Indian university rather than Amherst, USA; Damascus, Syria and Cambridge (for Ph.D. in, of all topics—composite cultures of UP i.e. "Ganga-Jamni Tahzeeb," which surely could have been done in India), he would not have felt like a stranger in India. [Same holds for his younger brother, who is reading for Ph.D. at Cambridge in Indian History (!), and plays polo with a fellow taluqdar student of ... well, Indian history.

As for the Amadabad properties, they would not have been declared as 'enemy property' had the late Nawab Dawood Ahmad of Amadabad trusted his wife and his younger brother, Haidar Ali, and transferred the properties to them when he decided to leave for Pakistan. But alas, he did not and today the Amadabad family in India is a subject of pity, ridicule and lament.

Ironically, Daddhoo's father, Ibn Dawood (one-time admirer of Jawaharlal Nehru), argued for the caste system in 1980s during a conversation with his late brother-in-law, and glorified its rigid class structure while defending its brutality with the words "but the world is not a fair place." He rejected any notion of principles of social justice that his late brother-in-law put forward, even though exemplified by the martyrs of Karbala as advocates of justice. In 2012, his late brother-in-law had remarked "Ibn Dawood has fallen victim to his own system of belief"; which evidently resonates with the manifesto of the BJP [Bharatiya Janata Party].

[At the time of writing this post, Ashoka University made no mention of Dudhoo Khan in its list of teaching staff].

As Jafar remarks on reading excerpts that Raza sent him, what this story shows is how during the last 80 years or so the whole history of Amadabad has been turned upside down.

ACKNOWLEDGMENTS

A number of people edited, commented, and reviewed the manuscript. This include various family members: Anita Saddler, Natalia Filippova, Olga Filippova, Valentin Filippov, either read portions and/or discussed the manuscript. Special thanks for the artist John Fraser for the brilliant cover art. The various verbatim accounts came together from joint discussions, participant observation in bars, Parisian café's, London pubs, assorted hangouts in Normandy, and Bristol, England, restaurants in Little Africa in Harlem, and wineries near the Champ Elysees. We discussed and spent time reading in Penne, France, Raz's flat in London well into the early morning hours. Even before the discussion was made to record the life history of the family, I was already recording witticisms, poems, by ee cummings, Basil Bunting, Omar Khayyam, and Jean-Joseph Rabearivelo.

Thomas Gerry editing one version of the manuscript and Kirti Varma performed some of the heavy lifting, critiquing parts that needed fixing whether it was names of foods, or Indian proverbs; they all worked to make our manuscript better. These random conversations later turned into seven years of prose work, notes, scribblings, anecdotes, capturing a life history too complex at times to consider possible. I can never fully thank all those who made this volume possible and I sincerely apologize for anyone we may have left out. We are especially appreciative of the anonymous reviewers for their gracious assistance and the wonderful work of Anthem Press production team.

In that regard the following individuals are gratefully appreciated and kindly noted:

Zain Abdullah, Andrew Arato, Beverley Brown, Chaya Bhuvaneswar, Benoit Challand, Jean Cohen, Jean Pierre Demange, Roumiana Tatarova Demange, Cristina Dragomir, Stephen Feuchtwang, Natalia Filippova, Carlos Forment, John Fraser, Peter Fraser, Tom Gerry, Linda Gerry, Megan Greiving, Hakim Hasan, Kazim Mohammad Amir Khan, Yumna Khan, Lawanna Kimbro,

Dara Levendosky, Chloe McAlpin, William Milberg, Abi Pandey, Anwar Shaikh, Anita Saddler, Tej. P. S. Sood, Joel Simundich, Kirti Varma, Harte Weiner.

Two student cohorts from the New School for Social Research are noted: The original Organic Novel Course: Scott Beck, Jussara Raxlen, Wendy Washington, Maria Elekidou and the present Living Book: From Research to Manuscript course: Jules Ostro, Patrick Devitt, Melanie Samad, James Farner, Aissata Fernandez Taranco, Jordon Marco, Jacob Yusufov, Alexa Dobre. Although all of the people mentioned here assisted in some way to the completion of this book, we take sole responsibility for any of its shortcomings.

BIBLIOGRAPHY

Anderson, Perry. *The Indian Ideology*. London: Verso, 2013.
Baldwin, James. *Another Country*. New York: Doubleday, 1962.
Becker, Howard. *Outsiders. Studies in the Sociology of Deviance*. Glencoe, IL: Free Press, 1963.
Campbell, Joseph. *The Power of Myth*. New York: Doubleday, 1988.
Chaudhuri, Nirad C. *The Autobiography of an Unknown Indian*. London: Macmillan, 1951.
Daynes, Sarah, and Terry Williams. *On Ethnography*. London: Polity Press, 2018.
Deb, Siddhartha. *The Beautiful and the Damned: A Portrait of the New India*. New York: Farrar, Straus, Giroux, 2011.
di Lampedusa, Giuseppe. *The Leopard*. New York: William Collins Publisher, 1960.
Faulkner, William. *Absalom, Absalom*. New York: Modern Library, 1964.
Fernea, Elizabeth. *Guest of the Sheik*. New York: Doubleday, 1965.
Flaherty, Frances. *The Elements of Story*. New York: Harper, 2009.
Freud, Sigmund. *Delusion and Dream. An Interpretation in the Light of Psychoanalysis of "Gradiva" a novel by Wilhelm Jensen*. Reprinted. New York: New Republic, 1917.
Ghosh, Amitav. *The Glass Palace*. New York: HarperCollins UK, 2000.
Ho, Engseng. *The Graves of Tarim: Geneology and Mobility Across the Indian Ocean*. Berkeley: University of California Press, 2006.
Hosain, Attia. *Sunlight on a Broken Column*. London: Penguin Books, 1992.
Jessal Smita, Tewan. "Primogeniture in Awadh: Sociological Implications for Class and Gender." *Economic and Political Weekly* 32, no. 22 (May 31–June 6, 1997): 1255–1264.
Kazantzakis, Nikos. *The Odyssey: A Modern Sequel*. New York: Simon and Schuster, 1958.
Kornblum, William. *Discovering Ink: A Mentor for an Historical Ethnography*. Annals. AAPSS, 595, September 2004.
Lewis, Oscar. *The Children of Sanchez. Autobiography of a Mexican Family*. New York: Vintage Books, 1963.
———. *La Vida: A Puerto Rican Family in the Culture of Poverty*. New York: Vintage Books, 1965.
Mehta, Ved. *Daddyji*. London: Penguin Books, 1972.
Mills, C. Wright. *Listen Yankee: The Revolution in Cuba*. New York: Ballantine Books, 1960.
Mount, Ferdinand. *The Tears of the Raja: Mutiny, Money and Marriage in India 1805–1905*. London: Simon and Schuster, 2015.
Prawer Jhabvala, Ruth. *Heat and Dust*. New York: Counterpoint Books, 1975.

Robinson, Alan. *Narrating the Past: Historiography, Memory and the Contemporary Novel.* London: Macmillan, 2011.

Roy, Anuradha. *The Folded Earth.* London: MacLehose Press, 2011.

Seth, Vikram. *Two Lives: A Memoir.* New York: HarperCollins, 2005.

Singh, Khushwant. *Train to Pakistan.* London: Chatto & Windus, 1956.

———. *Truth, Love and Malice.* New York: Penguin Books, 1995.

Thomas, W. I., and Florian Znaniencki. *The Polish Peasant in Europe and America.* Chicago: University of Chicago Press, 1918.

Thomas, W. I. *On Social Organization and Social Personality.* Chicago: University of Chicago Press, 1966.

Turgenev, Ivan. *Fathers and Sons.* New York: W.W. Norton, 1996.

Wood, Michael. *In Search of Myths and Heroes.* Berkeley and Los Angeles: University of California Press, 2005.

———. *India.* New York: Basic Books, 2007.

Woodruff, Philip. *The Men Who Ruled India and the Founders of Modern India.* New York: St. Martin's Press, 1954.

Yourcenar, Marguerite. *Memoirs of Hadrian.* New York: Farrar, Straus Giroux, 1954.

———. *Oriental Tales.* New York: Farrar, Straus, Giroux, 1983.

INDEX

Abid (twin brother of Khan, Raza Mohammed) 32
   Alexander technique and 62
   anglicization of 106
   Arabic poetry and 180–81
   at boarding school 93–95
      visits home from 100–6
   burial of 328
   at Cambridge University 168
   death of 325–26
   early life of
      family visits 33
      servants as element of 36
   in forced exile, in London 276–80
      Ibn Dawood as cause of 278
      as undesirable in India 278
   Jafar and 269
   letters to twin brother 84, 309–10
   Mohammad, Nawab Ali Haidar, and 267
   with mother 102–3
   post-primary school education, in England 63–64
   primary school years
      Loretto Convent School for Girls 40–41
      at La Martinière College 49, 53–56
   request for piece of family estate 275
   siblings of. *See* Jafar; Khan, Raza Mohammed; Zahra
   social isolation of 62–63
   Tess and 268–70, 326
Absalom, Absalom (Faulkner) 190

Adler, Alfred 62
Ahmad, Nawab Dawood (uncle) 7, 45–48, 56–57
   accession of, 27
   Ali, Nawab Haidar, and 47, 48–49
      commitment to sanitorium, 57
      in Lucknow 49
   Bhai, Hurr, with, in Iraq 105
   children of 28
   expectations of 28
   Ibn Dawood and 3, 4, 5, 28
      birth and infancy of 50–52
      lack of photos of 7–8
      polio and 51–52
      special diet for 52
   Indian Muslim League
      and 45–46, 47
   Indian National Congress and 47
   in Iraq 105
   Jinnah and 45, 59–60
   Khan, Raza Mohammed, and 44, 49–50
      visits by 33
      in Lucknow 49–50
   on Muslim homeland, establishment of 47–48
   Naidoo and 28
   Nehru, Jawarharlal, and 45
   in Pakistan 59–60, 145, 173, 208–10
      regional divisions in, involvement in 125
      self-exile in 90
   photographs of 27–28

Ahmad, Nawab Dawood (uncle) (*cont.*)
  pilgrimage journey of 28–29
  political focus of 47–48
  return from Iraq 112
  self-exile of 89–91
    family reaction to 91
    in Pakistan 90
    political reasons for 90
  as Shi'a Muslim 45–46
  visit to Haidar, Nawab Ali, in
    psychiatric hospital 125–26
Amadabad, India
  Tess in 270–72
  zenith of 19. *See also* Mohammad,
    Nawab Ali
Amadabad Estate 21
"Alam" (standard of Tamerlaine) 218
Alexander, Mathias 62
Alexander technique 62
The Alexandria Quartet (Durrell) 172, 231
Ali, Moazzam 86
Amma, Bajia 30
Anderson, Perry 309
Anglo-Indian culture 42
  in Lucknow 54
Anis, Mir 15–16, 208, 231
Annie (friend) 239–40
anti-imperialism 173
Aparajitao 230
Arabic poetry, Abid and 180–81
Arberry, Arthur 180, 181, 252–53, 306
aristocracy, membership in,
    embarrassment over 3–4
Arrow in the Blue (Koestler, 116
Ashcroft, Peggy (Dame) 97
al-Askari, Hasan (Imam) 61
Attenborough, Richard 14
Awami League 208–9

Bahgdad, Iraq 60–61
Baji, Bari (Zainab) 253, 303–4, 323
  children of 118. *See also* Maysam
  financial support by 291
  Qais 243–44, 275, 278–80, 290,
    291, 308–9
  death of 305–8, 327–28

marriage to Bhai, Hurr 82, 84–89
  banquets after 88
  date of wedding 84
  invited guests 85
  in Lucknow 88–89
  pranks as element of wedding
    celebration 87–88
  "rukhsati" event 86
  traditional Indian ceremonies
    in, 86–88
Maysam and 290
Baji, Chhoti 305
Begum (wife of Ibn Dawood) 278,
    280–81, 283–85
  family accusations against 299–304
  Zahra and, visit during illness 315–22
Bergman, Ingmar 175, 230, 231
Beyle, Marie-Henri. *See* Stendhal
Bhai, Hashim (cousin) 143–45, 215–16,
    223–24, 254, 329
  Ibn Dawood and 145
Bhai, Hurr (cousin) 78, 199, 253, 268,
    303–4, 323
  children of 118. *See also* Bhai, Hurr
  financial support by 291
  Qais 243–44, 275, 278–80, 290,
    291, 308–9
  death of 305–8, 327–28
  impact on Khan, Raza Mohammed
    306–7
  in Iraq 105
  in London 80
  marriage to Baji, Bari 82, 84–89
    Abid and 85
    banquets after 88
    date of wedding 84
    invited guests 85
    in Lucknow 88–89
    pranks as element of wedding
      celebration 87–88
    "rukhsati" event 86
    traditional Indian ceremonies
      in 86–88
Marsiya poems and 208
Maysam and 290
Musaddas 303–4, 308

INDEX 339

Russell, Bertrand, and 207
  at Trinity College, Cambridge 82, 94
  visit to boarding school 82
Bhai, Husain (cousin) 84, 85, 117
  at Magdalen College, Oxford 118
  in Pakistan 145
Bhai, Qasim 214, 327–28
Bhashani, Maulana 125
Bin Laden, Osama 6
Bird of Paradise 94
Black Hole of Calcutta 17
Blair, Tony 253
boarding school
  Abid at 93–95
    anglicization of 106
    visits home from 100–6
  Khan, Raza Mohammed, at 64
    academic struggles of 99
    arrival at 70–71
    Bhai, Hurr, visit to 82
    Bhai, Husain, visit to 84
    Chapel at 74–75
    during Christmas holidays 94
    completion of studies for 111–12
    compulsory subjects for 107
    culture shock for 101
    disciplinary actions against 109
    as exile 82
    father's advice at 65
    friendships for 93, 95
    growing independence of 98–99
    homesickness and 82–83
    journey to 65–67, 69–70
    journey with 65–67
    lodging with English families during summers 82–83
    pen pals for 83
    racism at 81–82
    reading interests for 93–94
    rebellious nature of 107
    reverse assimilation issues 101
    running away from school 108–9
    student treatment of 72–74
    summers during 81, 83, 104
    visits home from 75, 100–6
  Kirkhall and 100, 110

Mohammad, Nawab Haidar Ali, at 107–12
  meeting with boarding school Headmaster 108, 110–11
Bolt, Robert 172
Bombay, India 221–26
Bose, Subbash Chandra 25, 46–47
Bourgeois, Monique 191–92
Braham, Gerry 175
Braithwaite, Edward 238–39
Britten, Benjamin 237
Buck, Andrew 54
Buck, Colin 54

Cambridge University
  Abid at 168
  Trinity College at 82, 94
Campaign for Nuclear Disarmament (CND) 173
  March from Aldermaston organized by 182, 183, 237
caste system
  among Hindus 41
  in Islam, lack of 11
  Khan on 11
Castro, Fidel 245
Cavafy, Constantine P. 172, 175, 187
Chacha, Mahdi 85
Chacha, Mantoo 86
Chacha, Taqi 85, 268
Chapelle du Rosaire de Vence 191–92
Chaplin, Charlie 54–55
Charterhouse of Parma (Stendahl) 251
The Chess Players 14
Christ Re-crucified 15
Chrome Yellow (Huxley) 116
claims to family estate, by Ibn Dawood 273–76, 280–87
  allies in 280–81
  Begum role in 278, 280–81, 283–85
  forced exile of Abid 278
  illegal monies taken from 275
  legal victories in 283–87
CND. *See* Campaign for Nuclear Disarmament
Collins, Canon John 237
Colvin Taluqdar College 40

Community Care Alliance
  consortium 273
Cosmopolitan Bank of Commerce and
  Debit (CBCD) 4
Crammers
  accreditation for 113
  international students in 127
  Khan, Raza Mohammed, in 113
    for 'A' level exams 121
    academic structure for 115
    D'Alroy-Jones and 114–16
    literary interests of 119
    Shireen and 128–29
    tutor for 114–16
  tutors in, 114–16
Cuba
  Jack in 250
  Khan, Raza Mohammed, and 245–51
    in Havana 246–47, 250–51
    support of Castro 245
    with Tess 246–51
    travel to Cuba 246–51
    Trinidad de Cuba 247–50
Cuban Revolution 183
culture shock, for Khan, Raza
  Mohammed 101
cummings, e. e. 175, 177

Dabir, Maysam 15–16
Dada Abba. *See* Mohammad,
  Nawab Ali
D'Alroy-Jones, Peter 114–16
Daragh of Hazrfat Buddhoo 60
Davis, Miles 175
Daynes, Sarah 241
De Carlo, Yvonne 94
Delhi, India
  Ibn Dawood in 271
  Tess in 261–62, 264–66
  travel to 261–62, 264–66
Dickens, Charles 108
Dostoevsky, Fyodor 165–66
Down and Out in London and Paris (Orwell) 116
"dowry fodder," women as 9–10
Dravidians 41
Durrell, Lawrence 172, 231

ECT. *See* electroconvulsive therapy
Eden, Anthony 173
education systems, in India. *See also*
  boarding school; primary
  school years
  Hindi as second language 63
Edward VII (Duke of Windsor) 192
Egypt, invasion of 173
electroconvulsive therapy (ECT) 124–25
Elizabeth (Queen) 62
Elvis 138–39
English, as second language, for Khan,
  Raza Mohammed 73
ethnographic excavation 9–10
ettihaad (unity) 59
European Commission 276, 293–94
Evans, Dame Edith 237
Exeter College, Oxford University
  157, 160
Eyeless in Gaza (Huxley) 116
Ezurum, Turkey, hitchhiking
  through 197–98

The Fair Bride of Perth (Scott) 93–94
Faisal (King) 173
Faulkner, William 116, 167–68, 190
Ferdie (friend) 185, 233, 237–39
Ferengi Mahal (religious sect) 28, 47
films, for Khan, Raza Mohammed,
  enjoyment of 54–55, 94, 105,
  138, 175
  Pathar Panchali 230
  The Seventh Seal 175, 230
  Smiles of a Summer Night 175
  Summer with Monika 175
  Wild Strawberries 175, 230
Fitzgerald, F. Scott 190
Flynn, Errol 53–54
For Whom the Bell Tolls (Hemingway) 116
Ford, Glenn 138
form of worship. See *namaz*
Forster, E. M. 172, 237
France. *See also* Paris, France
  Egypt invaded by 173
  hitchhiking through, on way to
    India 189–92

INDEX 341

    to Nice 190–92
    to Paris 190–91
    Nice, 190–92

Gandhi, Mahatma 25
    assassination of 63
    homespun cotton movement 46
    Nehru, Jawaharlal, and 57n1
    "Quit India" campaign 46
Gardner, Ava 152
Garner, Errol 175
"The Garret" (Pound), 177–79
Gibran, Khalil 171
Ginsberg, Allen 180, 214
Grant, Al 175
The Grapes of Wrath (Steinbeck) 116
Great Britain. *See also* London
    Anti-British activities, in India 55
    Egypt invaded by 173
    India as colony of 17
        land laws in 17
        requisition of homes in, during
            World War II 48–49
        Ryotwari system in 17
    Indian War of Independence and 16
    Islamophobia in 6–7
    race-relations legislation in 232–33
    requisition of New White Palace,
        during World War II 48–49
Greece, hitchhiking through 195–97

Habib, Irfan 13, 325
Haidar, Nawab Ali (father),
    at Tajposhi 20
Hakim, Ted 173
Halévie, Elie 116
Harrow-on-the-Hill 123–26
Havana, Cuba 246–47, 250–51
Hemingway, Ernest 116, 190
Hepworth, Barbara 237
Hindi
    as official language, replacement of
        English with 106
    as second language, for Khan, Raza
        Mohammed 63
Hindu mysticism 170–71

    Sufism as Islamic counterpart to 171
Hindus. *See also* Hindi
    assassination of Gandhi 63
    caste system among 41
    Muslims and
        religious clashes between 11
        violence between 58
hitchhiking to India 179–82, 189–203
    arrival in India 210–19
        through Bombay 221–26
        through Lucknow 212–14
    through France 189–92
        to Nice 190–92
        to Paris 190–91
    through Greece 195–97
    illnesses as result of 221–22
    through Iran 198–203
        local foods in 201
        Mustafa, Agha, and 201, 202
        Mustafa, Begum Mohammad, and
            201, 202
        to Tabriz 199–200
        to Tehran 201–3
    through Italy 192–94
        by boat 194
        to Rome 193–94
    through Pakistan 205–11
        Ahmad, Nawab Dawood, and 208–10
        Bhai, Hurr, and 206–7, 209
        Bhai, Husain, and 206–7
        to Karachi 205–10
        lodging in family homes of Khan,
            Raza Mohammed 206–7
        use of Urdu 206
    preparations for 179–80, 181–82
    return to London after 225–27
    through Turkey 197–98
        to Ezurum 197–98
homes, houses and
    Amadabad Estate 21
    in Lucknow 175
    New White Palace
        female section of 33–35, 36
        layout of 36–37
        location of 37
        male section 35–36

homesickness, at boarding school, for
    Khan, Raza Mohammed 82–83
Hosein, Attiya 16
"Howl" (Ginsberg) 180
Hussain, Attiyah 55
Hussein (Imam) 15–16, 218
Huxley, Aldous 116

Ibn Dawood, Mohammad (Shaikhoo) 3,
    4, 5, 28
  Begum and, marriage to 278,
    280–81, 283–85
    family accusations against 299–304
  Bhai, Hashim, and 145
  birth and infancy of 50–52
  claims to family estate 273–76,
    280–87
    allies in 280–81
    Begum role in 278, 280–81,
      283–85
    forced exile of Abid 278
    illegal monies taken from 275
    legal victories in 283–87
  in Delhi 271
  employee accusations against 303
  family accusations against 299–304
  Khan, Raza Mohammed, and 145–46,
    264–66, 294–95
  lack of photos of 7–8
  Maysam and 331–32
    fraud accusations by 299–300
    illegal theft of family estate 295–97,
      300–1
  polio and 51–52
  return from Pakistan 105
  Sahab as mentor of 105, 145
  special diet for 52
  Urdu lessons for 106
  visit to Zahra, during illness 315–22
Imambaras (female-only shrines) 33
In Search of Miracles (Ouspenskii) 170–71
India. *See also* hitchhiking to India;
    Lucknow, India; national
    movement
  Anti-British activities in 55
  Black Hole of Calcutta 17

  Bombay 221–26
  border conflict with Pakistan 211
  as British colony 17
    land laws in 17
    requisition of homes by, during
      World War II 48–49
    Ryotwari system in 17
  Delhi
    Ibn Dawood in 271
    Tess in 261–62, 264–66
    travel to 261–62, 264–66
  Dravidians and 41
  education systems in 63–64
    Hindi as second language 63
    English language in, Hindi as
      replacement for 106
    Hindi as replacement language for
      English 106
  Kerala state 263–64
  Tess in 261
    in Ahmadabad 270–72
    in Delhi 261–62, 264–66
    in Kerala state 263–64
    in Lucknow 266–70
  women in, subordinate treatment of 11
  Zamindari in, abolition of, 108
Indian Muslim League
  Ahmad, Nawab Dawood, and
    45–46, 47
  election successes of 58
  during independence movement 57
  Khan, Nawab Hasan, in 18
  lack of Muslim support for 57
  Mohammad, Nawab Ali, in 21, 25
  in national movement 57
Indian National Congress 18
  Ahmad, Nawab Dawood, and 47, 58
  Ali, Nawab Haidar, in 58
  boycott of World War II
    declaration 57–58
  elections for 57–58
  Mohammad, Nawab Ali, in 21, 25
Indian War of Independence (1857) 16
  India as British colony after 17
Indian weddings. *See* wedding
    celebrations

INDEX 343

inheritance laws
   Mohammad, Nawab Ali, and 19
      under Oudh Settlement Act 24
      under Taluqdari Sanads 21
   primogeniture, in colonial India 17
   under Shi'a Islam 9–10
   women as "dowry fodder" 9–10
Intruder in the Dust (Faulkner) 116
Iran, hitchhiking through, on way to India 198–203
   local foods in 201
   Mustafa, Agha, and 201, 202
   Mustafa, Begum Mohammad, and 201, 202
   to Tabriz 199–200
   to Tehran 201–3
Iraq
   Ahmad, Nawab Dawood, in 105
      return to India 112
   Bhai, Hurr, in 105
   military coup in 173
Islam. *See also* Muslims
   lack of caste system in 11
   Shi'a Islam 9–10
      Ahmad, Nawab Dawood, and 45–46
      Imambaras and 33
      inheritance laws under 9–10
      social justice and 11
      Zakat as pillar of 21
Islamophobia
   in Great Britain 6–7
   after 9/11 attacks 6–7
Italy, hitchhiking through, on way to India 192–94
   by boat 194
   to Rome 193–94
"Ithaka" (Cavafy) 187
Ivanhoe (Scott) 93–94

Jack (friend) 174–80 *See also* hitchhiking to India
   arrival in India 214–19
   artistic influences for 174–75
   Braham and 175
   in Cuba 250

   "The Garret" and 177–79
   Grant and 175
   Jazz music and 175
   movie-going with Khan, Raza Mohammed 175
   practical jokes against 177–79
   Zabelita and 234
   marriage of 234–35
Jafar (brother of Khan, Raza Mohammed) 101–2, 267, 269, 313–14, 328
   in Lucknow, 328–29
   Mohammad, Nawab Ali Haidar, and 267
   siblings. *See* Abid; Zahra
Jazz music 175
Jean Christophe (Roland) 190
Jean-Pierre (London employer) 293–94
Jinnah, 46
   Ahmad, Nawab Dawood, and 45, 59–60
   on Muslims in India 46
   Nehru, Jawaharlal, and, in conflict with 46
Joyce, James 116, 190, 241

Kaiserbagh Baradari 88
Karachi, Pakistan 59–60
   hitchhiking through 205–10
Kazantzakis, Nikos 172, 231, 241
al Kazim, Musa (Imam) 60
Kerala state (India) 263–64
Khan, Ayub 208–9
Khan, Liaquat, Ali 209
Khan, Nawab Ali (great-great grandfather) 14–17
   adoption of 14
   death of 17
   Marsiya poetry of 14–15
Khan, Nawab Hasan (great grandfather) 18
   family of 18
   in Indian National Congress 18
   in Lucknow 18
   in Muslim League 18
Khan, Raza Mohammed 189–92. *See also* hitchhiking to India; life history
   Ahmad, Nawab Dawood, and 44, 49–50

Khan, Raza Mohammed (*cont.*)
   visits to 33
  Alexander technique and 62
  anti-imperialist leanings of 173
  in Baghdad 60–61
  Bhai, Hurr, and, emotional reaction to death 306–7
  at boarding school. *See* boarding school
  on caste system 11
  in Crammers. *See* Crammers
  Cuba and, homage to 245–51
    in Havana 246–47, 250–51
    support of Castro 245
    with Tess 246–51
    travel to 246–51
    in Trinidad de Cuba 247–50
  earliest memories of 32
  early life of
    earliest memories 32
    family visits 33
    in female section of New White Palace 33–35
    first experience with death 35
    in male section of New White Palace 35–36
    servants as element in 36
  embarrassment about aristocratic background 3–4
  on familial legacy 331–32
  family expectations for 65
  family move from Lucknow 59–62
  family structure 4
    cousins and 39
    dynastic rulership and 30
  family wealth. *See also* claims to family estate
    descent from royalty 74
    origins of 16–17
  "The Garret" and 177–79
  Haidar, Nawab Ali, and, visits with 124–25
  hitchhiking to India, with Jack. *See* hitchhiking to India
  homes of. *See* homes; New White Palace
  Ibn Dawood and 145–46, 264–66, 294–95
  on Islamophobia after 9/11 6–7
  Jack and, friendship with. *See* Jack
  Jazz music and 175
  Jean-Pierre and 293–94
  leisure and play for 38
    cricket for 39
    films and. *See* films
  letter from father 257–60
  letters from twin brother Abid 84, 309–10
  in London 75–80
    Bhai, Hurr, and 80
    Indian friends in 148–50
    loss of employment in 275–76, 293–94
    Lyons Corner House 78
    "poly-photos" 76, 77–78
    restaurants in 78–79
    shopping in 76
  loss of virginity for 158–59
  March from Aldermaston and 182–85, 237–39
  Marsiyas and, relevance of 16, 208
  Maysam and 289–97
  medical issues for 42–43
    typhoid fever 43
  with mother 102–3
  Nadia (daughter) 251–54
  nanny for 32
  at Oxford University 156–60
    choice of studies at 170
    at Exeter College 157, 160
    exit from 168
    registration period for 157
    Shireen and 157–60
  in Paris 75–80, 96–98
    French language instruction in 96
    restaurants 79
    sexual interest for, awakening of 96, 97
    sightseeing in 79–80
  post-primary school education. *See also* boarding school
    in England 63–64
  primary school years 40–45
    Dravidians and 41

INDEX

learning English as second language 73
Loretto Convent School for Girls 40–41
at La Martinière College 49, 53–56, 64
in publishing 232–33
publishing of life narrative, outcomes from 8–9
during Ramazan 84, 105
return to Lucknow 141–46
  discussion of marriage with Shireen 142
  jungle safari with Bhai, Hashim 143–45
  thoughts of Shireen during 146
  visit with Ibn Dawood 145–46
School of Oriental and African Studies and 180, 181, 232, 234
Shireen and. *See* Shireen
siblings. *See* Abid; Jafar; Zahra
social isolation of 62–63
social justice for, Urdu poetry and 11
Sufism for, 171
Tess and, marriage to 243–45
  family attendance at 243–44
Urdu poetry and, social justice characterized through 11
work in prisons 294
ziyarat for, with family 60–61, 62
Zorba the Greek as influence on 172, 231, 241
Khayyam, Omar 171
Khojas, Ismaili 141
Kidwai, Rafi Ahmad 58
King, Martin Luther 90–91
Kipling, Rudyard 53–54
Kirkhall, Rodney, 100, 110
Koestler, Arthur 116

Ladd, Alan 98–99
Lady Chatterley's Lover (Lawrence) 190
Lampedusa, Giuseppe di 289
land laws, in colonial India 17
  primogeniture and 17
Lansky, Meyer 246
Le Lavandou 120–21
Lawrence, D. H. 190, 191–92, 231

The Leopard (Lampedusa) 289
life history, as narrative
  documentation for 5–8
  through photos 7–8
  social context for 10
London, England
  Bhai, Hurr, and 80
  immigration to 238
  Khan, Raza Mohammed, in 75–80
    Indian friends in 148–50
    loss of employment in 275–76, 293–94
    Lyons Corner House 78
    "poly-photos" 76, 77–78
    restaurants in 78–79
    shopping in 76
  Mohammad, Nawab Haidar Ali, in 107–12
    meeting with boarding school Headmaster 108, 110–11
    registration for Bar 108
  racism against non-whites in 149, 169–70
  return to, after hitchhiking to India 225–27, 229–30
  "white flight" from 238
  "Windrush generation" in 238
Loretto Convent School for Girls 40–41
Lucknow, India
  Ahmad, Nawab Dawood, in 49–50
  Anglo-Indians in 54
  arrival in, after hitchhiking journey 212–14
  blackouts in 46–47
  family homes in 21. *See also* Ahmadabad Estate; New White Palace
  Ali, Nawab Haidar, in 49
    travel to 49
  family move from 59–62
  Jafar in 328–29
  Khan, Nawab Hasan, in 18
  La Martinière College 40
    Abid at 49, 53–56
    establishment of 53
    during Indian independence conflicts 53–54

Lucknow, India (*cont.*)
   Khan, Raza Mohammed, at 49, 53–56
   religious tolerance in 16
   Tess in 266–70
   U. S. soldiers in 41–42
Lyons Corner House, in London 78

Magdalen College, Oxford 118
Maharishi Mahesh Yogi 180
Marable, Manning 238–39
March from Aldermaston
   Campaign for Nuclear Disarmament organization of 182, 183, 237
   international participation in 184
   Khan, Raza Mohammed, and 182–85, 237–39
   Steve and 183
Margaret (Princess) 115–16
marriages. *See also* Baji, Bari; Bhai, Hurr
   discussion of, with Shireen 142
   of Jack and Zabelita 234–35
   of Mohammad, Nawab Ali 19
   Mut'ah marriage of 21–22
Marsiya poems 14–16
   Anis and 15–16, 208
   Bhai, Hurr, and 208
   classical 15–16
   Dabir and 15–16
   Imam Hussein and 15–16
   for Khan, Raza Mohammed, relevance of 16, 208
   relevance of, for modern readers 16
   subject matter of 15
Martin, Claude 53–54
La Martinière College 40
   Abid at 49, 53–56
   establishment of 53
   during Indian independence conflicts 53–54
   Khan, Raza Mohammed, at 49, 53–56, 64
Maysam (second cousin, son of Baji, Bari) 280, 290, 327–28
   financial support for parents 291
   on Ibn Dawood 331–32
   fraud claims against 299–300
   illegal theft of family estate 295–97, 300–1
   Khan, Raza Mohammed, and 289–97
Maysam, Sikander 125, 208–9
Michael (friend) 239–40
Mody, Sir Homi 88
Mohammad, Nawab Ali (Dada Abba) (grandfather) 18
   death of 22, 23
   funeral and mourning period after 24
   family palaces of 21. *See also* New White Palace
      Ahmadabad Estate 21
   in Indian Muslim League 21, 25
   in Indian National Congress 21, 25
   inheritance issues for 19
      under Oudh Settlement Act 24
      under Taluqdari Sanads 21
   marriages of 19
      Mut'ah and 21–22
   Nehru, Motilal, and 19, 23, 25
   Nehru Commission and 22–23
   religious charities built by 21
      under Zakat 21
   Urdu poetry of 20
Mohammad, Nawab Ali Haidar (father) 27–28, 29–30, 47, 48–49, 61, 103
   Abid and 267
   Adler and 62
   Alexander technique and 62
   illness of, psychiatric elements of 121–26
      commitment to sanitorium 57
      electroconvulsive therapy for 124–25
      in Harrow-on-the-Hill 123–26
      physician in charge of 123–26
      in residential psychiatric home 123–24
      visit by Ahmad, Nawab Dawood 125–26
      visits by Khan, Raza Mohammed 124–25
   in Indian National Congress 58

INDEX

on Khan, Raza Mohammed, going to boarding school
  advice for 65
  journey with 65–67
  letter to Khan, Raza Mohammed 257–60
  in London 107–12
    meeting with boarding school Headmaster 108, 110–11
    registration for Bar 108
  in Lucknow 49
  redemption of 323
Moharram 15
  subject matter of 15
Moore, Henry 237
Mount, Ferdinand 255
Mountbatten, Philip (Duke of Edinburgh) 62
Musaddas (Bhai, Hurr) 303–4, 308
music. *See* Elvis; Jazz music
Muslim League. *See* Indian Muslim League
Muslims
  establishment of homeland 47–48
  Hindus and
    religious clashes between 11
    violence between 58
  Imambaras and 33
  in India 46
  Shi'as 9–10. *See also* Shi'a Islam
  Sunnis 16
Mustafa, Agha 201, 202
Mustafa, Begum Mohammad 201, 202
Mut'ah (temporary marriage contract) 21–22

Nadia (daughter) 251–54
  wedding of 251–53
Naidoo, Sarojini 28, 47
Naimy, Mikhail 162
Nainital resort 44–45
namaz (form of worship) 87
Namier, Lewis 116
al-Naqi, Ali (Imam) 61
national movement, in India
  Indian Muslim League and 57

Indian War of Independence and 16
  India as British colony after 17
  La Martinière College and 53–54
  partition strategy and 58–59
  as Muslim homeland 58–59
Nawab of Ahmadabad 14
Nehru, Jawaharlal 25, 90
  abolition of Zamindari under 108
  Ahmad, Nawab Dawood, and 45
  Gandhi and 57n1
  on Indian Muslims 46
  Jinnah in conflict with 46
  socialist leanings of 57n1
Nehru, Motilal 19, 90
  Nehru Commission and 23
Nehru Commission
  Mohammad, Nawab Ali, and 22–23
  Nehru, Motilal, and 23
New India 25
New School 13
New White Palace
  British requisition of, during World War II 48–49
  female section of 33–35
    layout of 36
  layout of 36–37
  location of 37
  male section 35–36
Nice, France, hitchhiking through 190–92
9/11 attacks, in U.S. 253
  Islamophobia after 6–7

On Ethnography (Daynes and Williams) 241
Orwell, George 116
Oudh Settlement Act 24
Ouspenskii, Pyotr 170–71
Oxford University
  Khan, Raza Mohammed, at 156–60
    choice of studies at 170
    at Exeter College 157, 160
    exit from Oxford 168
    registration period for 157
    Shireen and 157–60
  lateness penalties at 158
  Magdalen College at 118

Paget, Debra 94
Pakistan
   Ahmad, Nawab Dawood, in 59–60, 145, 173
      regional divisions and, involvement in 125
      as self-exile 90
   Awami League 208–9
   Bhai, Husain, in 145
   border conflict with India 211
   creation of 58–59
   hitchhiking through 205–11
      Ahmad, Nawab Dawood, and 208–10
      Bhai, Hurr, and 206–7, 209
      Bhai, Husain, and 206–7
      to Karachi 205–10
      lodging in family homes of Khan, Raza Mohammed 206–7
      use of Urdu 206
   as Muslim homeland 58–59
palaces, of Mohammad, Nawab Ali 37. *See also* New White Palace
   Ahmadabad Estate 21
Paris, France
   Abid in 96–98
   hitchhiking through 190–91
   Khan, Raza Mohammed, in 75–80, 96–98
      French-language instruction for 96
      restaurants for 79
      sexual interest for, awakening of 96, 97
      sightseeing in 79–80
      during World War II, lack of rationing in 80
partition strategy, for India 58–59
   Ahmad, Nawab Dawood, on 47–48
   as Muslim homeland 58–59
Pathar Panchali 230
Peck, Gregory 152
PEN International 231
Pierre, Jean 276
pilgrimage
   of Ahmad 28–29
   ziyarat 59
pilgrimage to sacred shrines. *See ziyarat*

poetry. *See* Arabic poetry; Marsiya poems
Poitier, Sidney 138
"poly-photos" 76, 77–78
A Portrait of the Artist as a Young Man (Joyce) 116
Pound, Ezra 177–79
primary school years
   for Abid
      Loretto Convent School for Girls 40–41
      at La Martinière College 49, 53–56
   for Khan, Raza Mohammed, 40–45
      Dravidians and 41
      learning English as second language 73
      Loretto Convent School for Girls 40–41
      at La Martinière College 49, 53–56, 64
primogeniture, as inheritance system
   in colonial India 17
   under Taluqdari Sanads 21
The Prophet (Gibran) 171
purdah 7–8

Qais (second cousin, son of Baji, Bari) 243–44, 275, 278–80, 290, 308–9
   financial support for parents 291
Quayle, Anthony 97
"Quit India" campaign 46
"The Quran Interpreted" (Arberry) 180

racism
   at boarding school, towards Khan, Raza Mohammed 81–82
   legislation in Great Britain 232–33
   against non-whites, in London 149, 169–70
Rahman, Habib-ur 88–89
Raja of Bilahra 31
Raja of Nanpara 28
Ramazan (Ramadan)
   Khan, Raza Mohammed, during 84, 105
   weddings during 84
Ray, Satyajit 14, 230
al-Raza, Ali (Imam) 61

religious charities, Mohammad, Nawab
    Ali and 21
  under Zakat 21
religious sect. *See* Ferengi Mahal
reverse assimilation issues 101
Rilke, Rainer Maria 177
Rob Roy (Scott) 93–94
Roland, Romaine 190
Rome, Italy, hitchhiking through 193–94
"ru numai" (showing one's face) 87–88
"rukhsati" event 86
Rumi 134, 171
Russell, Bertrand 207, 237
Ryotwari system, in colonial India 17

Sahab, Jawaid 268–69
Sahab, Kamal 47, 86
Sahab, Lalla 105, 145
Sahib, Nawab 86
Said, Nuri-al 173
School of Oriental and African Studies
    (SOAS) 180, 181, 232, 234
schools. *See* boarding school; Cambridge
    University; education systems;
    Oxford University; primary
    school years
Scott, Sir Walter 93–94
self-exile, of Ahmad, Nawab
    Dawood 89–91
  family reaction to 91
  in Pakistan 90
  political reasons for 90
Une Semaine à Paris (magazine) 79–80
Seton, Marie 170
"Seven Odes of Pagan Arabia"
    (Arberry) 181
The Seventh Seal 175, 230
Shah, Lalla Bum Bahadur 85
Shah, Surat Bahadur 85
Shaikhoo. *See* Ibn Dawood, Mohammad
Shi'a Islam 9–10
  Ahmad, Nawab Dawood, and 45–46
  Imambaras and 33
  inheritance laws under 9–10
  social justice and 11
Shi'a Muslims 16

Shireen (first girlfriend/first love) 127–39
  dates with 130, 136–39, 150
  end of relationship with 161–68
    causes of 161–62
  family background for 131
    parents 131–32
    siblings 131–32
  as first love 103
  first kiss with 132
  letters from 137–38
  as marital possibility 104
    discussion with parents 142
    meeting with parents 133, 134–36
  other romantic relationships for 151
  possible pregnancy for 163
  reunion with Khan, Raza Mohammed
    in Crammers 128–29
    after holiday in Lucknow 147–50
    rekindling of relationship
      through 153–54
    at wedding of Bhai, Hurr 82
  romantic rivals for 131
  sexual interest in 151
  loss of virginity to 158–59
showing one's face. *See* "ru numai"
siblings, for Khan, Raza Mohammed. *See*
    Abid; Jafar; Zahra
Sinatra, Frank 162
Singh, Ranbir 72
Smiles of a Summer Night 175
SOAS. *See* School of Oriental and African
    Studies
social justice
  Shi'a Islam and 11
  through Urdu poetry 11
socialism, Nehru and 57n1
standard of Tamerlaine. *See* "Alam"
Stanford, W. B. 241
Stein, Gertrude 190
Steinbeck, John 116
Stendhal 251
Steve (friend) 83
  arrival in India 214–19
  Hakim and 173
  journey to India 179–80. *See also*
    hitchhiking to India

Steve (friend) (*cont.*)
   preparation for 181–82
   literary influences for 190, 191–92
   in March from Aldermaston 183
   as playwright 172
Suez Canal 173
Sufism 171
Suhrawarfy, Husain 208–9
Summer with Monika 175
Sunni Muslims 16

Tabriz, Iran, hitchhiking through 199–200
Tajposhi 20
The Talisman (Scott) 93–94
Taluqdari Sanads 21
al Taqi, Mohammad (Imam) 60
Tatum, Art, 175
Taylor, A. J. P. 116
Tehran, Iran, hitchhiking through 201–3
temporary marriage contract. *See Mut'ah*
Tess (wife)
  Abid and 268–70, 326
  in Cuba 246–51
    in Havana 246–47, 250–51
    in Trinidad de Cuba 247–50
  in India 261
    in Ahmadabad 270–72
    in Delhi 261–62, 264–66
    in Kerala state 263–64
    in Lucknow 266–70
  letters about Zahra's illness 319–20
  marriage to 243–45
    family attendance at 243–44
  Nadia (daughter) 251–54
theosophy 170–71
Thompson, J. M. 116
Townsend, Peter 115–16
Trevor-Roper, Hugh 116
Trinidad de Cuba, Cuba 247–50
Trinity College, Cambridge 82, 94
Turkey, hitchhiking through 197–98
  to Ezurum 197–98
typhoid fever 43

Ulysses (Joyce) 190, 241
United Nations Food and Agriculture Organization (UNFAO) 201
United States (U.S.)
  military presence in Lucknow 41–42
  9/11 attacks in 253
    Islamophobia after 6–7
unity. *See ettihaad*
University Film Society 170
Urdu (language)
  Ibn Dawood and 106
  Musaddas 303–4, 308
  poetry
    of Mohammad, Nawab Ali 20
    social justice through 11
  use of, during hitchhike to India 206
U.S. *See* United States

Wajda, Andrzej 156–57
Webster, Ben 175
wedding celebrations, Indian. *See also* Baji; Bari; Bhai, Hurr
  banquets after 88
  during Ramazan 84
  "rukhsati" event 86
  traditional ceremonies in 86–88
What's On (magazine) 78–80
"white flight," from London 238
White Haiderbagh Baradari 47
The Wild Palms (Faulkner) 167–68
Wild Strawberries 175, 230
Williams, Terry 241
"Windrush generation" 238
Wisdom, John 306
women
  in India, subordinate treatment of 11
  under inheritance laws, "dowry fodder" 9–10
World War II
  Indian National Congress response to 57–58
  requisition of New White Palace during, by British 48–49

Zabelita (friend) 230–32
  in Brondesbury Park 233

Jack and 234
  marriage of 234–35
Zahra (sister of Khan, Raza Mohammed) 43–44, 101–2, 269, 270–71
  Beghum and 315–22
  Ibn Dawood and 315–22
  illness of 311–24
    Abid and 311–12
    death after 321–22
    letters to Tess about 319–20
  visit by Khan, Raza Mohammed 311–24
  siblings. *See* Abid; Jafar
Zainab. *See* Baji, Bari
Zainab, Baji 51–52
Zakat (pillar of Islam) 21
Zamindari, abolition of 108
ziyarat (pilgrimage to sacred shrines) 59
  Khan, Raza Mohammed, and 60–61, 62
Zorba the Greek (Kazantzakis) 172, 231, 241

www.ingramcontent.com/pod-product-compliance
Lightning Source LLC
Chambersburg PA
CBHW032016230426
43671CB00005B/106